# Why Would Anyone Want to Swing a Cat?

# Why Would Anyone Want to Swing a Cat?

**Daily Mail**

Compiled and edited by

ANDY SIMPSON

Constable • London

Constable & Robinson Ltd
55–56 Russell Square
London WC1B 4HP
www.constablerobinson.com

First published in the UK by Constable,
an imprint of Constable & Robinson Ltd., 2013

Copyright © Associated Newspapers Ltd. 2013

The right of Andy Simpson to be identified as the
author of this work has been asserted by him in accordance
with the Copyright, Designs & Patents Act 1988

A copy of the British Library Cataloguing in Publication
Data is available from the British Library

ISBN 978-1-84901-650-6 (paperback)
ISBN 978-1-84901-947-7 (ebook)

Typeset by TW Typesetting, Plymouth, Devon

Printed and bound by CPI Group (UK) Ltd, Croydon, CR0 4YY

1 3 5 7 9 10 8 6 4 2

**(1) QUESTION: Why doesn't the modern Army use flail tanks like those we used to destroy mines on the Normandy beaches in the Second World War?**

I helped invent and develop the wartime flail tank in Orford village, Suffolk, where it was my job to lay mines in front of the experimental flails and dig up those which didn't explode. This specialized tank is useful only in a properly prepared minefield, as on the beaches of Normandy, and would be ineffective in areas where mines have been laid haphazardly.

*Gordon Minshull, Clacton on Sea, Essex*

As a flail tank commander from June 1944 onwards, I know the limitations of these machines. The flail tank was designed to work in open ground, in line abreast or staggered line ahead to clear a specific minefield. Flailing a single track through a forest, for instance, would crater the track and make it impassable for other vehicles wherever a mine was blown.

In ground which is frozen solid, the chains of the flail may fail to explode a mine, leaving the 36-ton tank to run over and trigger it. This happened to my tank twice, fortunately without casualties.

*Thomas H. Yates, Heywood, Lancashire*

Coalition forces who first occupied the Afghan airfields at Bagram and Kandahar in 2002 were hampered by the presence of a large number of mines and UXO (unexploded ordnance). There was a limited availability of mine detectors, so early 'demining' was accomplished by deploying troops in line-abreast, using their bayonets to prod the ground. This led to several casualties and fatalities.

Eventually, Jordanian Army Aardvark flails and Norwegian-provided Hydrema flails were employed on this work. The British-designed Aardvark consists of an armoured cab with a front-mounted flail. It has seventy-two chains with sixty-six striker tips (fist-sized balls of steel) attached to a rotor. The chains whip round in front of the cab detonating mines as it travels.

The Hydrema system is made in Denmark and is similar to the Aardvark. During the mine-clearing process, the vehicle is driven by a hydrostatic system in the direction opposite to normal driving. The clearing can be done using joysticks or through a fully automated computerized steering system. An armoured-steel deflector plate behind the flail provides protection against blast and fragments, and prevents objects being thrown on the vehicle.

Both have been used extensively in demining land in Bagram and Kandahar but Coalition forces were soon exposed to the reality of flail operations: they can 'process' land (especially useful in areas where vegetation must be removed) and detonate mines but leave significant numbers of UXO and some mines in their wake.

Nowadays they're used in conjunction with mine-detection dog teams, and in areas where there are high concentrations of mines the system is very effective.

*George May, Nottingham*


Flail tanks have been around for more than sixty years. Originally used purely by the military to breach minefields so troops could gain access to their objectives, some losses were incurred but were deemed militarily acceptable. Flails have developed further since then but this technology has limited application to humanitarian demining which must be 100 per cent effective to allow the safe return of men, women and children to land which has been cleared.

Hand clearance, using mine detectors and probing for mines, is the only proven method to achieve this, regardless of the type of mine encountered or the ground on which the work is being done.

Flails aren't effective against all mines. Many modern antipersonnel mines are designed to resist this type of clearance and require a uniform rolling pressure, like a human footstep, to trigger the mine.

Ground which has been flailed still has to be 'proved' by deminers with mine detectors. After flailing, the area has mine debris, such as metal fragments, making the job of demining even more difficult. And flails can't work easily in areas with trees, large boulders, gulleys and terrain which doesn't allow access for large machinery.

Flails are expensive to buy and maintain in the field and the infrastructure in developing countries can't always support the movement of large, heavy machinery. There's often a problem with logistic support and spares for this high-maintenance equipment.

Future developments in flail technology could make them more adaptable but at present we subscribe to the proven method of trained men and women using mine detectors. At less than £10 a day (all from voluntary donations) for each deminer, this is a cost-effective way of helping to solve the daily problems of death and maiming caused by any of the hundred million mines worldwide.

*Steve Wilson, Mines Advisory Group, Cockermouth, Cumbria*

## (2) QUESTION: Why is a person who stops drinking alcohol said to be 'on the wagon'?

It's commonly believed that this saying came from the physical act of jumping onto one of the wagons from which members of the temperance movement preached against the evils of alcohol. 'Jumping on the wagon' was the first step in the reformation of the alcoholic.

In fact, the saying originated in the US at the turn of the nineteenth and twentieth centuries as 'on the water wagon', vehicles which sprayed town and city streets and pavements with water to reduce dust.

Water wagons also provided the communal water supply in times of drought and were a ready image for someone who had swopped the temptations of alcoholic drinks for 'Adam's ale'.

*John Lord, Preston, Lancashire*


## (3) QUESTION: Is it just coincidence or is it deliberate that Father's Day comes nine months before Mother's Day?

In Britain, rather than Mother's Day, we have Mothering Sunday, whose origins lie in ancient mythology when a spring festival was dedicated by rites and festivities to Rhea, mother of the gods. By medieval times, the custom of honouring Mother took the form of leaving gifts to Mother Church at the high altar in mid-Lent.

The day acquired its present significance in Charles II's time when it became the custom for young people living away from home, mostly in domestic service, to be allowed a day off to take gifts home, to 'go a-mothering', on the fourth Sunday in Lent.

The American Mother's Day arose after Anna Jarvis campaigned in 1914 throughout the US for a day to commemorate all mothers. It is observed on the second Sunday in May.

Father's Day originated in America through the efforts of Mrs John Bruce Dodd, of Spokane, Washington, inspired by her father, Civil War veteran William Jackson Smart, who raised her and five sons after being widowed. She campaigned for recognition of the efforts of all fathers and the day was officially recognized by President Wilson in 1916. It was popularized in Britain in the early forties through the influence of American service personnel based here in the war.

The nine-month gap in this country between Father's Day and

Mothering Sunday, while amusing, is purely coincidental and isn't the case in most other countries.

*Lesley Grace, The Greeting Card Association*

**(4) QUESTION: Four out of the last five American presidents have been left-handed but will Prince William, when he becomes king, be the first British left-handed monarch?**

Six of the eleven US presidents since the Second World War – Harry Truman, Gerald Ford, Ronald Reagan, Bill Clinton, George Bush and Barack Obama – have been left-handed and one in four of the Apollo astronauts was left-handed, although only about one in ten of the total world population is left-handed.

Britain has had sixteen monarchs since Cromwell, of whom Queen Victoria, Edward VIII and George VI are known to have been left-handed and others may have been. Other famous left-handers have included Joan of Arc, Napoleon Bonaparte, Julius Caesar, Alexander the Great and Terry Venables.

*Deborah Knight, Anything Left-Handed Ltd, Brewer St, London*

George VI was left-handed but his left hand was tied behind his back when he was a child to make him use his right and this caused the stammer which plagued him all his life.

I studied this issue when I was a college elocution teacher. In a right-handed person, the left side of the brain controls movement and the right side controls speech. If a left-handed person is forced to use the right hand – the speech side – there is overload and speech suffers.

My daughter is left-handed and was never made to use her right hand. I stressed this when she started school at the age of five. Many great artists were left-handed, including Leonardo da Vinci, and in my college classes at least a third were left-handed.

*Evelyn Colledge, Markfield, Leicestershire*

I was forcibly changed to right-handed writing when I started school in 1948. My left arm was tied behind my back and I was thrashed with a cane if I was seen putting my left hand on the desk, even to hold my book steady when we progressed from a writing slate.

When I went to night school for pleasure in my mid-forties, the teacher held up a page of my writing to the class and criticized it. I explained that I had been converted to being right-handed and offered to show the class how it was done if she would take the place of the pupil. After my explanation of the method, she went white and declined.

*W. R. Hall, Sutton Coldfield, West Midlands*

My brother was born left-handed in 1900 and forced to write with his right hand. He developed a stammer which remained with him all his life. As a result of this practice, it was far more common to hear stammering in those days.

*Mrs A. Henciley, Chester*

I'm naturally left-handed and my memory of infant school is of being rapped on the knuckles for writing with my left hand. Since then, I've used my right hand to write but I do almost everything involving knives, tools, brushes, etc., with my left hand.

I have a slight speech impediment, which my mother said was caused by me being made to use my right hand to write.

*I. L. Sutton, Downend, Bristol*

When I was ten, my teacher suddenly decided that none of the children in his class should be different and that I should write exclusively with my right hand.

As a natural left-hander, I couldn't change and was ridiculed in front of the whole class. With the knowledge of the head, I had to spend several days with the 'babies' in the infants until I summoned the courage to tell my parents and they intervened.

This happened not, as you may think, in the early part of the last century but as recently as the mid-1960s. The humiliation remains with me to this day.

*Paul Smith, London*

When I was at school in Yorkshire in 1929, our class teacher offered a 6d (2 ½p) reward to any left-handed boy or girl who could successfully change to using their right hand. Not being left-handed, I couldn't benefit from this but I knew several who did and, in due course, collected their rewards.

I'm not aware of any of them having developed a stammer as a result of this unnatural practice.

*Trevor Barker, Prestwick, Ayrshire*

I was one of three left-handed boys in my school in the earlier 1940s made to write with our right hands. We all developed stammers.

*T. Strangeway, Nailsea, Somerset*

## (5) QUESTION: Who was Nelly, in 'not on your Nelly'?

This refers to Nelly Duff, a fictional creation of mid-nineteenth century devotees of Cockney rhyming slang. Nelly was a common name at the time and Duff was both a common surname and a word meaning useless or no good.

Nelly Duff rhymes with 'puff' – the breath of life. So 'not on your Nelly' means 'not on your life'.

*George Wardrop, Canterbury, Kent*

**(6) QUESTION: What kind of goat is a 'scapegoat'?**

The origin of the scapegoat lies in the Old Testament sacrificial system. In Leviticus 16, verses 18–22, we read that after offering blood sacrifices on the altar, high priest Aaron was instructed to take a live goat, lay hands on it and confess the sins of the people.

The 'scapegoat' was then sent into the wilderness, taking the people's guilt away. Christians see this as a picture of Jesus Christ, as prophesied by Isaiah: 'The Lord has laid on him the iniquity of us all.' (Isaiah 53:6)

*Geoff Chapman, Yeovil, Somerset*

Not all Christians agree with the interpretation of Leviticus 16 which makes Christ the scapegoat. 'Scapegoat' is an approximation of the Hebrew *azazel*-goat, which some scholars say refers to a place of demons, perhaps associated with the modern Hebrew '*La'azazel!*', meaning 'Go to the devil' or 'Damn you'. Others surmise a derivation from the root *azal*, to depart or remove, hence departing-goat or [e]scape-goat.

For the ceremony of the Day of Atonement (Yom Kippur), Leviticus describes two goats selected by lot, 'one for Yaweh and the other to be the azazel-goat'. The first was offered as a sacrifice for the people's sins, as Christ's blood atones for humanity's, while Satan is cast out as unforgivable. The original 'scapegoat' may stand for ultimate guilt, rather than guilt falsely attributed.

The word 'atonement' (constructed from 'at-one-ment') was invented by sixteenth-century Bible translator William Tyndale to translate the Hebrew and Greek terms for reconciliation with God, for which there was no English equivalent.

*Allan McGregor, Cambuslang, Glasgow*

**(7) QUESTION: Why 'Ferris' wheel?**

The Ferris wheel takes its name from its inventor, contractor and bridge builder George Washington Gale Ferris (1859–96). His invention, based on a huge bicycle wheel, first appeared at the Chicago World Columbian Exposition of 1893, intended to rival the 1,050 foot Eiffel Tower, built four years earlier in Paris.

His 250-foot-diameter wheel, turned by two 1,000 horse power reversible steam engines, had a circumference of 825 feet, was 30 feet wide and raised 15 feet off the ground on two 140-foot towers.

The whole structure weighed 1,200 tons and the axle was the largest single piece of steel forged at that time. It had thirty-six plushly fitted cars, each holding up to forty people, so 1,440 passengers could be carried round once every ten minutes. It reappeared at the St Louis Fair in 1904.

By comparison, the giant London Eye wheel on London's South Bank since the Millennium celebrations is 500 feet high and can carry 960 passengers on a twenty-minute revolution.

The success of the Ferris wheel in Chicago at the World's Columbian Exposition of 1892 made inventor George Ferris very rich and he set up an amusement park in the city. The severe economic depression of 1894, however, caused the demise of the park and Ferris auctioned the wheel for just $1,800. He became very ill with depression and died in Pittsburgh aged thirty-seven.

The original Ferris wheel reappeared at the 1904 Louisiana Purchase Exposition in St Louis, Missouri, but there wasn't enough money to dismantle it, and it became a rusting eyesore. The wheel was ignominiously dynamited on 11 May 1906.

*Aidan Smyth, Department of American Studies,*
*Keele University, Staffordshire*

(8) QUESTION: Both sexes wear their wedding or engagement rings on the third finger of the left hand but what do rings worn on other fingers, or thumbs, on either hand, signify?

A bishop's ring is worn on the fourth finger of the right hand because the thumb, index and middle finger are used by the bishop to bless his subjects. At the Royal Coronation, a bishop presents the king or queen with the Coronation ring which is placed on the fourth finger of the right hand, signifying that the monarch is head of the Church.

Traditionally, the signet ring was always worn on the little finger of the left hand. This was considered the easiest finger to turn to seal documents. The trinity ring, made of three bands of yellow, white and red gold, signifying friendship, fidelity and love, is worn on the little finger of either hand.

*Sally Goldsby, World Gold Council, Haymarket, London*

The Germans wear the wedding ring on the third finger of the right hand. The wedding band is presented as an engagement ring, worn on the ring finger of the left hand and transferred to the right during the wedding ceremony.

*Nina Achenbach, South Norwood, SE25*

An Edwardian etiquette book says: 'If a gentleman wants a wife, he wears a ring on the first finger of the left hand; if he be engaged, he wears it on the second finger; if married, on the third, and on the fourth if he never intends to be married.

'When a lady is not engaged, she wears a hoop or diamond on her first finger; if engaged, on the second; if married, on the third, and on the fourth if she intends to die unmarried.

'When a gentleman presents a fan, flower or trinket to a lady with the left hand, this is an overture of regard. Should she receive it with the left hand, it is considered an acceptance of his esteem, but if with the right hand, it is a refusal of the offer.

'Thus, by a few simple tokens, the passion of love is expressed and the most timid man may, without difficulty, communicate his sentiments to a lady and, in case his offer should be refused, avoid experiencing the mortification of an explicit refusal.'

*Mrs Sarah Threlfall, Southam, Warwickshire*

**(9) QUESTION: Is it known who invented the handkerchief or when it first appeared?**

In Britain, hankies date back to the fourteenth century. Household accounts of Richard II, who died in 1400, list 'little pieces made for giving to the lord king for carrying in his hand to wipe and clean his nose'.

This detailed explanation suggests they were new at the time, though whether fastidious Richard invented the hygienic alternative to sleeve or neckcloth is another matter.

*Geoff Hughes, Swindon, Wiltshire*

The word was current by 1600. Listed among the hundreds of public declarations associated with what was then Ilchester Gaol, in Somerset, is judgment passed on a young boy 'for stealing her ladyship's silk handkerchief'.

*Mrs S. Cave, Yeovil, Somerset*

According to Acts 19:12, handkerchiefs were brought to the Apostle Paul so he could pray over them and people could then place them over the body of a sick person. This practice has been used in recent times when a sick person has been unable to attend a church service.

*Anthony Marshall, Sheffield*

The Chinese devised the handkerchief when they invented silk cloth. An Oriental riddle asks: 'What does the poor man throw away that the rich man carries in his pocket?' The answer being that the poor man thumbs his nose while the rich man carries a silk handkerchief.

*E. Nicoll, Nuneaton, Warwickshire*

(10) QUESTION: How come flamingos and salmon are said to derive their pink colour from eating shrimps when shrimps turn pink only when boiled?

Shrimp are scavengers. London Zoo shrimps feed on detritus, a diet which contains nutrients including beta carotenes which give shrimps their pink colour.

Though the shrimp stay white/brown while alive, when boiled the beta carotenes change with the increasing temperature to a pink hue. Flamingos feed on shrimps, passing the carotenes up the food chain and giving the birds their pink colouring.

*Lilamani de Silva, London Zoo, Regent's Park, London*

(11) QUESTION: What is the meaning and origin of the expression to 'cut the mustard'?

This saying originated in nineteenth-century America, as part of cowboy jargon during cattle drives. However, I'm not convinced by *Brewer's Dictionary of Phrase and Fable*'s explanation of 'cut' meaning harvesting or gathering in.

Use of the term 'cut' for diluting or adulterating a dry powder is still common in drug culture where heroin, for instance, is 'cut' with another powder to reduce its potency while increasing the bulk.

Powdered mustard was a standard condiment on the trails, complementing an otherwise unrelenting diet, and had to be cut with water to produce the right strength of paste. Getting it right every time took a steady hand and good judgement: an ability to 'cut the mustard'.

*Graeme Donald, Stockport, Cheshire*

(12) QUESTION: I saw a group of giraffe-necked women from Africa parading at circuses shortly after the War. Is the tribal custom of ringing women's necks still practised?

Adorning women's necks with brass rings in the belief that they would ward off evil spirits wasn't an African custom but was practised by women of the Padaung people in Burma. It had almost disappeared when it was revived by those Padaungs who took refuge from civil war by crossing the border into northern Thailand.

Many impoverished fathers resumed the custom of collaring their daughters with twenty or more rings, increasing their neck length to more than 1ft, because tourists will pay to have their picture taken with these long-necked women, just as the circus used them to attract customers.

After a time, the weight of the neck rings can crush the wearer's collarbone and ribs. Removing them after many years can also have tragic consequences.

*Jack Hutton, Bromley Cross, Greater Manchester*

In 1944, my unit of Royal Engineers in the XIVth Army was in Ping Jin, which was known, in typical Army fashion, as Pink Gin, north of Mandalay, and our commanding officer told us it was the area where the giraffe-necked women came from.

I recall seeing these some of these women in Britain before the war.

*R. Hulse, Winsford, Cheshire*

## (13) QUESTION: Was Pope John Paul II the biggest ever crowd-puller?

The largest ever papal event was at Rizal Park, Manila, in the Philippines, on 15 January 1995, when Pope John Paul II celebrated World Youth Day with an estimated crowd of just over two million people. Pope Benedict XVI has drawn record crowds in some countries – notably Australia in July 2008 – but nowhere near his predecessor's numbers.

The greatest crowd-pulling feat of all must be the reported 3.5 million people who massed on Copacabana Beach, Rio de Janeiro,

Brazil, for a free Rod Stewart concert on New Year's Eve 1994 – though whether they were there to see him or just to celebrate New Year is open to conjecture.

The greatest recorded number assembled with a common religious purpose was the estimated fifteen million at the Hindu Festival of Kumbh Mela at the confluence of the Yamana, Ganges and invisible Saraswati rivers at Allahabad, Uttar Pradesh, India, on 6 February 1989.

The largest mass assembly to pay final respects to one person was the fourteen million who attended the funeral of the Madras chief minister, C. N. Annadurai, in February 1969.

The greatest number of spectators for any sporting event is the estimated 2.5 million who annually line the route of the New York marathon.

*Katrina Tate, Perth, Tayside*


**(14) QUESTION: Reading Stella Gibbons's *Cold Comfort Farm* reminded me that in my youth there was a farm in my area known as Labour In Vain. What other wry names for farms exist?**

A local farm at Ugthorpe, Whitby, has always been known as Land O'Nod.

*Carol Barker, Saltburn, Cleveland*


There used to be a Starve-All Farm near Sutton Coldfield but the name has been changed in recent years.

*Norman Green, Sutton Coldfield, West Midlands*


Crowthorne Farm in Berkshire was known as Starve-All Farm, because the ground there was so poor.

*Shirley Peckham, New Milton, Hampshire*

In the West Yorkshire village where I was born seventy-five years ago, there was one farm called Waste Not Want Not and another known as Grow Nowt.

*Mrs D. Fuller, Keighley, Yorkshire*

When I lived on the Dengie Marshes in Essex almost seventy years ago, there were farms there called Small Gains and Bad Knocks.

*Ron Kemp, Colchester, Essex*

Locally, I can find No Man's Friend, Cleaving Grange, Sheep Walk, Frog's Nest, Workhouse, Old Harbour, Moneypot Hill and Sober Hill farms.

*Ron Farley, Selby, North Yorkshire*

Driving between Honiton and Sidmouth, Devon, I always shiver when passing Gobsore Farm on Gobsore Hill.

*Hazel Martin, Taunton, Somerset*

When I was delivering grass seed in the area of high security around Long Lartin prison, I noted a nearby property called Long Stretch Farm.

*Alan Szkudlarek, Cheltenham, Gloucestershire*

## (15) QUESTION: Are animals left- or right-pawed in the same way as humans are left- or right-handed?

Some animals, such as sheep or birds, do nothing in which they could express a tendency to use one side more than the other but some animals certainly do. Male fiddler crabs have one small and one large claw and use the large one for signalling to females. Some males have the large claw on the left and others on the right.

In a study, captive orang-utans tended to be left-handed when scratching but used both hands equally when eating. Some capuchin monkeys tend to be left-handed while others are right-handed. It is also said that elephants have a preference for which side of their trunk to use when moving logs or digging.

*Dr Peter Cotgreave, Zoological Society of London*

We've discovered recently that parrots are either right- or left-footed – and the majority of them favour their left side.

My researchers studied 320 parrots from sixteen Australian species to see which eye they used to view potential foods. We found that roughly 47 per cent were left-handed, 33 per cent right-handed, and the remainder ambidextrous. In some cases, young birds appeared to experiment with both sides before finally settling on one.

You can see a very close relationship between the eye they use to view the object and the foot they use to grasp it. It's very consistent across all parrot species studied, except for a couple.

*Dr Calum Brown, from Macquarie University, Sydney*

**(16) QUESTION: When foreigners speak English with an accent, we often find it attractive, even sexy. Do we British sound attractive to them when we speak their language with an accent?**

People speaking French with an English accent do sound attractive. The best example I know of is actress Jane Birkin, whose accent is delightful. I could listen to her for days.

*Jocelyn Leboucher, Romford, Essex*

As a German who has lived in England for some time, I find it most charming to hear German spoken with an English accent. It doesn't matter if you confuse the German articles, *der*, *die* and *das*, or don't know how to pronounce certain words, the effort is greatly appreciated.

*Katharina Froemming, Swindon, Wiltshire*

When I worked for a multi-national firm in Munich, though fluent in German, I was teased mercilessly because I couldn't roll my Rs. I was told my French accent was about as sexy as fish and chips, my lisping attempts as Spanish comparable to a rainy day in London and my Italian had as much temperament as our national anthem.

My French colleague, meanwhile, could stop traffic with her voice, whichever language she used.

*Lynn Bruce, Chippenham, Wiltshire*

I don't know whether I sounded sexy but when I spoke Dutch to the Dutch, I was mortified to be answered in French.

*Mrs J. Foxon, Hinckley, Leicestershire*

My husband worked in Algeria for six years and spoke French all the time. He was once in a bar in Marseilles when the barman asked him to leave. When my husband asked why, he was shown a notice which said: 'No North Africans.' Perhaps the Lancashire accent and the big moustache didn't help.

*Mrs S. Myerscough, Westhoughton, Greater Manchester*

## (17) QUESTION: How do moles get all that dirt to the surface?

The European mole, 10 cm long and weighing 100 g (4 in and 3½ oz), is common in Britain but seldom seen because it spends most of its life underground in an elaborate tunnel system.

Each mole builds a tunnel complex, insulated from extreme temperatures and weather conditions on the surface, providing a ready source of earthworms and other invertebrates the mole eats.

The ovoid tunnels are generally 4 or 5 cm wide, maybe a metre deep and hundreds of metres long. Unfortunately for gardeners and farmers, moles generally inhabit soft ground.

They make their tunnels by moving through the soil, packing it behind with one paw and pushing it upwards with the other. They create many openings to minimize the distance they have to push the spoil out of their tunnels.

Moles are very strong and appear almost to swim through very soft soils. In normal soil they can travel at around 5 metres an hour. When a quantity of soil has collected behind it, the mole turns round and pushes it to the nearest opening, creating the unsightly mounds of soil so dreaded by gardeners.

*Martyn Gorman, The Mammal Society, London SW8*


**(18) QUESTION: If fiscal is to do with money, why are Scottish prosecutors called procurators fiscal?**

The office of procurator fiscal was first recorded in 1584, though it certainly existed before that.

Until 1746, the sheriff, roughly equivalent to a combination of an English crown court judge and a stipendiary magistrate, kept the fines collected in his court. The procurator fiscal was his agent, collecting fines and paying them into his treasury, the fisc.

The role of procurator fiscal developed gradually into that of public prosecutor in the sheriff court until he no longer had any responsibility for fines, though he has retained his historic title.

*Alastair Brown, Senior Procurator Fiscal Depute, Edinburgh*


This makes one wonder how the South African bird, the fiscal shrike, got its name. Shrikes are small, predatory birds, with hooked beaks, which feed on insects, small mammals and birds, often impaling their prey on thorns or pointed branches, leaving it to hang there as a type of 'larder'.

An 1872 book on African birds says the fiscal shrike earned its name from the title of the Dutch magistrate, the *fiskal*, of former times who, as well as collecting revenue, was the keeper of public order, responsible for hangings. One nickname for the fiscal shrike is Johnny Hangman.

In the UK, the closely related red-backed shrike is nicknamed butcher-bird for similar reasons.

*Chris Harbard, Royal Society for the Protection of Birds,*
*Sandy, Bedfordshire*

## (19) QUESTION: Who were 'the Four Marys'?

In 1542, six days after the birth of Mary Stuart, only child of King James V of Scotland and Mary of Guise (or Lorraine), the king died at Falkland Palace and the throne passed to the small child, who later became Mary Queen of Scots.

In 1548, when Mary was six years old, her mother arranged for her to be sent to France for education at the French court. Four Scottish girls, all of the same age, were chosen as her companions. These girls were Mary Fleming (or Flemyng), Mary Seton (or Seyton), Mary Beaton (or Bethune) and Mary Livingston (or Leuson). The girls stayed with Mary throughout her time in France and one, Mary Seton, stayed in service with her for more than thirty years.

The Four Marys are noted in many well-known folk ballads and even children's nursery rhymes, such as 'Mary, Mary, Quite Contrary', where they are referred to as 'pretty maids all in a row'.

*Mary Sinclair, Dundee*

When Mary Queen of Scots' maidservants, the Marys Livingstone, Seaton, Beaton and Fleming became the original Four Marys, the application of the name Mary to an attendant on a Scottish Queen wasn't new. It derived from the Icelandic *maer*, a virgin or maid, and had previously been applied to an attendant on James V's wife.

Three of the Marys left the Queen when they married but Mary Seton never wed and followed the Queen to her English captivity until ill-health forced her to leave her mistress and retire to France.

The personnel and story behind the ballad 'The Four Marys', however, which has been traced to the eighteenth century, refer to a different story: 'Last night the Queen had four Maries/Tonight there'll be but three/There's Mary Seton and Mary Beaton And Mary Carmichael and me.' There was no Mary Carmichael in the Scottish Queen's entourage.

This song is believed to refer to an incident at the court of Tsar Peter the Great. Mary Hamilton (the subject of the ballad), a Scottish-born attendant on the Russian Empress, was executed for the murder of her illegitimate child following a liaison with Peter.

The well-known fact that Mary Queen of Scots had four Marys became superimposed on the tragic story of Mary Hamilton.

*Howard Pizzey, Staplehurst, Kent*

In the 1950s and '60s, The Four Marys appeared in the girls' comic *Bunty*. They were Mary Radleigh, Mary Cotter, Mary Field and Mary Simpson who attended St Elmo's boarding school where they had the usual schoolgirl adventures.

They were known by their abbreviated surnames Raddy, Cotty, Fieldy and Simpy. Raddy was of aristocratic descent, Cotty was a scatty girl, Fieldy was the hockey and games champion and Simpy was middle class, having a father who was 'in trade'.

Their headmistress was Dr Gull, who wore mannish suits, and their teacher Miss Creef, resplendent in pince-nez and flowing gown.

*Jenny Payne, Sittingbourne, Kent*

**(20) QUESTION: Under which Minister of Education were the most grammar schools closed?**

Although the Labour Government of 1964–70 is credited with

ending selective education, only 235 out of 1,273 grammar schools in England and Wales were closed or turned into comprehensives during its term in office.

In the subsequent Conservative Government, Margaret Thatcher was Education Secretary from June 1970, beginning with just over 1,000 grammar schools, a further 463 of which had gone by the time the Conservatives lost power in 1974, leaving Lady Thatcher with the record for closing most.

A further 111 grammar schools disappeared by January 1975, approval for their closure having come from Margaret Thatcher.

In her biography, Lady Thatcher admits that during her tenure at Education, she received 3,600 proposals for schools to go comprehensive and accepted 91 per cent of them.

*Olive Forsythe, National Union of Teachers, London*

**(21) QUESTION: Living on the coast, I'm acutely aware of how we use the sea to dispose of sewage. How do landlocked countries such as Switzerland deal with their sewage?**

The more treatment stages sewage goes through, the cleaner the final waste water. UK sewage is often discharged into the sea after only minimal treatment, though greater treatment is common where sewage works discharge into rivers.

Sewage causes considerable pollution in Britain and it has recently been reported that many lakes are severely affected by nutrients in sewage encouraging thick growths of algae.

Switzerland has a very high standard of treatment plants at its lakesides, including requirements for nutrient removal, an advanced form of sewage treatment installed at only a very few sites in the UK.

*Mary Taylor, Friends of the Earth, London*

**(22) QUESTION: As a beer drinker since 1937, I'd like to know whether my favourite tipple was stronger before the Second World War, when it used to cost 6d a pint.**

The effects of two world wars have left modern brews weaker. In both conflicts, the original gravity of beer was reduced through lack of raw materials and the need for sober armaments workers.

The 1932 average was 1041 original gravity, dropping to 1032.7 in 1948. It moved up slightly in 1950 and has gone up slowly in the past twenty years. The rising diversity of premium products, continental-style lagers and characterful cask ales on offer today has seen a gradual increase in beer strength.

*Richard Gibb, Corporate Affairs Director,*
*Scottish & Newcastle plc, Edinburgh*

Guinness Extra Stout cost 6d in 1916 and 1917 and was 10d a pint between 1928 and 1939. Its alcoholic strength was reduced during both world wars in reaction to huge increases in excise duty.

It was 1073.8 original gravity (7.7 per cent Alcohol By Volume) in 1917, falling to 1047.8 (5 per cent ABV) by 1919. By 1940 it was back up to 1054 (5.7 per cent ABV) but by 1946 it was down to 1041.3 (4.3 per cent ABV) again, increasing to 1048 (5 per cent ABV) by 1950. Apart from duty increases, technical developments increased the stability of lower gravity beers, which has meant that their strength has never climbed back to their original levels.

A perfect pint of draught Guinness today is brewed to 1038 (4.1 per cent ABV) and Guinness Original in bottles and cans at 1040.5 (4.3 per cent ABV). Guinness Foreign Stout, brewed in Dublin and available in bottles, is brewed to 1072 (7.2 per cent ABV).

*Jeremy Probert, Guinness Brewing GB,*
*Park Royal Brewery, London*

**(23) QUESTION: 'A frog he would a-wooing go, Heigh ho! says Rowley.' What is this nursery rhyme about and who is Rowley?**

This popular nursery rhyme runs to at least fourteen verses, the first of which, according to the most recent version popularized by Grimaldi and comedian John Liston, begins: 'A frog he would a-wooing go, Heigh ho! says Rowley/A frog he would a-wooing go/Whether his mother would let him or no/With a Rowley, powley, gammon and spinach/Heigh ho! says Anthony Rowley.'

It's suggested that Rowley refers to Charles II who was nicknamed 'Old Rowley' after his favourite stallion but the rhyme was first noted earlier.

A more likely explanation is that Rowley comes from 'rowley powley', a name given to a plump fowl, a tasty dish served with gammon and spinach. The forename Anthony was added later.

The rhyme can be traced back at least four centuries from 'The frog cam to the myl dur' in *The Complaynt of Scotlande* (1549) through to 'A Most Strange Weddinge of the Frogge and the Mowse', a ballad licensed by stationers Edward White in 1580.

No deep meaning relating to the rhyme has been developed.

*Iona Opie, editor:* Oxford Dictionary of Nursery Rhymes, *Oxford University Press*

**(24) QUESTION: Why are slices of toast dipped in boiled eggs called 'soldiers'?**

Most dictionaries define a 'soldier' in this context as a 'narrow strip of bread or toast, given to children to dip in a boiled egg'. The name came from the understanding of a soldier as something straight, upright and in ranks, as 'soldiers' are when cut up into straight pieces like soldiers on parade.

*Lorna Gilmour, Collins Dictionaries, Glasgow*

To qualify as a 'soldier' the bread must be soft and oblong in shape. Untoasted bread, preferably buttered is ideal. Next, it must be lightly dipped, not thrust in. Finally the whole process must be carried out responsibly, leaving no stains on the tablecloth. There you have it: a Soft Oblong Lightly Dipped In Egg, Responsibly.

*K. Harrow, Lambeth Walk, SE11*

**(25) QUESTION: My male voice choir is learning 'The Whiffenpoof Song'. What are its origins and what on earth do the words mean?**

From February 1909, an informal Yale University singing group consisting of Meade Minnigerode, George Pommeroy, James Howard, Carl Lohmann and Denton Fowler began holding regular Monday-night meetings at Old Mory's, in New Haven, Connecticut.

'Manager' Robert Mallory and 'trainer' Richard Hosford, whose primary duties were to supply food and drink, were added and they called themselves The Whiffenpoofs, after a fish character in the popular musical comedy *Little Nemo*. The eighth member, Ted Guest, joined from 1910 with the official title of Perpetual Guest.

The Whiffenpoofs, their numbers rising gradually to the current fourteen, are Yale seniors chosen to continue the tradition. They travel extensively, giving concerts as far from Yale as Japan, Greece, Singapore and the UK.

*Gerry Hughes, British Association of Barbershop Singers*

The Whiffenpoof Anthem is a skit on Rudyard Kipling's 'Gentlemen-Rankers':

*To the tables down at Mory's*
*To the place where Louis dwells*
*To the dear old Temple Bar we love so well*
*Sing the Whiffenpoofs assembled with their glasses raised on high*
*And the magic of the singing casts its spell. Yes!*

24

*The magic of the singing of the songs we love so well*
*'Shall I Wasting' and 'Mavourneen' and the rest;*
*We will serenade our Louis while life and voice shall last*
*Then we'll pass and be forgotten with the rest.*
*We are poor little lambs who have lost our way, Baa, baa, baa.*
*Little black sheep who have gone astray, Baa, baa, baa,*
*Gentlemen songsters off on a spree*
*Damned from here to eternity,*
*God have mercy on such as we, Baa, baa, baa.*

The Temple Bar in Mory's was their meeting place. Louis is Louis Linder, first honorary Whiffenpoof and proprietor of the bar until his death in 1913. 'Shall I Wasting' and 'Mavourneen' were popular Whiffenpoof songs.

*John Reach, Whiffenpoof member and tour manager,*
*Connecticut, US*

Kipling's 'Gentlemen-Rankers' told the tale of well-bred gentlemen who, having been convicted of a crime, enlisted in the Army as privates to mitigate the disgrace they had brought on their families.

The words were changed by US students to tell the tale of those who spent more time enjoying themselves than studying. Their 'Whiffenpoof Song' became something of an anthem among aircrew of the American 8th Air Force in Britain during the Second World War.

*Reg Murphy, London SE22*

## (26) QUESTION: How did Britain come to own and then give away Heligoland?

Heligoland is Germany's only high-seas island, 38 miles out into the North Sea from the state of Schleswig-Holstein. It measures just over 2 sq km and has a population of almost two thousand whose main language is German, plus a distinct dialect.

Its first inhabitants are thought to have been Frisian fishermen before 1402 when it came under the control of Schleswig-Holstein. Danes took over in 1714 until the Napoleonic Wars when the British occupied it to keep it from French control.

After the abdication of Napoleon in 1814, the Congress of Vienna gave control of the island to Britain.

In 1890, the Anglo-German Convention handed Heligoland and the Caprivi Strip in Africa to Germany in exchange for acceptance of British control over Zanzibar and Uganda.

The island became a major German naval base during both world wars. In 1945 it fell under British control again and its population was evacuated to mainland Germany before the destruction of all fortifications on the island in 1947 in the largest non-nuclear explosion in history. The inhabitants were allowed to return from 1952.

The island today (known as one of the major pollen-free areas in Germany) is regularly visited by millions every year.

*Thomas Wulfing, German embassy, London*

After Britain took over the island in 1814, Hamburg postage stamps continued to be issued there until replaced by Queen Victoria stamps in 1867.

These were highly unusual among British stamps in that, until 1890, they were printed in Berlin, with values in German currency. Later issues had the equivalent value in pence and shillings alongside the German amount. Many are now scarce collectors' items.

*D. A. Tyrrell, Crewe*

**(27) QUESTION: Why 'sideburns'? What is so inflammable about such facial hair?**

Sideburns were originally 'burnsiders'. 'Mutton chop' or sidebar whiskers with a shaved chin and full moustache, were popularized

26

by General Ambrose Everett Burnside (1824–1881) in the American Civil War.

Though an innovative strategist, Burnside was dogged by misjudgement and bad luck and his spectacular failures and occasional victories kept his portrait in the papers. Though popular with his men, so many of whose lives he cost, he was less well regarded by the White House and Federal Command.

Apart from sideburns, he gave his name to the Burnside carbine and Burnside hat. He went on to become Governor of Rhode Island for three terms and was twice elected to the Senate.

*Maurice Wedgewood, Darlington, Co Durham*

General Burnside had a bridge named after him after the Battle of Antietam on 17 September 1862, when his Union troops spent more than two hours and lost 500 men for just 160 Confederate dead trying to cross a bridge over Antietam Creek. In all, the day saw the deaths of more than 23,000 men – the bloodiest day in American history.

Burnside commanded the main Union force, the Army of the Potomac, at the disastrous Battle of Fredericksburg in December 1862 and was relieved of his command a month later.

*Anne Dawson, Blackpool*

Apart from his sideburns, in the 1850s Ambrose Burnside invented a very accurate, fast breech-loading cavalry carbine. But his company went into liquidation. In 1860, nine months before the American Civil War started, the company which had bought his patent was selling two thousand of these guns a month but Burnside never profited from his invention.

*D. J. Hearn, Gravesend, Kent*

General Ambrose Burnside, whose name was applied to what were otherwise known as 'mutton chop' whiskers, was succeeded as commander of the main Union army by General Joseph Hooker – from whose female camp-followers we derive the term for prostitutes.

When military provosts tried to drive them out of the camp, they were prevented from doing so because 'the women were Hooker's'.

*Euan Grant, London N10*

While on holiday in Canada, I visited a historic pioneer village where there was a gunsmith's shop. The expert there told us that sideburns were grown to prevent the face being burnt when the powder in a rifle exploded to expel a shot.

*Janice Chalmers, London SE16*

## (28) QUESTION: What is stargazy pie and where does it originate?

Cornwall lays claim to this dish though details of its origin are obscure. According to F. W. P. Jago's *Dialect of Cornwall* (1882), star-gazing, staare-gaase or starry pie is made of leek and pilchards with the fish heads protruding star-wards through the crust. R. Morton Nance's 1963 *Glossary of Cornish Sea Words* says this once familiar delicacy has now become a legend.

The legend has its roots in the Cornish fishing village of Mousehole. About two hundred years ago, Mousehole fishermen were prevented from putting to sea by a terrible storm which raged for many weeks and supplies of fish ran low. With Christmas approaching, Tom Bawcock put to sea in the storm and his voyage produced a huge catch of seven kinds of fish. The villagers were fed and among the dishes made was star-gazy pie, with fish showing through the crust to demonstrate the abundance of the catch.

Thereafter, each 23 December, Tom Bawcock's Eve is celebrated in Mousehole with merriment, drinking, eating star-gazy pie and singing Tom Bawcock's song: 'A merry place you may believe/Was Mouzel 'pon Tom Bawcock's Eve/To be there then who wud'n wish/To sup o' seb'm sorts o' fish./When morgy brath [sand fish] had cleared the path/Comed lances [tiny fish] for a fry/And then we had a bit o' scad [mackerel]/And Starry-Gazy pie.'

This tale is somewhat suspect as an origin for the pie but recipes for it appeared in Cornish cook books of the twenties when it was suggested the arrangement of fish belonged to a time when no one minded seeing an animal, like the boar's head, peacock or hare, cooked as if it were alive. It was also noted that tilting the heads upwards means that the nourishing oil from the fish head drains into the body to enrich the pie.

The legend was given new life by Antonia Barber and Nicola Bayley's children's story *The Mousehole Cat*, also made into a short film in which the inhabitants of Mousehole can be seen celebrating Tom Bawcock to this day.

*Graham Lang, Menheniot, Cornwall*

**(29) QUESTION: Do historians have any clear idea of the total human population of the Earth around the year of Jesus's birth?**

Total population for the first two million years of human history is generally considered to have remained stable at about ten million, consistent with a global hunter-gatherer existence.

The period 9,000 to 2,400 BC, with an increase in the number of permanent settlements as people began to establish animal husbandry and develop farm systems so that less land was needed to sustain larger communities, saw great population growth. By the time of Christ's birth, global population is thought to have risen to twenty-five times its Neolithic size, or around 250 million.

Today's population is about 7 billion – more than twenty-seven times the population at the time of Christ.

*Bruce Bannerman, Edinburgh*

**(30) QUESTION: Why 'virger', not 'verger', at St Paul's Cathedral?**

'Virger' comes from the Latin *virgarius*, someone who uses a *virgula*: a small rod. Among other roles, today's virgers still carry a small silver rod to lead processions.

Verger with an 'e' is simply another English spelling, found in the Rolls of Parliament as early as 1472: 'Henry, late Duke of Lancaster, funded a church with a Deane and six Choristers and a Verger perpetuell . . .'

Spelling of many words has changed over the years but our cathedral statutes have always spelled virger with an 'i' rather than an 'e' and this tradition is upheld today.

*Canon John Haliburton, Chancellor of St Paul's Cathedral, London*

**(31) QUESTION: What is the shortest number of years it would take, in theory, to get from the lowest amateur football league to the Premier League?**

In theory, the non-League pyramid system allows a team playing in the first division of a county league to be taking on Manchester United in the Premier League within six years.

Promotion would have to be achieved in consecutive seasons. At each stage, the ground criteria established by the immediately senior league would have to be met, with promotion through the leagues entailing considerable financial outlay.

Below county level, there are thousands of teams playing in amateur leagues on park pitches whose dreams of playing in the Premier League remain inaccessible.

*David Barber, Football Association, London*

Bradford Park Avenue was once members of the Football League First Division, equivalent to today's Premiership, but had dropped out of the League by the time they went into liquidation in 1974.

On reformation in 1988, the club had to start in Division Three of the West Riding Country Amateur League, twelve levels below the Premiership, surely the greatest fall from grace in football history.

Bradford is now halfway back, playing six levels higher, in the Northern Premier League Premier Division. But it all might have been different: they once interviewed Bill Shankly for the manager's job – and turned him down.

*Pete Zemroch, Little Sutton, Shropshire*


**(32) QUESTION: I was one of nine bridesmaids at a wedding. What is the highest number of bridesmaids at a single wedding in Britain?**

When my mother had nine bridesmaids at her wedding in 1959, it made the front page of the local paper because bride and bridesmaids were all sisters.

*Bill Wilson, Watford, Hertfordshire*


In April 1954, a Miss Hughes of Basingstoke had ten bridesmaids at her wedding at St Michael's, Basingstoke. Hundreds of people turned out to see this 'wedding of the year' as she was the daughter of a local man who had won £75,000 on the football pools earlier that year, a considerable sum in those days.

The great number of bridesmaids was the talking point among local folk for weeks.

*Robert Brown, Basingstoke, Hampshire*


The twelve bridesmaids at Queen Victoria's wedding to Prince Albert at the Chapel Royal in St James's Palace in 1840, all daughters of the highest in the land, were referred to as Train Bearers.

*Ida Mary Goodrick, Tadcaster, North Yorkshire*

On 23 October 1936, when I was fifteen, I stood outside the door of Durham Cathedral to watch Sir Alec Douglas Home and his bride, Miss Elizabeth Arlington, with her fourteen bridesmaids.

*Mrs D. U. Smith, Luton, Bedfordshire*

Dame Barbara Cartland's daughter by her first marriage, Miss Raine McCorquodale, had sixteen bridesmaids when she married the Hon. Gerald Legge, the future Earl of Dartmouth, at St Margaret's Westminster on 21 July 1948. I was one of the thirty-two ushers, two to each bridesmaid when it came to taking them out for the evening after the reception.

*Gordon Fergusson, Tarporley, Cheshire*

Prominent in British wedding culture since the marriage of Princess Alexandra in 1863, the bridesmaid's traditional role is to protect the bride from evil spirits. The saying 'three times a bridesmaid, never a bride' is said to arise from the idea that a bridesmaid of three weddings will never marry because she has cushioned too much of the bad luck that would otherwise have gone to each bride.

The average number of bridesmaids today is three, but our files reveal weddings where there were more. Maria Gay, of Bedford, married with thirteen bridesmaids which, she assures us, was not unlucky. Sharon Howett, of Barking, Essex, had sixteen, while Patricia Seymour, of Kidderminster, had eighteen. The record goes to Tina Frost, of Rotherham, who married in June 1982 with twenty-one bridesmaids.

*Jane Bruton,* Wedding and Home *magazine, London*

My mother had twenty-two bridesmaids at her wedding when she married my father in St Patrick's Cathedral, Dublin, on 8 December 1938. She had one bridesmaid for each year of her age plus one to even up the numbers.

As Patricia Kennedy, she married Dermot McGillycuddy, second son of Senator, Lieutenant Colonel, The McGillycuddy of the Reeks, DSO. He held all three honours then, having served in the First World War, resigned his commission to inherit from his father in 1921 and re-enlisted for service in Northern Ireland following the outbreak of the Second World War.

*Donough McGillycuddy, Welford, Northamptonshire*

As a child, I knew a lady who taught at my local primary school who had her entire class, around thirty, as pageboys and brides-maids when she married.

*Mrs L. A. White, Herne Bay, Kent*

**(33) QUESTION: In about 1950, when petrol was still rationed, a Mr Baxter of Oxfordshire invented a substitute called Baxtrol. What became of Mr Baxter and his substitute fuel?**

When war ended in 1945, private motoring petrol rationing continued with an allowance of 270 miles a month. In 1948, this was slashed to a miserly 90 miles a month.

Mr Baxter had no need to invent anything. Well-known alternative fuels existed in the form of alcohols obtained from coal-fed gas works. Pre-war motorists used Cleveland Discol and National Benzol Mixture as blends with petrol.

I bought the odd gallon of Baxtrol in Leeds during 1948/49 for my 1934 Riley 9 Kestrel, paying 5 shillings a gallon, more than twice the cost of ration-book petrol at 2s a gallon. The real cost was higher because, for good combustion, Baxtrol's alcohol mix required one to keep the choke out much of the time.

*Mr P. Albericci, Heaton Mersey, Cheshire*

Petrol and diesel, refined from oil, have dominated the transport fuel market for 100 years but during oil shortages such as the

Second World War and the seventies' oil crisis, alternatives derived from coal have been explored. British Coal developed a technically efficient process to convert coal into transport fuel but it was too expensive to compete with oil-derived fuels.

Petrol and diesel engines can be converted to run on renewable fuels derived from biomass. Ethanol, made by fermenting sugar cane, wheat or barley has been widely used and methanol, from landfill gas or sewage plants, and vegetable oils, such as rapeseed oil, can be used in adapted diesel engines.

There are alternative transport fuels but while oil is cheap and plentiful and politicians work in days, rather than in years, these are of only academic interest.

*Dr Brian C. Williams and Dr David McIlveen-Wright, Centre for Energy Research, Northern Ireland*

**(34) QUESTION: A large brain is supposed to distinguish Homo sapiens from less intelligent species but is there any evidence that brain size in individual humans relates to their intelligence?**

In October 1907, a man called Daniel Lyon died of a throat infection in New York. He had spent more than twenty years as a night watchman and labourer and could read and write and appeared normal in every way but at post mortem his brain was shown to weigh just 680 g. The normal weight of an adult male brain is around 1,500 g and Mr Lyon's lightest of brains is now entered in the *Guinness Book of Records*.

The theory of evolution has assumed that the increased size of human brains has been one of the reasons why humans have succeeded so well on Earth but even with a brain of half normal size, Daniel Lyon lived a normal life. One explanation of this case is that life as a night watchman in turn-of-the-century New York was less demanding intellectually than that of a hunter gatherer two million years ago.

*Dr Peter Rowen, Medical Consultant, Guinness Book of Records*

It's been known for many years that human intelligence is related to the number of grey brain cells, the 'grey matter', found mainly on the surface of the Great Brain, the cerebrum: the greater the number of grey cells, the greater the intelligence.

Sheer brain weight isn't normally significant to intelligence. An average adult male brain weighs 1,500 g, heavier than the average female brain at 1,335 g, but it would be dangerous to infer any male claim to intellectual superiority due to the weight of his brain.

*Peter Fraser, Norwich, Norfolk*

### (35) QUESTION: Do we really know what Jesus Christ looked like? Who first painted or drew the likeness we are used to today?

We don't know what Jesus looked like, though we know he was a first-century Palestinian Jew, and therefore presumably had the characteristics of his people. Christian imagery varies enormously, particularly as artists have often symbolized the Christian teaching that Jesus is God-made-man by representing Jesus as belonging to their own race. Hence the rather European-looking Jesus figures we're familiar with.

Some artists have been influenced by relics which are claimed to show 'imprints' of Jesus, such as the Turin Shroud, which may account for some similarities between different artists' representations.

Most of the depictions of Christ up to the sixth century were thought to have been of a young, beardless man with short hair. When St Augustine of Hippo wrote in the fifth century, he noted there were no pictures of Christ.

In the next century, this all changed as throughout the Middle East, moving into Eastern Europe, hundreds of depictions of a long-haired, bearded man were seen.

One of the first of these is the 'Christ Pantocrator' dating from the sixth century, found at St Catherine's Monastery in the Sinai.

*B. Jennings, Manchester*

It's intriguing that the New Testament doesn't give any hint as to Jesus Christ's physical appearance. Many biblical heroes and heroines are vividly described: Joseph was 'well-built and handsome' (Gen. 39); King Saul – 'no-one among the Israelites were handsomer than he' (Sam., 1, 9); David was 'ruddy, bright-eyed and fair to look upon' (Sam., 1, 16).

With these descriptions in mind, one wonders what describing Jesus as 'presumably having the racial characteristics of his people' tells us. The Children of Israel, then and now, exhibit a sturdy variety of appearance and personality. Jesus wouldn't have described himself as 'a Palestinian Jew' but as a Jew from Galilee or Judaea.

*Rona Hart, Board of Deputies of British Jews, London*

The only record we have of what Jesus looked like is the prophesy in Isaiah 53:2, which says: 'He hath no form nor comeliness and when we shall see Him there is no beauty that we should desire Him.'

This is quite different from the tall, handsome man with long hair and beard depicted in the Turin Shroud and the thousands of pictures painted by artists through the ages. Jesus was so indistinguishable in a crowd that Judas Iscariot had to point him out to the soldiers who came to arrest him.

*Dr Philip Jones, Parkstone, Dorset*

## (36) QUESTION: Which is the most common bird on the planet? And the rarest?

The most numerous bird is probably the tropical African finch known as the Red-Billed Quelea of which there are in excess of 100,000 million, at least seventeen times the human global population.

This tiny creature is also the world's worst bird pest. Flocks of millions of them descend on crops and wipe them out as effectively as swarms of locusts. Quelea control is a huge problem in many African countries.

More than 1,100 of the world's 10,000 bird species are endangered. Rarest of all is probably Spix's Macaw, a South American blue parrot which has suffered from the loss of its tropical woodland habitat and, more recently, from the ruthless, illegal, bird trade.

*Mike Everett, Royal Society for the Protection of Birds,*
*Sandy, Bedfordshire*

**(37) QUESTION: Was that a male stand-in I spotted doing a stunt for actress Madeleine Carroll in Alfred Hitchcock's 1935 version of *The 39 Steps*?**

Alfred Hitchcock's assistant in 1935, Penrose 'Pen' Tennyson, donned a dress and blond wig to replace Ms Carroll for a scene in which her character has to leap a stream.

Great-grandson of Poet Laureate Alfred, Lord Tennyson, Pen soon graduated from actor's stand-in to England's youngest film director and made his first film, the boxing drama *There Ain't No Justice*, in 1939.

A studio joke at the time was that he shouted 'Break, break, break!' (in honour of his famous forebear's poem 'In Memoriam') instead of the usual 'Cut!'

He directed two more feature films and several shorts but a promising career was terminated by the Second World War when volunteer Naval Reservist Sub-Lieutenant Tennyson was killed in a flying accident.

*Harry Grace, Edgbaston, Birmingham*

I was enchanted to read about Pen Tennyson doing a stunt for Madeleine. Had he lived, Pen would certainly have been one of the great film directors. I looked on him as an elder brother.

A few weeks before he was killed in the Blitz, he gave me his watch and 12-bore shotgun, both of which I still have. I also have several hilarious letters he wrote to my late father from his training ship HMS *King Alfred*. When he married actress Nova Pilbeam, they honeymooned at our house in Sussex.

*Jonathan Balcon, Sevenoaks, Kent*

**(38) QUESTION: To start early flying machines, the mechanic and pilot called 'Switches off!' and 'Contact!'. What did this mean?**

Early aircraft engines were started by swinging the propeller – like cranking a car engine with a starting handle – and had two switches for the two magnetos. The complex system of calls was to ensure safety for the mechanic during starting.

With no brakes, the wheels were wedged with wooden chocks as the mechanic called 'Switches off, throttle set, suck in' and the pilot repeated the call, making sure both switches were in the off position while the propeller was rotated a few times to draw petrol mixture into the cylinders.

The mechanic would then call: 'Switch on. Contact', as the pilot switched on the impulse magneto and repeated the call, often shortened to 'Contact'. The mechanic would then pull down on the prop blade and quickly step aside. When the engine had fired up, the pilot would switch on the running magneto and call 'Chocks away!' as he opened the throttle to increase slipstream over the rudder to gain directional control on his way to the take-off point.

Today's light aircraft are started with parking brake applied and a shout of 'Clear props!' before turning an ignition key as in a car.

*A. F. Harris (ex-RAF pilot), Lower Bosoughan, Cornwall*

**(39) QUESTION: What was the Anselmo trial often referred to in American TV crime series?**

On 13 December 1971, the Supreme Court of Louisiana ruled, in the case of the State of Louisiana v Philip J. Anselmo Jnr and Terrance C. Lee, that a substantial amount of drugs and guns seized by police officers at the defendants' rented apartment in New Orleans couldn't be used as evidence against them because of the manner in which it had been obtained.

The court was told that police officers Jerry Faulkner and James Lewis, both of good standing, obtained the search warrant on the affidavit of an informer who said he had attended a 'pot party' there – but this was easily disproved. The court decided that as the warrant had been obtained on false grounds, any evidence it helped to supply should be omitted from the court case.

*Cindy Watson, Chicago, Illinois*

## (40) QUESTION: Why are strict laws characterized as 'draconian'?

Draconian, meaning particularly harsh or severe, comes from the code of laws drawn up in the seventh century BC by Athenian lawgiver Draco. He was appointed in 621 BC with the main task of replacing the practice of individual revenge with public justice and punishment.

Almost all offences listed were punishable by death because Draco is said to have claimed: 'Small crimes deserve death and for great crimes I know of no penalty more severe.'

Draconian law, though successful in stemming crime, was highly unpopular and was replaced in 594 BC when Solon, one of the fathers of Athenian democracy, became the law-giver.

*David Gordon, Perth, Scotland*

Seventh-century BC Athens didn't benefit very much from law-giver Draco's reforms. The story goes that he met his end when the Athenians threw their cloaks over him, pretending it was a sign of affection but in fact depositing so many of them that they crushed him to death.

*John Thorpe, Urmston, Manchester*

**(41) QUESTION: Was an amateur football team once mistaken for Wolverhampton Wanderers FC and obliged to play a top German Bundesliga team in front of 40,000?**

When our Wolverhampton Sunday League side, Oxbarn Sports and Social Club, went on a tour of Germany in summer 1973, someone at the German end took our description 'from Wolverhampton' to mean that we were Wolverhampton Wanderers.

We realized something was wrong when we arrived at FC Mainz to find large crowds turning up for the match. The mistake was rapidly realized by the Germans and announced over the loud speakers to a very amused crowd of about 10,000.

The crowd and officials insisted the game went ahead and we got good support from the home fans every time we got near their goal – which wasn't often. We eventually lost 14–0 but we had a fantastic reception from our hosts after the game, followed by huge media interest.

Wolverhampton Wanderers' then manager, Bill McGarry, promised to take his side to Germany to avenge our defeat but he was sacked shortly afterwards and it didn't happen. Perhaps our present manager Mick McCarthy would like the challenge?

*Phil Horton, Bridgwater, Somerset*

A similar misunderstanding occurred in April 1970 when Birmingham-based Twenty Two Youth Club toured Scotland, playing other youth clubs. The team were mistakenly thought to represent Birmingham City FC and arrived in Glasgow to find themselves lined up against a selection of Celtic and Rangers youth players, including George Stein, son of former Celtic manager Jock Stein.

This was the first time the two Glasgow clubs had co-operated in this way and they played in Celtic kit for the first half and Rangers strip for the second.

The match took place in front of five thousand at Lochburn Park and the enormous gulf in ability was soon apparent. Every time the Scottish team scored there was a mini pitch invasion, which initially frightened the Birmingham team. But in the end it worked to their advantage, restricting playing time so they conceded only seventeen goals.

*J. S. Parkes, Birmingham*

The same thing happened in reverse when Great Britain were drawn to play Bulgaria in a two-leg qualifying round of the soccer finals for the 1972 Munich Olympics.

The Olympics in those days were purely amateur and the Bulgarians were able to field their World Cup side, technically not full-time professionals. These players came here expecting to face the likes of Banks, Moore and Charlton, before a full house at Wembley.

The match was indeed at Wembley, in front of a crowd of three thousand, but the Great Britain team consisted of amateurs from clubs like Hendon and Skelmersdale United. In a giant-killing feat, Great Britain beat Bulgaria 1–0, with Joe Adams of Slough Town scoring with a fifteenth-minute header. But they succumbed 5–0 in the return match in Sofia.

*David Barber, The Football Association, London*

(42) QUESTION: The late Colin Reid used to refer to his wife in his *Daily Mail* column as 'The Chief Fairy' and Arthur Daley called his wife ''Er indoors'. I call mine 'The Management'. What do other men call their wives?

Since we married forty-nine years ago, I've called my wife 'Princess' but she's not so pleased with the title these days.

*B. C. Russell, Windsor, Berkshire*

I call mine 'Treasure' – because she has a sunken chest and people keep asking me where I dug her up.

*David Millard, Walsall, West Midlands*

Eccentric racing commentator John McCririck, no prize himself, calls his wife 'The Booby'.

*Neil Kendall, Blackpool*

I call my wife Dear – because she costs me a fortune.

*Ronnie Thomson, Girvan, Ayrshire*

My husband always calls me 'Baby'. As I'm now seventy, I wonder if he means I have as many wrinkles as when I was one.

*Margaret White, Cardiff*

My husband calls me 'Till' because, as he explains, he puts all his money in but never gets any out.

*Audrey Williams, West Byfleet, Surrey*

The late Roy Castle referred to his wife Fiona as his PLW: Perfect Little Woman.

*Mrs M. Lendon, Buxton, Derbyshire*

During the last years of his life, my husband called me 'You there', and would call out: 'You there, you forgot the Worcester sauce'; 'You there, you forgot the marmalade'; 'You there, I've got the wrong size knife and fork.' I used to shout back: 'There's no one in the kitchen by the name of "You there".'

*Mrs G. Joel, St Margaret's Bay, Kent*

My long-time friend is married to a German lady and for years referred to her, in her absence, as 'The Führer'. I recently noticed that he calls her 'Hun', claiming this is a term of endearment, an abbreviation of honey, but I have my doubts.

I take my orders from 'Brown Owl'.

*Mike Kay, Chelmsford, Essex*

For the first year of the war, I was evacuated to Brety, in Derbyshire, where I was surprised to discover that the local farmers' wives referred to their husbands, without sarcasm, as 'The Master'.

In the case of one retired couple who entertained me to tea, the wife addressed her husband as 'Master'.

*John Crossley, Sutton Coldfield, West Midlands*

### (43) QUESTION: Has there existed, within living memory, a poisonous species of spider native to Britain?

Almost all British spiders produce venom to deal with insects but only about thirty of our 640 native species can give even a modest bite capable of causing a human any pain or swelling.

There's no record in Britain of a human mortality resulting from a spider's bite, though potentially dangerous species occasionally turn up in imports from abroad.

*Paul Hillyard, Spider Specialist at the*
*Natural History Museum, London*

### (44) QUESTION: In my childhood, my family used 'Mazawattee' as a joke name. I came across it again in Nelson Mandela's autobiography, where he says he wore 'rimless Mazawattee tea glasses' as a disguise. Who or what is Mazawattee?

Mazawattee tea, packed by Densham & Sons, was first sold in Britain in 1870. The name, invented by Harrisons & Crosfield buyer D. F. Shillington, proved catchy and Densham's commissioned the granny and grandchild trademark which became as popular as the tea itself.

Calendars and posters featuring 'Granny's Tea' soon became familiar sights and are collector's items today. Gifts including tea caddies and clocks were offered in exchange for coupons from the packets.

John Densham sold the company to a grocery wholesaler just after the Second World War but Mazawattee tea was sold in Britain until the early 1960s.

*Illtyd Lewis, the Tea Council, London*


My husband says the name Mazawattee stood for 'Ma's away to tea', which is why grandma and granddaughter are shown having tea together.

I have a battered tin box which I acquired from my late mother-in-law, who was South African. It dates from the days when tea was expensive and the lady of the house would go out for afternoon tea.

I believe the Mazawattee brand name survived in South Africa after it disappeared from the shelves in Britain.

*Sandra van Eeden, Hayling Island, Hampshire*


As a lad in Deptford in the early 1930s, I played on the banks of the old Grand Surrey Canal alongside the factory producing and packing Mazawattee tea. Parts of the old factory remain, including a large brick clock tower which used to say 'Mazawattee Tea' down its side.

The tea was often sold in hinged-top tea caddies and featured a picture of an old lady sitting in a chair, with rimless glasses perched on her nose, drinking a cup of tea.

*S. Smart Bromley, Kent*

The Mazawattee Tea Warehouse stood on the site now occupied by the Tower Hill Pageant in London. The seven-storey premises were built around 1864.

Much of the part above ground was destroyed during the Blitz but the vaults survived. After the war, these fell into disuse until we took over the lease in 1987.

The remainder of the building, which is listed, was refurbished in Victorian style and now houses the Tower Hill Pageant visitor attraction and shopping arcade.

*Anita Waddell, Tower Hill Pageant*

My great-grandfather John Boon Densham founded the company in the 1860s and it was his son, John Lane Densham, who commissioned the famous 'Old Folks at Home' advertisement in about 1887.

The granny in the oil painting was Mary Ann Clark, wife of an Islington bootmaker. Young Adelaide, her grandchild, was to sit as the little girl but she was overcome by shyness and her place was taken by Alice Emma Nicols, a next-door neighbour.

John Lane was also responsible for the evocative brand name, after a day in the Guildhall Library, working out something snappy and memorable. He eventually settled on a shortened combination of the 'Hindoo' *mazatha* meaning luscious, and the 'Cingalese' *wattee*, a garden of growth.

The company hit the headlines in the late 1890s when it beat other tea companies in a fiercely competitive auction to buy the best 'golden tips' from Ceylon – and again when it deposited the biggest ever cheque for tea duty.

Ironically, it was steep tea duties, not abolished until 1967, which contributed to the eventual decline of the brand, particularly during the Depression years.

*Diana James, London NW11*

There may be other versions of the famous granny and grandchild trademark picture for the Mazawattee tea brand. Commissioned in 1917, there's an oil painting by Harry Gawthorne RA with the artist's mother as granny and myself, aged four.

*Mrs Dora Carter (née Watkins), Kent*

**(45) QUESTION: Why do so supermarkets issue plastic carrier bags with the handles at the ends rather than at the sides?**

Tesco introduced this type of carrier bag, known as the 'vest' style because the handle forms part of the bag, making it much stronger. Bags are made from a continuous tube of film which is flattened to have bag shapes punched out and the open ends sealed.

Bags with handles at the sides have to have them added, making the bag weaker, or handle holes punched out, in which case a reinforcement must be incorporated around the hole, which can come away.

Customers prefer box-shaped bags for easy packing and like the wide handles, which don't cut into their hands.

*Karen Marshall, Tesco, Cheshunt, Hertfordshire*

**(46) QUESTION: To buy a replacement set of wheelnuts for my car would cost 2 per cent of its total new price. How much would it cost to buy an entire vehicle as spare parts at standard retail prices?**

Most theoretical costings for building a car using spare parts come in at between 2 ½ to 3 ½ times the standard retail price of the complete car. And this doesn't account for the labour, space and equipment necessary to do the job.

Additionally, most modern cars consist of hundreds of components which would make assembly very difficult.

The high cost of car spares has concerned consumer groups for many years – car manufacturers make a large proportion of their profits from spares and repairs.

*Terence Jones, Chester*

In 1983, I built a complete Mini, starting from just the body shell. I used spares, mostly from scrap yards, but had to buy some brand new. The project took just over a year and cost me far more than I expected, though it was still less than buying a new car.

However, this doesn't take into account the time and frustration spent on the project and the near-collapse of my marriage. After all that effort, the car gave me nothing but trouble and I soon had to sell it on at far less than it cost to make.

*Kevin Sykes, Huddersfield, West Yorkshire*

A Morris Minor two-door saloon was built entirely from new spare parts by Dutton Forshaw's Swindon Garage for a Rod Law in 1974 for £3,625. The list price for the last car of this type, coming off the BMC production line three years earlier, was only £741, including tax – but this was the period of the 'Barber inflation'.

*Chris Howard, Morris Minor Owners Club*

## (47) QUESTION: Why would anyone want to 'swing a cat' and how much room would they need?

The 'cat' referred to is not your everyday tabby or tom but the cat-o'-nine-tails, an instrument of punishment used by the Royal Navy from the seventeenth to the nineteenth century.

The punishment was always carried out on the upper deck of the ship. A flogging could not be carried out between decks because the low beams prevented the bosun from swinging the cat high enough to get the required force to mete out the punishment properly.

*E. C. Smith, former guide: HMS* Victory, *Warrington, Cheshire*

A 'cat' or 'catch' was a strongly built merchant ship of Scandinavian design, once a common sight sailing up the Thames laden with such cargoes as salt. Sir Richard (Dick) Whittington, Lord Mayor of London in 1397, used cats to carry coal from Newcastle to London.

The expression 'no room to swing a cat' dates from this period and refers to congestion in the Thames when manoeuvring these vessels.

*Faith Hines, curator, Laundry Mangle Museum,*
*Newton Abbot, Devon*

As an ex-sailor, from a seafaring family, I regard the cat-o'-nine-tails explanation as a reasonable theory but find the Thames catch suggestion unconvincing.

I believe the true derivation is a corruption of an original saying, 'no room to swing a cot', 'cot' being the sailor's word for his hammock. To swing it, the nineteenth-century tar was allowed a beam (width) of just 14 inches.

The many mariner-inspired terms and sayings which, sometimes corrupted, have been absorbed into the language, came about by everyday use among the tars. Many hundreds of thousands of sailors would have swung their cots or hammocks, but few would have swung a cat-o'-nine-tails or a catch boat on the Thames.

*C. L. Lloyd, Gomshall, Surrey*

## (48) QUESTION: Why are people from Sunderland called 'Makkems'?

Locals in Sunderland and the surrounding former pit villages in County Durham are called 'Makkems' to distinguish them from 'Geordies', who hail from Newcastle and the former pit villages in Northumberland.

In the 1830s, Sunderland was the greatest shipbuilding town in the world. Lloyd's Register of Shipping for 1834 listed its output as almost equal to that of all the other British ports put together.

Sunderland's men were divided into two groups, those who made ships and those who took them all over the world – in the local accent, 'them as makk'em' and 'them as takk'em'.

Sunderland people are proud to be called 'Makkems and Takkems' or simply 'Makkems' in honour of the now defunct shipping industry.

*Peter Budson, Sunderland, Co. Durham*

In the past twenty years, 'Makkem and Takkem' has been shortened to 'Makkem' by Newcastle football fans who use it disparagingly of the people of Sunderland to suggest they can't finish the job. Wearsiders know better and are proud of the 'Makkem' label.

*Phil Young, Chester-le-Street, Co Durham*

**(49) QUESTION: Stories abound that the foundations of St Paul's Cathedral are either amazingly deep or ridiculously shallow. Is either true?**

The great cathedral rests on foundations that go to $4\frac{1}{2}$ feet below crypt floor level. Beneath this is a bed of sand and gravel with blue London clay far below.

In 1831, sand was pumped out from below the cathedral to make a sewer and this is thought to have contributed to the dome settling nearly six inches to the south-west in the 1920s.

*Canon John Halliburton, Chancellor of*
*St Paul's Cathedral, London*

An engineering book in my possession says St Paul's was deemed unsafe in 1925 and closed for five years for repairs. The three-layered dome, weighing 70,000 tons, was $5\frac{3}{4}$ inches out of perpendicular.

The piers carrying this weight were discovered to be hollow – they were made of facing stone 4 to 6 inches thick filled with debris – and had subsided by 2 to 6 ½ inches. To make them safe, they were bolted and filled with cement. The dome had bolts fitted through it so two 450-foot stainless-steel chains weighing 35 tons could encircle it to prevent any further spreading.

The £400,000 for these repairs was raised by public subscription, with no Government contribution.

*D. F. Green, Bourne End, Buckinghamshire*

## (50) QUESTION: Did Roald Dahl invent Gremlins when he was a Second World War fighter pilot?

'Gremlins', mythical, mischievous little gnomes, were commonly blamed for mechanical malfunctions on British air bases from at least the First World War. This was part of regular RAF slang in the twenties and was first used in print in a 1929 edition of *The Aeroplane*.

Claims for the etymology of the word include a corruption of the Kent beer Fremlins with the word goblin and an older suggestion that it stems from the Irish *gruaimin*, a small, bad-tempered person.

Roald Dahl, one of Britain's greatest children's authors, wrote his first stories while he was a fighter pilot in the early years of the Second World War, based around his experiences in the RAF, including the 1943 story 'The Gremlins'. Steven Spielberg took the theme of these mischievous little things further in his 1984 film of the same name.

*Oliver Gibson, Addlestone, Surrey*

## (51) QUESTION: What is meant by the 1570 Elizabethan rhyme 'Multiplication is vexation, division is as bad/The Rule of three doth puzzle me, and practice drives me mad'?

The 'rule of three' first appeared in the *Chiu Chang* manuscript

(Nine Chapters on the Mathematical Arts) in China more than two thousand years ago. Its purpose is to solve proportional problems of the 'If eight oranges cost 40p, how much would ten be?' type.

It states that the answer is found by multiplying the last two figures, in this case 40 and ten, and dividing by the first, in this case eight, giving the answer 50p.

*Dr Alan Jones, Manchester University*

*The Young Man's Companion*, published in 1748, gives a lengthy explanation of the Rule of Three. It's called the Rule of Three because from three known numbers we find out a fourth, unknown, number which is in the same proportion to the third number as the second is to the first.

The example given is instantly recognizable: 'If 12 gallons of brandy cost £4.10s, what will 134 gallons cost at that rate?' Today's young man or woman would be very familiar with this type of problem, though the name has been lost in the last two hundred years.

*P. J. Lazard, Milton Keynes, Buckinghamshire*

I use the technique known as 'practice' to calculate VAT on any amount. Write down 10 per cent of the amount, add half that below it (5 per cent) and half again below that (2 ½ per cent). The three values added together give the truly horrible percentage – 17 ½ VAT.

*Nick Hartland, Bedfont, Middlesex*

'Practice' in the Elizabethan rhyme refers to the mathematical process by which long multiplication could be simplified. For example, to multiply anything by 14, you multiply it first by eight and write it down, halve the answer and write it underneath, then halve this answer and write that underneath, then add the three up. The total is 14 times the original.

This was a neat method to use, especially when dealing with the old pounds, shillings and pence.

*Kathleen Eck, London SW15*

**(52) QUESTION: What happened to Archie Scott-Brown, a one-armed racing driver of the fifties?**

Born in Paisley on 13 May 1927, with a withered arm and short legs, W. A. 'Archie' Scott-Brown was a courageous driver and great character who overcame his problems to become a top racing driver.

Driving in an international sports car race at Spa, Belgium, on 19 May 1958, he lost control on a wet patch under the trees and crashed in flames at exactly the same spot that Dick Seaman had in 1939. He did not survive his injuries.

Scott-Brown was a former tobacco company representative who opened a garage and drove in the 1956 British Grand Prix. Oulton Park race stewards once banned him from the grid for being 'unfit to drive' but an immediate drivers' strike by his fellow competitors got Archie reinstated.

*Peter Miller, racing journalist, Banbury, Oxfordshire*

I recall Archie Scott-Brown from the fifties when I first saw him competing at Felixstowe, Suffolk, in a TD MG. He was spotted by Brian Lister, of Cambridge, when he drove the first Cooper MG at Snetterton on 3 April 1954, and then drove Lister MGs, Lister Bristols and the famous Lister Jaguars when, in 1957, he beat the Aston Martin works team.

He was born with a stump of a right hand which he used to stick in the steering wheel while he changed gear with his left hand. He was a cheery little man and drove with a zeal which bordered, at times, on crazy.

His last race was the sports car Grand Prix at Spa in Belgium on

18 May 1958, the same day as the Monaco Grand Prix. He crashed heavily approaching La Scourse, his car caught fire and he succumbed to his injuries.

*Michael Crow, Stamford, Lincolnshire*

I first met Archie Scott-Brown in motor sport in 1952 and he so impressed me that I loaned him my competition car. His successes inspired me to design and build cars for him to drive from 1954 to 1958.

His best year was 1957 when, driving the Lister Jaguar, he won eleven races out of fourteen, setting up the fastest lap on all the circuits visited – all against the finest opposition, including the entire Aston Martin works team.

Archie's heroic story is told in moving manner in Robert Edwards's *Archie and the Lister*s, published by Patrick Stephens Ltd.

*Brian Lister, Cherry Hinton, Cambridge*

Archie Scott-Brown wasn't one-armed, his hand was simply vestigial and his forearm foreshortened. He had no shinbones and had feet only after extensive surgery in childhood.

He was such a good driver that in his first test in a Formula One racing car in 1955 he broke the all-out lap record at Goodwood circuit.

*Robert Edwards, author,* Archie and the Listers, *London*

Archie Scott-Brown died many years ago but his spirit lives on for me. Archie captured me as one of his many admirers not just because of his amazing driving skill but because he was such a nice chap. As a fifteen-year-old schoolboy in 1954, my life-long passion for motor racing had just been born at the new Aintree Circuit, near Liverpool.

The likes of Stirling Moss, Mike Hawthorn, Peter Collins and

Juan Manuel Fangio were there, at the peak of their abilities, but only Archie took the time to talk to me. He was my hero.

*A. E. D. Burke, Wickford, Essex*

**(53) QUESTION: Harold Wilson's name is associated with the phrase 'This will not affect the pound in your pocket' and Harold Macmillan with 'You've never had it so good'. What phrases bring to mind Margaret Thatcher, John Major, Jim Callaghan, Tony Blair and Gordon Brown?**

Future years will surely know Margaret Thatcher (prime minister from May 1979 to November 1990) for her phrase 'There is no alternative', from which she earned the nickname 'Tina'.

James Callaghan (April 1976 to May 1979) will forever be associated with something he didn't say. After leaving the country in a mess to go to a conference in Guadeloupe during the 'winter of discontent', he was quizzed on his return about the rubbish piled high and dead bodies left unburied. He gave a long statement, to be greeted next day by the headline: 'Crisis? What crisis?'

John Major was more difficult because he was so 'grey' but I suggest remembering his infamous 'bastards' outburst, referring to Euro-sceptic Cabinet colleagues.

*C. J. Cooper, Beverley, East Yorkshire*

Lady Thatcher would no doubt like her prime ministership to be best remembered for her speech to the Conservative Party Conference about the possibility of switching policy. As she put it: 'You turn if you want to. The lady's not for turning.'

*Tim Mickleburgh, Grimsby, Lincolnshire*

Margaret Thatcher may be remembered for saying: 'Nobody would have heard of the Good Samaritan had he not been rich', or perhaps for: 'Home is a place you go when there's nowhere else to go'.

John Major could be remembered for this gem: 'When you have your back to the wall you turn round and fight.'

*Mrs J. Simmonds, Aintree, Liverpool*

Whether he meant it or not, John Major will probably be remembered for the phrase 'back to basics'.

*Louise Kinworth Gordon, Co Mayo*

Perhaps Tony Blair regrets his early mottos 'Education, education, education' and 'Tough on crime, tough on the causes of crime', but if he wakes up in a sweat at night it's probably to hear himself intoning: 'I'm a pretty straight sort of guy' when accused of protecting Formula One from the tobacco sponsorship ban in exchange for a £1 million donation to the Labour Party.

'Son of the manse' Gordon Brown will no doubt be remembered for claiming to have 'abolished boom and bust' shortly before the biggest bust-up in history.

*A. Simmons, London*

**(54) QUESTION: The English word 'dog' bears no resemblance to *hund*, *chien* or its equivalent in other languages. Where does it originate?**

*Collins English Dictionary* gives its etymology as: 'Old English *docga*, of obscure origin', while the *Oxford Dictionary* says the word's history and origins are unknown.

The generic name for a dog in Old English, as in other Teutonic languages, was *hund*, giving us the modern hound. The word 'dog' first appeared in English around 1050, translating the Latin *canis*.

It was originally used to define a powerful breed of dog and remains in this sense in various continental languages, like the

Swedish *dogge*. It has been used in English in a more general sense since its first appearance in 1050.

*Lorna Gilmour, Collins Dictionaries, Glasgow*

'Dog' is the phonetically altered remains of the Old English *deoga*, originally two words meaning 'teach' and 'jaw', expressing the domestication of a formerly wild animal.

The Latin *caninus/canis*, meaning dog, provided the *chien* of modern French by a process of phonetic decay and subsequent dialectic regeneration. The German word *hund* arises from the animal's use in hunting and may originally have been *hundoc* or even *hundocgo*.

*C. Wood, Edinburgh*

**(55) QUESTION: Why do Rugby Union players have pockets in their shorts but Rugby League players and footballers don't?**

Traditionally, Rugby Union players were gentlemen who needed somewhere to keep the handkerchiefs they carried onto the field. Some of today's players have their pockets sewn up lest an opposing player should catch a hand in them.

*Rex King, Museum of Rugby, Twickenham*

Rugby League players and footballers, as professionals, were paid by cheque but Rugby Union players, as amateurs, would be slipped their appearance money in cash.

*Rodney Jones, Branston, Burton on Trent*

Having just ironed my son's Rugby Union shorts and found his gum shield in the pocket again, I know that's why they have a pocket.

*Mrs Wendy Smith, Ewell, Surrey*

**(56) QUESTION: In parts of Norfolk they call a ladybird a Bishop Barnaby. Who was Bishop Barnaby?**

I wus readin th'other day about Bishop Barnaby an I sed ta my ole gal, 'Look 'ere, Missus, ya c'n tell he ent from Norridge dew he woun't a spelt that like that.' When I wus totty we called 'em Bishy Barny Bees; an if he think thas a lot a ole gammarattle he'll hat ta keep his lugs open for dodman (snail), pishmare (ant) and pishmare barny bee (earwig) an orl, dew he 'ont ever mek out wot we're orl on about.

Howsomever, if he want a know some more Broad Norfold he c'n git hold on me whenever an' I'll pass the seal o' day with him.

*Paul Turner, Diss, Norfolk*

Bishop Barnaby is one of several versions of this nickname for the ladybird, still common in Norfolk, Suffolk and further afield in Sussex, where it was first recorded in 1875 by W. D. Parish in his *Dictionary of Sussex Dialect*.

As the ladybird is named for the Virgin Mary, there's a remote possibility of a religious connection, perhaps from St Barnabas, whose feast day is 11 June.

*Rachel West, Norfolk*

We used to say the rhyme: 'Bushy bishy-barneybee, Tell me when your wedding be. If it be tomorrow day, Flap your wings and fly away.'

*Colin Coleman, North Fambridge, Essex*

**(57) QUESTION: Is there instant tea powder in tea bags to help them brew quickly?**

The tea bag has existed commercially in this country since 1953. Once considered humble, it is now an integral part of the British lifestyle and is used to brew around 147 million cups every day, about 86 per cent of all tea brewed in the UK.

Despite their convenience, tea bags need no instant tea powder to make the tea brew quickly.

Very small particles of tea leaves in the bag ensure that the maximum surface area is presented to the boiling water, and the bag itself is designed to present the minimum barrier to the excellence of the infusion.

*Illtyd L. Lewis, The Tea Council, London*

**(58) QUESTION: I was amazed by the incline on the football pitch at Uckfield, East Sussex. Which pitch has the steepest slope in the country?**

Having visited every British league ground while researching my book *The Football Grounds of Britain* (Harper Collins), I suggest the steepest pitch incline of any professional team must be Barnet's Underhill ground whose playing surface slopes 8 ft from end to end.

The most irregular pitch in the country is probably Oxford United's Manor Ground, which slopes 7 ft from corner to corner and 4 ft from side to side. Other grounds with slopes include Sheffield United's Bramall Lane, which drops 8 ft from side to side; Bath City's ground, which has a 5 ft slope from side to side; and Watford, which slopes 5 ft from end to end. Sloping grounds are a legacy from the early century, when many sites were chosen, and they mean a hefty bill to correct them when building modern stands without ruining spectators' sightlines. Most teams with sloping pitches are attempting to eradicate them, a good example being Hibernian, where two stands were constructed before levelling of the pitch.

League regulations state that pitches must be 'flat and free from surface depressions and excessive undulations'. The maximum permissible slope is 5 ft from side to side, 8 ft from end to end, and

10 ft from corner to corner. The most famous uneven ground in history was Yeovil's old Huish Park, which sloped 6 ft from side to side and 8 ft from corner to corner. It's now buried under a supermarket and the team plays on a new ground with a level pitch.

*Simon Inglis, London*

Some years ago, I watched a football match between New Quay and Felinfach at the latter's ground near Aberaeron. The Felinfach pitch sloped down from the centre spot towards all four corners, and no corner flag was visible from the one opposite.

I understood nothing could be done about the problem because, had the bump been flattened, sewage pipes would have been too near the surface.

*J. C. Diment, Dudley, West Midlands*

**(59) QUESTION: Have any credible theories been put forward to explain the mysterious disappearance of two pupils and a teacher on a school outing to Hanging Rock in Australia?**

Peter Weir's beautiful 1975 film *Picnic at Hanging Rock* about the disappearance of two pupils and a teacher at Hanging Rock, Victoria, on St Valentine's Day 1900, was based on Joan Lindsay's 1967 novel of that name which assumed a factual manner but was fiction. Lindsay herself hints at this in the book's preface.

Further investigation by the critic Yvonne Rousseau in her 1980 book *The Murders at Hanging Rock* show up inconsistencies in the novel and the film. The disappearance occurs on a Saturday, St Valentine's Day in 1900, but 14 February fell on a Wednesday that year. There was no ladies' college in the locality until 1919 and examination of newspapers covering the area between 1897 and 1905 shows no such accounts of either disappearances or murders.

*R. A. Cox, London SW18*

Australian novelist Joan Lindsay's *Picnic at Hanging Rock* describes the mysterious disappearance of, and search for, three people at a school Valentine's Day picnic in 1900.

The first chapter is prefaced by an author's note: 'Whether *Picnic at Hanging Rock* is fact or fiction, my readers must decide for themselves. As the fateful picnic took place in the year 1900 and all the characters who appear in the book are long since dead, it hardly seems important.'

'Took place' and 'long since dead' make it sound like fact but she was writing fiction. Lindsay was horrified by the flood of enquiries and irritated by demands to know whether the novel was based on real events. As published in 1967, the book was without its final chapter 18, but after the author's death the missing part was published, in 1987, as a separate book, *The Secret of Hanging Rock*, with an introduction by the writer's literary agent John Taylor and commentary by Yvonne Rousseau, author of a previous book on the mystery.

John Taylor writes: 'Her account was that the story came to her as she lay awake at night, but what came to her included the ending. It was meant to be part of the book but the publishers thought it should be deleted. As time went on, and particularly after the making of the film, many theories were put forward about what really happened. The book and film have a great air of authenticity.

'One day she handed me some letters from people who had been researching fruitlessly through old newspapers, hoping to find the real events. I remarked that it was sad that they wasted so much time. "Yes," said Joan, and then, absently, "but something did happen." Whether the something happened in the newspapers, in some anecdote she had heard or in her imagination, I have no idea and knew better than to ask.'

Chapter 18 explains why the three didn't return to the picnic. It's clearly imaginary and I prefer not to give away the contents.

*Philip Brown, Hempsted, Gloucestershire*

**(60) QUESTION: From where does the phrase 'clean as a whistle' come? Does it have anything to do with steam whistles?**

The whistle in this expression was of the reed or wooden variety. A good whistle, made correctly, emits a clear tone but its clarity is corrupted by even the slightest damage. Small bits of dirt or moisture affect the sound – hence 'clean as a whistle'.

The saying is thought to have originated as 'clear as a whistle' but 'clear' had become 'clean' by the early 1800s. The *Craven Glossary*, compiled by William Carr in 1828, describes the expression as 'a proverbial simile'. The introduction of steam engines, with steam whistles, into daily life helped reinforce the expression.

*Kirsi Laurio, International Phrase and Fable Society, London*

**(61) QUESTION: At what point in the year should we stop feeding the birds?**

There's normally no need to feed garden birds after the end of April but there's no harm in continuing to do so, provided you don't put out peanuts. Bits of peanut may get stuck in the throats of young blue tits. Sunflower seeds and other recognized bird food can top up their summer diet of insects.

*Derek Niemann, Royal Society for the Protection of Birds,*
*Sandy, Bedfordshire*

Through our window we used to watch blue tits in a nesting box. One day the parent birds kept going to the box but it became obvious that the food they were bringing wasn't being taken by their little ones. They left the box and we examined the baby birds, which had died.

On opening their crops, we found three pieces of peanut in each. They had clearly found these impossible to cope with and had died of starvation. Since then we've always removed peanuts from any bird food we put out at nesting time.

*Joan Cool, Lyme Regis, Dorset*

Naturalist Phil Drabble said scientists had discovered that birds have far more common sense than we give them credit for. They know not to feeds nuts or dried bread to their young. They keep it for themselves and feed their offspring on things like insects and spiders. Desisting from giving them food in spring makes life much harder for the parent birds: without an easy supply they have to work twice as hard to find food.

*Derek Bennett, Walsall, West Midlands*

**(62) QUESTION: When the aerial broke off my radio and the reception went fuzzy, I jammed a potato on the stump and the sound cleared up. It also worked with a carrot. Why should this be?**

Any reasonable conductor of electricity can receive electromagnetic energy – radio waves. The same effect can be created by holding an aerial or its remnants. With a strong enough signal, a clear improvement in reception should be evident.

Most vegetables, and the human body, have a high water content. The relative moisture of the outer skin will dictate the efficiency of the potato or human being to function as an aerial. There are, however, far more durable conductors for use as aerials, hence the lack of potatoes and carrots on chimneys.

*Tim Jenks, Confederation of Aerial Industries,*
*Wembley Park, Middlesex*

**(63) QUESTION: Was the Battle of Britain Spitfire really so superior to its Me109 counterpart?**

The Me109 was conceived in early 1934 at Bayerische Flugzeug-werke AG, in Augsberg, where Willy Messerschmitt was co-manager. It survived political squabbles to take its first flight in September 1935, six months before the Spitfire first flew.

After combat experience in the Spanish Civil War, it was subject to continued improvements which, along with its fuel injection and supercharger, gave it superior performance to R. J. Mitchell's Spitfire above 20,000 feet. It also had heavier, far more destructive armament. The Spitfire's domed cockpit hood, however, was superior to the flat glazing of the Me109 and the greater wing area, with its lower wing loading, meant the Spitfire could out-turn its adversary.

In the Battle of Britain, differences between the two planes involved their different uses. German aircraft had to fly further, reducing their effective combat time, and were forbidden to leave the bomber formations they were charged to protect, robbing them of their freedom of action. They were harassed by the Spitfires while the Hurricanes attacked the bombers.

*Alan G. Shepherd, Leicester*

Contrary to popular belief both during and after the Battle of Britain, the much vaunted superiority of the Spitfire MkI over the Me Bf109e could be described, at best, as marginal. This was borne out in trials carried out at RAE Farnborough in May 1940 using a captured Me109 in mock combat with a Spitfire.

The outcome of encounters between the two in battle depended more on the skill of their pilots than on any technical difference in the aircraft. It must also be remembered that The Few were fighting over home territory.

*Roy Redfearn, Colne, Lancashire*

The very name of the Spitfire gave it a psychological advantage over its Battle of Britain adversaries. The respect which German fighter pilots had for the Spitfire led them to underestimate the fighting qualities of the Hawker Hurricane. The late Sir Douglas Bader used to tell how German airmen always insisted they had been shot down by Spitfires, never Hurricanes. He called this 'Spitfire snobbery'.

*Bruce Catt, Burgess Hill, West Sussex*

Wartime competitive trials of Spitfires versus Me109s used identical fuels but this was unlikely to pertain in battle. As a 'sprog' joining the BP Research Centre at Sunbury-on-Thames in 1956, I was told by the old hands that research and development done there had 'won the war'.

BP invented the alkylation process, in one example of which two molecules combined to form iso-octane. This aero-fuel component gave our planes extra speed at crucial moments in combat. *The Story of British Petroleum*, published in 1959, states: 'The alkylation process contributed dramatically to the Allied air supremacy in the war.'

A similar book, from 1959, states: 'In 1936, the Research Laboratories of the British Petroleum Company developed the alkylation process to produce saturated iso-octanes. It was this process which formed the backbone of the production of high-grade aviation spirits in vast quantities in the 1939–45 war.'

We still await reports of interrogations of German scientists and others immediately after the war which might give information on German aviation fuels and/or opinions of their relative merits.

*Dr P. Gould, Sunningdale, Berkshire*


**(64) QUESTION: We're told there are eight indigenous languages, other than English, in use in the British Isles. What are they?**

Eight indigenous languages, older than English, are still in use in the British Isles: Welsh, Cornish, Scots, Irish, Manx, Channel Islands patois, Shelta (or Sheldru – the tongue of itinerant tinkers) and Romany.

*Cathy Brooks,* Guinness Book of Records, *Enfield, Middlesex*


**(65) QUESTION: Why did Jack and Jill go up the hill to fetch their water?**

They were obviously fetching water from a hill spring. There's no mention at all of a well in the nursery rhyme, though nearly every illustration includes one.

*Lorna Edmunds, Stratford-upon-Avon, Warwickshire*

Lewis Spence's 1947 book *Myth and Ritual* traced an ancient mystic ceremony in the Jack and Jill rhyme: 'No one in the folklore sense climbs to the top of the hill for water unless that water has special significance' – dew water, for instance.

Revd. S. Baring-Gould, in *Curious Myths of the Middle Ages* (1866), says the verse isn't nonsense but refers to a Scandinavian myth about two children, Hjuki (pronounced Juki in Norse) and Bill, who were captured by the Moon while they were drawing water.

This myth is said to account for the markings on the full moon, which include the children with a bucket on a pole between them.

*Sara Holden, Mumbles, Swansea*

Jack and Jill are drawing water from dew ponds, once common on the South Downs, and still found in parts of the British Isles.

Dew ponds were depressions lined with flint, slate and clay to make them watertight and work on the principle of condensation collecting in the form of dew to fill them, generally sited on top of a hill for best results.

They were full in times of drought when lowland water supplies ran dry.

*Eryl Griffiths, Wrexham*

I believe this is an example of one of our many courting rhymes which Victorian high moral attitudes almost completely destroyed.

Known since at least Elizabethan times, the rhyme was first printed in 1765 with further verses added around 1800 and 1820. Going 'up the hill to fetch a pail of water' was just an excuse, like 'going to the woods to pick flowers', for Jack and Jill, typical names for a courting couple. The original has Jill falling and breaking her crown: a bride wore a virgin's crown. 'And Jack came tumbling after' – the double meaning is clear.

'Then up Jack got and home did trot/As fast as he could court her/Jill lay still her pail did fill/With milk and not with water.' This second verse, not the one generally known, has been part of folklore for many a year.

*Peter de Loriol Chandieu, Clapham, London*

## (66) QUESTION: Has a judge in this country ever refused to accept a jury's verdict?

The key case is that of A. Bushell, a foreman of the jury who acquitted the Quakers William Penn and William Mead of unlawful assembly in 1670.

The Recorder of the City of London refused to accept this verdict and fined and imprisoned the jury. Bushell applied to the Court of the King's Bench for a writ of habeas corpus and was successful. The jurors were set free.

This case established the independence of the jury from the presiding judge in returning its verdict.

*W. H. Walker, Canvey Island, Essex*

## (67) QUESTION: How many years are generally held to comprise a generation?

A generation is any period of time from which a created object, person or thing is superseded by something regarded as better and/or newer. Some of the shortest 'generations' are for electronic gadgetry like computers, phones and cars, and in fashion, etc., while the longest are found in geology, astronomy, civilizations and language.

There is much debate about the recognized length of a human generation. Webster's Dictionary puts it at twenty-five to thirty years, the Oxford Dictionary suggests thirty years and Collins says thirty-five years.

A human generation can be regarded as the average time in which a society's children are ready to take the place of their parents, generally twenty-five to thirty years in Britain but as short as twenty years in developing nations.

*Suzanne Campbell, Kirkcaldy, Fife*

**(68) QUESTION: Scientists have announced that they have created anti-matter. What do they keep it in?**

Everything is made from matter, whose basic building blocks are the electron, proton and neutron. In 1929, British physicist Paul Dirac proposed that there would be a mirror image for each of these basic building blocks: a positron (or anti-electron), an anti-proton and anti-neutron. Together these would make up the mirror image of matter: anti-matter.

In 1995, scientists at CERN research centre in Geneva, Switzerland, created the simplest form of anti-matter, anti-hydrogen, by smashing protons together at very high speed to create anti-protons. These are charged and can, therefore, be controlled by a magnetic field. By combining the anti-protons with Xenon gas, anti-hydrogen was produced. This had no charge and simply flew into the equipment's detectors. Fractions of a second later the anti-hydrogen had reverted back to being anti-protons and positrons.

Scientists will have to think of new ways of controlling anti-matter if we are to ever see it used practically.

*Tudor Gwynn, Museum of Science and Industry, Manchester*

**(69) QUESTION: Who has/had the highest-recorded IQ?**

There are many different IQ tests worldwide all using an average IQ of 100, but according different values to the required entry level for Mensa, the high IQ society.

Mensa uses two tests to identify people's IQ scores in the UK: the Cattell B and Culture Free tests. Passing these at a level putting you in the top 2 per cent of the population qualifies you for Mensa membership. The minimum test mark to get into Mensa is 148 on the Cattell B Test, equivalent to 132 on the Culture Free Test.

The highest mark a middle-aged adult can score on the Cattell B Test is 161, and 1,257 of our 38,000 members have achieved this. The highest mark for children is 178, which 385 of our young members have achieved.

*Richard Milton, Mensa, Wolverhampton*

The highest-recorded IQ was achieved by Marilyn vos Savant, born 1947, in St Louis, Missouri, US, whose IQ was measured at 228 at the age of ten.

The limitations of the Cattell B test, used by my school thirty years ago, are still a source of discussion among more intelligent Mensa members.

*Tim Mickleburgh, Grimsby, Lincolnshire*

My school tested the IQ of every child in a face-to-face interview, lasting an hour and three-quarters, long acknowledged as the only way to obtain an accurate result. My score of 183.5 was not the highest recorded.

*Jeremy Wright, Liverpool*

(70) QUESTION: How does a flock of about two hundred starlings manage to take off at exactly the same time?

Large flocks of birds, such as starlings, often appear to act simultaneously though there are actually split-second differences in their timing.

Most birds have very rapid reflexes and can respond very quickly to a close movement. Birds, with eyes on either side of their head, have a wide field of view and can easily detect movements of other birds in the flock.

Slow-motion film reveals how the movement of one bird, normally on the edge of the group, causes a wave of movement throughout the flock, even when flying, allowing them to avoid mid-air collisions.

*Derek Niemann, Royal Society for the Protection of Birds,*
*Sandy, Bedfordshire*

It may be that all the birds are reacting to the same stimulus, an alarm call or a cat on the prowl. No doubt starlings wonder about human behaviour, all emerging from a train at the same time, or roaring and rising to their feet when a goal is scored at football. That must be just as much of a mystery to them.

*Daphne Ramsdale, Wigan, Lancashire*

### (71) QUESTION: Are professional footballers allowed to buy or own shares in football clubs?

The Premier League has no specific rules relating to players owning or trading shares in football teams. We do, however, have regulations relating to club officials acquiring a financial interest in more than one team.

If the issue needed to be examined, we would first look to the rules which govern club officials as a point of reference.

*John Zerafa, FA Premier League, London*

### (72) QUESTION: Why 'British Racing Green'?

The Gordon Bennett Trophy began in 1900 as an international race between teams chosen by the national automobile clubs of France, Belgium, Germany and America. The French raced in blue, Belgium in yellow, Germany in white and the US in red.

The following year, Britain was included, represented by S. F. Edge in a green 50 hp Napier, and a year later Edge and his Napier won the Gordon Bennett Cup, establishing green as our national motor racing livery.

The shade of green varied over the years with the colour which is now regarded as racing green emerging after the Second World War. This persisted until sponsorship of cars and drivers increased to a point where national colours made way for corporate logos and colours.

In the 1912 French Grand Prix, the Arrol-Johnston team represented Scotland in a blue car with the Gordon tartan.

*Enid Smith, British Automobile Racing Club, Thruxton Circuit,*
*Andover, Hampshire*

## (73) QUESTION: Is there anyone alive today who was made to wear a dunce's cap at school? When did this practice end?

I have vivid memories of my first week in school when a shamefaced boy from the top class was brought into the room and made to stand, head bowed and weeping, wearing a dunce's cap and a notice on his chest which I was told read: 'I am a dunce.'

When I started waking at night, screaming with nightmares, our doctor shrewdly concluded I was disturbed by something at school and advised my parents to move me. They did, but it was years before I could explain to anyone that I was sure the notice around the boy's neck was going to choke him.

*Beryl Coulon, Isle of Wight*

I can recall having to wear a black dunce's cap at the age of six. I was in an orphanage for boys where our night attire consisted of long white linen gowns. As mine was rather long, I tripped over it and made a large hole. Our clothing was inspected when it went in the laundry basket and I was given the dreaded cane and made to wear the dunce's cap, complete with a letter D, front and back. A double D is also my initials, though at the time I was too young to appreciate the irony.

*Douglas Dunning, Redditch, Worcestershire*

My school in the thirties had not only a dunce's cap but also a 'chatter box', a large cardboard box with a long red tongue, invariably heavily tear stained, which was hung around the neck. This punishment was inflicted on children aged four and a half to seven years old.

*Mrs D. Morton, Sheffield*

When I was five years old, I went to a small private school for a time and remember children having to stand in a corner wearing a dunce's cap, though I never had to suffer it.

*Mrs K. V. Crow, Hoddesdon, Hertfordshire*

**(74) QUESTION: My father-in-law used to recite a child's poem which begins: 'January brings the snow, makes your toes and fingers glow . . .' How does it go on?**

Sara Coleridge (1803–1852), daughter of Samuel Taylor Coleridge, wrote the poem 'The Months', also known as 'The Garden Year':

*January brings the snow/Makes our feet and fingers glow,*
*February brings the rain/Thaws the frozen lake again.*
*March brings breezes, loud and shrill/Stirs the dancing*
*daffodil,*
*April brings the primrose sweet/Scatters daisies at our feet.*
*May brings flocks of pretty lambs/Skipping by their fleecy*
*dams,*
*June brings tulips, lilies, roses/Fills the children's hands with*
*posies.*

Hot July brings cooling showers/Apricots and gilly flowers,
August brings the sheaves of corn/Then the harvest home is
borne.
Warm September brings the fruit/Sportsmen then begin to
shoot,
Fresh October brings the pheasant/Then to gather nuts is
pleasant.
Dull November brings the blast/Then the leaves are whirling
fast,
Chill December brings the sleet/Blazing fire and Christmas
treat.

Jane Priestley, Evergreen Quarterly, *Cheltenham,
Gloucestershire*

This poem, learned by many children, was parodied by Michael
Flanders and Donald Swan:

January brings the snow/Makes your feet and fingers glow.
February's ice and sleet/Freeze the toes right off your feet.
Welcome March with wintry wind/Would thou wert not so
unkind.
April brings the sweet spring showers/On and on for hours and
hours.
Farmers fear unkindly May/Frost by night and hail by day.
June just rains and never stops/For thirty days and spoils the
crops.
In July the sun is hot/Is it shining? No it's not.
August cold and dank and wet/Brings more rain than any yet.
Bleak September's mist and mud/Is enough to chill the blood.
Then October adds a gale/Wind and slush and rain and hail.
Dark November brings the fog, Shouldn't do it to a dog.
Freezing wet December then . . ./Bloody January again.

John Lewis, Babbacombe, Devon

**(75) QUESTION: After the Second World War top snooker professionals tried unsuccessfully to introduce an advanced version of the game. How did it work and what happened to it?**

Snooker Plus, brainchild of Joe Davis, was launched at London's Burroughes Hall in October 1959, when Joe compiled the first 100 break in this version of the game in a match against his brother, Fred.

The new version involved adding an extra orange ball, worth eight points, midway between the blue and pink, and a purple, worth ten, between the blue and brown.

The new maximum break went from 147 to 210, but with the purple so far from the reds, no maximum was ever recorded at Snooker Plus, the highest break being 156 by Ireland's Jackie Rea.

*Ian Morrison, sports author, Calvia, Majorca*

I recall seeing some forty years ago an exhibition match of Royal Snooker. This included two extra coloured balls, orange and purple, which I believe scored eight and nine points respectively, and were potted between blue and pink, and pink and black.

I have played unofficial variations of the normal game: Contract Snooker, in which the pocket had to be nominated, and another variant in which yellow, green and brown scored only if pocketed in bottom pockets, blue only in middle pockets, pink in top pockets and black anywhere.

Between the wars, Walter Lindrum experimented with four-ball billiards, the extra ball being pink.

*Eric Thomas, Purley, Surrey*

'Volunteer snooker', in which a player could choose any colour after potting a red, was played in the mid-forties and called 'progressional snooker'.

I recall a game in which Sam Craig was involved on the Newtownards Road around 1947. Potting the first red, he lined up the blue ball for the middle pocket and proceeded to put blue after blue in both centre pockets. Getting tired of going around the table, he would often just pull back the white, hardly waiting for the blue to be replaced on its spot as the break went on for many hours and added up to many thousands.

Onlookers swore he'd worn a groove in the cloth but I suppose it was just the chalk off the white ball which created that impression.

*S. Clarke, Camberley, Surrey*

## (76) QUESTION: Has a billiard table ever been designed and installed on a ship?

I don't know about cruise ships but the 26,000 ton, 15-inch gun battleship HMS *Resolution* had a full-size billiard table in the wardroom in 1939. The table was converted at sea for use as one of the wardroom's three dining tables.

In harbour, with polished cover removed, its level was adjusted by built-in ratchet wheels and measured on spirit levels set in the woodwork around the cushions before play. Play at sea, even in the calmest conditions, would have been highly problematic.

*Commodore R. W. Garson, CBE, RN, Hunstanton, Norfolk*

As an engineer on tankers in the sixties, I remember we had a 6 ft by 3 ft billiard and snooker table which we used with flat discs instead of balls. The seas had to be pretty rough before the discs started sliding around.

*D. M. Horsman, Bridgwater, Somerset*

When I was a cadet on the training ship HMS *Worcester* in the late forties, we had two billiard tables which functioned well in the calm waters of the Thames at Greenhithe, Kent.

They had adjustable feet for levelling and the only problem came when large numbers of the 220 cadets suddenly moved to one side of the ship to see some passing attraction. Those playing had to wait until the cadets dispersed and we returned to even keel.

*Graham Hay, Haverfordwest, Dyfed*

### (77) QUESTION: Who was the first British serviceman killed in the Second World War?

Twenty-year-old Aircraftsman Kenneth G. Day of No 9 RAF Squadron was shot down on 4 September 1939, the second day of the war, while bombing the *Scharnhorst* and *Gneisenau* battleships at the Kiel Canal.

Ten days later, his body was found near the Elbe lightships and buried with full military honours at Cuxhaven cemetery. After the war, he was reburied at Becklingen war cemetery, Saltau.

Day, nicknamed 'Talkie', was brought up in Alexandra Orphanage, in London's Haverstock Hill and was known as a happy-go-lucky chap. He joined both the RAF and Mosley's Blackshirts. Had he not perished, he might have been detained in the wartime round-up of fascists in 1940.

*John Christian, London SW11*

The War Graves register confirms that the first casualty was Cadet David Stewart Cox, aged seventeen, killed on 3 September 1939, the day war began. Petty Officer Reginald Bargrove was killed in HM Submarine *Oxley* when it was torpedoed in error on 10 September 1939.

By the time the first soldier was killed in action in December 1939, HMS *Courageous* had lost 518 crew, the *Royal Oak* 786, including 100 boys (ratings under eighteen), the armed merchant cruiser *Rawalpindi* 270 and many other ships had been sunk.

While the British Army was still singing about 'hanging out their washing on the Siegfried Line', the Royal Navy was taking the brunt of the war.

*Gus Britton, Royal Navy Submarine Museum,*
*Gosport, Hampshire*

## (78) QUESTION: Why is 6 July called Cherry Day?

The only cherry day recognized in the folk calendar is Cherry Pie Sunday, observed on the first Sunday of August, especially in Buckinghamshire, which is very proud of its jet-black cherries, known locally as 'chuggies'. This celebrates completion of the cherry harvest, with a cherry pie served in the afternoon.

The Japanese celebrate Hanami in spring. Cherry blossom, which blooms for just a few days each year, is the national flower of Japan and the Japanese attach great importance to the daily cherry blossom report in newspapers and broadcast media, predicting the best day for celebration. As soon as it's announced, people find a good spot to sit under a favourite cherry blossom and eat, drink and make merry. The celebration welcomes the beginning of spring and reminds people of the impermanence of the world.

If 6 July has any significance to the biological world it's as the birthdays of botanist Sir William Jackson Hooker and ecologist Jonathon Porritt.

*Gill Ivisan, Brogdale Horticultural Trust, Faversham, Kent*

## (79) QUESTION: What does a tailgate spoiler do for a car? If they are so good, why doesn't every car have one?

Tailgate spoilers are either aerodynamic or aesthetic. Wings on racing cars produce downforce, pushing the car against the ground for faster cornering but very few, if any, road cars have spoilers big enough or of the right shape to be effective at this. Their spoilers are most effective in reducing drag, making a car more fuel efficient.

Spoilers can assist the high-speed stability of hatchback-style cars, particularly in cross-winds. The Ford Sierra had mini-spoilers added at the back edge of the rear-side windows shortly after its launch after complaints about the car in cross-winds.

Most spoilers are added to make a car look more sporty, though in some cases this can be counter-productive, for example the 200 mph McLaren FI has a higher top speed without the rear wing fitted to the racing versions. Adding unnecessary parts to a car to make it appear more sporty is no new fashion. In the thirties and forties the retention of leather straps to hold the bonnet was more of a fashion statement than a structural necessity. The symbolism was of such speed that it needed the leather straps to keep the bonnet closed when in fact the catches were adequate.

*Scott Brownlee, Cosworth Engineering, Northampton*

I owned a 1983 rear-engined Skoda 120LE Super Estelle, which I dubbed Foxbat, whose most irritating fault was disconcertingly to change lanes in cross-winds, especially on motorways. I accidentally cured the problem when, for cosmetic reasons, I fitted a big tail spoiler that I picked up for £1 at a jumble sale. To my surprise, Foxbat immediately stopped wandering around in cross-winds and I no longer had to wrestle with the steering to keep a straight course.

*Toyin Akingbule, London, W5*

When Ferrari began developing a mid-engined sports racing car in the early 1960s, test driver Richie Ginther found the 246P type almost undriveable at speed. During practice for the 1961 Monza Race, weight distribution and aerodynamics combined to cause instability, especially in the banked Curva Grande which was hair-raising enough anyway. Ginther and his mechanics riveted a rough but effective strip of aluminium across the rear deck: thus was the spoiler invented.

*M. H. Boyask, Hove, Sussex*

The Porsche Carrera 911 has a most effective spoiler. Used as a picnic table it includes a lip to stop plates slipping off.

*Warren Lewis, Dagenham, Essex*

(80) QUESTION: Many people claim to be able to 'make rain'. Are they just cranks or is it possible that they have some measure of success?

Red Indian methods aside, scientists have studied rain making by 'cloud seeding', using artificial condensation nuclei, for many years. A few of the many methods employed include dropping frozen carbon dioxide pellets into clouds from aircraft or by burning silver iodide.

'Cloud seeding' has been followed by rain, though it's impossible to tell whether the rain might have happened anyway.

When a large part of Mongolia was being devastated by forest fires in May 1996, under the direction of meteorologists, silver iodide shells were fired into clouds by the Mongolian military and within a short time it began to snow. But would it have snowed anyway?

*Sean Clarke, Meteorological Office, Bracknell, Berkshire*

(81) QUESTION: One of my friends excuses himself by saying he is 'going to shed a tear for Nelson'. What other historical euphemisms are there for spending a penny?

In the 1950s, when a gentleman left the room to answer the call of nature, he said he was going to turn his bike round.

*Margaret Wright, Leicester*

When my mother was in a rather self-consciously literary class of schoolgirls at Thomas Carlyle School, Fulham, in the late thirties, they used to paraphrase W. B. Yeats: 'I will arise now and go to Innisfree . . .'

P. Browne, Tunbridge Wells, Kent

Women brought up in this area say: 'I'm just going to empty my clog.'

Michael J. Boardman, Newton Le Willows, Merseyside

I once heard a soldier say: 'I'm just going to shake hands with the unemployed', which I thought was quite funny.

Edwin Palmer, Farnborough, Hampshire

My brothers always used to claim they were going to scuttle the *Graf Spee*.

Helen Laine, Norfolk

A very early expression must be that used in the Authorized Version of the Bible. In Judges 3, Israelite hero Ehud assassinates the immensely fat Moabite king Eglon with a concealed weapon and leaves the palace while the king's guards assume he's in the toilet.

Seventeenth-century translators rendered the phrase '. . . he is relieving himself . . .' '. . . he covereth his feet . . .'

E. Fuller, Edinburgh

## (82) QUESTION: Why don't we eat blue food?

Likes and dislikes are learned through personal and cultural associations. Blue food is simply seen as culturally inappropriate.

The cultural association probably arose from the fact that blue food occurs less regularly than other natural food colours, such as brown, red, yellow, white, etc. Today, all foods can be given any colour imaginable, but only very few are blue, such as blueberry pie and children's sweets.

*Catherine Reynolds, Institute of Food Research, London*

*Truite en bleu* (blue trout) is a classic French dish, achieved by placing a freshly caught trout (often held alive in a tank in the restaurant) in a little vinegar, making it turn a delightful bright blue colour.

The trout is then gently poached and served with freshly boiled vegetables and melted nut-brown butter.

*Barrie Newland, Kirksland Hotel, Hawick, Roxburghshire*

**(83) QUESTION: What is the longest word in English which doesn't use the same letter twice?**

Two examples are unproblematic and unpredictable, each of which has thirteen letters.

*Richard King, Huntingdon, Cambridgeshire*

The longest I can find are the thirteen-letter documentarily, endolymphatic, pneumogastric, subordinately and troublemaking and the fourteen-letter ambidextrously.

*P. Fuller, Norwich*

The longest I can find has fourteen letters: hydropneumatic.

*Mrs G. P. Burgoyne, Windsor, Berkshire*

I can make dermatoglyphics (fifteen letters) which are skin patterns, especially on the palms of the hands and soles of the feet.

*Rajiv Boval, Bournemouth, Dorset*

How about the sixteen-letter uncopyrightables?

*Derek Browett, Peterborough, Cambridgeshire*

## (84) QUESTION: Did the ancient Greeks or Romans spot any flying saucers or similar extra-terrestrial activities?

There's good evidence that there have always been sightings of what we now call UFOs. An illustration in the Swiss Library in Zurich, for example, depicts globes of light being seen by amazed onlookers above Basle on 7 August 1566.

Perhaps the most intriguing story concerns the Dogon tribe of Mali in Africa. Early in the twentieth century, two French anthropologists spent nineteen years living among them and discovered that the Dogon possessed extraordinary knowledge of astronomy. They knew of the rings around Saturn and the moons of Jupiter, despite these being relatively recent scientific discoveries.

Sceptics claim such knowledge may have come from missionaries. The Dogon say the information was given to them ten thousand years ago by an alien race that came in starships from a planet around Sirius. They were reputedly given details of the Sirius System, which wasn't formed from a single star like our sun. It seems the Dogon were aware of details which only very modern astronomical techniques have verified – including some alleged aspects which our science still has to confirm or disprove.

There are numerous other references in almost every ancient culture to visitation by a race from the stars. One of the most scholarly researchers – albeit rather unsung – was Sunderland man Raymond Drake – whose books during the fifties and sixties pre-empted Von Daniken.

Drake found various references in Greek and Roman writings. The terminology was typical of the day, with blazing swords, shields and the like crossing the sky. Often they were thought of as omens for battle, but sometimes the accounts simply refer to what today would be one-off sightings.

81

The big problem with ancient UFO reports is that in those days very few people were able to read or write so things weren't documented. Much went by word of mouth and became distorted over the centuries.

*Jenny Randles, Paranormal Research, Fleetwood, Lancashire*

Ancient Egyptians witnessed many strange phenomena. H. Brinsley le Poer Trench's book, *The Flying Saucer Mystery*, says the first recorded UFO sighting was 3,500 years ago in the reign of Pharaoh Men-Khepper-Ka Tehuti-Mes (Thothmes II, whose obelisk, nicknamed Cleopatra's Needle after the barge that brought it to Britain, stands on the Embankment). He is said to have recorded a sighting of 'circles of fire', which descended from the sky, whose occupants conversed with him.

*Eva Coomber, St Cleer, Cornwall*

**(85) QUESTION: What was the significance of the three big glass bottles containing different coloured liquids most chemists' shops used to have in their windows?**

These unusual-shaped glass containers are known as 'carboys' and are thought to have been used by apothecaries to demonstrate their ability to formulate a potion which kept its form while everything else in the Middle Ages was going off.

The carboy later became a distinguishing sign of a chemist in much the same way as the barber's pole. Jesse Boot first displayed carboys 120 years ago and you can still see the symbol in more than 1,200 Boots stores today.

It's thought there were four rather than three colours used, symbolizing the four elements: earth, fire, air and water, often related to the four humours (blood, phlegm, choler, melancholy).

*Tim Legge, Boots, Nottingham*

**(86) QUESTION: Why does a kettle go quiet just before it boils?**

The familiar noise of the 'singing' kettle comes from two similar sources. All water contains dissolved air which is released as gas as the water heats. As the water increases in temperature, the noise that predominates is caused by the boiling of the water around the source of heat – the electric element or the base of the kettle on the stove. Close to this intense heat, bubbles of steam form briefly before contact with the colder water immediately around condenses it again. It is the collapse of the small steam bubbles that causes the noise.

As all the water reaches boiling point, the steam bubbles don't re-condense. In the brief interval while these bubbles build up enough size to escape to the surface, there's a moment of comparative calm, only to be broken as the new noise of bubbling begins at the surface of the water.

*Keith Matthews, Crystran Ltd, Poole, Dorset*

The point at which a kettle goes quiet is the best time to use the water to make instant coffee. If the coffee froths, the flavour is deliciously enhanced.

*R. Fairman, Welwyn Garden City, Hertfordshire*

**(87) QUESTION: Who, or what, were Z Men?**

Soldiers demobilized from full-time service after the Second World War but retained in the Z Reserve were commonly known as Z Men.

In 1952, the Z Men were mobilized for a fortnight's camp with the Territorial Army. I was a young National Service NCO doing my three years compulsory part-time service at the time and found myself in charge of men with war medals, which didn't go down well.

The comedy film *Down Among the Z Men*, starring Peter Sellers,

Harry Secombe, Michael Bentine and Spike Milligan, was made at the time, adapting the popular song 'Down Among the Dead Men'.

*Geoff Pitcher, Littlehampton, Sussex*

I was posted to Tewkesbury in Gloucestershire as a Z Man in the RAOC. We were former servicemen who had been demobbed after the Second World War but were needed for the Korean War and were sent to camps for two weeks' re-training. We wore blue flashes on our shoulder tabs and were paid Army pay on top of civilian wages. The local girls soon discovered this and I found out how the GIs felt when they came over here in the war.

*Stanley Haywood, Thornhill, Cardiff*

Not all Z Reservists got double pay. I was sent for a fortnight's training with 318 Battery RA. Hustled onto a Glasgow train by military policemen, we disembarked at Carlisle and boarded trucks to go to Otterburn Ranges.

Allowed a pass out until midnight on the Saturday, we spent the time in Newcastle and went home the following Friday. Being in the building trade, I got no Army pay or civilian wages and lost two weeks' contributions to my National Insurance stamps.

I've never been told that I'm no longer a Z Reservist.

*J. R. Carlin, Whireinch, Glasgow*

On demobilization, we old fellows who served in the Second World War weren't discharged but transferred to the Z Reserve. I have never, so far, been discharged from the Z Reserve and I know nobody who has.

We await the call of duty, ready to converge on the nearest barracks with our crutches and Zimmer frames . . .

*Revd. Peter Sutton, Holsworthy, Devon*

**(88) QUESTION: Does any other family have a surname like mine – Noon – which is the same (in capitals) back to front or upside down?**

Many names form palindromes (words that read backwards as they do forwards), including first names Eve, Hannah and Lil, and the surname Mallam. Names that read both back to front and also upside down are very rare but one example is the late John Lennon's wife Yoko, whose surname was Ono.

*Nell Allen, Seaton, Devon*

Our family surname is Ede, the same backwards or forwards, and my first name is Lee, making my name a bit of a mouthful. When our daughter was born, one of the midwives commented that her whole name is a palindrome: Hannah Ede.

*Mrs Lee Ede, Eastbourne, Sussex*

My maiden name was Noxon, which can also be read backwards and upside down.

*Pamela West, Worth, Kent*

There's an American political activist called Revilo P. Oliver, which is both an anagram and a palindrome.

*Francesca Legge, Christchurch, Dorset*

I went to school with a girl called Ingrid Riding.

*J. Sherman, Blackburn*

My dad's name is Eric Rice. My grandmother was superstitious and believed giving him a name which was an anagram of his surname would bring him luck throughout life.

*Martin Eric Rice, Kilmarnock, Ayrshire*

We're told Ronald Roland Arnold is the only possible three-name anagram. But Arnold, too, is a common Christian name and one could be called Ronald Roland Arnold Aldron.

*Ronald Sanderson, Blackpool*

A friend named Harry Rose married a young lady called Rose, making her Rose Rose. When she stood up, I wonder if he was tempted to say: 'Rose Rose rose.'

*Charles Mason, Birmingham*

## (89) QUESTION: What is the origin of the place name Good Easter in Essex?

The county of Essex has both Good Easter and High Easter, two miles to the north. This place name comes from the Old English *eowestre* – a sheep fold – and there's reference to the general locality in the Domesday Book (1086) under the name Estra.

A distinction had been made between the villages by the thirteenth century, the 'High' prefix referring to its elevated situation while the 'Good' prefix stems from the woman's name Godgifu (Godiva).

*Adrian Room, author,* Dictionary of Placenames in the British Isles, *Bloomsbury, London*

## (90) QUESTION: How did a diamond ring come to symbolize an engagement?

A plain iron hoop was the forerunner of today's engagement ring. In Roman times, a ring symbolized the cycle of life and love running out at the circle's end. Gold replaced iron and betrothal rings have traditionally been worn on the third finger of the left hand because it was believed that the *vena amoris* (vein of love) ran from that finger to the heart.

The first recorded diamond ring was given by Archduke Maximilian of Austria to Mary of Burgundy in 1477. He was advised to have a gold ring set with a diamond – a symbol of purity and conjugal fidelity – if he wanted to win Mary's heart. That ring is now in Vienna's Kunsthistorisches Museum.

The practice really became popular from the late nineteenth century, when diamonds were discovered in South Africa and became marginally more affordable.

More than 80 per cent of brides in the English-speaking world have an engagement ring, and Japan has also adopted the habit.

*Susan Farmer, Diamond Information Centre, London*

**(91) QUESTION: William the Conqueror, William II, the Angevins and Plantagenets were Norman French. The Tudors were Welsh, James II Scottish, William of Orange Dutch, the Georges and Windsors German. Since 1066, has England had an English king?**

Richard III, last of the Plantagenet line which ruled England for more than three hundred years, can claim to be the most English king.

He was the only truly English monarch, born of English parents, Richard, Duke of York, and Lady Cecily Neville, with four English grandparents – maternally, Ralph, Earl of Westmorland, and Joan Beaufort, and paternally, Richard, Earl of Cambridge, and Anne, daughter of Roger, Earl of March.

As proved by extant documents, he was born in 1452 at Fotheringhay Castle in Northamptonshire. He had an English queen, Lady Anne Neville, younger daughter of Richard and Anne Neville, Earl and Countess of Warwick.

He died in 1485, leading his army into battle at Bosworth – the last English king to die on English soil doing so.

*Mary Goose, Wisbech, Cambridgeshire*

**(92) QUESTION: When my mother was a child, her father used to cut bark from a tree which glowed in the dark when she hid it under the stairs. What sort of tree would this have been?**

This phenomenon is most likely to be associated not with a particular type of tree, but with the common wood-rotting honey fungus having colonized the bark. The phosphorescence this fungus emits by its metabolic activities can be quite dramatic in the dark.

Several species of honey fungus (Armillaria) throughout Britain are wood-rotting and capable of attacking live trees as well as dead wood. They're woodland fungi but, as many gardeners know to their cost, also attack garden trees and shrubs. They often kill young conifers in forests, causing gaps in plantation.

*Dr Steve Gregory, Forestry Commission Research Division,*
*Roslin, Midlothian*

**(93) QUESTION: When placing a credit card order by phone, why is the card's expiry date always required?**

About 3 per cent of the many millions of plastic card transactions authorized by Barclays Merchant Services are by people ordering by telephone. It's important that all means of security be employed by ourselves and retailers to protect against fraud, especially for phone orders where retailers can't see the card, 'swipe' it to check its validity, check its chip-and-pin or be given a signature for authentication. So retailers must ensure they take enough information from a caller to authenticate that they are who they say they are and that they hold a valid card.

A caller is asked for the expiry date to establish whether their card is up to date, and may also be asked for things which don't appear on the card, such as their address. When all this information is relayed back to the credit card centre, it helps authorize the orders of valid callers or reject invalid requests or fraudsters.

*Sara May, Barclays Bank, London*

**(94) QUESTION: Is there any factual story behind the Rip Van Winkle folk tale?**

This character first appeared as a short story by New York-born Washington Irving (1783–1859) in his *Sketch Book of Geoffrey Crayon, Gent*, published in 1819. It told how happy-go-lucky and often well-oiled Rip Van Winkle escaped his nagging wife on a trip with his dog, Wolf, to the Catskill Mountains in New York State one September day in 1769.

There he encountered a band of little men playing ninepins and sneakily drank from their keg, which made him fall asleep. On waking, he found that his dog had left him and his musket was rusty. He returned home to discover that twenty years had passed, his wife had died and no one knew who he was. The country had achieved independence, with George II being replaced by George Washington.

Irving is believed to have visited the place associated with Rip Van Winkle's sleep, known as Kaaterskill Clove, near Haines Falls, ten miles from Catskill.

There is no documentary proof of Rip Van Winkle's existence at the time but similar tales involving meetings with 'little men' and disappearances for long periods are told all across Europe and North America.

*Nancy Petramale, Green County Tourism and Info Centre,*
*Catskill, New York*

I've seen Rip Van Winkle. From the east side of the Hudson River – where I was brought up – as young children, we were told we could look west and see old Rip, west of the Hudson in the Catskill Mountains.

Every child brought up there is told to look across the beautiful mountains behind which the sun sets every evening and, with a bit of imagination, pick out Rip Van Winkle's silhouette – his feet, legs, middle, chest and head – in the outline of the Catskills. Little boys, as I was seventy years ago, who had glorious grandmothers like mine, had the old fellow pointed out to us and felt very comfortable living in his shadow.

*Charles West, Bath, Somerset*

**(95) QUESTION: I have a cat called Gilbert and have heard this name was commonly used for cats in the Middle Ages. Is this true, and if so, why?**

A castrated male cat was known in the Middle Ages in England as 'gib cat', the 'gib' being said to have been derived from Tibert or Tybalt, the French form of Gilbert.

*The Romaunt of the Rose*, the medieval translation of *The Roman de la Rose*, renders the phrase '*Thibert le cas*' as 'Gibbe, our cat'.

*Joan Moore, Cat World magazine, Shoreham-by-Sea, West Sussex*

**(96) QUESTION: Our school was built in 1717, can any state school beat that? Which is the oldest state school in Britain?**

As a pupil in the 1940s at the Royal Free School in Windsor, founded in Queen Anne's time in 1705, I was told it was the first state school in Britain, although the original building is no longer used by the school.

Over the years, the school has produced several outstanding academics and sportspersons, most notable being Sir Sydney Camm who, at a very young age, became chief designer with the Hawker Aircraft Company and designed more than fifty aircraft, of which the Battle of Britain Hurricane was just one.

*Clifford Smith, Bognor Regis, Sussex*

My husband's old school, Northampton School for Boys, now a state school, was founded by Thomas Chipsey in 1541.

*Shirley Watson, Northampton*

Here in Barnsley, we're very proud of Peniston Grammar School which, having been founded in 1392, is, we believe, the oldest state school in the country.

The school is still changing with the times, having had a £1 million extension in the 1990s to house a new library.

*Diane Bell, Barnsley Metropolitan Borough Council,*
*South Yorkshire*

The primary school in Ewelme was built in 1430 by the Earl of Suffolk and his wife, Alice, granddaughter of Geoffrey Chaucer. It's probably the oldest school in the country still in its original building.

*Mrs H. J. Sim, Ewelme, Oxfordshire*

I still have a small notebook from St Saviour's and St Olave's Grammar School, New Kent Road, London SE1, containing notes dictated by my headmistress, Mrs Frodsham MA, in 1917.

She told us that around AD 800, the Christian Prince Olaf of Norway landed near London Bridge to invade England. A small colony of monks he established there founded a grammar school for boys which grew into St Olave's School. Olaf is recalled in the school badge – a crown, cross and battleaxe.

At the turn of the nineteenth/twentieth centuries, a girls' section was founded as St Saviour's and St Olave's Grammar School, which I attended between 1912 and 1918.

*Kathleen Lutman, Ledbury, Hertfordshire*

Beverley Grammar School, in Yorkshire's East Riding, was founded in about AD 700 by St John of Beverley, who died in AD 721.

We were taught we were the third oldest school in the country, behind King's School, Canterbury, and St Peter's, York. Since neither of these is now a state school, Beverley Grammar must hold the record.

*Dr R. Michael Scrowston, Beverley Grammar School*
*Old Boys' Association*

## (97) QUESTION: When the Jews established themselves in Palestine fifty years ago, why did they choose to be Israelis, descended from the Israelites, rather than Judah?

When the name of the Jewish state in Palestine was discussed by the Settlement Council just before the Declaration of Independence in May 1948, the two possibilities, Israel and Judah, were considered.

The former was associated with the ten northern tribes of ancient Israel which seceded from the rule of descendants of King David and were lost to Jewish history after deportation by the Assyrians in 721 BC. The latter relates to the Kingdom of Judah, the remaining two tribes, from whom descend the Jewish people of today.

The decision to call the modern state 'Israel' was seen by the first prime minister, David Ben-Gurion, as a unifying symbol, expressing the desire of the state to act as a focus for the 'ingathering of the exiles', descendants of the two tribes of Judah or of the lost ten tribes of Israel.

*Mark Faber, Embassy of Israel, London*

## (98) QUESTION: Why is a picture falling off a wall supposed by the superstitious to portend a death in the family?

I'm not superstitious but recent events have made me think very hard about such matters.

On Sunday 9 June, my wife had a nasty accident. She had been adjusting the pictures above our mantelpiece when one fell down, breaking its glass and an ornament. I put the matter aside as just one of those things. Four days later, the *Daily Mail* posed this question about falling pictures being a portent of death in the family. That evening, my wife received a phone call from her father's nursing home in Richmond, North Yorkshire, to say he was unwell. In the early hours of Sunday her father passed away, peacefully, in his sleep.

The pictures above our mantelpiece are of locations with which we have associations. The one which fell was of Harrogate, in North Yorkshire.

*A. E. D. Burke, Wickford, Essex*

It's still commonly believed that if a picture falls from the wall for no apparent reason, it foretells the death of someone in the house. Some say the omen won't be fulfilled unless the glass breaks but usually the fall of a picture alone is deemed to be enough.

This well-known superstition is a relic of the old belief that a person's portrait is somehow magically connected with its subject. This link between a man's soul and his pictorial representation is now largely forgotten but the fear lives on in the ominous regard attributed to the fall of a picture.

*Eric Hoare, Chepstow, Gwent*

As a child, my nanny told me that a picture falling off the wall was an omen of death. Visiting our son one night a picture did just that and I was the only one who knew what it meant but didn't tell anyone at the time. My husband died ten days later.

*Nora Stott, Pinner, Middlesex*

**(99) QUESTION: Two of the US Navy's nuclear-powered aircraft carriers are called *Carl Vinson* and *John Stennis*. Who are/were they?**

Born in Kemper County, Mississippi, on 3 August 1901, John Cornelius Stennis graduated from Mississippi State University in

1923 and from the University of Virginia Law School in 1928. After serving in the Mississippi state legislature he was elected to the Senate in Washington, DC, in 1947.

He retired from the Senate in 1988 after forty-one years' service, which included chairing the Senate Armed Services and Senate Appropriations Committees, and died in 1995.

Carl Vinson (1883–1981) was born in Milledgeville, Georgia, became a student of law and was admitted to the Bar in 1902. Elected to Georgia State Senate in 1906, he represented his state in Washington, DC, as a member of the House of Representatives from 1914 to 1965. He served as chairman of the Naval Affairs Committee and later the Armed Services Committee.

The USS *Carl Vinson* was the first US ship to be named after a living person since the American Revolution. The Nimitz class of aircraft carriers, to which both USS *Stennis* and *Vinson* belong, are nuclear powered, displace about 100,000 tonnes and carry more than 100 aircraft and helicopters each.

The full list of the Nimitz class and their completion dates are as follows: *Nimitz* 1975; *Dwight D. Eisenhower* 1977; *Carl Vinson* 1982; *Theodore Roosevelt* 1986; *Abraham Lincoln* 1989; *George Washington* 1991; *John C. Stennis* 1995; *Harry Truman* 1997, *Ronald Reagan* 2003 and *George H. W. Bush* 2009.

*Ian Richardson, High Shincliffe, Durham*

## (100) QUESTION: Who were the Committee of 100?

Within two years of its founding in 1958 by philosopher Bertrand Russell and Canon John Collins of St Paul's Cathedral, the Campaign for Nuclear Disarmament (CND) split over its tactics for trying to rid Britain of nuclear weapons. Some members were adamant that all protest should be strictly within the law. Others advocated non-violent direct action, principally the 'sit-down protest' which was interpretable as causing an obstruction.

The latter group met at Friends House on 22 October 1960, and formed themselves into The Committee of 100. In fact, there were ninety-seven at the meeting, including Russell, Revd. Michael Scott, playwrights John Arden, Robert Bolt, Sheila Delaney, John Osborne and Arnold Wesker, film-maker Lindsay Anderson, poets Christopher Logue and Hugh MacDiarmid, musician George Melly, actor Bernard Miles and writers John Braine, William Gaskill and Doris Lessing.

On their first demonstration on 18 February 1961, two thousand people sat down outside the Ministry of Defence in Whitehall, while three thousand others demonstrated on foot. On 29 April, two thousand protesters sat down in Parliament Square to coincide with the annual CND Aldermaston march and the police made 826 arrests.

The Trafalgar Square sit-down of September that year involved twelve thousand people of whom the police arrested 1,300. This coincided with blockades of nuclear bases such as the US submarine base at Holy Loch.

Soon after this, Special Branch officers raided the Finsbury Park offices of the Committee of 100, seizing documents and arresting many of the group's leaders. The organization was decapitated.

The thawing of international relations after the Cuban missile crisis took the wind out of the sails of the nuclear disarmament groups and the committee was disbanded in 1968.

When a revitalized CND emerged in the early eighties in reaction to the deployment of US Cruise missiles in the UK, it espoused the non-violent direct protest techniques of the Committee of 100 as its major weapon. These days, though direct action is still a feature of our protest, our methods concentrate more on increased lobbying for a change in society.

*Lionel Trippett, Campaign for*
*Nuclear Disarmament (CND), London*

## (101) QUESTION: What are Schiller's words to Beethoven's 'Ode To Joy'?

The poem 'An Die Freude' ('Ode To Joy') was written by Johann

Schiller (1759–1805) in 1785. Ludwig van Beethoven (1770–1827) wanted to use it as early as 1793 and produced an original arrangement in 1812 but did not complete his Ninth Symphony incorporating the *presto-allegro* which is now used as the European Anthem until 1824. It had its first public performance in Vienna on 7 May that year.

The words, translated from the German are:

> *Joy, though spark from flame immortal/Daughter of Elysium*
> *Drunk with fire, O heav'n-born Goddess/We invade thy*
>   *halidom*
> *Let thy magic bring together/All whom earth-born laws divide*
> *All mankind shall be as brothers/Neath thy tender wings and*
>   *wide.*

It continues in this vein for another twenty-six lines before concluding:

> *Seek him o'er yon stars of heaven/O'er the stars rise his*
>   *pavilions.*

*Sean Allerton, Sherburn in Elmet, Yorkshire*

Ralph Hill's book *The Symphony*, first published by Penguin in 1949, refers to an article about sixty years ago in the *Radio Times* by a Professor Abraham. This pointed out that Schiller's ode was written in 1785, on the eve of the French Revolution, at a time when liberal ideas were beginning to make themselves felt.

The ode was really addressed not to *An die Freude* (To Joy), but *An die Freiheit* (To Freedom). Owing to political necessity, Schiller was forced to substitute *Freude* for *Freiheit*, somewhat to the detriment of the poem. It is clear, however, that Beethoven, and probably numerous other people, were aware Joy was merely a thin disguise for Freedom.

*J. D. Lowes, Bedhampton, Havant, Hampshire*

Beethoven's Ninth Symphony was a favourite of mine until the EU adopted it as the European anthem. I propose some new lyrics: 'Pencil-pushing admin boys and unelected bureaucrats, Rule-book writers, business blighters, red-tape strangling fatty cats, Come to Strasbourg, come to Brussels, join us here in Fairyland. If it moves we'll regulate it, pass a law and kill it now.

'All traditions, ancient wisdoms, stamp on them until they're dead. All that's free and easy-going, regulate it. In its stead. We'll think rules up, legislation, grind them down most ruthlessly. So: come to Brussels come to Strasbourg, MEPs and office boys. Huge pay rises, constant crises justify your lot in life.

'Nations tremble, leaders humbled facing Euro-bureau threats. We're in power, we're in charge and will be till they throw us out.'

*John Hardy, Packington, Leicestershire*


My college, St Chad's, of Durham University, uses this tune for one of the cleaner of its songs. Founded as a theological college at the turn of the century, we maintain High Church traditions, despite admitting undergraduates of both sexes to read for all degrees.

The song goes: 'St Chad's College architecture may not be fantastical/But we have a long tradition that's ecclesiastical.

'See our young potential bishops, never heard of actresses/ Sanctimoniously performing, Anglo-Catholic practices.'

*Martin Jubb, St Chad's College, Durham*


## (102) QUESTION: What is the significance of the three scimitars on English county badges and coats of arms?

The three weapons on the arms of Middlesex aren't scimitars but notched sword *seaxes*, traditional emblems of the East Saxons.

Since the fifteenth century, the sovereign has delegated power to grant new arms to senior heralds or kings of arms who make the grants by letters patent, registered in the College of Arms. New grants in Scotland are entered in the Public Register of All Arms and Bearings in Scotland in the Lyon Office, Edinburgh.

County councils set up by Act of Parliament in 1888 were allowed to apply for coats of arms and, in November 1910, the Garter, Clarenceux and Norroy (first, second and third Kings of Arms) granted the County of Middlesex: 'Arms of Gules (red) three Seaxes fessewise in pale proper pomelled and hilted Or points to the sinister and cutting edge upward in a chief of Saxon Crown of the last (i.e. Or).'

*Thomas Woodcock, Somerset Herald, College of Arms, London*

## (103) QUESTION: From sea level, on a clear day, across a calm sea, how far away is the horizon?

About three miles. For practical purposes, the distance in nautical miles to the sea horizon can be found by: 1.15 × the square root of H – where H is the height of the observer's eye above sea level. Nautical miles (of 6,080 ft) multiplied by 1.1515 gives statute miles (of 5,280 ft).

So for a 6 ft man at sea level it would be 1.15 times the square root of 6, which gives 2.8 nautical miles or 3.2 land miles. If he stood on top of a 100 ft cliff, it would be 1.15 × the square root of 106, giving 11.8 sea and 13.6 land miles.

*Capt. R. H. Wills, Wimborne, Dorset*

The figure which takes the distance in miles to be 1.225 times the square root of the height in feet can be used in reverse.

For example, at sea level the summit of a 1,000 ft hill 38.7 miles away would be just visible above the horizon. And the figures can be combined: thus, an observer standing on a boat 25 ft above sea level would just see the top of a cliff 100 ft high, 18.4 miles away. But this formula doesn't apply for very large heights of, say, hundreds of thousands of miles.

*David Roberts, Three Crosses, Swansea*

**(104) QUESTION: How many pints does the traditional yard of ale hold?**

A yard of ale holds about 2 ½ pints and the secret to drinking one is patience. Drink very slowly, revolving the glass as you swallow and keeping an eye on the level of liquid. Towards the end, watch out for the bubble that forms in the bulb at the end of the glass. Drink even more slowly to stop the bubble rushing up the glass and spilling the ale down you.

*Michael Speake, Easton, Norfolk*

The idea for the yard of ale came from the 'yard of tin', the long coach horns sounded by the guard to let passengers know the coach was setting off, to warn others of its presence and alert turnpike keepers to open their gates. Many 'half-way houses' along coaching routes had old horns used during celebrations as drinking vessels; the glass yard is an imitation of the horn.

*Graeme Cobb, Saltcoats, Ayrshire*

**(105) QUESTION: How did Michael Bentine produce his amazing special effects on TV in the days before computer graphics?**

Thank you for the compliment about my 'amazing special effects' which, I take it, refers to my 'invisible flea circus' and not my use of make-up.

The 'invisible fleas' weren't special effects but genuine fleas, trained in the art of camouflage. We resorted to special effects only in rare moments when the fleas considered a stunt too dangerous. When this happened, the backroom boys and I worked with great ingenuity, using gravity, electromagnets, springs, balloons, steam engines and all-important bits of string. I recall we also found use for the odd drop of alcohol.

I first used these effects on ATV's *Dave King Show* in September 1957. In 1959, they became a regular feature on the ABC programme *After Hours*, which I wrote and presented, on the TV shows *It's A Square World* and *All Square* during the 1960s and the 148 *Potty Shows* in the 1970s and early 1980s.

*Michael Bentine, CBE*

I joined the BBC visual effects department in 1965 and worked on his *Square World* series. Most of the effects were pretty simple: footprints made by 'invisible men' involved cutting holes in a cardboard base, sticking a paper strip underneath and covering it with sand. At the right moment the strip was peeled off and the sand fell through (usually into the operator's eyes) and footprints appeared.

Other models were animated by tiny electric motors, nylon lines, magnets, small explosive charges and bits of old clocks. There were usually two of us jammed uncomfortably under the model with an array of switches, buttons, cords and wires.

We rehearsed twice but Michael was prone to change everything as inspiration came. As the countdown started, panic and perspiration prevailed. When chaos descended, the result was often funnier than intended and Michael was a brilliant ad-libber.

I once prematurely erupted a small volcano by releasing a balloon-full of mauve porridge up the crater. His comment was too rude to transmit and had to be edited out.

Computers can do wonderful things at trifling cost but elastic bands and string were more fun.

*Tony Oxley, London W13*

(106) QUESTION: Men in Edwardian novels are sometimes described as wearing 'wideawake' hats. What was this?

The wideawake – a round, low-crowned informal felt hat, with a wide brim, worn mostly in the country, evolved during the mid-nineteenth century and was given its name from the fact that it was made of material without a nap.

*Avril Hart, Victoria and Albert Museum, London*

**(107) QUESTION Were Spitfires made at Salisbury bus station during the Second World War and transported by bus to Grovelly Woods for assembly?**

Several versions of Spitfire, including the Mks V, IX, XII, XIV and the Seafire, were built in Salisbury. Wings were made in the Wiltshire & Dorset Bus Garage, fuselages at the Wessex garage and tails at Anna Valley garage. Engines were installed in fuselages at Castle Road factory and final assembly and test flying of Salisbury-built Spitfires took place at Chattis Hill and High Post.

This method of dispersed component manufacture, necessitated by security, was a forerunner of Tornado and Airbus aircraft projects which have components manufactured in various places.

*Frank Crosby, Imperial War Museum, Duxford, Cambridgeshire*

Wiltshire and Dorset Bus Garage did manufacture Spitfires. Wings, sailplanes and fuselages were transported to Highpost Airfield, between Salisbury and Amesbury, before each aircraft had machine guns fitted and tested by a visiting test pilot. The aircraft was then flown by ferry pilot to its appointed RAF station. Some test pilots and many employees making Spitfires at Salisbury were women. It was claimed they were better at welding the aluminium fuel tanks than the men.

*B. Woodgate, Harefield, Middlesex*

**(108) QUESTION: Do vessels have to pay for Tower Bridge to be opened when they pass underneath it?**

Money donated to build the first London Bridge accumulated over eight hundred years into the Bridge House Estates Fund, managed by the Corporation of London, and was used to build Blackfriars, Southwark and Tower Bridges at no cost to the taxpayer. The fund also covers the cost of lifting the bridge and its maintenance.

Tower Bridge was the response to a desperate need for a road bridge east of London Bridge which wouldn't interfere with shipping. Lifting the bridge takes just a few minutes. Completed in 1894, it was lifted 6,160 times in the first year.

Vessels must now give twenty-four hours' notice but the bridge can still be opened at any time and is lifted an average five hundred times a year. Its history is told in an exhibition inside the bridge, where visitors can also see the fantastic view from the towers, 140 ft above the Thames.

*Keith Patterson, Bridge Master, Tower Bridge, London*

**(109) QUESTION: Signs at Bexhill, Sussex, claim it as the birthplace of British motor racing. Does it have a better claim than Brooklands?**

The banked circuit at Brooklands was built in 1906 as a high-speed test centre for the infant British motor industry and the first races held there were in 1907.

Five years earlier, Lord Montague's forefather, John Montague of Beaulieu, introduced his friend Lord De La Warr to officials of the Automobile Club of Great Britain and Ireland (now the RAC) at the 1902 Nice Speed Trials. The Laird of Bexhill was keen on staging an event on the paved cycle track on his De La Warr estate at Bexhill and within weeks had organized an international there for Whit Monday, 1902.

The Bexhill Races attracted 35,000 to see great sporting motorists like Australia's Selwyn Edge in his race-bred Napier; the Hon. Charles Rolls of Monmouth, co-founder of Rolls-Royce, in a Mors; Louis Renault in a car of his own name; Alfred Harmsworth, founder of Associated Newspapers, in a Mercedes, and Charles Jarrott in his Darraq.

102

Honours went to Frenchman Leon Serpollet in his steam-driven car which averaged 54 mph. After the event John Montague launched the *Car Illustrated* magazine, recording 'Bexhill; the scene of Britain's first official motor race'.

*Max Le Grand, author* Brands to Bexhill, *Cheltenham, Gloucestershire*

**(110) QUESTIONS: I've read that post is still addressed to my great-uncle, John Christie, at 10 Rillington Place. What happens to these letters?**

The location no longer exists. Its name was changed to Ruston Close before the street was demolished. John Christie was hanged in 1953 for the murders of his wife and six other women.

A handful of letters are sent to this address every year and are passed to the Royal Mail's National Return Letter Centre in Belfast, where staff attempt to return them. Some 270 people process 175,000 items of mail a day, opening and examining it to establish a sender's address. About 61,000 are returned, the rest are recycled. The content of all letters remains confidential.

*Eugene Wallace, National Return Letter Centre, Belfast*

As a sixteen-year-old trainspotter at Paddington Station, I took the short ride to Ladbroke Grove with some friends and visited 10 Rillington Place after six bodies had been discovered there in 1953. The landlord charged 2s 6d (12½p) to look over the house. I've never forgotten the evil feeling in that place.

*John Hobbs, Earley, Berkshire*

**(111) QUESTION: Are the football shirts sold to supporters the same as those worn by players?**

Yes, though some badges and logos are printed, rather than

embroidered, as on players' shirts. All our replica and professional shirts are made from 100 per cent Jerseytex, a hard-wearing polyester which returns a shirt to its original shape, regardless of how much it's stretched or pulled during a game.

*Simon Woollard, Umbro, Manchester*

**(112) QUESTION: Why is it considered unlucky to change a boat's name? Has anyone ever suffered as a consequence?**

This is one of many superstitions surrounding seafaring and ships. In 1926, my marine engineer father, Joseph Thames Barraclough, sailed out of Cardiff on the *Loyal Citizen*, which was lost at sea in a hurricane off the coast of Baltimore on 14 September. Several superstitions were involved in that voyage. Because of the General Strike, insufficient coal was available in Cardiff to take them to their South American destination, so they were obliged to make the detour to Baltimore to take on more coal.

This coal load wasn't trimmed, as it would have been in Britain, so when they ran into the hurricane, the coal shifted and the ship foundered with all forty-four men. Seven other vessels were also lost.

The *Loyal Citizen* had changed owners and was previously named *The Marquis of Bute*. She sailed on a Friday and backed out of the dock. This is how such superstitions arise.

The shipping company was dilatory in telling wives and families, and my mother read the news in the papers before being officially informed. The company stopped my father's pay from the day the ship went down.

*Miss Patricia Barraclough, Bridlington, Yorkshire*

My father was one of seventeen killed when HMS *Arctic Pioneer* was bombed at the entrance of Portsmouth harbour on 27 May 1942. The Royal Navy raised her to clear the harbour entrance and she was returned to her original owners, Boyds Fishing Co, of Hull, in 1946/47 and renamed *Arctic Viking*.

A fisherman who had worked for Boyds before and after the war saw the *Arctic Viking* coming back to Hull, recognized her as the *Pioneer* and refused to sail on her. She sank with all hands in a gale off Flamborough Head in 1961.

*Arthur Hovell, Goring by Sea, Sussex*


I've been on many ships which have had their names changed, including the *Express of Japan* which became the *Empress of Scotland* when used as a troopship in 1942.

My wife and I have noted name changes on most merchant ships in African ports, the original names often being welded on for easy removal. A shipping agent told us it was obligatory to change a ship's name when it changed owners.

*L. Charlwood, West Byfleet, Surrey*


In the late thirties, the submarine HMS *Thetis* sank in Liverpool Bay with tragic loss of life but was recovered and renamed *Thunderbolt*. She was then lost in action in the Second World War.

A vessel named *Robert Barton* was renamed *Hayburn Wyke* and requisitioned for minesweeping duties. She was torpedoed at anchor near Ostend, Belgium. Official sources show this as 2 January 1945, with the loss of two officers and twenty ratings. There were two survivors. My brother, George William, was one of the unfortunate casualties.

*L. W. Carrington, Bingley, West Yorkshire*


I served on five ships which changed names without any adverse result – and one of them was very lucky. The *Halls of Montezuma* had been renamed *Esso Bristol* when we docked in Texas City for repairs on 16 April 1947. In the early hours of 17 April, the French

10,000-ton freighter *Grand Camp*, loaded with fertilizer, exploded with huge force. The American cargo vessel *Higher Flyer*, while being towed from the scene, blew up too, setting off more fires and explosions. This disaster, with the loss of more than six hundred lives and countless injuries, was for many years America's worst man-made disaster.

The *Esso Bristol* was tugged to safety and needed only some hard work and paint before she was her old self.

*Don Riddle, Felsted, Sussex*


Despite the anecdotal evidence, a larger statistical sample appears to refute this superstition. About three hundred ships a month have their names changed, the changes being published in the monthly *Marine News*, the periodical of the World Ship Society.

Most of these changes are brought about either by a new owner wishing to change the name or the vessel being chartered by a new charterer.

*Derek Blackhurst, World Ship Society, Salcombe, Devon*


In the forties, I was sent to join an American ship called the *Samuel Horman*, anchored with other ships off Gravesend. It was freezing cold and I had to pay a boatman 2s 6d (12½p) to row me out to the ship.

We could find no ship of that name there, so I returned to the seaman's pool where they told me the ship's name had been changed the day before to the *Francine Clore*. So I had to pay another 2s 6d (more than a day's wages) to be rowed out again. Pretty unlucky, I'd say.

*B. Reynolds, Herne Bay, Kent*

**(113) QUESTION: What happened to racing tipster Ras Prince Monolulu who used to mingle with the crowds on Derby Day chanting 'I gotta horse'?**

Self-styled Ras Prince Monolulu, otherwise known as plain old Peter Carl McKay, was the most flamboyant of all racing tipsters of the last century. His line 'I gotta 'orse!' proclaimed at every race track in Britain, France and America, was second only to his colourful red and blue robes with matching ostrich-feather head-dress.

Born in 1881, he left his early years very much a mystery. He claimed to have been born in Addis Ababa, capital of Ethiopia, the descendant of a chieftain of a Jewish tribe but with Scottish blood. All official files on him registered his citizenship as Danish.

In his early teens, he is supposed to have become a stoker in a ship out of Djibouti, bound for America. On his arrival there, he jumped ship and over the next few years had a number of jobs including bar cleaner, dentist and lion-tamer before being 'shang-haied' into the US Navy.

After his stint working for Uncle Sam, he had a short period as a gospel preacher on behalf of Salvationist General Booth but he soon became bored and sought new adventures in Europe after making his way here as an escort and carer for horses being shipped for racing.

Monolulu is known to have spent time in Denmark, Germany and France before coming to Britain in 1902. He soon became a stablehand and within a few years was an accomplished tipster. In 1920, he is supposed to have won more than £3,000 on the Derby when he put all his money on Spion Kop. His reputation as a tipster was established and from that point he was feted by racing's rich and famous the world over.

He claimed acquaintance with the Duke of Windsor, the Aga Khan and Lord Derby. Over the next twenty years, he claimed massive fortunes came in through his winners but went out through his extravagances.

After the Second World War, he continued his success as a tipster until, in 1965, at the age of eighty-four, he died on Valentine's Day: an appropriate day for a man who is supposed to have been married six times.

*Simon Clare, British Horseracing Board, London*


Besides tipping the occasional winner, Ras Prince Monolulu regularly entertained at Speakers' Corner. I always made straight for his platform, even at the expense of missing Baron Thompson, Charlie the Shorthand Professor or the Caveman – all actors of great note in the 1930s.

Monolulu's speeches were humorous and informative. I recall him saying he had named one of his children Raymond, the name of a winning horse he'd tipped for The Cambridgeshire.

*Alec Cottrell, London W12*


The last time I saw Prince Monolulu was at Westminster Cathedral in October 1956 at the requiem mass for the jockey Michael Beary, which Monolulu attended in his full regalia.

Michael wanted to be interred at Epsom, where he had won the 1937 Derby on Mid Day Sun. To the delight of all those present, Prince Monolulu climbed in beside the driver of the hearse to escort the jockey to his final resting place.

No one would have appreciated it more than Michael, even if the famous tipster was simply cadging a lift.

*Gordon Fergusson, Tarporley, Cheshire*


Jeffrey Bernard's biography includes a claim to have choked him to death: 'In February 1965, Hackett sent Bernard to interview racecourse tipster Prince "I gotta a horse" Monolulu, the 82-year-old Abyssinian, who was seriously unwell in Middlesex Hospital.

'Bernard took a box of Black Magic chocolates and when

Monolulu proved too weak to help himself, Bernard pushed a strawberry cream into his feeble mouth. The prince tried to swallow it, coughed and started choking. A nurse sent Bernard out of the ward and drew a screen around the bed, but it was too late. Monolulu choked to death.'

*Davina Ramsay, London, WC2*


## (114) QUESTION: Why the irrational song 'Ashby de la Zouch by the Sea'?

The local explanation is that during the Second World War, when American soldiers were trying to explain the location of this small town to the folks back home, they told them to look for the county name Leicestershire on the map and Ashby would be found just by the letter C. Hence 'Ashby de la Zouch, by the C' – which had nothing to do with the sea.

*Marjorie Collis Hastie, Ticknall, Derby*


## (115) QUESTION: On which stretch of rail line was the comedy film *The Titfield Thunderbolt* filmed? Does it still exist?

T. E. B. Clarke, writer of *Passport to Pimlico*, *The Lavender Hill Mob* and other great Ealing comedies, was intrigued by vintage machinery and the 1952 film *The Titfield Thunderbolt*, about a village trying to keep its branch line open against competition from a bus company, reflects that.

Despite featuring the likes of Stanley Holloway, its biggest star was *The Lion*, a historic loco. This 1838 engine, with a 6 ft smokestack and leather buffers stuffed with horse hair ('Horrible to drive, a barrel on wheels', said one of the production team) was borrowed from a Liverpool museum and given a new livery for this first Ealing comedy in Technicolor.

Limpley Stoke, near Bath, with several miles of disused railway line, doubles as the imaginary village of Titfield. In those years,

Tibby Clarke's vision of locals replacing British Railways seemed far-fetched, though he claimed it was viable. These days, his idea looks rather more sound. Sadly, *Thunderbolt* proved less hilarious than his earlier hits.

*Don Coppins, Edgbaston, Birmingham*

Two other notable films were made on the seven-mile stretch of line between Limpley Stoke and Camerton before it lost its trackbed as part of the Beeching cuts. *The Ghost Train*, made in 1931, starred Jack Hulbert and Cicely Courtneidge, and the 1938 *Kate Plus Ten* starred (and was written by) Jack Hulbert alongside Genevieve Tobin and Noel Madison.

*John P. Love, Solihull, West Midlands*

### (116) QUESTION: When was the last cavalry charge in battle?

It's generally accepted that the last classic, full-scale cavalry charge by the British Army was by the 21st Lancers, Duke of Cambridge's Own, at Omdurman during the battle of Khartoum on 2 September 1898.

I have a print showing Lieut. Newham leading his troop in that charge, during which he was seriously wounded. He died in 1901 and is buried in a family vault in Brookwood Cemetery where I have maintained his grave for many years.

*Charles Cracknell, Woking, Surrey*

In 1917, the 14th Australian Light Horse Brigade secured the water wells at Beersheba, Palestine, from the Turks. Capturing the wells intact was essential for General Allenby's advance on Jerusalem. The 18 ALH Regiments in Allenby's force of 58,000 weren't strictly cavalry but mounted riflemen who used horses for battlefield mobility but generally fought on foot.

In a controversial decision, the 4th and 5th Regiments charged the Turks, using the speed of their horses to get under the guns and secure the wells from demolition while the enemy were expecting a dismounted assault.

At sunset on 31 October, 832 mounted riflemen armed with 18 inch bayonets instead of cavalry sabres, formed up in three extended lines 1,100 yards long and 1,000 yards apart. The charge soon passed the 1,500 metre range at which the Turkish artillery had been calibrated, preventing the enemy from adjusting their fall of shot. Though fortified with wire and machine guns, the trenches were quickly overrun and the wells made safe. The objective secured for the loss of thirty-one killed, thirty-six wounded and seventy horses lost, made the charge at Beersheba one of the most successful in history.

*S. A. Kirkwood, Woking, Surrey*

The last cavalry charge against the British Army was by just sixty horsemen on 21 January 1941, in Eritrea. In his book on the 1940/41 Abyssinian Campaign, military historian Michael Glover writes: 'Dawn on January 21 found the leading vehicles probing the mouth of the Keru Gorge in Eritrea where the road, running between steep cliffs, had been heavily mined and blocked by demolition.

'The whole of the Italian 41st Colonial Brigade, under General Fongoli, had been deployed to hold this defile and Brigadier Frank Messervy, underestimating the enemy strength, sent the Sikhs from the 4th and 5th Indian Divisions against them, supported by his field battery. It was not enough. The infantry, suffering 150 casualties, were pinned down short of their first objectives and even the gunners were in imminent danger. They were then charged from the rear by a squadron of Ethiopian cavalry led by two Italian officers on white horses.

'There was a moment of stupefaction before the guns were swung round to engage the horsemen while parts of Skinner's Horse, a motorized cavalry regiment, the Sudan Defence Force, under Allied command, and the 25th Field Regiment of the Royal Artillery joined in. The cavalry withdrew but charged again before being driven off leaving twenty-three dead and sixteen wounded.'

*Richard Symons, Imperial War Museum, London*

The *1st Grupo Squadron*'s charge against the Royal Artillery at Keru, in Eritrea, on 21 January 1941, was led by Baron Amedeo Guillet.

*C. K. B. Taylor, Surrey Yeomanry Regimental Association,*
*Sanderstead, Surrey*

In Burma on 19 March 1942, Captain Arthur Sandeman of the Central India Horse led his Sikh sowars of the Burma Frontier Force towards what he thought were friendly Chinese troops. By the time he realized he had ridden into a Japanese ambush it was too late and, ordering his trumpeter to sound the charge, he led his troop at the gallop towards the enemy machine guns. Sandeman and many of his men were killed.

*Brian Nicholls, Maidstone, Kent*

The last charge by a cavalry unit of the British Army was at Isolio, Kenya, in 1953. During the Mau Mau emergency, a detachment of British-led North Frontier Tribal Police came across a guerrilla camp and successfully rode it down.

*James Dann, London E3*

Polish cavalry made the last large-scale classic cavalry charges of modern times. German general Heinz Guderian's swift advance into Poland in 1939 took him across the Polish corridor into East Prussia, cutting off in the north sizeable Polish forces including the crack Pomorske Cavalry Brigade. The cavalry spearheaded an attempt to rejoin the main Polish forces.

As the Germans looked on in disbelief, the troopers came riding towards them on splendid horses as white-gloved officers signalled the charge, trumpets sounded, pennons waved and sabres flashed. The brigade, lances at the ready, rode straight into the fire of Guderain's tanks and soon lay in a smoking, screaming mass of dismembered men and horses.

According to a German account, some survivors being taken off to prison camps were seen rapping incredulously on the sides of the German tanks: they had been told the armour was cardboard.

*F. G. Grisley, Barry, South Glamorgan*


**(117) QUESTION: How can one differentiate the call of a cuckoo from that of a collared dove?**

The male cuckoo has a loud, emphatic, far-carrying, two-note 'cu-coo' call, with a short first syllable higher than the longer second, repeated ten to twenty times or more. In late summer, this may become 'cu-cu-coo' but is still unlike the collared dove's three-note song. The female has a distinctive loud bubbling call.

Slim, grey, with pointed wings and long tail and resembling a hawk in flight, the cuckoo arrives in mid to late April and has normally left by the end of August. A calling male droops its wings and tail in collapsed posture on branches or wires.

The collared dove, rounded with longish tail, in blends of pale pink/buff to grey/brown, with a narrow black half-collar, dark wingtips and brownish tail with whitish edges, has a less emphatic (though still far-carrying) three-note 'co-coo-cu' call, with the emphasis on the second syllable, which is three times as long as the first and third.

It lives in this country all year round, in pairs or small flocks, and is far more common around human habitation than the cuckoo.

*Mike Everett, Royal Society for the Protection of Birds,*
*Sandy, Bedfordshire*

Both collared dove and cuckoo call the same sound over and over again but each collared dove has a different message. Our local one seems to say 'My bowel's stuck' while one further down the lane says 'Bye bye, May'. The cuckoo is less intelligent and repeats what it is – a cuckoo.

*Geoffrey Garside, Cumbria*

When you hear a dove, you think you might have heard a cuckoo. When you hear a cuckoo you know you have.

*Jim Snell, Crawley, Sussex*

**(118) QUESTION: With athletics records being separated by hundredths of a second, how sure can we be that all tracks are exactly the same length?**

Important venues such as the National Indoor Arena in Birmingham have certificates recording the exact length of the lanes for each event. Measurement must be repeated whenever the track is resurfaced or re-marked. World and European record forms require the exact distance of the race to be certified by a qualified surveyor or the record claim is invalidated.

*David Littlewood, Rules Revision and Records Committee,*
*British Athletic Federation*

**(119) QUESTION: Is there really a book that starts: 'It was a dark and stormy night . . .'?**

This phrase opened Edward George, Lord Bulwer-Lytton's 1830 novel *Paul Clifford*: 'It was a dark and stormy night; the rain fell in torrents, except at occasional intervals when it was checked by a violent gust of wind that swept up the streets, for it is in London that our scenes lies, rattling along the housetops, and fiercely agitating the scanty flame of the lamps that struggled against the darkness.'

*Martin Pollard, Torrington, Devon*

Bulwer-Lytton has a contest named after him, the winner of which has to pen the most appalling opening to an imaginary novel.

Sponsored by San Jose State University, a recent winner was Janice Estey of Aspen, Colorado with: ' "Ace, watch your head," hissed Wanda urgently, yet somehow provocatively, through red, full, sensuous lips, but he couldn't, you know, since nobody can actually watch more than part of his nose, or a little cheek or lips if he really tries, but he appreciated her warning.'

*N. Sutherland, Edinburgh*

*It was a dark and stormy night and raining it will be,*
*By the cheerful fire's spark the cat sleeps peacefully.*
*'Puff! And the wind blew off the rain and the Moon shone out.*
*Mousey! Go to bed again: the cat will be about.'*

I learned this verse in childhood in the twenties but don't know where it came from.

*Marguerite E. Stone, Herne Bay, Kent*

The children's picture book by Janet and Allan Ahlberg entitled *It Was a Dark and Stormy Night* was published by Puffin in October 1993. It begins: 'It was a dark and stormy night . . .'

*Peter Campbell, March, Cambridgeshire*

When I was a small child, my uncle taught me to recite a story which used to drive my parents up the wall. It must be told as dramatically as possible and goes: 'T'was a dark and stormy night, the wind blew and the rain came down. On the sea there was a ship and on the ship was a Captain and his Mate.

'The Captain said to the Mate: "Mister Mate, tell us a story," and so the Mate began: "T'was a dark and stormy night; the wind blew and the rain came down. On the sea there was a ship . . ."' and so on for as long as you like.

*Sandra Elsom, East Ham, London*

**(120) QUESTION: What are the regiments of the two characters pictured on the Camp Coffee bottle? Is it true that earlier pictures showed the servant bowing?**

It's said that R. Paterson & Sons of Glasgow produced Camp Chicory and Coffee Essence in 1885 after some Gordon Highlanders asked Robert Paterson's son Campbell to create a drink for easy use by the armed forces on campaign in India, where the process of grinding and brewing real coffee was too complicated for field kitchens. The result was the world's first instant coffee.

The liquid coffee and chicory concentrate proved such a success it soon spread to home-based Britons and by the first decade of the twentieth century, Camp coffee was being drunk from Russia to Australasia, in the Americas and South Sea islands.

The original label was said to show General Sir Hector MacDonald, hero of India, the Sudan and the Boer War, being approached deferentially by his Sikh bearer. The drawing was such that it was impossible to identify the officer with any particular regiment. Modern labels show the two men in conversation.

The motto 'Ready aye Ready' was well known, widely used in Scotland and not associated with any particular family.

Camp continued to thrive through the First World War, its producers becoming a private limited company in 1927 and a public company in 1952. It's still produced in Paisley today, as a hot drink and as a flavouring for icings, fillings, cakes, etc., where coffee flavour is required. In the eighties it was recognized as the ideal ingredient for iced coffee.

*Hugh Evans, Product Group Manager, The Jenks Group,*
*High Wycombe, Buckinghamshire*

**(121) QUESTION: Whatever happened to the Powderhall Sprint? How did the competitors' times compare with the leading runners of the day?**

Edinburgh's New Year Athletics Gala, one of the top events on the Scottish sporting calendar, incorporates the former Powderhall Sprint, which has survived without a break since 1870.

The race is a handicap event, originally run on grass at Powderhall greyhound stadium. It became the foremost professional race in the world, boasting crowds of up to 16,000 before the First World War. It moved to the new Commonwealth Stadium in 1971.

It's difficult to compare professional athletes, who competed on grass fields in the cold New Year, with the Olympic amateurs of their day.

George McNeill once ran the 110 metres off scratch in 11.0 seconds in his heat, but came second in the final to Wilson Young, who was given a six-metre start. McNeill was never able to represent Scotland in amateur athletics because he played professional football for Hibernian FC.

Some betting syndicates are said to have won £25,000 on the race in the thirties. Training squads explored every avenue to beat the handicapper and the bookmakers and, until 1949, runners were allowed to enter under assumed names, adding to the mystique of the event.

*M. Boon, Edinburgh*

**(122) QUESTION: What are the rules of the French game of *boules*?**

Like football, *boules* is a generic term covering four games. The best known is *petanque*, the rules of which are comprehensive. Put simply, the game is played in singles or doubles, where each player uses three *boules*, or triples, where each has two.

The starting team is decided by toss of a coin. One player draws a circle on the ground, 35 cm to 50 cm across, in which both feet of a thrower must remain until the *boule* lands. The first player throws the *cochonnet* (jack) 6 to 10 metres away, not less than one metre from any obstacle.

The first player then throws his *boule* as near as possible to the *cochonnet* and an opposing player then tries to throw his *boule* closer to the *cochonnet* or knock away the leading *boule*. The *boule* nearest the *cochonnet* leads and it's up to the players of the non-leading team to throw their *boules* until they get closest.

When a team has no more *boules* the players of the other team throw theirs and try to place them as close as possible to the *cochonnet*. When both teams have no more *boules*, a team is awarded as many points as it has *boules* closer to the *cochonnet* than any of the losing team's. A player of the winning team throws the *cochonnet* from where it is and the game proceeds until one team reaches 13 points.

*David Kimpton, British Petanque Association, Coventry*

**(123) QUESTION: Why Coronation chicken?**

In 1953, Rosemary Hume and Constance Spry of Le Cordon Bleu School, London, were invited by Sir David Eccles, Minister of Works, to prepare and serve luncheon for visiting Foreign Heads of State after the Coronation of Elizabeth II. It was to be served in the Great Hall of Westminster School, where kitchen facilities were too small to serve hot food beyond soup and coffee.

The food had to be simple because most of the waitresses were inexperienced students at Cordon Bleu. Thus was created Poulet Reine Elizabeth, chicken cooked in a light curry mayonnaise and served cold, which became known as Coronation Chicken.

*Justine Hughes, Le Cordon Bleu, London W1*

## (124) QUESTION: Who was the first British woman to win an Olympic track or field gold medal?

Female track and field events were introduced to the Olympics in Amsterdam in 1928 when Halina Konopacka of Poland became the first woman to win gold, in the discus.

Britain's first gold in a track or field event came at the Tokyo Olympics on 14 October 1964, when Mary Rand (née Bignall) broke the world long jump record with a 6.76-metre leap. Later that week she won a silver medal in the pentathlon and a bronze in the 4 × 100 m relay.

The first British woman to win any Olympic gold was Charlotte Cooper, who won the women's lawn tennis final in Paris in 1900 when there were no female track or field events.

*Stan Greenberg,* Guinness Book of Olympics Facts And Feats, *Enfield, Middlesex*

## (125) QUESTION: How were huge woollen tapestries protected from moth damage in the centuries before insecticides?

Many were not adequately protected and are lost to us now, but before the introduction of modern insecticides, insect-repelling herbs, dried and ground into a powder, were sprinkled around a tapestry to protect the fabric.

Sometimes leaves were used whole, strewn around the area, or placed in small muslin or linen bags tied near the fabric.

The common herbs artemesia, alecost, camphor, mint, santolina and sweet woodruff have insect-repelling properties.

The strong scent of camphor is a major ingredient in mothballs.

Dried sweet woodruff and sweet clover leaves were placed under carpets and rugs and between linens to deter insects.

Mint was strewn in cupboards and beds to deter ants and fleas, and santolina or cotton lavender was hung in closets and placed in books to deter moths. Artemesia was ground into powder and infused in water to create a liquid moth repellent.

*Julie Taylor, Conservation Unit, Museums and Galleries Commission, London*

**(126) QUESTION: My mother-in-law used to cover all mirrors in the house during a thunderstorm. Does anyone know the origin of this practice?**

My mother also did this and, when asked why, answered darkly that 'lightning comes after its own reflection'. My aunt, who lived in the Welsh mountains and didn't cover her mirrors during thunderstorms, had what she called a thunderball come down her chimney and skitter across the room. She had the presence of mind to open the door and it vanished outside.

They talked about it for years: Mother maintained that it was looking for the mirror.

*Mrs L. M. Chapman, Irthlingborough, Northamptonshire*

As a child, I remember my grandmother being terrified of thunder and lightning. She always discouraged me from looking into or standing near mirrors during thunderstorms. She explained that a flash of lightning may reflect from the mirror, causing as much damage as a direct strike.

*Miss A. E. Seaward-Birchall, High Bebington, Merseyside*

My mother, born in 1890 in Westbury-on-Trym, Bristol, dreaded thunder and lightning and I recall that in the late 1920s and early

1930s, at our home in Battersea, London, she would reverse or cover all the mirrors and place a cloth over the cutlery to prevent, as she explained, lightning being attracted into the house by the polished metal or reflected via the mirrors.

During really bad storms, she used to sit in the passageway facing the open coal store under the stairs to avoid seeing flashes through the windows.

Surviving the bombs and gunfire of the London Blitz helped lessen her dread but until her death in Crawley in 1959 she retained a lively aversion to storms.

*S. C. Gooch, Swansea*

The Children's Encyclopaedia of 1924 says we must be on our guard against lightning in a thunderstorm and take practical precautions: 'Indoors, keep away from conductors of electricity, metal grates, fenders, fire irons, iron bolts and fasteners, and mirrors which are strong conductors of electricity because of the quicksilver on their backs . . .'

I presume this is why they were covered. Apparently, the safest place indoors is in the middle of the house on a thick rug.

*Joan Smith, Bognor Regis, West Sussex*

In the late 1920s or early 1930s, while living in Defford, Worcestershire, during a particularly severe thunderstorm, what looked like a ball of fire dropped outside our sitting-room window. Afterwards we noticed on the mirror of an old-fashioned sideboard, a diagonal purple mark about 4 inches wide. It remained there ever after.

*Mrs G. P. Dyer, Cheltenham, Gloucestershire*

**(127) QUESTION: Having paid off my mortgage, I was disappointed to find that the deeds for my hundred-year-old property were typed. When did typed legal documents replace handwritten ones?**

Typed documents overtook handwritten ones only gradually after the invention of the typewriter. I've seen hand-scripted legal documents from as late as the fifties and typed documents from as early as the thirties.

I believe the document referred to here is the land certificate, introduced by the 1925 Land Registration Act to simplify conveyancing. This certificate was to be a 'logbook', recording changes of ownership of the property. Before 1925, a pile of old deeds were passed from the seller's solicitor to the buyer's and had to be checked to ensure there were no problems with the title. The land certificate should be a précis of the old deeds. Deeds used to be retained with the land certificate, but this practice has died out.

*Adrian Sutton, Bromsgrove, Worcestershire*

**(128) QUESTION: Can my pet goldfish experience emotions, such as happiness and sadness? How could we know?**

Goldfish may not be very bright but they certainly show emotion. They react to their owner's presence with excited swimming, take a lazy siesta after feeding, and males chase the females in springtime.

If unhappy, in a crowded tank or dirty water, a goldfish clamps its fins and its bright eyes go cloudy. It may gasp at the surface or sulk in a corner.

Having helped more than 50,000 owners, I can assure you that if goldfish are unhappy, they can feel it enough to give up and die. Healthy goldfish are happy goldfish and will live for twenty or more years.

*Dr David Ford, Aquarian Advisory Service, Elland, West Yorkshire*

In an indoor aquarium, we had two large goldfish which had been together for about eighteen years. When one died, the other spent the twenty-four hours before we could get a replacement dashing round in a demented fashion as though looking for her.

When we went on holiday and left my four goldfish with a food block, my son looked after them and was upset to find them all huddled in a corner, hardly moving. He thought they were dying.

Shortly after I arrived home, they were back to normal: they just missed me.

*Doreen Dennet, Poole, Dorset*

We used to have a variety of fish in our pond, including a beautiful shubunkin and a goldfish, twice its size, which teamed up and became inseparable.

Several times Shu had to be put into a tank for treatment and Goldie moped in a corner of the pond until Shu came back. One day Shu was very ill and had to stay in a tank for three days. We put him back in the pond on the fourth day and were rewarded with a beautiful, touching reunion scene which brought tears to my eyes. The two fish swam towards each other and touched noses like humans kissing before swimming around each other in great excitement.

They were together for four more years until Shu died and Goldie followed just a few days later, obviously of a broken heart.

*Mrs B. Perry, Bristol*

My mother's pet goldfish showed its annoyance if she was late feeding it. It would flick its tail against the side of the bowl to make a tiny ringing sound and soon had us trained. He eventually died of over-eating, having got the family trained a little too well.

*D. Smith, Weston-super-Mare*

When my old goldfish's mate died, he went into a corner and wouldn't eat. I tried putting him in a pond with other fish and he fainted with fright, so I returned him to his tank.

Then I fixed a mirror to the end of his tank and he immediately fell in love with his reflection. He kisses it, dances to it and sleeps next to it. He's very happy.

*Mrs Jo Elkins, London NW10*

**(129) QUESTION: Who is Francis Gay and how long has he been publishing his *Friendship Book*?**

Francis Gay was the pen name of Herbert Leslie Gee, from Bridlington, Yorkshire, who contributed articles under the heading 'The Friendly Man for the Methodist Recorder'.

Just before the Second World War, he was the inspiration behind *The Friendship Book*, which first appeared for 1939, providing a thought a day for the year.

*The Friendship Book* appeared every year, published by D. C. Thomson & Co of Dundee, for whom Herbert Gee wrote from 1935 to 1973. He died on 19 March 1977, at seventy-five.

*Ken Bowden, Bacup, Lancashire*

Francis Gay was probably best known for his weekly page in the *Sunday Post* newspaper. As part of my journalistic training, I spent a day a week phoning round Scottish ministers to get from them any 'couthy, heart-warming stories' about parishioners for Francis Gay's page.

In those days Francis Gay (pen name of Herbert Gee) wrote most of the page himself and it became so popular that after he died in 1977, the page was continued by experienced writers.

*Ian Brown, Chislehurst, Kent*

**(130) QUESTION: I have a 'tallboy'. Why do we call them that?**

A tallboy is one chest of drawers on top of another. Originally known as a double chest or chest-on-chest, they were first produced around 1700.

A typical tallboy has three wide drawers at the base and two or three narrower ones above. Some hybrid pieces have a secretaire drawer and others may have a brushing slide, a flat piece of wood which pulls out on which clothes may be brushed.

Designed for bedroom clothes storage, they declined in popularity from the mid-eighteenth century and were seldom produced after about 1810.

The descriptive word 'tallboy' emerged in the Victorian period, the 'tall' part referring to the height of the piece – up to 6 ft – and the 'boy' perhaps to a male servant, reflecting the serviceable nature of the piece.

*Brian Austen, Furniture History Society, Haywards Heath,*
*Sussex*

'Tallboy' is allied to the name of the woodwind oboe, itself a corruption of the French *hautbois*, 'tall wood'. The instrument arrived in England in about 1560 as the *hautboy*, pronounced ho-boy.

This was fully Anglicized to 'tallboy' as early as 1676, after which it was used of anything tall, wooden and useful. The earliest appearance of 'tallboy' noted by the *Oxford English Dictionary* is from 1676 and clearly alludes to the musical instrument. The same dictionary shows the first furniture use as 1769.

It's also possible that the American itinerant worker, the 'hobo', is named after the original *hautboy* in that he is useful at harvest time.

*Graeme Dodd, Cheadle Hulme, Cheshire*

**(131) QUESTION: Considering that most of the First World War was fought in trenches, what did the Cycle Corps do in it?**

Cyclists first appeared in the British Armed Forces when the 1st Volunteer Battalion, Royal Sussex Regiment used them as scouts on manoeuvres in 1885. In 1887, Colonel Stracey of the Scots Guards, commanding the Dover Marching Column, used cyclists on his flanks when he found himself short of cavalry.

Cycle corps were formed for the Boer War of 1899–1902, at one stage making up 3 per cent of active British troops, used mainly for dispatch riding. They often rode ahead to link cavalry to infantry or to reconnoitre roads for transport wagons. An eight-man 'war cycle' with detachable rims on its pneumatic tyres was used on railway lines.

The immobile trench warfare of the First World War gave cyclists little opportunity to practise reconnaissance and most cyclist units reverted to infantry, their machines being used for battlefield mobility.

The end of the war meant the end of the cyclists as a body; by 1920, the fifty-one yeomanry cyclist regiments and twenty-three territorial force cyclist battalions had been demobilized or disbanded.

*Lucinda Brown, National Army Museum, Chelsea*

My father, born in 1882, was a keen cyclist and served with the Army Cyclist Corps from 1916 to 1918 in the campaign against the Bulgars. He told me they used to patrol a 7-mile-wide no man's land on bicycles, supported by the yeomanry on horseback. He said it was surprising how long it took to mount a bike and ride off under fire.

*Douglas Collard, Cockermouth, Cumbria*

British Army cyclist troops weren't entirely disbanded after the First World War. When I arrived for training at Mansfield Royal Army

Service Corps garrison, Nottinghamshire, in September 1940, I encountered an infantry company of cyclists with new Raleigh bikes.

I believe they were the only troops in our Army issued and equipped with real leather battle accoutrements, including gaiters and ammo pouches. On parade, they cycled 'in step' – wonderful stuff, from a soldier's point of view.

*Frank Broadley, ex-driver T/222272 No 3 Company RASC,*
*Chandlers Ford, Buckinghamshire*

Infantry cycle troops were among those who landed in Normandy in 1944. I saw hundreds of cycles abandoned in a field during the break-out from the bridgehead. Once we had broken out and gone to liberate the rest of their country, our French allies took full advantage of these gifts.

*H. Day, Northfleet, Kent*

**(132) QUESTION: In the rhyme 'Monday's child is fair of face . . .' why are all the days blessings except Wednesday's child who is full of woe?**

Wednesday's child is not 'full of woe' as is usually thought but is Woden's child. Woden (Odin), father of Thor, was the principal god of the Teutonic people, the Norse god of war, learning and poetry. He possessed great magical powers.

Wednesday is also associated with Mercury and suggests a lively mind and appreciation of learning. Far from being 'full of woe', Wednesday's child should be a bright spark and a mine of information, even if only on a superficial level.

*Audrey Atkinson, Eastbourne, Sussex*

There are several versions of the rhyme, some of which came to light when Prince Charles was born on Sunday 14 November 1948,

127

and the First Lord of the Admiralty, Viscount Hall, suggested to the House of Lords that congratulations should be sent in the form of the rhyme.

At the time, this started an argument about the correct wording. My own favourite is the 1849 *Notes and Queries* version, which goes: 'Born of a Monday, fair of face, Born of a Tuesday, full of grace, Born of a Wednesday, merry and glad, Born of a Thursday, sour and sad, born of a Friday, godly given, Born of a Saturday, work for your living, Born of a Sunday, never shall we want, so there ends the week and there's an end on't.'

In most versions, the prediction for Sunday's child is a favourable one, which reflects an old belief, but the other days change from rhyme to rhyme.

*Sara Holden, Mumbles, Swansea*


**(133) QUESTION: How much did the 1951 Festival of Britain and Battersea Funfair cost, and what would that be at today's prices?**

The 1951 Festival of Britain was the nation's first attempt to celebrate the exciting new post-war era, with events all over the country and a main festival site on the bomb-damaged area now known as London's South Bank. The permanent Festival Hall, as well as several temporary features including the Dome of Discovery and the futuristic Skylon pylon, was built on the site and the event is fondly remembered by those who attended. Like the Great Exhibition of exactly one hundred years earlier, it ushered in a new generation – in this case the 'never had it so good' fifties that many of today's grandparents seem to yearn for.

Festival organizer Sir Hugh Casson reported the full cost of the event as just over £11 million, representing £277 million at 2009 prices.

*Toby Wilson, Sutton, Surrey*

**(134) QUESTION: In the film *The Godfather*, Vito Andolini took Corleone as his surname after his birthplace. Are there any real-life Corleones called Michael?**

Directed by Francis Ford Coppola, the 1972 film *The Godfather* starred Al Pacino in the role of Michael Corleone. A thorough examination of the Palermo, Sicily, phone book shows this name is popular, with thirty-one listings, including a Massimo, a Matteo and a Mario but no Michael.

The name is used in other parts of Italy, including Rome but the UK has no phone book listing for any Corleone.

*Graham Harris, Newcastle*


**(135) QUESTION: Did the Italian Air Force raid mainland Britain in the Second World War?**

When the RAF bombed targets in Northern Italy in June 1940, it upset Mussolini and he pressured Goering into allowing the *Regia Aeronautica* to take part in the Battle of Britain. Goering reluctantly agreed and on what was effectively the last official day of the battle a strange formation appeared over southern England: fifteen twin-engined bombers escorted by seventy open-cockpit, fixed-undercarriage biplanes, all painted bright green and blue and flying in close formation, as if at an air show.

They passed over Ramsgate, dropped a few bombs and, apparently happy with the propaganda effect, and still in perfect formation, turned for home.

Two weeks later, on 11 November, as the Fleet Air Arm, flying open-cockpit, fixed-undercarriage, biplane Swordfish torpedo bombers, destroyed half the Italian fleet at Toranto, the Italians attempted another raid on Harwich and lost thirteen aircraft. The crew of a shot-down bomber were discovered wearing steel helmets and armed with rifles and bayonets.

*T. F. Downs, Thong, Kent*

The *Corpo Aereo Italiano* (Italian Air Force) moved a number of aircraft to bases in Belgium in October 1940 and their first attack was a night raid on Harwich on 25 October.

On 11 November, fifty aircraft attacked a convoy off Lowestoft. Three Fiat CR42 fighters and three BR20 bombers were shot down. One CR42 force-landed at Orford Ness in Suffolk and is preserved in the Battle of Britain Museum at Hendon.

On the night of 17/18 November, six BR20s attempted a raid on Harwich.

On the night of 2/3 January 1941, four BR20s attempted a raid on Ipswich.

On 14 January, the *Corpo Aereo Italiano* redeployed to its Italian bases.

*D. Goodes, Barnstaple, Devon*

On the morning of 11 November 1940, the Italian Air Force took part in a raid over south-east London and one bomb scored a direct hit on an Anderson shelter in the garden of 13 Kenward Road, Eltham SE9. Fortunately, there was no one in it.

During the Abyssinian War in the thirties, feelings had run high and the local Italian hokey-cokey seller had stones thrown at him and had to return to his homeland. After that bomb landed, everyone joked that he'd joined the Air Force and had flown back to get his revenge.

*Mervyn Haisman, Tenby, Pembrokeshire*

**(136) QUESTION: Why do guns and ammunition come in such odd sizes –.303, .22, .475, 9.5, etc.?**

In the seventeenth and eighteenth centuries the bore (calibre) of a gun was determined by the number of its projectiles which could be cast from 1 lb of lead. Thus the regular British Army 'Brown Bess' musket was a 12-bore because twelve of its lead balls could be cast from 1 lb of lead, giving a shot size of .76 in. The gradual replacement of the old black powder with powerful smokeless powders in the late-nineteenth century led to smaller bullets with much greater velocities.

There was much divergence of opinion on the perfect bullet size for each use and a bewildering proliferation of calibres appeared. The specific design and dimensions of each gun mathematically determined its barrel calibre, producing some very odd sizes.

To complicate matters further, common calibres are often referred to in either metric or imperial dimensions and sometimes both: the .223 in cartridge is also a 5.56 mm.

*M. Pegler, senior curator, Royal Armouries, Leeds*

Not all calibres were developed using imperial measures; many were originally developed under the metric system. For example, a 6 mm bullet size translates to .243 when converted to imperial and a .30 in imperial measure translates to 7.62 mm in metric.

The other reason for the variety is that the calibre isn't the only factor. A bullet size may be used by several manufacturers, each using a different powder charge and a different cartridge case design. For example, both the American and the British chose a .30-calibre bullet size in the early twentieth century. The Americans chose a cartridge case without a rim and called it a .30 and the British chose a cartridge case with a rim and called it a .303.

A .303 wouldn't load into a .30-calibre rifle but a .30 would load into a .303, with unpleasant consequences.

*Edward Chambers, Wellingborough, Northamptonshire*

## (137) QUESTION: Have any parents called their twin children Adam and Eve?

I do not have twins but my children are named Adam and Eve and they didn't mind as they went to separate schools after the age of eleven.

I have heard, however, of a pair of twins called Mark and Spencer.

*Angela Jenshil, Hendon, Middlesex*

In my family, there is a record of twins having been christened Adam and Eve, in Brixton, Devon. They were born on 27 May 1806, and christened on 15 June of that year. Sadly, Adam died on 24 August 1806 and Eve on 21 August 1808.

Their parents were George Townsend and Susannah Gloyn who married on 22 April 1785, and had three children before they had the twins: George, who lived to the age of five, John Gloyn, who died in infancy, and another George who lived to the ripe old age of seventy and had six children. So, out of five children, only one grew up to marry and have children of his own.

*Robert John Gloyn Townsend, Northampton*

Colonel Guy Buxton and Mrs Ruth Buxton had a daughter called Eve Buxton whose twin brother was called Adam.

In 1944, Eve Buxton became my stepmother when she married my late father, Squadron Leader Keith Marten, while they were both stationed at Biggin Hill, in Kent.

*Peter Marten, Paignton, Devon*

My mother's family tree reveals that her great-grandparents, John Miller and Elizabeth Notting, married in 1802 in the village of Winterborne Kingston, Dorset. They had ten children, including two boys born in 1822. They survived only a few days, but long enough to be baptized Moses and Aaron.

*Jack Read, West Byfleet, Surrey*

My grandfather lived next door to a man who was known as

Sheddy. This turned out to be short for Shadrach. His brothers were called Meshach and Abednego.

*Mrs S. Myerscough, Westloughton, Greater Manchester*

Those brothers Shadrack, Meshach and Abednego were my great-uncles and were known as Shad, Mesh and Ben for short. Their eldest sister, my grandmother, was christened Faith and her two sisters were Hope and Charity. Their family name is Critchley and they came from Leigh in Lancashire.

*G. Speakman, Westhoughton, Manchester*

My late husband had identical twin brothers who were christened Romulus and Remus. I wonder if there are any other twins with the same names.

*Mrs C. Day, Barton-upon-Humber, North Lincolnshire*

**(138) QUESTION: My son doesn't believe me when I tell him racing cycles used to have bamboo wheels. Are any still used?**

Wheel rims made sometimes of laminated bamboo but more often of maple, and known as 'woods', were normally used in racing though some cyclists liked them for ordinary cycling.

They were lighter than steel, used for ordinary road wheels, and were used with special lightweight tyres which had the inner tube sewn inside the outer covers.

Some of the fastest men in my old cycling club were still using them in the early 1950s when they were overtaken by more reliable alloy wheel rims. An old club colleague told me he still has a set of wooden wheels in his loft and has recently rebuilt them. He assures me they look very smart.

*Brian Bateman, formerly of Advance Wheelers CC,*
*Romford, Essex*

Bicycle frames of bamboo with lugs and brackets of steel were commonly made in the 1890s.

*Bill Pryor, Colchester, Essex*

Wooden cycle rims are still crafted in beechwood by the Ghisallo family in the depths of the Italian countryside and sold by Johannes Resseagmier of Bremen, in Germany.

*A. Deramore, Pickering, North Yorkshire*

## (139) QUESTION: How big a pile would all the 24ct gold in the world make?

Gold is so dense that all the 130,000 tonnes ever mined would fit in a 23-metre cube. This would fit easily under the arches of the Eiffel Tower, inside four jumbo jets or five or six houses.

More than half the gold mined has been made into jewellery, bars, coins or ornaments. The rest is held by central bank reserves and private investors. The gold stockpile grows each year by around 3 per cent with the addition of up to 2,500 tonnes of newly mined gold.

Gold's beauty, scarcity, indestructibility and mystical appeal has meant demand for gold, mainly for jewellery, has more than doubled in the past fifteen years and now exceeds 3,000 tonnes a year. One in every seven adults bought something gold last year.

*Deborah Cookson, World Gold Council, Geneva, Switzerland*

## (140) QUESTION: Why is a nautical mile longer than a statute mile?

A nautical mile is the distance of the Earth's surface subtended by one minute of latitude at the Earth's centre. Were the Earth a perfect circle, one nautical mile would be an arc length of one minute at all places and in all directions. In fact, the Earth is flatter at the poles and its axis of rotation, at the Equator, has the least diameter. As a result, the nautical mile varies slightly with the latitude, being shortest at the Equator and longest at the poles.

On average, and for all practical purposes, a nautical mile is 1,852 m (6,075 ft) compared with 1,609 m (5,280 ft) for a statute mile on shore.

*Arabella Perugini, National Maritime Museum,*
*Greenwich, London*

**(141) QUESTION: In detective fiction, did the butler ever actually do it?**

In *The Sign of Four*, Sherlock Holmes remarks: 'By the way, apropos of this Norwood business, you see that they had, as I surmised, a confederate in the house who could be none other than Lal Roa, the butler . . .'

As 'they' included the Andaman islander Tongo, who shot Lal Rao's employer Bartholomew Sholts with a poisoned dart from his blowpipe, the butler, though he didn't actually do it, was at least an accessory to it.

*M. Foley, Aylesbury, Buckinghamshire*

**(142) QUESTION: Who introduced apples to Britain? Have places like Appleby, Appledore or Appleton any historical bearing on this?**

The apple, fruit of *Malus pumila*, a tree of the Rosaceae family, has been cultivated into several thousand varieties in three categories: cider, cooking and eating.

All varieties are derived from the wild crab apple; the Romans introduced cultivated apples to Britain. The Roman Empire had about thirty varieties, one of which, grown in Britain at the time, the *decio*, is among the two thousand or so varieties held in the national collection by the Brogdale Trust.

*Joanna Wood, English Apples and Pears Ltd, Faversham, Kent*

Most common of apple place names in Britain is Appleton, from the Old English *aeppel* (apple) and *tun* (farm). Northern England has several places called Appleby where the *by* is the Scandinavian word for farm.

Appledore, found mostly in the south, means 'place at the apple tree', from the Old English *apuldor*. There are also places named for other fruit such as Pyrton, Oxfordshire ('farm with pear trees'), Plumstead, London ('place where plum trees grow') and Cherry Hinton, Cambridgeshire ('high farm with cherry trees').

*Adrian Room, author,* Dictionary of Placenames in the British Isles,
*Bloomsbury, London*


## (143) QUESTION: In what sense is patriotism 'the last refuge of a scoundrel'?

This aphorism is normally attributed to British lexicographer Samuel Johnson (1709–1784) who also gave us such well-used gems as: 'When a man is tired of London, he is tired of life', 'It matters not how a man dies, but how he lived', and 'I look upon every day to be lost, in which I do not make a new acquaintance'.

Although the quotation was first coined in the popular magazine *The Idler* more than two centuries ago, it didn't sink in with later generations.

It refers to those who wrap their intentions in a nationalistic package to enlist the support of people whom they have failed to convince by normal means.

Nationalism is then presented as an acceptable defence of culture and society rather than what it really is: a leeching of the people through manipulation of their fears of foreign influences.

*Geoffrey Manning, Sutton, Surrey*

(144) QUESTION: What was the Hokey-Pokey sold to us as children before the war by a man on a motorbike and sidecar in South Yorkshire?

The word for ice cream in Italian is *gelate* and the proffered *poche* should perhaps be *pochi*.

Italian ice-cream sellers certainly called out something like this to sell their wares and my old Italian teacher, Dr Umberto Morelli, from the Romanza, said 'hokey-pokey' meant something like: 'Hurry, there aren't many left.'

As children we used to sing and skip to the rhyme: 'Hokey-pokey, penny a lump, the more you eat, the more you jump.'

'Hocus-pocus', meaning trickery, chicanery or magic incantation, seems to be an alternative to 'hokey-pokey' and is shown as a corruption of such in Collins's English/Italian dictionary. I recall using 'It's all hokey-pokey' to mean it's a load of rubbish, deceit, untruth, etc.

*Miss I. D. Davison, Sutton*

This is probably one of the bits of British culture to be enthusiastically adopted abroad while being quietly forgotten in the home country. As a New Zealander living in Britain, I can report that hokey-pokey is alive and well on the opposite side of the planet.

It's a crunchy, sticky bar of confection not unlike the inside of Crunchie bars and may be bought in slabs. Particularly cosmic is hokey-pokey ice cream which has to be eaten to be believed. If any British ice cream firm produces this, let me know. The motorbike and sidecar aren't included in the following New Zealand recipe but could be added as a decorative garnish.

Ingredients: 5 tbsp sugar, 2 tbsp golden syrup, 1 tsp baking soda. Put the sugar and syrup into a saucepan. Heat gently, stirring constantly until sugar dissolves. Increase the heat and cook until mixture just starts to boil. Stir occasionally if necessary, to prevent burning. Remove from heat. Add baking soda. Stir quickly until mixture froths up. Pour into a buttered tin immediately. Leave until cold and hard. Break into pieces. Eat as slowly as you can manage.

*Kate Daniell, Selborne, Hampshire*

Hokey-pokey is an ice cream. I believe the crunchy, sticky bar called hokey-pokey in New Zealand is what we knew before the war as honeycomb. A man would ride around with large chunks of this on the back of his horse and cart and chop off a halfpenny or a penny's worth. For a halfpenny you received a huge lump about three to four inches cubed. Very nice it was too.

*C. R. Hornsby, London N9*

My brother, who died in 1988, wrote in his memoirs: 'Francis Valley, an Italian who settled here, used to come round in the summer sitting up in a little pony trap with a canopy over it shouting "Hokey-pokey, penny a lump!", and the kids answered him with "And the man who sells 'em is off his chump!"

'These lumps of ice cream were about 2 in by 1½ in and 1 in thick. Of course, there were no wafer biscuits so we used to collect it on a saucer and eat it with a spoon. This was in about 1920.'

I recall us singing, 'Hokey-pokey penny a lump, That's the stuff to make you jump.'

*Ken Jackson, St Brelade, Jersey*

**(145) QUESTION: Apart from the well-known matches, I believe England played Germany at soccer at the Expo '67 world fair in Montreal. Who played and what was the result?**

The year after our 1966 World Cup success, the England team, managed by Alf Ramsey, did indeed play in Montreal but not against the German national team. They played German club side, Borussia Dortmund, beating them in the final 3–2 on 11 June 1967.

Frank Wignall scored two goals and Norman Hunter one. The game was part of a mini-competition and was regarded by the Football Association as an exhibition, rather than competitive, match.

In earlier stages, England beat Mexican club side Leon 3–0 (3 June) and FK Austria 2–1 (9 June).

*Ray Spiller, Association of Football Statisticians, Basildon, Essex*

The England squad chosen for the 1967 Canadian Centenary Tournament in Montreal comprised goalkeepers Gordon Banks and Peter Bonetti; backs George Cohen, Ray Wilson and Keith Newton; half backs John Hollins, Mike Bailey, Brian Labone, Norman Hunter and Jack Charlton, and forwards Mike Summerbee, Alan Ball, Derek Temple, Johnny Byrne, Colin Bell and Frank Wignall.

*David Barber, Football Association, London*

**(146) QUESTION: The heroine of the Jane Austen novel *Northanger Abbey* is said to prefer baseball to books. What was baseball in those days?**

There are references to games being played five thousand years ago in Egypt having characteristics which could lay claim to being forerunners of baseball. By the Middle Ages, the Cathedral of Rheims wound up its Easter services with games in which a ball was swatted with a stick. These made their way to Britain and evolved into a game called stoolball, in which a pitcher tried to hit an upturned stool with a ball while a batter tried to hit the ball away with a stick.

Once the game moved out of the churchyard and into the countryside, legend has it that milkmaids were responsible for adding more stools, or 'bases', which the batter had to circle after striking the ball.

When a rule was added that a base-runner could be out by being struck with a thrown ball, the children's game of rounders was born. Posts driven into the ground called 'goals' or 'bases' were incorporated, and there are references to the game of 'goal ball' or 'baseball' as early as 1700.

A publication printed in London in 1744 called *A Pretty Little Pocket Book* contained a rhymed description of the game and a picture captioned 'Base-Ball'.

*Northanger Abbey* was published around 1800, so the reference must be to this early, simple version of today's game.

In the first half of the nineteenth century, the game was being played in America by the elite classes at gentlemen's clubs on the East Coast, and it was here that the new rules came into being, which transformed the game from its 'rounders' origins into the modern professional game.

*Trevor Kendall, Baseball Briefing, Grimsby, Humberside*

### (147) QUESTION: Was the 'Teddy Bears' Picnic' tune specially composed to test radio audio frequency?

The 'Teddy Bears' Picnic' tune was composed in 1908 by American John W. Batton as a tribute to Teddy Roosevelt after a bear hunting expedition in Dakota during his 1903 election campaign.

In 1930, songwriter Jimmy Kennedy, who later wrote the words of such hits as 'Isle of Capri' and 'South of the Border', added words for a Manchester pantomime, at the request of his boss, publisher Bert Feldman.

In 1932, BBC music arranger Tony Lowry bought a copy of the song from Feldman and had it recorded by Henry Hall, with vocals by Val Rosing. The recording was chosen by the International Radio Convention at Geneva in 1933 as the ideal music for testing high and low sound frequencies.

*J. G. Hughes, Richmond, North Yorkshire*

**(148) QUESTION: Would an enclosed room whose internal surfaces were covered by mirrors, lit by a single bulb, be appreciably brighter than the same room with no reflective surfaces?**

What we see as brightness is actually light reflected off a surface. So the brightness of a room depends largely on the brightness produced by light reflecting off its surfaces.

If all the surfaces in a room are mirrored, it will seem less bright than a room with all the surfaces painted white. A mirror is normally made of glass with a silver backing. So light reflecting from a mirror first has to travel through the glass to the mirror.

Every time this happens, a small amount of light energy gets lost. Because the surface of the mirror is smooth, the light will travel in straight lines and get reflected in straight lines.

Walls painted white are slightly rough by nature and never as smooth as a mirror. This means the light that hits the wall in one place will be reflected back in different directions. Some of this reflected light will hit the walls again and again, creating a diffused light. Because the light does not have to travel through any surface before getting reflected, all the light comes back. Thus a room with mirrored surfaces will appear less bright than one with surfaces painted white.

*Bhagwant Singh, Museum of Science and Industry, Manchester*

**(149) QUESTION: What is the origin of the services slang 'jankers' for punishment?**

The term 'jankers', familiar to the thousands of British Army, Navy and RAF personnel as a military punishment or punishment detail, was particularly popular during the 1950s in the heyday of National Service.

The origins of the term are obscure, with the first references to its use dating from the late 1910s and early 1920s. Consensus of opinion suggests the word may be related to the word 'jangle', which in earlier times meant 'to grumble', hence a 'jangler' or 'janglers' being a person complaining about his punishment. The term later being applied to the punishment itself.

*Graeme Cobb, Saltcoats, Ayrshire*

When I served in the RAF for five years in the Second World War, I was told this word was a corruption of 'janitor's chores', the distasteful punishment for a culprit who had done something wrong.

*Mrs G. Pollard, Plympton, Devon*

**(150) QUESTION: How do those twists get into a previously perfect telephone cord, and is there a neat trick to remove them?**

Although knotted curly cords rarely result in an electrical failure, the shortening effect has led to telephones being pulled off tables as well as customers taking up very strange positions while taking calls. The knotting is usually caused by picking up the phone with one hand, transferring the handset to the other hand before replacing on the rest at the end of the call.

An easy solution to this problem is to hold the curly cord near the instrument end allowing the handset to dangle free. The cord will then untwist itself. Although not available from BT, devices are sold that connect between the handset and cord with a joint which allows the handset to rotate without twisting the cord. If all else fails you could buy a cordless phone.

*Dave James, quality and reliability engineer, BT Labs, Martlesham Heath, Ipswich*

**(151) QUESTION: Is it possible to live without a pancreas?**

The pancreas is a long, thin organ, five or six inches long, nestled within the curve of the duodenum, stretching across the posterior abdomen behind the stomach and terminating near the spleen under the left diaphragm. It has both digestive and endocrine functions and therefore contains two different types of cells.

Its digestive function is performed by several small lobules which contain numerous cells that secrete electrolytes and three important enzymes: trypsin, amylase and lipase. These enzymes digest proteins, split fat and break down highly polymerized nucleic acids and polysaccharides such as starch, amylopectin and glycogen.

The pancreas's endocrine function is performed by numerous small groups of cells called the islets of Langerhans, which release hormones into the blood.

The hormone secretin controls the amount of fluid secretions. The islets of Langerhans also secrete two hormones, insulin and glucagon, which regulate carbohydrate metabolism: one decreases blood sugar; the other increases it.

*Hugh Franks, London W1*

I was diagnosed as having a tumour in the pancreas and had a Whipple operation (named after the surgeon who conducted the first procedure of this type), which involved the removal of not only the pancreas but also the duodenum and the bottom of the stomach and then the fastening of everything together again.

As a result of the operation, I'm diabetic. I have insulin injections twice a day and Pancrex capsules before each meal to give my stomach the necessary enzymes and digestive juices.

I'm more than satisfied with my quality of life and am very grateful to the staff at the County Hospital in Lincoln.

*Peter Bowness, Glentham, Lincolnshire*

**(152) QUESTION: What kind of traffic used the Blackwall Tunnel in East London when it was made 113 years ago? How was it lit?**

The Blackwall Tunnel, running beneath the Thames from Blackwall to East Greenwich, was formed under the Thames Tunnel

(Blackwall) Acts of 1887 and 1888. The project was begun under the supervision of A. R. Binnie in 1894 and completed in 1897 when it was officially opened to the public on 22 May by the Prince of Wales (later King Edward VII) on behalf of Queen Victoria.

The cost of the 6,200-ft tunnel amounted to £1,323,663, of which £869,476 went on construction and the rest on acquiring the necessary land and property and creating approach roads from the East India Dock Road to the north and the Trafalgar Road to the south.

When the tunnel was opened, the main traffic was horses and carts, and the fact that the tunnel isn't straight (having been dug out from four vertical shafts which fitted local geological conditions) made the down-tunnel journey easier for horses with heavy loads. According to local legend it was also useful because the horses couldn't see the natural light at the end of the tunnel and bolt for it.

After construction, the four shafts were retained for ventilation. An electric lighting station was erected at the Northumberland Wharf on the north shore of the river. This cost £30,000 and remained in use until 1912.

*Alan Ali, Greenwich Council, Woolwich, London*

**(153) QUESTION: Why is cancer, the crab sign of the zodiac, also the word for carcinoma, cancer of the body?**

Cancer is the Latin word for both the crab and the malignant tumour. According to Greek physician Galen in the second century AD, the medical sense developed because the swollen veins surrounding the affected part resembled a crab's limbs.

The word cancer was adopted for the disease in Old English times, and became canker in the Middle Ages. Around 1400, the original Latin form cancer was revived for the zodiac sense.

By about 1600, canker had come to be applied to corroding

ulcerations in plants and animals generally, and around this time, cancer was re-introduced as a more technical and specific term for the malignant tumour.

*Lorna Gilmour, Collins Dictionaries, Glasgow*

**(154) QUESTION: Why did the German airship *Hindenburg* stop over Yorkshire in 1936 to drop a small parcel by parachute?**

Along with hundreds of others, I saw this incident over Keighley on 22 May 1936. The *Hindenburg* dropped a small parcel with trailing ribbons, which landed in a yard behind a shop in the High Street, and was picked up by a couple of Scouts on their way to an evening meeting.

The parcel turned out to be a small cross and some carnations, dropped by a German priest with a request that it be placed on the grave of a prisoner of war relative who had died in a local hospital, known as the Fever Hospital, during the First World War.

I remember the airship looking enormous – it was more than 800 ft long – and at the time of the drop was only a few hundred feet above the ground. Hundreds of amateur photos were taken, but most people arrived too late to capture the event and none of the stills appear to have survived.

Some years ago, the German PoWs' bodies in the local cemetery were exhumed and returned to Germany or moved to the main German cemetery in Cannock Chase, Staffordshire. The small chapel at the graveyard, where the cross had been placed, was demolished.

The *Hindenburg* passed over the area again on 16 June 1936, and the general suspicion was that she was really on a photographic mission, since Keighley at the time had many engineering works, later used for the production of war materials.

*Bill Hensman, Keighley, West Yorkshire*

**(155) QUESTION: Does any creature other than man intentionally eat or drink certain substances to get drunk or high?**

Not intentionally – but the amarilla tree in South Africa produces a fruit which ferments when ripe, producing an alcohol-like substance enjoyed by elephants, giraffes and monkeys, who are affected by it in the same way that humans are by alcohol.

Most animals have a tolerance level higher than humans to toxic and hallucinogenic substances.

*John Pullen, primates section, London Zoo*

Serving in India in the Second World War, I attended the jungle fighting school at Gundalar in the Nilgiri Hills, near a camp where elephants were used to help work forest teak. My battalion was invited to watch a demonstration by an old bull and cow elephant working together as a couple.

We were told that every few months the bull broke his chain at night and vanished into the jungle, only to reappear three days later in a bleary condition.

His 'wife' would berate him with angry trumpeting and beat him severely with her trunk. He would go meekly to his place and be excused work duty for a couple of days as he was obviously suffering from a hangover.

It was discovered that the bull used to go to a spot in the jungle where a small stream flowed into an abundance of rotting vegetation which fermented into an alcoholic salt lick. The bull would get well and truly plastered and sleep it off before returning to the compound to face his 'rolling pin' reception.

Many of my former 2nd Battalion the King's Own Royal Regiment comrades will confirm this story.

*Gerry O'Neill, Preston, Lancashire*

Some years ago, my mother bought me a hamster as company in my college digs. I would often feed Foggy little pieces of apple and pear, which disappeared rapidly into his sleeping quarters for later devouring (or so I thought).

When he started to show some balance problems and began hanging bat-like from anything and everything, I took him to the vet. At first he suspected lead poisoning from the paint in his cage, but as there were no signs of any paint nibbling he investigated further. 'Ah,' he said, pushing aside Foggy's bedding. 'Your hamster is drunk.'

Foggy had been putting his apple and pear under the bedding and sleeping on it, thus becoming a cider/perry lout. My vet's advice was to wean him off the apple and pear slowly.

*Karen Carmichael, Chelmsford, Essex*

According to *All About Elvis*, by Fred L. Worth and Steve D. Tamerius, among Elvis Presley's many pets was a chimpanzee called Scatter which acquired a taste for bourbon and eventually died of cirrhosis of the liver. It was with Elvis at both Graceland and Los Angeles.

*Alasdair Riley, London W4*

In *How to Shoot an Amateur Naturalist*, Gerald Durrell describes the effect of eating fly agaric, a poisonous fungus: 'Reindeer apparently adore it, treating it rather as we would treat a bottle of whisky or gin found under a tree and, when fly agaric is in season, lose no opportunity to get plastered.'

He describes how Laplanders watching the reindeer 'possibly envied their regrettable state of intoxication and found out – one shudders to think how – that if you imbibe the urine of someone who has been on an agaric bender you can obtain the same effect through the "distilled" potion'.

*N. Millner, Balham, London*

**(156) QUESTION: What are the seven basic plots in literature and which Shakespeare plays illustrate them?**

I was always under the impression that the seven basic plots in literature are: Achilles – the fatal flaw, as in *Macbeth*; Cinderella – rags-to-riches saga, poor heroine gets handsome prince; Circe – thrillers of the chase/pursuit genre as in *The 39 Steps*; Faust – variations on the concept of a debt to be repaid; Orpheus – the gift that is taken away, for example, wife, health, money, life; Romeo and Juliet – the love story that doesn't have a happy ending and Tristan – the eternal triangle (Tristan, Iseult and King Mark).

It's difficult to attribute any one plot to any one Shakespeare play or novel as most consist of a combination.

*S. L. Protheroe, Fortrose*

**(157) QUESTION: A letter from my uncle – serving in France in the First World War – thanks his mother for the safe arrival of a parcel containing 'sunpoker'. He says the boys had some on sugar but it was too hot for them. What is sunpoker?**

The sunpoker spoken of in the letter refers to samphire (*Crithmum maritimum*), a plant found mainly along the seashore. The young fleshy leaves, which are lightly scented, made an excellent pickle when salted and preserved in vinegar.

The plant is also known as St Peter's Herb, and the pickle was referred to by my relatives on the Kentish coast as sanpeter or sunpeter.

*Eric Thomas, Purley, Surrey*

**(158) QUESTION: What are the eleven towns referred to in the name of the village of Ruyton-Eleven-Towns, Shropshire?**

This pleasant village on the River Perry, north-west of Shrewsbury, was built in the thirteenth century by the Norman family of

Fitzalans. More correctly known as Ruyton of the Eleven Towns, it was so named to distinguish it from other Ruytons and Rytons in the area (a common name from the Old English *ruye tun* meaning 'rye farm').

The eleven 'towns', including Ruyton, were the medieval towns of Ruyton Manner, namely: Coton, Eardiston, Haughton, Rednal, Shelvock, Shotatton, Sutton, Tedsmore, West Felton and Wykey.

The young Arthur Conan Doyle worked here for a time as medical assistant to a Dr Eliot. On arrival he is said to have commented: 'Ruyton-Eleven-Towns? There is scarcely enough here for one good one!'

*Gerard Mackay, Nesscliffe, Shropshire*

The eleven 'towns' all still exist, though many now consist of only a farm or small settlement.

*Mrs Dorothy Payne, Stevenage, Hertfordshire*

**(159) QUESTION: Is there a limit on how many and how long the upcoming-programme 'ads' can run on BBC and ITV? How many programmes per year do they replace?**

There's no statutory limit to the number of trails the BBC can broadcast between programmes but it's not in our interests to overload the junctions between programmes. We recognize there's a natural limit to the amount of information viewers can take in at any time.

Trails don't displace the programmes that surround them – indeed, they often help a broadcaster start a programme closer to the billed start time than would otherwise be possible. They provide an opportunity to find out more about forthcoming programmes and, as such, are a cost-effective way of allowing the audience to make a better-informed decision when choosing what to watch.

Research shows that the overwhelming majority of our audience value the information that trails provide and use this as a key element when planning their viewing.

*Adam Hume, BBC, London*

The BBC and ITV both use the fact that they're allowed to show as many upcoming programme 'trailers' as they wish but the main over-subscriber to this technique is the BBC, which seems to use its advert-free position to fill the between-show space with its own 'ads'.

Taking just a slow day on the BBC, there will be at least seven upcoming programme trailers with a duration of about thirty seconds each. This may not seem much but when tallied up it's quite alarming. Over one day this totals just 3.5 minutes, which over a week means about 24.5 minutes, or roughly one episode of, say, *Keeping Up Appearances*.

Over a month this becomes almost two hours, and over a year a staggering 1,277.5 minutes or 21.3 hours – enough time to show almost sixty episodes of *Neighbours*, or a full series of *Murder One*. Still, it could be worse, I'd rather see a trailer for a programme than have someone attempt to brainwash me about what type of washing powder I should use.

*James Hunter, Maida Vale, London*

(160) QUESTION: What good are we doing rinsing fruit and vegetables with cold water before eating them? Does this really remove pesticides?

There is no need to rinse fruit and vegetables to remove pesticides. Safety procedures ensure that the small amounts of pesticides which reach the food chain are harmless – and it should be remembered that almost 60 per cent of fruit and vegetables contain no pesticide residues at all. The residues which are found are generally measured in parts per million or billion, and wide safety margins are set to allow for the occasional exceeding of levels fixed by international bodies.

It is this cautionary approach which enables us to be confident about their safety. The good that you can do by rinsing fruit and vegetables is in removing any dirt that may remain on them.

*Pat Hindley, Fresh Fruit & Vegetable Information Bureau,*
*London SW7*


## (161) QUESTION: Has any couple made love in outer space?

Authors of futuristic works have recognized the need to simplify traditional techniques of procreation if the challenge of space love-making is to be tackled successfully. In the film *Barbarella*, set well into the twenty-first century, Jane Fonda and David Hemmings make love in transit by simply touching hands.

*Rosemary Manning, London W8*


There have been at least five husband-and-wife couples among NASA's shuttle astronaut corps since the first flights in the early 1980s, and the first couple to go on a space mission together were Jan Davis and Mark Lee, launched aboard space shuttle *Endeavour* in September 1992.

Membership of what might be termed the '200-mile-high club' is a delicate subject but on relatively short earth orbit missions astronauts face a workload busy enough to ensure such matters are not their highest priority.

However, any future flight to Mars, for example, would take a very long time and the physical and psychological well-being of the crew may drive this subject onto the agenda.

At this point, Isaac Newton's Third Law of Motion – 'to every action there is an equal and opposite reaction' – will come into play. Lack of anticipation of the effects of zero gravity caused the first space-walking astronauts to start rotating themselves when trying to undo nuts with spanners. They have now been provided with handholds and foot restraints, leading to the thought that intimacy in space may require appropriately positioned restraining bands.

*H. J. P. Arnold, Space Frontiers, Havant, Hampshire*

In the 1979 James Bond film *Moonraker*, Roger Moore, as Bond, and Lois Chiles, as Holly Goodhead, make zero-gravity love, watched, with growing anger, by Q, M, the Minister for Defence and Russian General Gogol.

An American technician says because of the importance of the joint US/UK mission, he has patched the video live to the White House, Buckingham Palace and 10 Downing Street.

*Mr B. R. Shacklady, Lostock, Bolton*

The Russians have been rather more forthcoming than NASA and admit that intercourse in outer space took place in their spaceships, in particular in June 1982 when cosmonaut Svetlana Savicka shared the confines of *Jaljut 7* with two colleagues from Russian space town.

The Russians had given themselves the far more ambitious plan of conceiving the first space child but this scheme remains unfulfilled. Svetlana Savicka gave birth to two healthy daughters but neither was the longed-for space child.

*M. Zastava, Chelmsford, Essex*

When *Soyuz 4* successfully introduced its docking probe into *Soyuz 5*'s receptacle on 16 January 1969, *Soyuz 5* commander Volynov exclaimed, 'You raped me!'

*P. Smith, London N5*

**(162) QUESTION: Do countries other than France have foreign legions?**

At least one other country has a foreign legion – Spain. I joined the Spanish Foreign Legion (*Legion Estranjeras*) in February 1960 in Valencia, and was posted with my regiment to Villa Cisneros in Spanish Sahara.

Together with the Colonial Troops, it was the main force behind General Franco's invasion of mainland Spain from Morocco during the beginning of the Spanish Civil War.

Discipline and punishment were more fierce in the Spanish than the French Legion and, unlike the French Legion which did not accept its own citizens, the Spanish Legion accepted Spanish soldiers as well.

*Niels E. Winkel, Horncastle, Lincolnshire*

The Spanish Foreign Legion, formerly stationed in Spanish Sahara, is now based in the Canary Islands. It was posted to Bosnia as part of the peacekeeping operations there.

*Keith Kennedy, Manchester*

**(163) QUESTION: In the opening titles of the American comedy series *Cheers*, a newspaper headline 'We Win' was held up. Who won what?**

Here at the Bull and Finch in Boston, the bar (which originated in Britain) on which Cheers was based, we have the 'We Win' photograph on display. The picture of a forties scene in an unknown pub in Boston has been edited so that few details are clear. Until recently it was thought it related to the November 1948 Presidential election between Republican Thomas E. Dewey and Democrat Harry S. Truman.

Pre-poll ratings insisted Dewey would win convincingly and voting through the night appeared to be going that way. Newspaper editors lined up headlines such as Dewey Wins, Dewey Beats Truman, We Win, etc. But dawn, when most of the papers were on the streets, brought a final flurry of results going Truman's way, making him President in the biggest political upset of the century.

Closer inspection of the cutting shows it refers to an October 1946 World Series baseball game in which Boston Redsox beat St Louis Cardinals. Sadly, the Cardinals clinched the series by four games to three.

*Kate Huggins, Bull and Finch Pub, Boston*

## (164) QUESTION: Did a British submarine once return from patrol with a train and a bus painted up as 'kills'?

These were not 'painted up' but emblazoned on the boat's flag. British submarines returning from successful patrols fly the Jolly Roger (emblem of the Royal Navy Submarine Service) onto which are embroidered symbols denoting the activities of the patrol.

It wasn't unusual for submarines on the surface to fire their guns at enemy trains where the railway line ran close to the coast, and buses, tanks, planes and bridges were all engaged, in addition to enemy ships, when the opportunity offered.

A white bar denoted merchant ships sunk, a red bar success against an enemy warship and a red bar with a 'U' through it the sinking of an enemy submarine. A dagger was the symbol for a successful commando or spy insertion or pick-up.

Rarer symbols included HMS *Sybil*'s Jolly Roger sporting a scarlet pimpernel flower after a French woman agent, instead of uttering the expected password, quoted 'They seek him here, they seek him there' to be allowed on board.

HMS *United* returned to Malta with a white flag depicting a stork carrying a baby in its beak after its captain, Lieutenant John Roxburgh (later Vice Admiral Sir John Roxburgh KCB CBE DSO DSC), became a father while on patrol.

We have a large collection of original Jolly Rogers in the Royal Navy Submarine Museum, Gosport, many of which are on display.

*Commander Jeff Tall OBE, Royal Navy Submarine Museum,*
*Gosport, Hampshire*

HMS *Turbulent* surfaced three times near enemy coasts in the Eastern Med in the Second World War and shot up a goods train, a road convoy and an electric train. Insignia on its Jolly Roger flag commemorated this.

The sub was commanded by Commander John Wallace 'Tubby' Linton, posthumously awarded the VC for his exploits after *Turbulent* failed to return to base in May 1943.

*Mrs J. Hassell (formerly Mrs Linton), Plympton, Plymouth*

I was first aware of the history of this highly successful wartime submarine when serving as engineering officer on the current HMS *Turbulent*, her nuclear-powered successor, under Commander A. T. Lightoller.

While 'standing by' during construction at Vickers in Barrow in 1982/3, I took on the task of researching our illustrious predecessor's history. I have now retired from the service but I believe 'Train Night' is still celebrated at sea in the present *Turbulent* with a formal dinner, when a model train graces the wardroom dining table.

*Commander C. V. Hanna MBE, Kirkby in Furness, Cumbria*

**(165) QUESTION: What are the biggest examples of people gaining property by squatters' rights, and how long does this take?**

Squatters' rights (more properly called Adverse Possession) can be claimed over someone else's land when the statutory time limit for recovering that land runs out.

For example, if you move a boundary fence to take part of your neighbour's garden, the neighbour must take action to recover the land within twelve years or his ownership of it is lost.

Most land claimed by Adverse Possession has been abandoned and is of little value, though the *Daily Mail* recently drew attention to a case where a couple obtained Adverse Possession of a house which had belonged to a local council.

Adverse Possession acquisitions are more common in Ireland than in Great Britain, perhaps due to high levels of emigration in the late nineteenth and early twentieth centuries. The Land Register of Northern Ireland receives several Adverse Possession applications each month, about half of which are successful.

The properties involved vary from small pieces of garden to building sites, dwelling houses and, occasionally, whole farms. The most unusual application which we have received from a squatter related to a portion of a lake.

*Arthur H. Moir, chief executive and registrar of titles,*
*Land Registers of Northern Ireland, Belfast*

## (166) QUESTION: Who was Zarathustra and what did he 'also sprach'?

Zarathustra, also known as Zoroaster, was an east Persian prophet from about 628–551 BC who preached the worship, through fire, of Ahura-mazda (or Ormazd), the god of creation, light and goodness. The sacred writings of the Zoroastrian religion, the Zend-Avesta, had great influence on Persian kings of that time.

*Also Sprach* (Thus Spake) *Zarathustra* was the title of Friedrich Wilhelm Nietzsche's abstract philosophical work published in 1892, promoting self-realization for the (super)man. The theme of this work was adopted by Richard Strauss in his 1896 tone-poem.

*Hadrian Rochester, Reigate, Surrey*

The faith founded by the Persian prophet Zoroaster is still practised by a significant minority in and around Iran. It's a form of dualism, in which good and evil are in perpetual conflict and good can prevail only with the help of mankind.

Zoroaster 'spake' much and his thoughts, brought to prominence by Nietzsche, found musical expression not only through Richard Strauss (the opening of whose piece was featured in the film *2001 Space Odyssey*) but through Mahler, Delius and Vishnegradsky.

Most quoted is his declamation to the rising sun, which roughly translates: 'Oh mighty star, what would be your joy if men were not here to see your light?' In short, God needs man as much as men need God. The twelve climactic chimes at the end of Strauss's 'Also Sprach Zarathustra' express this thought.

*Jack Nickle Smith, Taplow, Buckinghamshire*


As a Zoroastrian, I object to the way in which our prophet, Zarathustra, is often associated with the philosopher Nietzsche. Zarathustra's teaching, laid down in ancient Avestan scripts, was prominent long before Nietzsche. In his work *Also Sprach Zarathustra*, Nietzsche used the prophet's name to support his own philosophy.

Followers of Zoroastrianism feel no affinity with Nietzsche and have no special place in their hearts for Richard Strauss's works. There are about 150,000 Zoroastrians in the world, the largest concentration being in India. There are between 5,000 and 7,000 adherents in the UK.

*Miss Tehmina Bhote, Bayswater, West London*


**(167) QUESTION: How do satellites and newly launched space-craft avoid 'space junk' surrounding Earth?**

Despite an estimated orbital debris population of 35,000 objects, ranging in size from 1 cm to less than 10 cm, most satellites do not manoeuvre to avoid collisions.

In terms of American space launches, the US command 'screens' to protect satellites and spacecraft already in orbit from vehicles about to be launched.

An empty box of clear space is used as protection – 50 km around unmanned spacecraft and 200 km for a crewed spacecraft, like the Space Shuttle or Russian Mir Space Station.

A ground launch may be delayed for a few minutes to allow an orbiting spacecraft or satellite to move out of the trajectory of the launching craft.

*Eileen Hawley, NASA, Johnson Space Center, Houston, Texas*

## (168) QUESTION: How did 'quack' come to be used for a bogus or incompetent doctor?

This term comes from the Dutch *quackensalf* or *quackensalver*, a person who falsely claimed medical knowledge or skills, often seen at markets and fairs dispensing potions, creams and other 'cures'.

The word is made up of the Dutch *quacken*, meaning to chatter or prattle (making a lot of pointless noise, as a duck might) and *salf*, which is similar to our 'salve', a cure.

*Keith Bassett, Windsor, Berkshire*

In the days when the plague was killing millions with no treatment available, the disease needed more doctors than were available and some men, though unqualified medically, were allowed to treat victims.

To protect themselves, doctors treating plague victims wore beak-like masks, sometimes filled with herbs as folklore suggested the disease was spread by its smell. The masks made the doctors look duck-faced and people nicknamed them 'quacks'. As many of these 'doctors' were unqualified, the word stuck to any unqualified or bogus physician.

*Dr Anand Deshpande, Westhoughton, Lancashire*

**(169) QUESTION: Is a professional footballer under an obligation to retrieve the ball when it goes out of play?**

No, though players normally fetch the ball quickly when they're losing. Ball boys are employed to bring the ball back and players of a losing team will encourage them to retrieve it more quickly.

Referees and linesmen are advised not to retrieve the ball in case they should find themselves out of position for the subsequent play.

*Arthur Smith, Referees' Association, Coventry*


**(170) QUESTION: Why is it traditional to stand for the 'Hallelujah Chorus' during a performance of Handel's *Messiah*?**

Many people still take the traditional view that at the first London performance of *The Messiah*, at Covent Garden in 1743, the religious intensity of the 'Hallelujah Chorus' caused the audience to rise spontaneously as a mark of respect.

Its first performance in Dublin had caused great acclaim but London was pretty cool about Handel's great work. German-born George II enjoyed Handel's company and no doubt felt obliged to support his compatriot. Speaking poor English, George probably understood little of what was happening in the concert and, under the influence of a big meal and plenty of wine, dozed off halfway through.

At the electrifying opening of the 'Hallelujah Chorus', Handel uses trumpets and timpani to jolt the work into life, and this may have woken the sixty-year-old king, perhaps starting him to his feet in anticipation of the National Anthem, and obliging everyone else to do the same.

These days, many conductors encourage their audiences to remain in their seats.

*P. Spratley, Peterborough, Cambridgeshire*


Evidence for this tradition comes from 1779, some thirty-seven years after the first London performance of *The Messiah*, when

James Beattie wrote in a letter to Revd Laing that 'when the oratorio was first performed, the audience was exceedingly struck with the music in general but when that chorus struck up For The Lord God Omnipotent Reigneth they were so transported that they all, together with the King, started up and remained standing until the chorus ended: and hence it became the fashion in England for the audience to stand while that part of the music is performing'.

*Simon Evans, Sevenoaks, Kent*

## (171) QUESTION: My wife and I have retired with no ties. Which area of Britain is the healthiest place to live?

The regional trends survey, compiled by the Office For National Statistics, shows the South-West is best if you want to live longest, followed by East Anglia.

Ozone levels are linked to respiratory problems and the healthiest amounts can be found in Northern Ireland and Scotland. If you want to avoid radon gas which seeps from the ground, it is most prevalent in the South-West and parts of Northern Ireland, the East Midlands and Scotland. Infant mortality is often a good test of the general health of a population, and East Anglia comes out healthiest. It also has the fewest cases of neurotic disorder.

Taking all factors into consideration, East Anglia comes out best, followed closely by the South-West.

*Bill Wallace, Dundee*

George Bernard Shaw saw the gravestone of an eighty-year-old woman in the churchyard in Ayot St Lawrence, Herts, which read 'Her time was short' and so moved there in 1906.

His biographer, Hesketh Pearson, wrote: 'Shaw felt that a place where inhabitants who died at eighty were considered short-lived had the right climate for him.'

His instinct proved correct: Shaw lived to the age of ninety-four.

*Anthony Underhill, Folkestone, Kent*

**(172) QUESTION: What happens if someone on a live TV show gets the hiccups? Has this ever happened?**

Most viewers have seen a presenter hiccup on live TV. I recall seeing former *This Morning* presenter Richard Madeley do so and the show just carried on. Obviously a severe hiccuping bout would mean switching to another presenter or pre-recorded material.

The most memorable case of hiccuping affecting a film production was that of Graham Moffatt, best known for co-starring in many Will Hay films, who spent two weeks of March 1951 hiccuping at a rate of six a minute and had to be treated in Kettering Hospital.

The saddest case must be that of thirty-three-year-old pianist Iolanda Montalbano, of Palermo, Sicily, who had suffered several hiccuping bouts and was so depressed at the thought of starting them again during a concert that she committed suicide by shooting herself in February 1991.

Early discussion of the matter was reported more than seventy years ago in *The Lancet* by Dr C. F. T. East, who quoted Plato in describing how Aristophanes couldn't speak his turn for hiccuping at a symposium. The three-stage cure put forward by Eryximachus involved holding the breath, gargling water and, if the hiccuping persisted, irritating the nose until sneezing occurred. After one or two sneezes the hiccups disappear.

*Harry Pickering, Oldham, Lancashire*

**(173) QUESTION: Are rhubarb leaves really so poisonous?**

Rhubarb contains oxalic acid, which is corrosive and interferes with calcium absorption. Even the stems contain enough acid to take the shine off your teeth, and about 10 lb of rhubarb would contain a lethal dose. The same applies to spinach, but not even Popeye could get through 10 lb at one meal. Many natural foods are toxic in large quantities. The best approach is moderation.

*Peter L. G. Bateman, Society of Food Hygiene Technology, Lymington, Hampshire*

My father would never eat rhubarb, since the time when he was a Royal Marine. He and his colleagues were served rhubarb which had been cooked in a chipped enamelled container, exposing the iron underneath. This caused at least one death and, according to my father, the pain the survivors experienced was excruciating.

*P. W. Watson, Littlehampton, Sussex*

There's no doubt about this. My mother's sister, a fifteen-year-old trainee nurse in a Yorkshire hospital in 1917, died after being served rhubarb leaves as a vegetable. No doubt someone would have been heavily sued if this had happened now, but in those days it was treated as an awful tragedy.

*Mrs A. Mathews, Ladybridge, Banffshire*

**(174) QUESTION: On which stretch of line was the classic comedy *Oh, Mr Porter!* filmed? It starred Will Hay and centred on Buggleskelly Station.**

*Oh, Mr Porter!* was filmed on the Basingstoke & Alton line of the Southern Railway in 1937. The line had been closed in 1936 and was actually being demolished as filming took place. The supposedly Irish station of Buggleskelly was, in fact, Cliddesden Station, about two miles out of Basingstoke.

The Basingstoke & Alton line had an unhappy history. It opened as late as 1901, largely as a commercial-political ploy to block plans by the rival Great Western for a line from Basingstoke to Portsmouth. Traffic was light and the railway company grabbed the chance to close the line so that its track could be sent to France for the 1914–18 war effort.

To its consternation, the Southern Railway was forced to rebuild and re-open the line in 1923 but managed to close it to passengers in 1932 and then to goods four years later.

*Oh, Mr Porter!* gave the line a final moment of glory but it had been used for at least one other film, *The Wrecker*, in 1928.

*Handel S. Kardas, editorial consultant,* Railway World *magazine*

The windmill sequences were filmed at my great-aunt's and great-uncle's windmill in Terling, Essex. It was a working mill and my aunt recalls her husband crawling along the walls to untangle the stuntmen's ropes for the scene in which Will Hay and his sidekicks Moore Marriott and Graham Moffatt spin uncontrollably on the end of each sail.

*Rowena Brown, Waltham Cross, Hertfordshire*

Hertford can share some of the glory from this film. The opening shots show the star trio with the *Silver Link* locomotive taking on water at Hertford North station early one Sunday morning in 1937. The wheel tapper, Moore Marriott, was asked why he tapped the wheels and responded: 'To make sure they're still there.' It was a red-letter day for train spotters in Hertford.

*Fred Chunk, Hertford, Hertfordshire*

**(175) QUESTION: How do you set a sundial to read the correct time?**

First, the plate must be perfectly horizontal and the gnomon, the bit that casts the shadow, set at the correct angle for your latitude. Some examples are: Brighton/Plymouth 50½ deg. London/Bristol 51½ deg. Ipswich/Hereford 52 deg. Norwich/Birmingham 52½ deg. Lincoln/Liverpool 53½ deg. York/Lancaster 54 deg. Newcastle/Carlisle 55 deg. Edinburgh/Glasgow 56 deg.

Then set your watch to solar time on the day you set the sundial. This is Greenwich Mean Time, plus or minus the equation given in a nautical almanac, available in your local library.

At noon on your adjusted watch, set the dial so the shadow falls on the XII mark.

*Roy Andrews, Sanderstead, Surrey*

**(176) QUESTION: When I was a sailor it always raised a laugh when somebody recited 'Eskimo Nell', 'Dead Eye Dick' or 'Mexican Pete'. Who wrote them?**

The scandalous humorous recitation 'Eskimo Nell', extending to around sixty verses, tells the story of Mexican Pete (Mohican Pete in some versions) and Dead-Eyed Dick bursting into a Rio Grande saloon and demanding satisfaction from the local ladies. They enjoy forty or so encounters before meeting Eskimo Nell, a woman of massive stamina and proportion, from the frozen north. The story, familiar to almost every serviceman since the Second World War, relates in great detail how they are worsted by her – and modesty forbids me to relate any more.

Sadly, no author has come forward to claim this most influential of twentieth-century poetic works, though it's often suggested credit should be given to Noël Coward.

Another suggestion is that it was the work of Anglo-Canadian poet Robert William Service (1874–1958) or a collective effort by Cambridge students of the 1920s, based on Service's 'The Shooting of Dan McGraw'.

*Mike Williams, Rugby Song Cassettes Unlimited,*
*Colyton, Devon*

'Eskimo Nell' must be the work of Robert Service, who composed many ballads set around the Yukon. My copy of his *Ballads of Cheechako*, includes titles such as 'The Ballad of Pious Pete', 'The Ballad of One-Eyed Mike' and 'The Ballad of Hard-Luck Henry', all very amusing, well-written verses.

*Mrs J. Gibbins, Chingford, London*

**(177) QUESTION: If the Tour de France is the world's third-largest sporting event, which are the first and second?**

The greatest number of live spectators for any sporting spectacle is the estimated 2,500,000 who line the route of the New York Marathon. However, spread over three weeks, it's estimated that more than ten million spectators see the Tour de France.

The largest-ever crowd in one place to view a sporting event was the 199,854 at the Brazil versus Uruguay football match, in the Maracana Stadium, Rio de Janeiro, Brazil, on 16 July 1950.

*Carole Jones*, Guinness Book of Records, *Enfield, Middlesex*


I believe the 1950 Brazil v Uruguay football match, which attracted 199,854 spectators, has been exceeded as the world's largest sports audience for a single event.

The accolade must go to the Indianapolis 500, billed as 'the world's greatest race'. Practice and qualifying take place throughout May, with Pole Day (when the front of the grid is decided) boasting 300,000 spectators. The race, usually on the last Sunday in May and run for 500 miles at speeds well above 200 mph, annually attracts a crowd of just under half a million.

*Jason Humphries, Rochester, Kent*


The laurels in this contest must surely go to the Italian *tifosi* race fans who lined the route of the old Mille Miglia, Italy's classic 1,000-mile motor race held twenty-four times between 1927 and 1957. Italian motor sport authorities claimed this annual race held on ordinary roads, starting and finishing at Brescia on the central Lombardy plain, was watched each year by at least ten million fans and possibly as many as fourteen million in the early fifties when at least 530 two-man cars took part. With crowds up to twenty deep at many corners, the ten-million figure is widely accepted.

*Peter Miller, Banbury, Oxfordshire*

**(178) QUESTION: The lyric of Cole Porter's song 'You're the Top'** **mentions Harry Preston. Who was he?**

Cole Porter (1893–1964) composed and wrote 'You're the Top' in 1934 and it became one of the few hits he enjoyed at the time.

Its nine verses include references to obscure things such as Ovaltine, Pepsodent, the Zuider Zee, Whistler's Mama, the Steppes of Russia, even a Roxy usher – but don't appear to mention a Harry Preston.

However, the song lends itself to the addition of the singer's own favourite things and recordings by entertainers including Bing Crosby, Ella Fitzgerald, Ethel Murman, Mel Torme and Dionne Warwick could well include Harry Preston. The most likely Harry Preston would have been the diarist, sportswriter and hotelier who died in 1936.

*Betty Barron, Sutton Coldfield Music Library, West Midlands*

When he was a child around the end of the First World War, my father was a great friend of Harry Preston who owned the Royal York and Albion hotels in Brighton. My sisters and I often used to accompany our parents to the Royal York and would play with Harry's daughter Nancy while our parents were socializing.

*F. A. Desutto, Crawley, Sussex*

When I was born, in 1932, I was christened Raymond Harry Preston, but it was only in later years that I discovered Harry had been included because of my grandfather, John Henry Preston of Southport's long friendship with Sir Harry Preston.

My grandfather, a director of Southport Football Club, stayed at one of Sir Harry's hotels in Brighton in the 1920s and, through a mix-up over their names, they became friends, discovering a mutual interest in sport. I've appeared in a production of Cole Porter's

*High Society*, but I'm sorry to say Harry Preston wasn't mentioned in the song 'You're the Tops'.

*Raymond Harry Preston, Stockport, Cheshire*

I was secretary to Sir Harry Preston in the 1930s and was with Lady Edith Preston and their daughter Nancy after his death when they sold the Royal Albion Hotel.

I called there recently. Gone were the uniformed porters and page boys, along with the original reception office, on the counter of which used to be a heavy, silver-framed photograph signed by Edward, Duke of Windsor, as Prince of Wales.

The glitterati of the day used to come and go and I have a 1936 photograph of Sir Harry with musical comedy star Frances Day. In Coronation Year (1937), all lady visitors were presented with a gold-tasselled commemorative box of chocolates.

*Mrs Audrey Cant, Cheltenham, Gloucestershire*

It's difficult to imagine now what the name Harry Preston used to evoke and why it might have been included in the composition. Brighton, in the inter-war years, was described as 'London by the Sea' and everyone who was anyone went there, including Cole Porter. The Royal York and Royal Albion Hotels, both owned by Harry Preston, were frequented by the smart set.

Harry was a raconteur, impresario and man-about-town, always raising money for charity. He had been one of the country's foremost amateur boxers and, in 1921, organized a charity boxing tournament patronized by the Prince of Wales.

Harry, a former featherweight, performed an exhibition bout with French light-heavyweight Georges Charpentier who fought Jack Dempsey for the world heavyweight crown in the US the following year.

Harry was a celebrity, photographed by the Press and sought out as a friend by successful people from the world of sport, film and stage.

*Brian Kenway, South Warnborough, Hampshire*

## (179) QUESTION: To what did Edward the Confessor confess?

The 'Confessor' accolade of the penultimate king of Anglo-Saxon England was the Church's term for someone who achieved sainthood not by martyrdom but by lifestyle, 'confessing' the Gospel to the world, as in the baptismal injunction: '. . . be not afraid to confess the faith of Christ crucified . . .'

According to contemporary accounts, Edward was known for his piety and purity of life, and when he died in January 1066, the Anglo-Saxon Chronicle recorded: 'Angels led his righteous soul to heaven's residence.'

More critical historians suggest that Edward might have confessed to being too close to his cousin William, Duke of Normandy, at whose court he had sheltered as an exile before becoming king. Edward's apparent equivocation as to whether William or his close advisor Harold Goodwinson should succeed him allowed the Norman to claim the throne.

Edward's canonization in 1161 was a gesture of reconciliation by the conquering Normans towards the Anglo-Saxons as Edward became, before St George, patron saint of England.

*Gordon Marsden, History Today, London*

## (180) QUESTION: Which was the small French seaside town featured in the 1953 Jacques Tati film *Monsieur Hulot's Holiday*?

This is the little seaside town of St Marc sur Mer, in the Loire-Atlantique, just east of St Nazaire, close to the Point de Chemoulin.

I saw the film in 1953 at the Continental cinema in Wallasey, Cheshire, not knowing that in 1972 I would be holidaying in the nearby town of Pornichet with my wife and our two children. The beaches in the area were excellent and it was a very happy holiday.

*A. E. V. Costello, North Ferriby, East Yorkshire*

*Monsieur Hulot's Holiday* (*Les Vacances de Monsieur Hulot*) was the first outing for Tati's M. Hulot character who innocently left comic devastation in his wake. It followed Tati's success with *Jour De Fête*.

The ninety-minute, black and white film, set in a supposed Breton coastal resort, featured archetypal holiday characters including the buxom, welcoming Martine (Nathalie Pascaud), the workaholic on holiday (Jean-Pierre Zola), the robust English spinster (Valentine Camax), the overworked and flustered waiter (Raymond Carl), the old military buffer (Andre Dubois) and the beach bum couple (Rene Lacourt and Marguerite Gerard).

It had no plot and very little dialogue and was produced and directed by Tati as well as featuring him in the star role.

*Emma Barret, Beith, Ayrshire*

My wife and I visited St Marc sur Mer's Hotel de la Plage, which features in the film, for dinner recently and found film posters and photos displayed there. The hotel has been slightly developed but most aspects used in the film are easily recognizable. St Marc is a small but delightful resort, quiet and pretty.

*Brian Mayes, Tiptree, Essex*

### (181) QUESTION: Why do we call potatoes 'spuds'?

Potatoes are commonly called 'spuds' in England and Scotland because the narrow fork with three broad prongs used to lift them from the ground was known as a 'spud' and the word transferred to the vegetable itself.

The word 'spuddy' was slang for a man who sold bad potatoes.

*Paul Oldfield, Potato Marketing Board, Oxford*

**(182) QUESTION: Can the Fresh Fruit and Vegetable Info Bureau tell us how to remove the wax from lemons so they can be grated?**

After picking, lemons are sent to the packhouse to be washed free of dirt, a process which removes their natural wax. An edible wax, made from beeswax or shellac, is applied to the lemon to protect and preserve it. The edible nature of this wax means it's perfectly safe to grate a lemon skin though, if you're at all uncertain about eating it, you can buy unwaxed lemons, wrapped in Cellophane, in many stores.

*Debra Pieri, Fresh Fruit and Vegetable Info Bureau, London*

**(183) QUESTION: Why do coroners look into cases involving treasure trove and mysterious deaths?**

The first written record of the office of Coroner comes from 1194 when Richard the Lionheart was looking for new ways to raise money for the Crusades. Historically, the coroner (or 'crowner') discharged various functions for the protection of the Crown's financial interests in judicial proceedings, particularly those arising from death.

In times of unsophisticated law enforcement, fines were exacted not only from criminals but from the local community for failure to prevent crimes, report deaths, etc. Provisions existed to enrich the Crown through forfeiture of sureties, seizure of possessions of felons and confiscation of deodands (instruments used to kill someone), wrecks and treasure trove. Most of these functions gradually fell away from the Coroner or were taken over by others, in particular by Justices of the Peace, leaving today's coroners with their responsibilities for investigating unnatural or violent deaths, which makes up about 99 per cent of the role, and examining finds of treasure trove.

*Fiona Hamilton, Home Office, London*

**(184) QUESTION: What gave German bomber aircraft their distinctive drone compared with our aircraft when I listened to them as a boy during the Second World War?**

The engines in twin-engined aircraft each drive one propeller. Internal combustion uses spark plugs to create a firing sequence for smooth running but two engines rarely fire at exactly the same speed. If the firing sequence of a pair of engines isn't synchronized, a vibration creates the distinctive drone.

*Nick Forder, air and space gallery, Museum of Science*
*and Industry, Manchester*

When two notes of different frequency impinge on the ear, they 'beat' with each other and produce two other frequencies, their sum and their difference.

Our fighter planes were single engined while the twin piston engined German bombers had two note-producing devices. Normally, when the aircraft reaches cruising height, the pilot synchronizes the engines by adjusting the speed of one of them while listening to the beat note until it slows to zero.

Petrol engines normally stay synchronized for many minutes. The pilot will readjust them when he hears the 'beat' return. Many of the German bombers were powered by Junkers Jumo diesel engines, which were virtually impossible to synchronize for more than a minute or two. Their pilots didn't bother, hence the distinctive 'wha-wha' note that sent us diving for shelter.

*Graeme Wormald, Bewdley, Worcestershire*

Early in the Second World War, British air defences included sound locators to warn of the approach of enemy aircraft. The remains of one, with its huge bowl-shaped walls, can still be seen near Dymchurch on the Kent coast.

In more general use were mobile locators, used by the Army in conjunction with searchlights and anti-aircraft guns. These were two pairs of metal, cone-shaped 'mirrors', each operated by a man wearing headphones. The operator aimed his 'mirrors' in the direction of the aircraft noise and used fine adjustment to set them on a bearing where the noise volume was greatest. The two operators provided converging bearings to give the height and position of the aircraft.

German pilots, in the twin-engined bombers of the period, desynchronized their engines to produce a characteristic 'beat' to prevent the sound locators getting a fix on a maximum sound position.

*Frank Green, Baldock, Hertfordshire*

In his book, *Enemy Coast Ahead*, Guy Gibson writes: 'We had de-synchronized our engines to that unmelodious "rhoom-rhoom" noise which we were told rendered the audio detection system for searchlights ineffective, but all it did really was to cause unnecessary vibration on board.'

*J. Eggleston, St Albans, Hertfordshire*

I believe the 'German drone' was more imagined than real. My hearing at the time, in common with other aircraft-recognition buffs, was good enough, with experience, to identify individual types by sound alone, but I could never detect any general difference between German and British engine sounds.

Just after dark one evening in 1940, a stream of aircraft passed overhead and my aunt judged them to be German by the characteristic noise. Looking through binoculars, I soon identified them with absolute certainty as outward-bound Armstrong-Whitworth Whitley bombers of the RAF. My aunt remained unconvinced that the distinctive drone emanated from good old British Rolls-Royce Merlins.

*E. Ellis, Shamley Green, Surrey*

Living in London's East End at the time, I knew the distinctive drone of German bombers, mainly He-111s, dropping bombs on London. This wasn't my imagination.

My friend, Captain E. M. Brown, RN, the greatest test pilot Great Britain has ever produced, was chief naval test pilot at Farnborough Royal Aircraft Establishment, where he test-flew all captured enemy aircraft for evaluation and held the record for having flown more types of aircraft than any other pilot.

He told me the distinctive sound was due to the two engines being desynchronized, and this was confirmed to me by a German pilot who escaped serious injuries after his Do-17 was shot down during the Battle of Britain by Spitfires over Kent.

*Bill Kerr, London N2*

London was bombed many times in 1917 and 1918 by German twin-engined Gotha bombers, and also on occasion by the colossal Staaken aircraft, the largest ever to operate over the UK in either world war.

The throbbing of the engines of the Gothas in particular led to them being known as 'Wong-wongs' and, according to my grandmother, a veteran of both wars, the 1941/43 sound was almost identical.

*D. R. Bennett, Horsham, Sussex*

### (185) QUESTION: Why is red wine served at room temperature, not chilled?

The temperature at which a wine is served has a profound effect on its bouquet. Flavour components in a wine are released as the temperature of the wine increases so the more complex the bouquet of the wine, the warmer it should be served to fully appreciate its subtleties. The ideal temperature for most red wines is 'room temperature', 16–18 degrees Celsius. Temperature has a marked

173

effect on the tannin which gives red wine its astringent, mouth effect. Immature clarets and heavy Italian red wines have high levels of tannin and serving them slightly warm helps soften the tannin, making the wine more approachable.

Not all red wine is best served at room temperature. Those with soft or low tannins, simple bouquets and noticeable acidity, such as Beaujolais Nouveau or Lambrusco Rosso, benefit from a slight chilling, 10–12 degrees Celsius.

The best way to ensure you serve your wine at the correct temperature is to learn more about the subject from a body like the Wine and Spirit Education Trust.

*Janet Bangs, Wine & Spirit Education Trust, London*

### (186) QUESTION: What are the advantages of the pantograph and overhead wires over a third rail for electric railways?

Overhead wire electrification systems operate at 25,000 volts, supplied directly from the regional electricity companies, at intervals of about 50 km, without need for conversion. This makes the system more economic for mainline, long-distance electrification operating high-speed, high-power trains at relatively low frequencies.

Third rail systems, using direct current of 750 volts, are best suited for metro-type railways where the need is to run a high-frequency service over relatively short distances at speeds of up to around 120 kph. In general, the all-round weather performance of the overhead system is better than the top contact third rail type, the latter being particularly susceptible to the effects of ice and freezing rain.

*Henry Puntis, Railtrack, London*

The low maximum voltage, about 750 volts DC, which can safely be used in a third rail, can transfer only limited power to trains. Low voltage necessitates a larger current for a given train power, resulting in large voltage drops and pick-up problems: hence the sparking that goes on in frosty weather or when leaves fall on the third rail.

Higher voltage means a lower current for a given train power and more powerful trains but, for safety reasons, high voltages have to be in overhead wires, out of people's reach.

*R. Barnes, chartered electrical engineer, Longfield, Kent*

Overhead systems produce more injuries and deaths among maintenance staff and overhead wires are more prone to vandalism and accidental damage.

In train performance, there's no clear winner: the world speed record was held for many years by an experimental third-rail-supplied train at a test centre in Pueblo, USA. The sheer flexibility of catenary overhead wires can create serious problems at very high speeds.

*Tony Hobbs, Brecknell Willis & Co Ltd, Chard, Somerset*

The biggest disadvantage has to be the ugly overhead wires and their associated steelwork, a blot on the landscape and an environmental disaster. It surely cannot be beyond the skills of science to build a train motor that utilizes the environmentally friendly third rail system to produce much greater power than existing outdated units.

*Charles Harrison, Bexhill, Sussex*

One advantage is wildlife conservation. My husband works in track maintenance and is often shocked by the number of badgers, foxes, their cubs and other animals he finds dead near the third rail. These animals have obviously been killed by the power supply rather than by being hit by trains.

*Mrs E. A. Edbrooke, Hastings, Sussex*

**(187) QUESTION: If lightning strikes a body of water, does it affect the fish or bathers in the locality?**

When lightning strikes water, its electric charge spreads out in all directions until dissipated. Part of the current may pass through the body of a swimmer or fish, causing unconsciousness, injury or death. If you're swimming when lightning threatens, make for the shore and seek shelter in a large building or a car. Don't be tempted to shelter under a tree, lightning is more likely to strike the trees along the shore than nearby water.

Records of recent lightning injuries and deaths in the British Isles, compiled by the Tornado and Storm Research Organization (TORRO), indicate that each year on average sixty-six people are struck directly outdoors or indirectly indoors, e.g. while using the telephone, of whom three are killed. No recorded lightning incidents in the last four years have involved swimmers and only a few strikes were water related, including three people whose fishing rods were struck and two people struck while on boats. TORRO would be interested to receive details from anyone who has been struck by lightning.

*Prof Derek Elsom, Oxford Brookes University*

**(188) QUESTION In Sussex, the alleyway between the backs of houses is a 'twitten', while elsewhere it's a 'snicket'. What is the origin of these terms and are there others?**

In Norfolk, a path of this kind is referred to as a 'hoke'. A common expression is: 'I'm just going up the hoke.' I presume this is Norse, its nearest equivalent in the dictionary is 'hoki', the Norse god of mischief and destruction.

The Norse language here also gives us 'pightle' for 'an odd-shaped piece of land'. Several houses go by this name.

*J. E. Price, Walsall, West Midlands*

At Kingston on Spey, near Garmouth, the lane between two houses is called a 'trochy'.

*Angus W. Currie, Gretna, Dumfries and Galloway*

Cassell's German Dictionary has: '*Twiete* – narrow side lane of alley (dialectic)'. It would appear the two words have a common etymological source.

*G. Hawthorn, Scarborough, Yorkshire*

I was told by a ninety-two-year-old lifelong resident of Hastings that the word 'twitten' means 'betwixt and between'. An alleyway running betwixt and between the houses.

*Amy Stephens, St Leonards-on-Sea, E. Sussex*

I believe the word 'jitty' may be derived from the French *jete*, a ballet step. Some of these very narrow lanes often had houses or shops on either side and people could step or *jete* from one side to another. The word probably came here with the Normans, though I can't prove it.

*Miss S. Herbert, Glenfield, Leicester*

In my native Warwickshire, we always called such an alleyway a 'sling'.

*R. Pearson, Twickenham, Middlesex*

In Beijing, alleyways between buildings are known as *hutongs*, a word which came into common use in the Yuan Dynasty about seven hundred years ago. At this time China was ruled by the Mongols and the word is the Mongolian term for the space between nomadic tents.

*Liam Brown, London SE13*

**(189) QUESTION: As white horses are called greys, why don't we see pubs called The Grey Horse?**

There is a Grey Horse pub in what was the main village street of Balerno, a few miles from Edinburgh, the history of which goes back almost two hundred years. It was the first inn travellers from Lanark and the south encountered on their way into the capital.

One wall of the small bar carries a portrait of Robert Burns, a possible clue to the origin of the name of the pub, which opened within a few years of Burns's death. One of his most famous poems is 'Tam O'Shanter', a drouthy (thirsty) character, who 'roade a grey mare'.

*J. F. Gray, Currie, Midlothian*

The Grey Horse is an unusual name for a pub, even rarer than the true white (albino) horse, which has blue eyes and no colour in its hair. One of the best-known Grey Horses is in Kingston-upon-Thames, Surrey, famed for its live jazz. Owned by Young's for 105 years, it was built in 1849 by local brewer George Nightingale, who was Mayor of Kingston in 1846. Its name may be connected with the grey horses often chosen to pull the mayoral carriage in official parades, a tradition that survives at the Lord Mayor's Show in London every November.

*Michael Hardman, Young & Co's Brewery, Wandsworth,*
*London*

We live by Kempton Park race course and presume that our pub, now nearly two hundred years old, was named after an old favourite. The name White Horse is usually heraldic in origin.

*Tony and Ingrid Miller, The Grey Horse,*
*Sunbury on Thames, Middlesex*

178

There's a Grey Horse pub at Raillur Lane, London W10, which has been there for a hundred years or so and still serves a joyous pint, plus good food.

*J. B. Johnson, Bushey, Dorset*

The Grey Horse pub is alive and kicking at Collingham, near Newark. They do a lovely roast beef Sunday lunch.

*Christine and Graham Cooper, Skellingthorpe, Lincolnshire*

A pub at the bottom of Kilgate, near the railway bridge at Wakefield, is called The Grey Horse.

*Mike Kitchen, Wakefield, Yorkshire*

## (190) QUESTION: What is this 'handcart' in which, according to Richard Littlejohn, we're apparently all going to hell?

As a written expression, the saying 'going to hell in a handcart' dates from only 1986, when it's recorded in Robert Sproat's novel *Stunning the Punters*: 'It wasn't long after that that rock music really went to hell in a handcart.' The saying is also recorded in the US in 1992 in George F. Will's political book *Restoration*: 'So, it is natural for Americans to decide that things are going to hell in a handcart.'

But these written examples are evidence that the expression was already commonly used in popular language. Similar sayings for strange modes of transport to describe the fact that we're all going to hell, include 'go to hell in a basket' (first noted in 1969), 'going to hell in a handbasket' (1971), and 'going to hell in a plumber's pail' (1993).

The handcart is the type used by street traders to sell fruit and vegetables and other goods.

*Jeremy Welsh, Streatham, London*

This saying goes back considerably further than 1986. *The Oxford Dictionary of English Proverbs* records the phrase 'going to heaven in a wheelbarrow' from 1629.

Since fiends, not angels, would be in charge of the conveyance, the phrase had the ironic implication that it actually meant going to hell but this irony has been lost to modern writers in an attempt to make the meaning plainer.

Also current were the similar sayings 'There's no going to heaven in a sedan' and 'You can't go to heaven on a feather bed'.

*N. R. Holliday, Sutton, Surrey*

**(191) QUESTION: Has the fifteen-year-old boy who won £10,000 on a Camelot scratch card been allowed to keep the money?**

Though a fifteen-year-old boy did buy a winning Instants ticket some time ago, it was his mother who claimed the £10,000 prize. That prize was correctly paid out as, at that time, there was no way of knowing that the ticket was originally purchased by a fifteen year old.

When this fact came to light, the matter was referred to the police who subsequently decided to take no further action.

Camelot was keen to get a legal ruling and took the case to the High Court, while agreeing to pay all the mother's legal fees, to ensure there was no confusion if this situation occurred again and to dissuade other people under the age of sixteen years from playing any National Lottery game. Camelot will not pay out any prize to anyone under sixteen.

*Camelot Group plc, Rickmansworth, Hertfordshire*

**(192) QUESTION: Why were life-sized models of Red Indians placed outside tobacco shops?**

Shopkeepers used specific signs to identify their trades for the many people who couldn't read. When smoking became popular and the sale of tobacco was a commercial enterprise in the seventeenth century, snuff and tobacco merchants advertised their trade with a carved human effigy.

London was obsessed with Native American Princess Pocahontas, who arrived in Britain with her husband Captain John Rolfe in 1616, and so, when a quick-witted tobacco merchant used an effigy of 'La Belle Sauvage' with a peace pipe in her hands as a sign for his shop, other merchants followed suit.

Her effigy was subsequently replaced by that of a male Indian, in a crown and skirt of tobacco leaves, carrying a plug of tobacco and a clay pipe. 'At the sign of The Black Boy' became a popular address for tobacco merchants. This scantily clad blackamoor gave way to other figures – a Turk, Saracen or Indian prince.

In 1720, Jacobite conspirators met secretly at David Wishart's snuff shop in Coventry Street, London, a location denoted by a wooden figure of a Highlander. After the rebellion of 1745, when Highland dress was seen as far south as Derby, a Highlander figure became the traditional sign of a snuff merchant.

*Clive Turner, Tobacco Manufacturers' Association, London*

## (193) QUESTION: Why are bits of exploding shells and bombs known as shrapnel?

This term is technically incorrect – they should be called fragments. General Henry Shrapnel (1761–1842) invented a case shot for artillery containing an explosive and musket balls that, on bursting, caused great casualties among enemy infantry. First deployed in the Peninsular Campaign in 1804 and favoured by the Duke of Wellington, it was used up to the First World War.

By that time the musket balls had been replaced by steel balls or ball bearings. After the First World War, explosives improved to a point where much heavier shell cases could be used, the shrapnel balls could be left out and the case fragments left to do the damage. But pieces flying from an explosion were still called shrapnel.

*A. R. Rice, Filton, Bristol*

A blue plaque has been placed on the General Henry pub, formerly The Foresters Arms, in Horsham Road, Littlehampton, saying: 'General Henry Shrapnel (1761–1842), inventor of the shrapnel shell, had a workshop on this site.'

*Geoff Pitcher, Littlehampton, Sussex*

## (194) QUESTION: I came across a personal telephone conversation on my radio. How is this possible?

Cordless telephones operate on two wavebands, one for the handset and one for the base unit. The band for the handset lies in the region of 47.5 megahertz, well away from domestic broadcast services. But the base unit, the box plugged into the telephone outlet, transmits on frequencies around 1.6 to 1.7 megahertz, only just off the high-frequency end of the medium-wave broadcast band.

Many broadcast receivers will tune to one or more of the eight channels used by cordless phones. It's illegal to eavesdrop in this way but cordless phones are a very insecure system of communication.

*Graeme Wormald, Bewdley, Worcestershire*

## (195) QUESTION: In about 1925 my father owned a car called a Sizaire-Berwick which was similar to a Rolls-Royce. Are there still any in existence?

Maurice and George Sizaire built their first cars in 1904 with Louis Naudin at 79 Rue de Lourmel, Puteaux, Paris. Financial problems forced them to sell out to the Duc d'Uzes in 1907 but they continued making Sizaire-Naudin vehicles until 1912 when the Duc sacked all three and set up his own car-making firm which continued until 1921.

Maurice and George were joined by F. W. Berwick and built Sizaire-Berwick cars at Courbeville, near Paris, until the Sizaire brothers joined the French Army in 1914 and Berwick went to London to build an aircraft factory. After the war Maurice moved to London and designed a new Sizaire-Berwick, a two-ton vehicle which failed to sell. Austin Motors bought him out in 1923 and continued making Sizaire cars until 1925 while Maurice became an employee of the Tecalemit Grease Company until he retired in 1960. George Sizaire stayed in France, building his own cars from 1919 to 1929 when he moved to Belgium and continued manufacture there until 1931.

*Alan Burrows, Ipswich*

There used to be a fine example of the Sizaire-Berwick car, produced by my great-grandfather, Frederick Berwick, at Beaulieu Motor Museum, but its whereabouts is now uncertain.

*Chris Knapman, Seaton, Devon*

## (196) QUESTION: What is the song 'Puff the Magic Dragon' all about?

This song, first released in 1963 by American folk trio Peter, Paul and Mary, was written by trio member Peter Yarrow and Leonard Lipton. It tells the story of a mischievous sea-dwelling dragon, Puff, who inhabits an area known as Honah Lee, where it befriends a young boy called Little Jackie Paper.

They share various adventures, involving strings and sealing wax, amongst other things, until Jackie grows up and doesn't come to play any more, whereupon Puff the mighty dragon stops roaring, sheds his scales and slips back into his cave.

The lyrics were condemned at the time for being drug related but, regardless of whether they were or not, millions of children warmed to the tune, a top-ten hit in most English-speaking countries.

*Betty Barron, Sutton Coldfield Music Library, West Midlands*

The words are well crafted to gain acceptance at face value, but I believe the song is about opium smoking. 'Magic dragon' has long been an alternative name for the drug; 'puff' is self-explanatory and 'Little Jackie Paper' is the strong brown paper, sometimes waxed, known in the trade as 'jack-paper', in which parcels of opium are traditionally circulated. Hence the strings and sealing wax of the lyric.

The line about frolicing in autumn mist is about inducing the mind to rove free in the smoke clouds produced from reclining and puffing one's self into insensibility.

Other lyrics include references to travelling on a boat with billowed sail and sorrow when Jackie Paper came no more and the mighty dragon ceased his fearless roar. Even the 'cherry lane' where Puff no longer went to play, is the cherrywood mouthpiece of the opium pipe.

I don't believe the song was written solely with this underlying theme – it may not have been a conscious process at all – but a resident of San Francisco's Haight-Ashbury district has assured me it was the anthem of the sixties hippie generation after publication by Blossom Music Ltd in 1963.

*Connell Bernard, Churchstoke, Montgomery*

The laid-back feel of the sixties persists on a section of the north coast of the island of Kauai, in Hawaii, which is popular with musicians, singers and movie people. It was the location of Taylor Camp (believed to have been named after Elizabeth Taylor's brother Howard), a community of tent and tree-house dwellers, renowned for all-night music, drugs and parties, cleared out by the authorities in 1977 after a drawn-out legal battle over squatters' rights.

This volcanic area's jagged coastline resembles the outline of a dragon's back and local dragon folk tales may be due to the Chinese influence of indentured labourers brought in to work the fields.

It's a popular place for sailing boats and a fantastic spot to watch the sunset and look across to Bali Hai of the movie *South Pacific* (actually the cliffs of the Na Pali coast). If you're lucky, you can sometimes see a moonbow in the mists and at the end of the bay is a beach which will be familiar to anyone who has watched Mitzi Gaynor 'wash that man right out of her hair'.

Just before the beaches give way to the fantastic Na Pali cliffs, there are caves, said to have been created by the goddess Pele, perhaps where Puff the Magic Dragon still mourns his friend?

The name of this whole area is Hanalei. So who was Little Jackie Paper? A child in Taylor Camp or Hawaiian pidgin English?

*Mr R. Duniec, Alwoodley, West Yorkshire*

## (197) QUESTION: Why do cricketers play on a bald patch instead of the nice green grass all round it?

Ideally, cricket should be played on a firm, true surface to allow the ball to bounce consistently. Clay soil is best suited to this because it can be moulded flat when moist and retains moisture, holding it together when dried out by sun and wind.

The grass is intended to reinforce it, its many millions of roots helping bind the soil together and prevent cracking. As much grass as possible is shaved off the top, which, together with rolling, produces a hard, firm surface.

After playing, the surface is watered and spiked to allow air and water into the turf to speed recovery.

*Dave Bracey, Bromley, Kent*

## (198) QUESTION: In the classic American TV series *Bewitched*, did Samantha (Elizabeth Montgomery) really wiggle her nose that dramatically to make spells or was it all a special effect?

The famous nose twitch was no fake. Elizabeth Montgomery could do it naturally and, of course, the show's producer, Montgomery's husband William Asher, put his wife's unusual talent to the best possible use. The comedy series, which ran from 1964 to 1974, was based on the 1942 film *I Married a Witch* and featured the late

Elizabeth Montgomery as Samantha Stephens, who confesses to her husband, Darrin, on their wedding night that she is a witch with amazing powers.

She promises not to use them, and the comedy stems from her attempts to lead a normal life, much interrupted by her mother, Endora (Agnes Moorehead), arriving on a broomstick and causing mayhem.

One of the unseen stars of the show was visual effects expert Dick Albain who, without today's computer technology, made people and objects appear and disappear or move around, mostly using freeze-frame techniques.

*Nick Sainton-Clark, Visual Effects Organizer,*
*BBC Television, London*

After watching the programme, I tried to move my nose in the same manner and could do it exactly. Had Elizabeth Montgomery not been able to do it, no doubt the show's producers would have settled for ear-waggling or some other physical ability.

*Pamela Nelson, Stockport*

### (199) QUESTION: Who was the first person to 'start the ball rolling'?

This expression is generally accepted as having been introduced into the English language in the late nineteenth century from the game of croquet.

Developed from a game first played by monks in Ireland, croquet arrived in Britain in 1851. By 1865 the first croquet club had opened in Worthing and the first open championships followed two years later. Two years after that the All England Croquet Club opened at Wimbledon, later to become the All England Lawn Tennis and Croquet Club.

In those days, a skilled player could begin the play and finish without their opponent ever picking up a mallet. The decision as to who went first – who 'started the ball rolling' – was therefore all-important. Croquet's huge popularity at the time secured a place for the saying in the language to apply to anyone who initiates an activity.

*Tony Antenen, National Secretary, Croquet Association, London*

Croquet arrived in Britain in 1851 after my great-grandfather saw the game in Ireland and introduced it to this country at the Great Exhibition, where he won a gold medal.

Another famous expression derived from croquet involves the finish when, to conclude a player's turn, he has to strike his ball against the winning peg.

This was called 'pegging out', an expression which passed into everyday language as a euphemism for someone dying.

*C. T. C. Jacques, Thornton Heath, Surrey*

**(200) QUESTION: When did town-twinning begin and which were the first to be twinned?**

Records from the local government international bureau show the first twinned towns were Keighley, in Yorkshire, and Poix du Nord in France on 2 August 1920, a relationship that continues to this day.

*Valerie Pitt, Solihull Twinning Association, West Midlands*

**(201) QUESTION: What is the difference between reverend, very reverend and right reverend?**

*The Oxford Dictionary of the Christian Church* says the style 'Reverend', from the Latin *reverendus* (worthy of being revered), is an epithet of respect applied to the clergy since the fifteenth century. It has been used since the seventeenth century as a title put before their names in correspondence.

Archbishops and the Bishop of Meath (as Premier of Ireland) are styled Most Reverend, other bishops Right Reverend, as is The Moderator of the Church of Scotland. Abbesses, prioresses and other nuns who have the title Mother are also styled Reverend.

The legal right of Nonconformists to be called Reverend was established by the 1876 Keat Case, when a faculty (a warrant in church law) was ordered for the erection of a tombstone on which a Wesleyan Minister was styled 'Reverend', the incumbent (local vicar) having previously refused to allow it to be set up.

In the Church of England, Reverend applies to anyone ordained as a priest or deacon, while archdeacons are Venerable. The senior priest of a cathedral, the Dean or Provost, is Very Reverend.

As a style rather than a rank, Reverend should always be prefaced with 'the' and never used with just a surname: 'The Revd John Smith' or 'Mr Smith', not 'Revd Smith'.

While Inspector Morse could solve a Cluedo crime, the suspect Revd Green has always been ungrammatical. Perhaps it's time to investigate this infamous priest's credentials.

*Steve Jenkins, Church of England Communications Unit,*
*London*

**(202) QUESTION: Whenever I took our Mazda for its MOT, the garage said its Wankel-type engine creates virtually no emissions. Why are these non-polluting engines not more widely used?**

I researched these engines for a school project and built a working model to demonstrate the principle most recently developed by Felix Wankel, whose first engines ran in 1957.

His licence went to only one manufacturer in each country. In Germany, NSU bought the licence and produced the Ro80, as well as teaming up with Citroën to produce rotary-engined vehicles.

In Britain, Rolls-Royce bought the licence and produced a twin-chamber design to develop higher compression ratios for diesel fuel with the intention of putting it in tanks.

Mazda, which bought the licence for Japan, was by far the most successful producer, particularly in sports car versions, where consumption is less important.

*John Mayo, Bicester, Oxfordshire*

Legislation now requires all cars to use catalyst and oxygen sensors, incompatible with thermal reactors but just as effective in cleaning exhausts. Emissions from most modern cars are now cleaner than the 1985 RX-7.

Several companies bought the rights to develop the Wankel rotary engine but most dropped it early on when it gained a reputation for poor fuel economy and unreliability due to ineffective gas sealing and rotor tips that wore out very quickly.

Only Mazda persevered and in 1967 produced a rotary-engined car which was both reliable and powerful. Since then, Mazda has produced almost two million rotary-engined cars and used the engine to great effect in becoming the only Japanese manufacturer to win the Le Mans 24-hour race.

*Graeme Fudge, Mazda Cars UK Ltd, Tunbridge Wells, Kent*

## (203) QUESTION: Why were crown coins regarded as unlucky?

First minted in August 1526, in the reign of Henry VIII, the crown (like the gold sovereign issued by Henry VIII a few years earlier) was inspired by the French *ecu au soleil* (crown of the sun). Its initial value of 4s 6d (22½p) was superseded by the more convenient 5s (25p) coin after three months.

After 1662, under Charles II, gold crowns gave way to silver, struck with machinery instead of a hammer, and the crown's high value proved useful for paying large sums through the rudimentary banking system until 1751 when production ceased.

Coinage reform after the Napoleonic Wars brought demands for a large silver coin and a new crown appeared in 1818 with a portrayal of St George and the Dragon. But its high value limited its use in everyday transactions, with many people refusing to carry it or accept it in payment. One shopkeeper famously threw a crown coin he was offered out onto the street.

This dislike generated superstition, particularly in the catering industry, where handling a crown came to be seen as a harbinger of impending dismissal. Minting of crowns ceased, though it resumed on a small scale between 1927 and 1936, mostly for numismatists.

A 1935 crown was struck to commemorate George V's Silver Jubilee and another was issued in 1937 for George VI's coronation, establishing the crown as a commemorative coin. Another was struck after the Second World War to commemorate the Festival of Britain and in 1953 crowns were issued in large numbers for the Queen's Coronation.

*Derek Slark, Royal Mint, Llantrisant, Glamorgan*

## (204) QUESTION: Has the capital of Wales always been Cardiff?

Before gradual conquest by the Normans and their successors, Wales was divided into tribal kingdoms with no one city regarded as a capital. The Normans established marcher-lordships to administer the country until the reign of Henry VIII, when Acts of Union incorporated Wales administratively with England.

It wasn't until 1954 that a conference of Welsh local authorities chose Cardiff as the capital over Swansea, Caernarfon, Aberystwyth and Machynlleth.

Cardiff stands on an ancient site dating back to the Romans. With the expansion of the coal industry, it became the largest and richest part of Wales and it boasts a Civic Centre worthy of a capital which none of its rivals could match.

It officially became a capital city on 20 December 1955.

*Carolyn Pugsley, Cardiff Marketing*

The ancient capital of Wales is Aberffraw on Anglesey, known in Welsh as Mother of Wales. The *Y Goron* (Crown) pub is reputedly built on the site of the Prince's dwelling.

*P. Davies, Lampeter*

**(205) QUESTION: Duck, salmon, trout, sardine, lamb, beef, chicken, turkey, rabbit and liver are all available in pet food. Why no pork?**

Our extensive research into new variety ideas has found that pork isn't very popular and pet owners are never very enthusiastic about it. Of all the familiar meats, pork is always well down the preference ratings.

*Evelyn Trundle, Spillers Petfoods, New Malden, Surrey*

Pork varieties are available from small retail outlets and pork is used extensively in prepared pet food.

*Barbara Shaw, Pet Food Manufacturers' Association Ltd, London*

I've concluded that pork is avoided in pet foods because it acts as a laxative to many cats and dogs.

*Sally Johnson, Northampton*

**(206) QUESTION: I'm told that the largest living thing in the world is a fungus. Is this true?**

Many people consider the 1,200-mile long Great Barrier Reef, off the coast of Queensland, Australia, to be the largest living thing in the world but it consists of billions of living and dead corals rather than one entity.

A single living clone growth of the underground Fungus *Armillaria ostoyae* was reported in May 1992 as covering 1,500 acres in the forests of Washington State, USA. The International Mycological Institute is debating whether or not this, and similar fungi found throughout the world, can be considered a single entity.

The most massive plant is a network of quaking aspen trees in the Wasatch Mountains of Utah, USA, growing from a single root system and measuring 106 acres with a mass of 6,000 tonnes. The giant sequoia tree, nicknamed General Sherman, in the Sequoia National Park in California, is more than 275 feet tall and weighs at least 2,000 tonnes.

The largest animal on the planet so far discovered is the blue whale, measuring up to 110 feet in length and weighing up to 190 tonnes.

*Tim Mickleburgh, Grimsby, Lincolnshire*

**(207) QUESTION: Ships have a plimsoll line to make sure they aren't overladen. How do airport authorities make sure aircraft aren't overloaded?**

Some shippers mark freight items with grossly wrong weights. It's been known for an alert forklift truck driver to express concern and a trip to the weighbridge reveals all.

Pilots can become aware of an imbalance as the controls become effective while accelerating for take-off. More than one disaster has been averted by an abandoned take-off, at the expense of much rubber and brake linings. Aircraft will fly while overloaded or with a centre of gravity outside the prescribed limits but it's not a pleasant experience.

*B. Pike, Grimsby, Lincolnshire*

Like humans, aircraft get heavier as they get older. The reasons are many, including the effect of modifications, repairs, collected dirt under floors, etc., but probably the biggest effect is from paint.

The Civil Aviation Authority insists that all commercial aircraft are weighed at regular intervals, usually every three years, or after any major modification or repaint, and recommends that privately owned light aircraft should be reweighed at least every ten years.

*Chris Fry, CAA approved weights engineer, Yeovil, Somerset*

**(208) QUESTION: How is Sister Wendy, the TV art historian, allowed to have a name which isn't a Biblical Christian name but was made up by J. M. Barrie for his *Peter Pan* book?**

Sister Wendy Beckett became an authority on art history and old masters after her BBC TV series, *Sister Wendy's Story of Painting*. Though born in Scotland, she spent much of her childhood in South Africa with her parents before returning to Britain at sixteen to join the Notre Dame nuns.

In an interview she explained that she had never had any great affection for her given name, Wendy, and on entry to her vocation had intended calling herself Sister Michael, after St Michael the Archangel but at the last minute she felt that to change her name would have been self-indulgent.

When not filming for the BBC, Sister Wendy spends her time in contemplation in her caravan at the Carmelite Monastery at Quidenham, Norfolk.

*Margaret Mellor, Norwich*

Many sisters in religious congregations choose or are given a saint's name to be known by when they become novices but in some congregations, such as the Society of the Sacred Heart, they have always kept their baptismal name. Since the Vatican II council of the Catholic Church (1963–65) some sisters have reverted to their baptismal names.

*Sister Margaret Byrnes, Society of the Sacred Heart, Hammersmith, London*

**(209) QUESTION: When and why did the spelling of such words as 'honour', 'colour' and 'theatre' change to 'honor', 'color' and 'theater' in America?**

The main force for changing English English to American English was author and lexicographer Noah Webster (1758–1843) of West Hartford, Connecticut. He believed words should be accepted on their merits, not bound by rules created on a different continent.

Examining the language of the newly independent America, without regard to the English used in Britain, he created in 1828 the first American-English dictionary, including new pronunciations and new spellings.

He felt that words ending in '-our' should be '-or' and deemed it more logical to put '-er' rather than '-re' at the end of words such as 'theatre' and 'centre'. And he removed the final 'k' from words such as 'musick' and 'traffick'.

After publication of his dictionary, the language of the Old and New Worlds became increasingly divergent, a process which continued until the late twenties when the two languages, and those of other English-speaking nations, became familiar to all, through the growth of international mass communication. Today, the English spoken in every part of the world is becoming increasingly homogeneous.

*Dr D. Simpson, Glasgow*

As an American writer in Britain, I sometimes refer to the UK as The Land of Extra Vowels but defer to my linguistic hero Bill Bryson, an American journalist living in Britain, author of *The Mother Tongue, English and How it Got That Way* (William Morrow & Co, New York, 1990).

He notes that the English gave up the 'u' in words such as terrour, governour and horrour but kept them in words such as honour and colour. He writes: 'There's no logic to it, no telling why some words gave up the "u" and others didn't. For a time it was fashionable to drop the "u" from honour and humour – Samuel Taylor Coleridge did it – but it didn't catch on.'

*Louis De La Foret, Wordsmith & Images, Northampton*


I wonder if an American is justified in calling Britain 'the land of the extra vowels'. In school English lessons, Americanized English was anathema and we were taught 'not to confound the language of the nation with words of -osity and -action'.

I used to take my medicine, now I take my medication. I used to move, now I relocate. Is it the US which is truly 'the land of extra letters'?

*S. Henderson, Barrow-in-Furness, Cumbria*


The way in which English has borrowed from other languages over the centuries has given rise to alternative spellings. For example, the original Latin form for colour is *color* for the noun and *colorare* for the verb.

Old French used *color* but later amended it *colour* and adapted the verb to *colourer*. The English spellings 'color' and 'colour' come from Latin, either directly or via Old French.

The British 'realise', modelled on the French *realiser*, is a recent change from 'realize', which reflects the original Greek ending used in the US as well as by many British, myself included.

*Paul Coxwell, Sutton on Sea, Lincolnshire*


## (210) QUESTION: They seem very popular these days, but what exactly is a judicial review?

Judicial review, as we now know it, is a relatively recent way by which an administrative decision, such as that made by a civil servant or minister, or a quasi-judicial or judicial decision, such as that made by a tribunal, may be reviewed by the High Court. The procedure is contained in Rules of Supreme Court (RSC) Order 53.

Grounds for such reviews include error of law and irrationality.

*Ian Millard, barrister, Little Venice, London*

**(211) QUESTION: Does anyone recall anything about the Penelope Ann newspaper adventure stories of sixty-five to seventy years ago, after whose heroine my mother named me?**

Penelope Ann first appeared in the *Evening News* in 1942, the creation of cowboy-turned-writer Philip Neville and based on his niece. More than fifty stories later she became the heroine of the novel *Me and Penelope Ann*, published in 1947.

*Philip Cakebread, Banstead, Surrey*

**(212) QUESTION: Alan Shearer was the first player to score 100 goals in the Premier League. Who was the first to score 100 goals after the Football League began in 1888?**

John Southworth achieved his 100th goal in the Football League in 1893. He scored sixteen goals for Blackburn Rovers in the 1888/89 season, twenty-two in 1889/90, twenty-six in 1890/91, twenty-three in 1891/92 and ten in 1892/93, making ninety-seven goals for Blackburn before moving to Everton for the 1893/94 season – when he scored another twenty-seven.

His 100th goal came in a match against Sunderland on 30 September 1893. He pulled off another record for Everton on 30 December 1893, when, playing in a 7–1 victory against West Bromwich Albion, he became the first League player to score six goals in a match.

Southworth may in fact have reached his 100th goal while still at Blackburn. Goalscorers in many early games were unidentified as matches ended as it was getting dark.

Born in 1866, John played three times for England as well as gaining two FA Cup winner's medals. His last League game was against his old side Blackburn Rovers before a knee injury forced him out of the game. He went on to play the violin in Llandudno Pier Pavilion Orchestra for thirty years. He died in Liverpool on 16 October 1956, aged ninety.

Between 1890 and 1894, Sunderland's Johnny Campbell became the first to score 100 goals for one club.

*Ray Spiller, Association of Football Statisticians, Basildon, Essex*

**(213) QUESTION: Have 'low-profile' tyres any advantage over standard radial tyres? Why are they so much more expensive?**

In the past, low-profile tyres have been used on high-performance vehicles, but now manufacturers are fitting them on some standard models as they can build in a bigger steering wheel and bigger brakes.

Owners of most cars can choose to fit low-profile tyres instead of standard radials for aesthetic reasons.

Low-profile tyres have advantages and disadvantages. They give better grip in dry weather, but transmit more of the bumps and holes in the road to the car's occupants.

They are generally dearer than normal tyres because their manufacture is longer and more complicated.

*Sally Warburton, Automobile Association, Basingstoke,*
*Hampshire*

**(214) QUESTION: Where does the word hocus-pocus come from – and does it have anything to do with the hokey-pokey ice-cream we used to enjoy as children?**

'Hocus-pocus', meaning rubbish or untrue, stems from the time when there was a strong opposition in this country to the Roman Catholic doctrine of transubstantiation – the idea that Christ is truly present in the bread and wine when consecrated in the Eucharist.

The words of the Latin mass '*Hoc est corpus meum*' ('This is my body') were characterized as 'hocus pocus'. Another anti-Catholic item dating from that era is the Jack-in-the-box toy, a jovial representation of the 'tabernacle' found in Catholic churches containing the Eucharistic elements.

*John Bowyer, Heath, Cardiff*

**(215) QUESTION: Why do we keep our car in a 'garage', not a 'carage'?**

In the early years of the twentieth century, cars were kept in out-buildings, such as stables or carriage houses. If a special building was erected for a 'horseless carriage' it was generally called a 'motor-house'. Around the same time, commuters to London could keep their vehicles during the day in large buildings like today's indoor car parks.

The *Daily Mail* of 11 January 1902, reports Harrington Moore, Honorary Secretary of the Automobile Club, opening the first one of these – with room for eighty cars – in Queen Victoria Street.

This new institution called for a new word: a 'garage', borrowed from the French for a shed for vehicles or a business which stored, maintained and repaired cars.

*E. S. C. Weiner, Oxford English Dictionary, Oxford*

There is some irony in our English adoption of the word 'garage' from French. The French verb *garer*, to protect or guard, had already taken on the new meaning 'to park' for the dawn of the motoring era.

Modern French now finds itself without a purely French term for a car park and has had recourse to English for *le parking*.

*V. M. Boon, Dover, Kent*

**(216) QUESTION: Does the UK have a national day as in other countries? If not, which would be suitable?**

The UK is one of the few countries with no national day. The four countries in the Union each celebrate their own national days: St David's Day (1 March) in Wales, St Patrick's Day (March 17) in Northern Ireland, St George's Day (23 April) in England and St Andrew's Day (30 November) in Scotland.

Empire Day, 24 May, was inaugurated in 1902 in honour of the late Queen Victoria's birthday but fell victim to our anxiety to forget our colonial past.

Renamed Commonwealth Day in 1958, its date was changed in 1966 to match that of Queen Elizabeth's official birthday. In 1976 the date changed again and it is now observed (or not) on the second Monday in March.

We're all aware of many countries' national days – few fail to realize what 4 July means to the US or that 14 July is Bastille Day in France. If the UK remains a union, now may be a good time to choose a new date. My favourite would be 1 May, date of the 1707 union of Scotland and England.

*Stephen Tewson, Torquay*

We used to celebrate Empire Day with a parade in the school playground, waving Union Flags and singing: 'We have come to school this morning, 'Tis the twenty-fourth of May, And we join in celebrating What is called our Empire Day.

'We are only little children, But our parts we gladly take, We all want to do our duty, For our King and Empire's sake.'

*Doris Wright, Bognor Regis, Sussex*

**(217) QUESTION: Who invented the cuckoo clock?**

In the seventeenth century, farmers around Baden-Wurttemberg in southern Germany took to carving complex wooden objects during the winter and began to produce their own clocks.

In about 1730, Franz Anton Ketterer produced a clock which used a bellows and a pipe to imitate a cuckoo call but it wasn't a great success and it wasn't for another fifty years that his idea was revived.

By the end of the nineteenth century, heavily carved imitation chalet cuckoo clocks were being made in large numbers in southern Germany and in Switzerland, which usurped Germany to become famous for them.

*Leigh C. Extence, antique clock specialist, Teignmouth, Devon*

**(218) QUESTION: I used to play football for Acton Garden Village Railway Tenants FC. Is this the longest named football club in the land?**

An even deeper breath is required to name Framwellgate Moor and Pity Me Working Men's Club FC, from the former mining village near Durham, regular participants in the FA Sunday Cup. During the Sunday Cup competition of 1994–5, they travelled to Edinburgh Park, Liverpool, to play a club at the opposite end of the verbal scale, A3, a name derived from Mersey Docks. Brevity prevailed over verbosity by four goals to three.

*Rob Ruddock, Liverpool*

**(219) QUESTION: The Beatles referred to 'mojo filters' in 'Come Together' and Paul Weller, in 'Into Tomorrow', sings: 'Your mojo will have no effect.' What is a mojo?**

A mojo was originally a magic spell or charm, intended to instigate or enhance sexual attraction. The word is thought to come from *moco*, a Gullah word used by African slaves in the US deep South.

It crops up frequently in blues tunes from the twenties such as Charley Lincoln's 'Mojo Blues' (1927) and Blind Lemon Jefferson's 'Low Down Mojo Blues', famous for the lines 'My rider's got a mojo and she won't let me see/Every time I start a'lovin, she ease that thing on me.'

Mojo developed to become a slang word for narcotics, especially morphine. Jim Morrison, of The Doors, nicknamed himself 'Mr Mojo Risin', a convenient anagram of his name.

*Carol Bentley, Colchester*

A Mojo is a magic charm, a lock of hair, stone or carved figure used to cause someone to fall in love with its owner. Possibly its most famous use is by bluesman Muddy Waters with his 'I got my mojo working but it just don' work on you.'

*Alan Higgins, London, SE25*

As a musician, I have encountered this word applied to the way people react to the music they're playing.

A mojo is a natural stimulant, like an adrenaline rush – not to be compared with a drug-enhanced performance. When the mojo kicks in, the performer becomes enveloped in their playing, expressing this by strange movements. A concert performance by Jimi Hendrix is a perfect example of a mojo at work.

*Vince Knight, Shenfield, Essex*

In sixties Liverpool, a 'mojo filter' was a stale loaf of bread. Down-and-out drinkers referred to methylated spirits or metal polish as their 'mojo' and filtered out some of the more toxic ingredients by straining the liquid through a stale loaf.

*Barry Woodward, Bispham Green, Lancashire*

(220) QUESTION: Why do the French say *'toutes les choses ont l'air au trente-et-un'* for 'everything appears to be in order'?

*Trente-et-un* (thirty-one) is a French card game in which you have to score thirty-one to win, finishing with two royal cards and an ace. It follows that thirty-one indicates something being correct, or in order.

The French expression '*sur son trente-et-un*' is the equivalent of our 'dressed up to the nines'.

*Bob Hanna, Crowborough, Sussex*

A common phrase in France is *se mettre sur son trente-et-un*, which translates as 'to dress yourself in your thirty-one'. During the reign of Louis XIV (1643–1715) in France, a *trentain* was an expensive ornate jacket worn on special occasions.

Construction of this jacket was supposed to involve 30 hundred threads. Over the years, *trentain* has been corrupted to *trente-et-un* and its meaning lost.

*Dave Hopkins, Deal, Kent*

## (221) QUESTION: Why is anyone called Ward nicknamed Sharkey in the Royal Navy?

Sharkey has been naval slang for anyone surnamed Ward for more than two centuries, since the notorious lives of two Barbary Coast pirates both named Ward.

A man called Ward, of unknown first name, was one of the first pirates to establish himself on the North African coast. By 1613 he had been joined by at least thirty known pirate captains, with a headquarters at the mouth of the Sebu River.

The second Ward was the notorious Captain Ward who, as a poor English sailor, travelled to the Barbary Coast and offered his services to the Moors. He became a Mohammedan soon after his arrival and was given command of a galley.

Details of his life are sketchy, though it's known he amassed great wealth and 'lived like a Bashaw in Barbary'.

*Tony Walters, Swansea*

**(222) QUESTION: Did actress Nanette Newman sing with The Rolling Stones?**

Credits on the 1969 Rolling Stones album *Let It Bleed* include backing vocalists Madeline Bell, Doris Troy and Nanette Newman for the song 'You Can't Always Get What You Want', and vocalists Nanette Newman, Mick Jagger and Keith Richards for 'Country Honk'.

Nanette Newman also appears in the credits for 'Salt of the Earth' on the Stones' 1968 album *Beggar's Banquet*, giving rise to the quaint notion that the Northampton-born Fairy Liquid Queen/actress/presenter and author Nanette Newman teamed up in the late sixties with Mick and the Stones.

In fact, the Nanette Newman in question was an American with several roles as an actress/singer to her credit. A friend of Jagger's girlfriend Marsha Hunt, she was drafted into the studio as a back-up singer.

*Jaap Hoeksma,* Shattered Magazine *(the Rolling Stones fanzine), London*

**(223) QUESTION: Cardinal numbers have one, two, three, four, etc., and ordinal numbers have first, second, third, fourth, etc., but are there any adverbs following in the sequence once, twice, thrice . . . ?**

English is a Germanic language, descended from an ancestor of which there are no surviving records though there are early records of Old (eighth century) English and older forms of the other languages in the group including German and the Scandinavian languages etc., plus fourth-century records of Gothic, a language which did not survive.

In Gothic and other old Germanic languages, ordinal numbers were formed by adding '-th' to cardinal numbers but numeral adverbs were made simply by adding sintham, the ancient word for '-times'.

In Gothic, 'thrice', for example, is *thrim sintham* and 'seven times' is *sibum sintham*. Old English used the same system: 'four times' was *feower sithum*.

In early Germanic languages, cardinal numerals were inflected, adding endings to show their relationship to other words, and Old English commonly added the genitive ending to adjectives to form adverbs. This ending was '-es', like the '-'s' ending of our modern possessive: 'queen's', 'princess's', etc.

In the twelfth century, this '-es' was added to the numerals one, two and three to make ones, twies and thries, which later became once, twice and thrice. We can only guess why it was never added to higher numerals but the first three numerals are irregular in other ways, for instance all other ordinals are formed with '-th' but first, second ('other' in Old English) and third are irregular.

*E. S. C. Weiner, Oxford English Dictionary*

### (224) QUESTION: Why is the lowest deck on a ship called the orlop deck?

Orlop, from the Dutch *overloopen*, to run over, is the platform that overlaps the bilges of a ship. On men-of-war, this dark and airless deck, usually below the waterline, held the powder magazine, storage space for coiled ropes and living quarters for junior officers.

On merchant ships, the orlop is the deck of the cargo hold.

*David Elias, Nottingham*

### (225) QUESTION: Does light weigh anything?

Albert Einstein published his theory of relativity – predicting that light had a mass – in 1905 and his ideas were proved correct in 1919 when, during an eclipse of the sun, scientists saw light from a star they knew was behind the sun.

Every object has mass, and weight is the force exerted on mass by gravity. The light from behind the sun could be explained only by the fact that light has mass and was attracted by the gravity of the sun, bending the rays around it, making its light visible from Earth.

*Bhagwant Singh, Museum of Science and Industry, Manchester*

When Einstein formulated his Special Theory of Relativity in 1905, his equation $E = mc^2$ predicted that light would have mass. As a result, he speculated that light would be bent by gravity, and in 1911, using Newton's theory of gravity, he calculated that the bending of light would be 0.83 seconds of arc.

By 1916, however, Einstein had developed his own theory of gravitation, called general relativity. Unlike Newton, he explained gravity in terms of the curving of space/time. Based on this theory, he calculated the bending of light as 1.7 seconds of arc.

Subsequent measurements of the bending of starlight, taken during solar eclipses, have validated this value.

*Glyn Phillips, Lake, Isle of Wight*

Einstein's theory of relativity predicts that light is bent in a gravitational field, but the theory accounts for this as a consequence of the curvature of space itself near a body of mass, not by gravitational attraction on light.

In the 1919 eclipse, light from a star normally hidden by the sun followed the curved path of space in the sun's gravitational field to become visible during the eclipse.

*Richard Levene, Ilford, Essex*

Referring to 'curvature of space' near a body of mass is merely a way of explaining how this attraction might work, not a separate phenomenon.

Curvature of light is caused not by the action of the mass of the sun but by the magnetic centre of the solar system, situated near the sun. Even within a solenoid one can see a stream of electrons deflected by a magnetic field.

If light were deflected when passing close to a mass, this could be clearly observed in the vicinity of planets. Eclipses of the moon would provide the best opportunity for such observation. But this curvature has been observed only at the precise magnetic centre of our system. Talking of 'curvature of space' is anti-scientific. Space has no form and isn't relative to anything. It can be neither curved nor straight because it has no dimensions and is infinite in all directions.

The weight of light, known to science as the Solar Wind, is equal to 4/10 the atmospheric pressure per square mile. Maxwell, in 1873, showed radiation exerts pressure and Lebeder and Nichols confirmed this.

But this poses a problem for scientists because the idea that the sun's light exerts a constant pressure on the Earth, repelling us from it, cannot be contained within current laws of gravity, either by Newtonian or Einsteinian physics.

*James Hardiman, Taunton, Somerset*

The scientist de Broglie believed that, as a consequence of quantum mechanics, a particle must also have a wavelength, and deduced this relationship for what came to be known as de Broglie waves: wavelength = Planck's constant/(mass of particle × velocity of particle).

So for a given wavelength a mass can be deduced. Rearrangement of the equation says that this mass would be equal to Planck's constant/(speed of light × wavelength).

By rounding up the figures and assuming blue light to have a wavelength of 4,000 Angstroms, the weight of the blue light would be approximately 0.000000000000000000000000000000000000-000006 of a gram.

*Steve Reay, Washington, Tyne and Wear*

**(226) QUESTION: Could Elvis Presley play the guitar?**

The idea that Elvis Presley couldn't play the guitar stems from a joke he cracked during a CBS special when he said he knew only three chords but 'had fooled everyone for a long time'. Many people took this seriously, though in fact he was quite an accomplished player.

Elvis learned guitar as a child, taught mainly by his uncle, Travis Smith, while growing up in Tupelo, Mississippi. Throughout his career he spent many hours taking pointers from some of the great guitarists of his era, including the legendary Chet Atkins, with whom he spent many hours improving his technique.

For his 1968 'comeback' tour, Elvis played his favourite guitar, a Gibson J200, on stage and live on TV. He also played the introduction to 'You're So Square' on a bass guitar after his bass player Bill Black apparently 'had problems getting it right' and left the studio for a break.

Here at Graceland, we have a collection of fifteen of Elvis's guitars, including the Gibson. Elvis could also play the violin and had his own Stradivarius.

*Patsy Andersen, Graceland, Memphis, Tennessee*


**(227) QUESTION: How much cornflour would be required to thicken all the oceans?**

The weight of the world, according to most scientific calculations since the first attempt by Neville Maskelyne in 1774, is regarded as 5.978 times ten to the power 24 kilograms; about 6,000,000,000,000,000,000,000,000 kilograms. A further estimate gives the world's oceans as 0.024pc of this weight, or 1,440,000,000,000,000,000,000,000 kilograms.

Home economists advise that 4 tbsp (60 grams) of regular cornflour is enough to thicken each kilogram (just less than 2 pints) of water to the recommended thickness for gravy or white sauce, so you would require 48,960,000,000,000,000,000,000,000 tablespoons or about 42,253,000,000,000,000,000 kilograms of cornflour to turn the seven seas to gravy.

Cornflour can be successfully mixed only with cold water and must be stirred while being brought to the boil so only a rapid acceleration of the greenhouse effect, accompanied by a series of global earthquakes, are likely to effect this particular recipe.

*Katey Holgate, Chigwell, Essex*

## (228) QUESTION: To what process have processed peas been subjected? How do they differ from garden or marrowfat peas?

Most peas in this country are supplied frozen or in cans because peas are prone to rapid deterioration and have a very short shelf-life unless suitably processed.

Both methods involve some type of processing, whether they be so-called 'processed peas', garden peas, marrowfat peas, or fresh frozen peas. With processed peas, the peas dry in the pod after maturity. They are 'wetted out' (soaked overnight in water) and then canned.

This canning process involves heating the filled can to sterilizing temperatures which destroy any potential microbiological spoilage organisms.

Marrowfat are larger mature peas that have been collected in the same way as processed peas.

Mushy peas are produced from field-dried peas which then have the pea surface mechanically worn down to assist moisture penetration in cooking, which gives them a characteristically soft texture.

Some brands of canned, processed, marrowfat peas and mushy peas may have some ingredients added, such as colouring, salt, sugar, mint or even curry.

*Keith Anderson, Institute of Food Science and Technology,*
*Shepherds Bush Road, London W6*

**(229) QUESTION: Is it true that only five people named Smith have played international football for England?**

A total of eighteen Smiths have played international football for England: Arnold Smith of Oxford University (1876); Charles Smith of Crystal Palace (1876); Albert Smith of Nottingham Forest (1891-93); Gilbert Smith of Oxford University and Old Carthusians (1893–1901); Stephen Smith of Aston Villa (1895); Herbert Smith of Reading (1905–06); Joe Smith of Bolton (1913 –20); Joe Smith of West Bromwich Albion (1919–22); Bert Smith of Tottenham (1921–22); William 'Billy' Smith of Huddersfield (1922–28); Jack Smith of Portsmouth (1931); Septimus Smith of Leicester (1935); Reg Smith of Millwall (1938); Leslie Smith of Brentford (1939); Lionel Smith of Arsenal (1950–53); Trevor Smith of Birmingham (1959); Bobby Smith of Tottenham (1960–63); Tommy Smith of Liverpool (1971) Alan Smith of Arsenal (1988–92) and Alan Smith of Leeds, Manchester United and Newcastle (2001–07).

Among almost 1,200 players who have put on an England strip, Smith is the most common name at 1.5 per cent, compared with 1.52 per cent as a proportion of the English population.

English footballers include ten Johnsons, nine Browns, seven Robertses, seven Joneses, seven Wrights, six Allens, six Wilsons, six Taylors, five Lees and five Hills.

*David Barber, Football Association, London*

**(230) QUESTION: Why was a Teddy boy's jacket called a 'drape'?**

'Zoot suit' fashion appeared in the US at the end of the Second World War. Popularized by jazz and big band musicians, it consisted of an over-length, unwaisted jacket, with very wide shoulders and long lapels, fastening on a single button, below waist height.

British clothing manufacturers referred to this unfitted style as a 'draped suit', later shortened to 'drape suit'. Produced mainly in grey or blue gabardine, with a single button fastening, it became the uniform at most dance halls.

High fashion in the early 1950s saw a resurgence in distinctly British style with the growing popularity of Edwardian modes, featuring a short, close-fitting four-buttoned jacket with velvet collar and dark blue or black slim trousers.

But this was the era when the teenager emerged as a fashion leader and by 1953 youngsters in Britain had combined the two fashions into a kind of Mississippi gambler style.

With a reputation for violence at the time, the Teddy boys wore clothes which were strictly speaking neither Edwardian nor in line with the 1940s 'drape' style, though this is the name by which their style of jacket has passed into the language.

*Mike Ellis, Shoreham-by-Sea, Sussex*

'Drape' wasn't coined by British manufacturers. The popular 1941 song 'Zoot Suit' refers specifically to its drape shape.

The zoot suit was first worn by black people in Harlem, New York City. When America entered the war, a declaration was issued saying zoot suits used an extravagant amount of cloth, which was needed for uniforms. They went out of style quite quickly and bore little resemblance to Teddy boy gear, apart from the 'draped' shape.

*Jack Nickle Smith, Taplow, Buckinghamshire*

## (231) QUESTION: Is the famous Old Ball Court on the Square in Nelson, Mid Glamorgan, the only example of a handball court in Britain?

There is evidence that this game was widespread until the early part of this century in many parts of Glamorgan. It resembles modern squash, with each player hitting the small rubber ball alternately against the wall, but with the palm of the hand rather than a racquet. It's a folk game, usually played on the gable end of a building, but purpose-built three-wall courts were constructed next to the pub in some towns and villages.

Nelson, which has hosted the World Singles Wall Handball championship, is the only place I know of where this game has an unbroken tradition.

The game has almost disappeared over the past half-century, but there is an excellent example of a ball court built in 1864 in Jersey Marine near Swansea. Dilapidated courts are found in Llantrisant, the Rhondda and many of the other Glamorgan and Gwent valleys.

*Tecwyn Vaughn Jones, Department of Welsh, Cardiff*

## (232) QUESTION: Why has Errol Flynn's last film, *Cuban Rebel Girls*, made in 1959, never been shown?

*Cuban Rebel Girls*, made in black and white in 1959 and starring Errol Flynn's girlfriend Beverly Aadland, was Flynn's last film.

Aadland played a girl who attaches herself to Fidel Castro around the time of his overthrow of the Batista regime, observed by Flynn as an American reporter.

Castro co-operated in making the film, believing it would be complimentary to his fledgling regime. He was promised a look at it but the crew gave him a blank tape before smuggling themselves out of the country. Their bravery was wasted. Critics said Flynn had 'saved his worst for last'. It was so poor it has never been shown in this country, though it was sold in some US video stores under the title *Assault of the Rebel Girls*.

*John Walker*, Halliwell's Film Guide, *HarperCollins, London*

*Cuban Rebel Girls* was a semi-documentary, filmed in Cuba by director Barry Mahon, who had worked with Errol Flynn on the never-completed *William Tell*. Flynn had some sympathy with Fidel Castro and wrote and narrated the story, appearing only infrequently in it as a reporter. It was intended to launch the career of his girlfriend, sixteen-year-old Beverly Aadland. Cheaply made and badly put together, it was a sad finale to the career of one of Hollywood's most dashing stars.

*David Small, Oadby, Leicester*

*Cuban Rebel Girls* was based on Flynn's time with Castro just before the fall of Batista. Weeks later, Hollywood's most fascinating legend died of a heart attack, aged fifty.

Errol Flynn was a much underrated actor. He was a very lonely man, searching, to the end, for his soul. He was buried in Hollywood in an unmarked grave and film director Raoul Walsh is said to have smuggled a case of whisky into his coffin. Errol would have liked that.

*Reg Otter*, Movie Memories Magazine, *Shepperton, Middlesex*

## (233) QUESTION: Can you still get passe-partout? Why was it so called?

Passe-partout was gummed paper or cloth tape used to fasten together glass, picture and backing board as an inexpensive form of picture frame, common throughout Europe from Victorian times but seldom practised today, though the tape can still be found in specialist stationers.

On the Continent, *passe-partout* refers to a picture mount, the card surrounding the artwork and spacing it from the frame.

*Collins Dictionary* says it's a seventeenth-century French word meaning 'pass everywhere'. First reference to it comes in 1645 when it meant a passport. It was used in connection with a master key and it seems to have been this idea of passing through, as vision does when looking through glass at a picture, that transferred its association to picture framing.

*Fiona Ryan, Fine Art Trade Guild, London*

Passepartout tape has been superseded by a self-adhesive tape known to stage and film crews and photographers as 'gaffer tape' and to heating engineers as 'duct tape'. Available in 25 mm and 50 mm widths, in black at photographic stores and in silver at builder's merchants, it's very strong and has a multitude of uses.

*Doug Streeter, Brighton, Sussex*

## (234) QUESTION: When were wristwatches first made popular?

Ladies' wristwatches were popular from the early Edwardian period. Some ladies adapted fob watches from 1900 onwards and I have seen wire loops added to them so they could be worn on the wrist.

It was considered effeminate for a man to wear a wristwatch before 1914. But men in the trenches in First World War found pocket watches impractical so wristwatches became acceptable. Early models had active luminous dials to be read at night in the trenches.

*Paul Hoffman, Old Coulsdon, Surrey*

Although the history of wristwatches can be traced to earlier times, they didn't become popular until the First World War when their sheer practicality made them desirable for members of the Armed Forces.

Many manufacturers produced military wristwatches, often with metal grilles to protect their faces and they were especially popular with pilots of the Royal Flying Corps and officers of all services.

As a result, wristwatches became ever more fashionable during the twenties and thirties while the use of pocket watches declined.

*Vernon Mills, Port Talbot, West Glamorgan*

From 1901, Parisians were fascinated by the exploits of a diminutive Brazilian living in their beautiful city. Alberton Santos-

Dumont made and flew a series of experimental airships, on one occasion circling the St Cloud racetrack and the Eiffel Tower and ending up in a chestnut tree in Edmond de Rothschild's garden. The baron helped rescue the aeronaut and invited him in for breakfast.

By 1906, several Frenchmen were building primitive aircraft aimed at winning the *coup d'aviation* prize for the first flight of 25 kilometres. On 19 May 1907, Santos-Dumont took off from Issy and covered nearly 24 miles of a circular course to win the prize.

The French Aero Club gave a banquet in his honour and at the meal he found himself sitting next to jeweller Louis Cartier, explaining how difficult it was to control an aircraft and fiddle with a pocket watch at the same time.

Cartier went away and designed the first wristwatch, which he presented to Santos-Dumont to help him keep track of the time while airborne.

*Terry Lunton, Standish, Lancashire*

I still have the Swiss-made wristwatch my uncle wore during the First World War, inscribed with his name and number: 'J. E. Kay, DPMH 1261'. The watch was also used by his son throughout the Second World War and inscribed 'E. B. Kay, RASG 207413'. He later became a Captain.

The watch is still working and keeps perfect time.

*Kathleen Kniveton, Lytham St Annes, Lancashire*

## (235) QUESTION: What does Kum By Yah mean? What is the history of this hymn?

This negro folk/gospel song originated in the southern states of the US as 'Come By Here, Lord'.

Exported to the West Indies, it was rephrased in pidgin English as 'Kum Bah Yah, Lord', before making its way to the British Isles, where it has become a favourite for many folksy churchgoers.

*Betty Barron, Sutton Coldfield Music Library, West Midlands*

**(236) QUESTION: What colour was the wine at The Last Supper, red, white or rosé? What would be its nearest equivalent today?**

The Gospel accounts (Matthew 26: 19–28 and Luke 22: 1–20) show the Last Supper was celebrated by Jesus and his eleven faithful apostles immediately following their annual observance of the Jewish Passover, using the remains of the Passover meal.

This would have included the flat, unleavened bread and plain red wine which Jesus used to symbolize his body and blood.

The nearest similar wine today would be an unadulterated red grape wine such as chianti, claret or burgundy.

*D. Rose, Northolt, Middlesex*

**(237) QUESTION: What became of Lieutenants Chard and Bromhead after their valiant efforts at Rorke's Drift?**

Both were awarded the VC and Chard was promoted captain and brevet major on 23 January 1879, the day Rorke's Drift was relieved.

John Rouse Merriott Chard, Royal Engineers, was almost killed in a 'friendly fire' incident that year before being present at Ulundi, the final battle of the Anglo-Zulu War. Lord Wolseley presented him with his medal at St Paul's, Zululand, in July and he returned to a hero's welcome in Plymouth and Exeter.

Summoned to Balmoral, he charmed Queen Victoria and was invited back several times. Serving in Cyprus and India as well as postings at home depots, he was promoted major in 1886 and lieutenant-colonel in January 1893, in Singapore. In January 1896 he was promoted colonel, commanding the sub-district of Perth, Scotland.

Afflicted by cancer of the tongue, he was on sick leave from August 1897. He suffered much distress and died at his younger brother Charles's rectory, St John the Baptist, in Hatch Beauchamp, near Taunton, on 1 November 1897, aged forty-nine. He never married.

Gonville Bromhead, who commanded B Company, 2nd Battalion, 24th (2nd Warwickshire) Regiment, the bulk of the Rorke's Drift defenders, was severely deaf. He received his medal from Lord Wolseley on 22 August at Utrecht, Transvaal, and was posted to Gibraltar.

On his return to England in 1880 he was feted by his home town, Lincoln, and given presents by Queen Victoria, though he missed meeting her because his invitation arrived while he was on a boating holiday.

He served in the East Indies before rejoining his regiment, now designated the 2nd Battalion, South Wales Borderers, at Secunderabad, India. Promoted major in 1883, he served in the Burmese Expedition of 1886–88 and in the East Indies again before dying of typhoid, in Allahabad, India, on 9 February 1891, aged forty-six. He never married.

*John Young, Anglo-Zulu War Research Society, Lower Sheering, Essex*

Of the other eight VC winners from Rorke's Drift, only Surgeon Reynolds AMC, who lived to be eighty-eight, Pte J. Williams (real name Fielding), seventy-five, and Pte W. Jones, seventy-two, lived long lives.

*Ron Larby, London NW10*

Many of the other British soldiers in the battle sank into obscurity. Henry Hook (played by James Booth in the film) ended up as a guard at the British Museum. Frederick Hitch (the wounded one who gave out the ammunition, played by David Kernen) was discharged from the Army for his injuries and become a London cabman. Corporal Schiess (the one with the bandaged leg in the film) was destitute and ill by 1884 and was finally given passage to England on a troopship but died on the journey and was buried at sea.

*Nicholas Scovell, Southsea, Hampshire*

**(238) QUESTION: In English, contractions such as 'can't' and 'don't' are straightforward. Why does 'won't' mean 'will not'?**

Won't is the contraction of 'wol not', an older form of 'will not'. In his preface to *Sylvie and Bruno Concluded*, Lewis Carroll insists on two apostrophes in 'ca'n't' by reasoning that the constituents 'can' and 'not' are each abridged. He extends this logic to 'sha'n't' for 'shall not' and 'wo'n't' though only for 'would not'. Both 'Won't you ...' and 'Wo'nt you join the dance ...' appear in *Alice's Adventures In Wonderland*.

*Barry Monks, Hitchin, Hertfordshire*

Contractions of common expressions generally follow the path of being easiest to say. 'Shall not' can't easily be rendered as 'shalln't' and quickly becomes 'shan't'. In speech, 'will not' shrinks to 'won't' and 'wouldn't have' becomes 'wunt've'.

*David Elias, Quiz Compiler, Nottingham*

**(239) QUESTION: Does the Secretary General of the United Nations have to be a French speaker?**

French is one of six official UN languages with Arabic, Chinese, English, Russian and Spanish. The working languages of the Secretariat are English and French.

It's not a requirement for the Secretary General to speak French but, as a permanent member of the Security Council, France can veto Security Council resolutions and insists the Secretary General be fluent in French.

The first six UN leaders, Trygve Lie (Norway) 1946–53, Dag Hammarskjold (Sweden) 1953–61, U Thant (Burma) 1961–71, Kurt Waldheim (Austria) 1972–81, Javier Perez de Cuellar (Peru) 1982–92, and Boutros Boutros Ghali (Egypt) 1992–96, were all able to speak French.

*Elizabeth Lee, UN Information Centre, London*

Kofi Annan (Ghana) 1997–2006 is a French speaker but Ban Ki-Moon (South Korea) 2007– is not and French President Jacques Chirac is said to have agreed to his presidency only on condition that he take French lessons.

*S. Andrews, London NW5*

**(240) QUESTION: Did butlers really iron their employers' newspapers as Sir Anthony Hopkins does in the film *The Remains of the Day*?**

The fifty new butlers a year who leave us to work for royalty, ambassadors, celebrities and the merely wealthy all over the world, are trained to create and maintain for their employers a perfect environment, to enable them to go about their important business free from diversion by the more mundane aspects of normal life.

Butlers trained to a professional standard still iron their employers' daily intelligences to effect a level of dryness in the printer's ink, sufficient to prevent it contaminating the hands of the person reading the journal.

Ink-stained fingers may make a fellow look dishevelled and are particularly unwelcome when meeting other people or dealing with other correspondence.

Ironing a newspaper to eliminate creases also renders it clearer to read, affording to a gentleman, in conjunction with other butlering skills, a smooth and unpressured course into the day ahead. A newspaper which has been ironed assumes the appearance of that great objective of the butler's art – perfection.

*Ivor Spencer, International School for Butler Administrators and Personal Assistants, Dulwich, London*

After a lifetime of domestic service, including twelve years before the last war in the top stately homes of England, Scotland and Southern France, I can tell you that newspapers were ironed simply because it was necessary to do so. Most papers were sent by post, directly from Fleet Street, Manchester or Glasgow, and when opened required a warm iron to flatten them. They were then folded once and held together with four stitches, two above and two below the fold.

I look back on a lifetime of such jobs and wonder why any person aspiring to be a butler would seek to learn by attending a training school for butlers. The finest school on earth is the school of experience – but its fees are exceedingly high.

*Martin Lloyd Jones, Seaton, Devon*

In 1934, when Wimpole Street houses were occupied by the gentry, my late brother Tony was employed as a footman at the home of the late great art collector Edward James, benefactor of Picasso and Salvador Dali.

His first job every morning was to iron the newspapers to be given to his master by the butler with the morning tea. The butler himself didn't iron the papers, a job which was beneath his dignity.

*Kenneth Maberley, London SW16*

In the 1950s, I was a Royal Navy steward, acting as butler to the ship's captain and had to iron his newspapers to dry the print to prevent it coming off on his fingers. Later I discovered it easier to leave the newspaper in the plate warmer.

*John Spiteri, Harrow, Middlesex*

**(241) QUESTION: Jimmy White has been World Snooker runner-up on six occasions and Plymouth Argyll were runners-up in the old League Division III South six years running. Has anyone come second more often?**

Cliff Richard has had thirteen British No 1 hits, putting him in third place behind Elvis Presley and The Beatles, who had seventeen each

219

– but he holds the UK record for the most discs which peaked at No 2: ten.

These were 'Move It', 'Voice In The Wilderness', 'Fall In Love With You', 'I'm Looking Out The Window'/'Do You Wanna Dance' (double A side), 'It'll Be Me', 'It's All In The Game', 'Don't Talk To Him', 'Wind Me Up (Let Me Go)', 'Daddy's Home' and 'The Best Of Me'.

*Tim Mickleburgh, Grimsby, Lincolnshire*

Apart from one dead heat, either Oxford or Cambridge have come second (or sunk) every time the University Boat Race is rowed.

*Derek Foxley, Manchester*

Between 1974 and 1991, Liverpool Football Club finished second in the First Division six times (1975, 1978, 1985, 1987, 1989 and 1991). But in every other season bar 1981, when they came fifth, they finished as champions. So much for 'Always the bridesmaid, never the bride'.

*Gerard Dunn, Huyton, Merseyside*

Jamaican sprinter Merlene Ottey gets my vote as most unfortunate runner-up. After 1980, Ottey ran in five World Championships and five Olympic Games, collecting eleven bronze and six silver medals. She's known to other athletes as 'Ms Bronze' because of her string of third places. She got three gold medals, too, but one of these was as a result of a disqualification of the original winner and one was as a part of a winning sprint relay team. Two of her silver medals were achieved when finishing only 1/1000th of a second behind the gold.

In 1996 she became the second fastest woman of all time over 100 metres, to go with the same achievement over 200 metres. In both she came behind Florence Griffith Joyner.

*John Reynolds, Weymouth, Dorset*

In the fifties and sixties, there was a racehorse called Parcel Post, which always finished second. I think it held the record for second place.

*J. J. Thomas, Newton Abbot, Devon*

## (242) QUESTION: When did Judaism reject polygamy?

Though polygamy is allowed in the Hebrew Bible, the ancient sages and rabbis rarely had more than one wife. In 4,761 (AD 1000), Rabbi Gershon of Mainz convened a council on the subject which issued a ban (*charem*) on Jews having more than one wife at a time. This ban operated among the Ashkenazim, Western European Jews, and was also accepted by the Sephardic Spanish and Portuguese.

Asian Jews, however, particularly those in Yemen who had no contact with European Jewry and knew nothing of the ban, can still have more than one wife. This caused a problem when many Yemeni Jews were brought to Israel. It was resolved by those with more than one wife being allowed to retain their polygamous state while those who were not already married were forbidden to have more than one wife.

*Rabbi Sidney Kay, Rabbi Emeritus, Southport New Synagogue*

Polygamy was allowed in the Hebrew Bible but wasn't sanctioned by God. He created only one wife for Adam and under His original purpose, a wife wasn't meant to share her husband with another woman.

After the rebellion in Eden, polygamy appeared in the line of Cain and was eventually adopted by some worshippers of God. Polygamy served to increase Israel's population and the position of women and their children were protected by many regulations. But God never abandoned his original standard of monogamy: Noah and his sons, to whom the command to 'be fruitful and fill the earth' was repeated, were all monogamous.

Symbolizing his relationship with Israel, God portrayed Himself as a monogamous husband and the original standard of monogamy was re-established by Jesus Christ and practised by early Christians. Overseers were to be men with not more than one wife.

King Solomon, renowned for his wisdom and for having many wives and concubines, violated God's clearly stated commandment that the king 'should also not multiply wives for himself, that his heart may not turn aside' (Deuteronomy 17:17). It was through the influence of his surfeit of foreign wives that Solomon turned to the worship of false gods and 'began to do what was bad in the eyes of God . . .' (1 Kings 11: 1–9).

*Nick Welham, Verwood, Dorset*

**(243) QUESTION: The current Duke of York has only daughters. Have the Dukedoms of York, Clarence, Gloucester and Albany always failed to maintain a male line?**

The Royal Family hasn't been very successful in maintaining the lines of its junior branches, with few titles getting as far as a fourth generation. The 4th Duke of York became Edward IV in 1461. The titles of Cumberland and Albany would have continued to this day but were forfeited in 1919 because the then holders were German princes.

Of previous Dukes of York, Edward, son of Edward III (born 1385), was the ancestor of Edward IV. Richard, son of Edward IV (1474), is thought to have been murdered as a child. Henry (1491) became Henry VIII. Charles (1604) became Charles I. James (1643) became James II. Ernest, brother of George I (1716), and Edward, brother of George III (1760), both died unmarried. Frederic (1784) died childless. The title was later held by George V (1892) and George VI (1920).

Clarence was equally unsuccessful. Lionel, son of Edward III (1362), left one daughter. Thomas, son of Henry IV (1411), was childless. George, brother of Edward IV (1471), was murdered in

1477. His son wasn't allowed to succeed and was executed, unmarried, in 1499. The title was later held by William IV (1789) and Albert Victor (1890), eldest son of Edward VII who died, unmarried, in 1892.

As for Gloucester: Thomas, son of Edward III (1385), was killed in 1397, leaving a son who didn't inherit and died in 1399. Humphrey, son of Henry IV (1414), was childless. Next was Richard III (1461). Henry, son of Charles I (1659), and William, son of Queen Anne (1689), both died young. Frederick, son of George II (1717), became Prince of Wales and, on his death in 1757, was succeeded by the future George III. His younger son William (1764) left one son, William, the 2nd Duke, who died childless in 1834.

Albany was originally a Scottish title. Among those who held it were Robert, son of Robert II, and his son Murdoch, who was executed in 1425. Alexander, son of James II, and his son John died childless in 1536. In Hanoverian times, the title was combined with the Dukedom of York, both titles traditionally going to the second son of the sovereign.

*Anthony V. Martin, Crediton, Devon*


## (244) QUESTION: Did Britain come close to war against the Northern States during the American Civil War?

On 8 November 1861, Charles Wilkes, captain of the US warship *San Jacinto*, overhauled the British mail packet *Trent* and forcibly removed two Confederate commissioners on their way to Britain to represent President Jefferson Davis. The commissioners were taken to Boston and interned.

This high-handed action provoked such indignation in Britain that Palmerston's government actually prepared for war against the North, forwarding troops to Canada and strengthening the Royal Navy in American waters.

Eventually, however, diplomacy prevailed, notably through the efforts of Lincoln's Secretary of State, William H. Seward. Captain Wilkes's action was disavowed by the US and the commissioners released early in 1862.

Britain never formally recognized the Confederacy and, despite the Trent Affair, maintained peaceful relations with the Union.

*A. Kinghorn, Edinburgh*

### (245) QUESTION: Which insect is fastest in its progress across the floor?

Large tropical cockroaches, with a recorded speed of 5.4 kph (3.36 mph) or fifty body lengths per second, are regarded as the fastest insects on land. Their performance was calibrated by Periplaneta Americana at Berkeley University, California, in 1991.

*Carole Jones*, Guinness Book of Records, *Enfield, Middlesex*

### (246) QUESTION: What is the connection between 'double carpet' and the odds of 33–1?

Many people believe 'double-carpet' for odds of 33–1 stemmed from nineteenth-century prison slang when, it's suggested, an inmate was allowed to have his own carpet after three years inside, two threes being 33 or 'double-carpet'. Another theory suggests carpets were made in prison workshops and a standard carpet took three months to produce.

A more plausible explanation, however, comes from the racing world itself. Any jockey accused of breaking the rules was called to the Jockey Club HQ to be 'carpeted' in front of a panel of three stewards. The number three became known as a 'carpet' so 'double carpet' was 33.

*Ed Nicholson, Ladbrokes, London*

**(247) QUESTION: Who were the 'green children' who came out of the ground near Bury St Edmunds?**

Two medieval chroniclers, William of Newburgh and Ralph of Coggeshall, record the story of the 'green children', a girl aged about ten and a younger boy, who mysteriously appeared near the village of Woolpit, Suffolk, in 1173.

They were described as having green skins, talking an unknown language and wearing clothing of a style and material never previously seen by locals. They were quoted as saying: 'We heard a sound like bells and then, suddenly, as if placed in some absence of mind, we found ourselves in the field where you were reaping.'

For a long time they refused to eat but eventually began to accept local food and their colour gradually changed to a more natural hue. The boy died after about a year, from depression it was said, while the girl, named Agnes Barre, was married four years later to one of Henry II's senior ambassadors.

The whole story has never emerged because Henry II annexed the village of sixty people and placed his vice-chancellor in control of it.

Robert Burton's *Anatomy of Melancholy*, published in 1651, says the children might have come from Mars or Venus.

*E. A. Freeman, Thorpe, Surrey*

William of Newburgh's Latin twelfth-century description of the children is No 3873 in the Harleian Collection in the British Museum.

Theories as to where the 'green' children originated include the idea that they were from Scandinavia. After the girl learned English, she said her home had prolonged periods when the sun never set and the children could have arrived at Ipswich, just 18 miles from Woolpit.

Another theory regards them as the original 'babes in the wood'. Their green colouring is thought to have been a result of eating arsenic, known to give a green tinge to the skin, and this could account for the death of the boy.

In recent years the story has also been turned into a series of children's books, a TV programme and a musical.

*Rod Jones, local historian, Woolpit, Suffolk*

Legend has it that one of the medieval derivations for the name of the village is its connection with wolves. The 'green children' were a feral brother and sister raised by wolves, discovered and introduced to civilization in the Middle Ages.

Raised in caves, it was said they had green-tinged skin after years spent underground. Both were said to howl at a full moon and were seen, at times, running on all fours.

*Laraine Bates, Brome, Suffolk*

## (248) QUESTION: Who won the Battle of Jutland?

By fair counting, the Imperial German Navy, with its superior optics and armour, won the 1916 Battle of Jutland, inflicting on the Royal Navy twice the losses in men and material it sustained – Britain losing fourteen ships to Germany's eleven.

The strategic outcome was that the German fleet remained sufficiently intact to require a Royal Navy presence in the area to counter it, but the Germans didn't venture into full-scale fleet battle again.

In the Second World War, the Germans named capital ships after their Jutland commanders, Hipper and Scheer, but Britain had no HMS *Jellicoe* or HMS *Beatty*.

*D. Fisher, Maidenhead, Berkshire*

## (249) QUESTION: Old stately homes and manor houses used to have ice houses. How did they make ice without refrigeration facilities?

Few estates were without a lake, the water of which froze to a good depth during the severe winters years ago. Blocks of ice were cut from the lake, loaded on carts and transported to the brick-lined ice house, built underground to keep it as cool as possible. With ice blocks stacked around the walls, the temperature held at just below freezing.

North-west Kent has several former ice houses marked on old maps, including a particularly fine one on Sundridge Park golf course, Bromley, reached by an underground passage. The huge chamber remained cold in the middle of summer, even without its icy contents.

*Fred Nixon, Sandy Cross, Heathfield, East Sussex*

The practice of storing ice in winter for summer use goes back to the ancient Greeks and Romans, and most country houses in England had ice-houses for storage. The ice-house floor sloped towards a central drain to allow water from the melted ice to pass away quickly.

Once it was discovered that the exclusion of damp was very important to the retention of the ice, ice-houses were built above ground, the outer walls being of massive brickwork and the inner ones of timber, with sawdust between the two.

Ice was imported in insulated ships from the lakes of North America in the early years of the last century; and by 1900 Britain was obtaining up to 150,000 tons of ice a year from Norway.

*Graeme Wormald, Bewdley, Worcestershire*

## (250) QUESTION: How many different combinations of coin can make £1?

Like many mathematical problems, this is best cut up into manageable chunks. First, note that the number of ways of making £1, using only 1p and 2p pieces, is 51, as the number of 2ps can be anything from 0 to 50. By similar observations we can see how many ways to make 95p, 90p, 55p and so on, out of only 1p and 2p coins.

In the table, the second column is the number of ways of making the amount in the first column out of 5p, 10p, 20p and 50p coins. The third column is the number of ways of making the remainder out of 1p and 2p coins. The fourth column is the second column multiplied by the third:

| | | | |
|---|---|---|---|
| 0p | 1 | 51 | 51 |
| 5p | 1 | 48 | 48 |
| 10p | 2 | 46 | 92 |
| 15p | 2 | 43 | 86 |
| 20p | 4 | 41 | 164 |
| 25p | 4 | 38 | 152 |
| 30p | 6 | 36 | 216 |
| 35p | 6 | 33 | 198 |
| 40p | 9 | 31 | 279 |
| 45p | 9 | 28 | 252 |
| 50p | 13 | 26 | 338 |
| 55p | 13 | 23 | 299 |
| 60p | 18 | 21 | 378 |
| 65p | 18 | 18 | 324 |
| 70p | 24 | 16 | 384 |
| 75p | 24 | 13 | 312 |
| 80p | 31 | 11 | 341 |
| 85p | 31 | 8 | 248 |
| 90p | 39 | 6 | 234 |
| 95p | 39 | 3 | 117 |
| £1 | 49 | 1 | 49 |

Totting up the fourth column and adding one because £1 can also be made with a pound coin, we get the surprisingly large answer 4,563. This was obtained without any electronic or mechanical calculating device and if you followed the working, your maths is probably better than you may have suspected at school.

*Gerard MacKay, Nesscliffe, Shropshire*

**(251) QUESTION: Has anyone kept track of the number of times an envelope has been re-used?**

During the Second World War, my brother and I regularly re-used envelopes. On receiving a letter from him I would open the envelope carefully, fold it in half and return it to him when I next wrote. The address remained the same so it required only another stamp. We used one envelope thirteen times.

*K. Burt, Eastbourne, Sussex*

As small businessmen, my partner in Lincolnshire and I in Wiltshire receive a lot of junk mail and try to re-use the envelopes. We can get about three uses from an average envelope but a few months ago a plastics company sent my partner its junk mail in a special plastic envelope. Before we eventually lost this, it had clocked up twenty-six separate postings.

*Robert J. Painting, Wingaway Ltd, Chippenham, Wiltshire*

During many years of playing chess by post, I've had several envelopes which made more than a dozen journeys. This year I've had an envelope which has travelled through the post twenty-six times.

*Owen Birch, Bexhill on Sea, Sussex*

My late friend Ian G. Tubby, of West Sussex, and I used padded envelopes to exchange our weekly chat cassette. I recorded the number of uses of our two envelopes on the back when posting it back to Ian including, on one occasion, a return posting to Australia. One envelope was used more than 100 times.

*F. H. A. Sweet, Basingstoke, Hampshire*

**(252) QUESTION: Did Mrs (now Lady) Thatcher in fact say: 'There is no such thing as society'?**

Baroness Thatcher is quoted in *Woman's Own* magazine of 31 October 1987, as having remarked: 'There is no such thing as society. There are individual men and women and there are families.'

*Miss Joan MacNamara, Redruth, Cornwall*

**(253) QUESTION: A popular country dance is called Gathering Peascods. Who or what are 'peascods'?**

Peascods are peapods. Here in Kent, I haven't heard the word used for a very long time but as a child in Hertfordshire I can remember Grandma, originally from Wales, remarking on the price of peas in the local greengrocers. My mother agreed they were expensive and Grandma added: 'Mind you, they had been codded.'

*May Hammond, Marden, Kent*

**(254) QUESTION: What's inside a Dalek?**

In the fictional universe of *Doctor Who*, the Dalek – or Mark III travel machine – was invented on the planet Skaro by crippled scientist Davros. Each Dalek contains, and is controlled by, one of the remains of a race called the Kaleds, turned into mutants during a nuclear war with their enemies the Thals. So Daleks aren't robots.

In the real world, a Dalek's innards consist of a seat, castors, controls for the eye stalk, gun and sucker arm – and an actor, usually small, who propels the Dalek with his feet.

The longest-serving Dalek operator was John Scott-Martin who played them many times from the mid-sixties. The Daleks, created by writer Terry Nation and realized by BBC staff designer Raymond Cusick, were first seen on 21 December 1963, when one of the now famous sink plungers appeared in the bottom left-hand corner of the screen to menace the Doctor's companion Barbara Wright, played by Jacqueline Hill. They were fully revealed in the following week's episode.

Often ridiculed for their inability to tackle stairs, they retaliated in their *Doctor Who* appearance in 1988 when one hovered up a flight of steps.

The word Dalek has entered the *Collins English Dictionary*, where it's defined as 'any of a set of fictional robot-like creations that are aggressive, mobile and produce rasping staccato speech'.

*Richard Hall, Bishopston, Bristol*

The name Dalek was made up by their originator, writer Terry Nation. He used to say he got it from the spine of an encyclopaedia covering DAL to LEK. The word means 'far and distant thing' in Serbo-Croat.

*Richard Hall, Bristol*

I recall with perfect clarity the horror I felt while watching *Dr Who* when a Dalek was destroyed and a wiggley, slug-like thing slithered away. It was many years ago but remains with me as the most frightening TV image I've ever seen.

*Alison Short, Braintree, Essex*

### (255) QUESTION: What happens to a homing pigeon when its owner moves house?

Racing pigeons are unreasoning creatures which respond to a love of home, loft, nest box and their mate and young in the nest. When racing, they respond most ardently to the last of these.

When moving home, a fancier's pigeons are 'broken out' to a new loft at the new address. They're first taken to the new loft to acclimatize them to a new environment. On release they instinctively return to the old loft. This is repeated for about a week, releasing the cocks and hens separately from the new address but feeding and watering them only at the new loft.

Sensible members of the flock soon accept the change and can fly out around their new loft within a few days. Slower-witted birds persist in returning to the old loft and have to be brought back for further releases from the new site.

After about seven days, the old loft is dismantled and the odd returning pigeon, finding its old home gone, should find its way to the new address. When released from race panniers on a pigeon transporter for racing, 'broken out' pigeons invariably return to their old loft site before flying on to their new loft. The fancier has to accept this delay in race times with pigeons which have moved home.

*Bill Dyer, London SE9*

I believe all the pigeons who don't find their way home again come to live at Windy Ridge Farm. This place is full of them, all ringed. They must fly over, look down and see a soft touch; plenty of food in the horses' food buckets and somewhere to roost in saddle racks and horses' backs.

If any pigeon fancier or racer has lost any pigeons they can come here and take their pick though I wouldn't be surprised if the birds simply flew back here again.

*Wendy Clinton, Windy Ridge Farm, High Peak,*
*Montgomeryshire*

**(256) QUESTION: Why is it considered 'unlucky to wive between the sickle and the scythe'.**

This expression was first noted in 1678 as 'who marries between the sickle and the scythe will never thrive'.

The most likely explanation for its use is simply that the time between the sickle and the scythe was one of the busiest periods of the year for agricultural communities. The sickle, a short-handled blade, was used to cut the grain, normally around late August, this was followed soon after by the scythe, which, being a long-handled blade, was used to cut the stem of the crop for use as winter feed.

The need to attend a celebration at this time of high workload was probably disliked by many and seen not to be a great starting point from which a new couple should begin their life together.

*Rosemary Rashid, Oxford*

This saying runs contrary to the well-known English rhyme on the best time of the year to marry:

> *Married when the year is new; he'll be loving kind and true.*
> *When February birds do mate, never wed or dread your fate.*
> *If you wed when March winds blow, joy and sorrow, both*
>     *you'll know.*
> *Marry in April when you can; joy for maiden and for man.*
> *Marry in the month of May and you'll never rue the day.*
> *Marry when June roses grow; over land and sea you'll go.*
> *Those who in July do wed, must labour for their daily bread.*
> *Whoever wed in August be, many a change is sure to see.*
> *Marry in September's shine, your living will be rich and fine.*
> *In October you do marry? Love will come but riches tarry.*
> *If you wed in bleak November, only joys will come, remember.*
> *When December's snows fall fast, marry and true love will last.*

*Mrs R. Pullen, Ely, Cambridgeshire*

**(257) QUESTION: In what way was the one episode of *The Waltons* series that was never shown deemed to be 'unsuitable for family viewing'?**

*The Waltons*, created by Earl Hamner, told the story of the Walton family of Walton's Mountain, Jefferson County, part of the Blue Ridge Mountains of Virginia, in 220 fifty-minute episodes made by

CBS between 1972 and 1981. Showing a proud family growing up in one of the poorest areas of America, with never a hint of sex or violence, it will be long remembered for its closing sequence – 'Goodnight, John-Boy', 'Goodnight, Grandpa', 'Goodnight, Mary Ellen' – often parodied at the time.

In a 1977 interview, Earl Hamner told a newspaper that one episode was censored and people have taken this to mean that a whole programme was dropped.

In fact, the episode which dealt with Mary Ellen reaching puberty originally included an implication that she may have 'gone all the way' with her boyfriend. The subject was sensitively handled by scriptwriters but US television networks thought it out of keeping with the tone of the series. The script was changed so Mary Ellen did nothing more than have her first kiss.

*May Kunge, Manchester*

### (258) QUESTION: On what basis were major A-roads classified?

Road numbering in England and Wales is based on a radiating zone principle, like a clockface centred on London. Six single-number A routes – A1, A2, A3, A4, A5 and A6 – ring the capital, making the boundaries for the zones. Zone 1 lies between A1 and A2, zone 2 between A2 and A3 so on, moving clockwise. Roads starting in each zone have numbers beginning with the figure corresponding to that zone.

In Scotland, a separate zone system divides the country not clockwise but from south to north, using the remaining single number A routes – A7, A8 and A9.

*Alison Langley, Department of Transport, London*

There are exceptions to the rule. The boundary between Zones 1 and 2 lies not at the A2 but at the Thames estuary. Strictly speaking, Kent roads north of the A2 are in Zone 1 but the A28, for example,

234

runs from Hastings on the south coast, south of the A2, to Margate on the north Kent coast, north of the A2 and retains the same number all the way.

*Dudley Turner, Westerham, Kent*

## (259) QUESTION: Why did the US have a military plan for war with Great Britain in 1940–41?

War between Britain and the US was narrowly avoided in the British Guiana (now Guyana)/Venezuela border dispute of 1905/6.

Venezuela demanded large tracts of disputed territory and Britain sent warships and threatened to invade Venezuela. The US objected, saying this would violate the Monroe Doctrine, under which the US claimed responsibility for anything that happened in the Americas. The US navy was dwarfed by the Royal Navy, so Congress threatened to send troops to invade Canada if the UK proceeded against Venezuela by force.

Invasion plans were drawn up but Britain agreed to arbitration, eventually receiving more land than she had originally claimed.

*Richard Owen, Southport, Merseyside*

During and after the First World War, Japan was an ally of Britain. The US and Canada feared Japan and obliged Britain to end this arrangement under the Washington Naval agreement of 1921.

Japan reacted with wrath. It pursued its own way, free of the West, leaving the League of Nations and moving towards a conclusion we know only too well. US military thinkers in the twenties concluded that any US war would be against either the British Empire or Japan.

It was only Germany's (then an ally of Japan) declaration of war on the US that brought America into the European war.

*Mr E. Barker, Southampton, Hampshire*

A plan was drawn up by the US for the invasion of Britain and its Empire in 1928–29, when it was believed conflict might arise over trade with US encroaching on British markets.

Washington envisaged landing troops on British soil after Canada and other parts of the Empire were severed. An expeditionary force would gain a foothold in Ireland. War plans were also drawn up for US conflict with China and Japan.

In July 1928, British Foreign Secretary Austen Chamberlain said war with Germany, Italy and Japan was 'inconceivable' but war with America was 'probable'.

Norman Longmate's 1972 book *If Britain Had Fallen* says American military planners thought a US invasion and liberation of a Nazi-occupied Britain in 1940 would have been so fraught with difficulties that no strategist could have recommended it.

*A. Martin, London SE15*


### (260) QUESTION: Why is the Queen's official birthday different from her actual birthday?

Since 1958, the Queen's 'official' birthday has generally taken place on the second Saturday in June. Before that it was normally on the second Thursday in June. She was actually born on 21 April 1926.

The idea of having two birthdays originated with Edward VII (1841–1910) who reigned from 1901 to 1910 and was born on 9 November. To ensure more clement weather for outdoor celebrations, he was given an 'official birthday' in the summer months.

The 'official birthday' is usually marked by Trooping the Colour at Horse Guards Parade and the Queen's Birthday Honours list, while the real birthday is celebrated simply, with the Union Flag flown on most public buildings throughout the kingdom.

*Ross Dalesworth, London W12*

**(261) QUESTION: I've heard of a dog which followed his master to France and tracked him down in the trenches during the First World War. Is this true?**

This story is recounted in *A Passion for Dogs*, published by Battersea Dogs Home. Irish Terrier Prince was devastated at being left behind in Hammersmith, London, when his owner, Private James Brown of the North Staffordshire Regiment, was posted to France in September 1914. Prince went missing and a few weeks later tracked down his master in the front line trenches at Armentières. This seemed so amazing that the Commanding Officer had Prince and his master parade in front of him. The accepted belief was that the dog had attached itself to some troops crossing the Channel and then used a sixth sense, combined with good sense of smell, luck, and the fact that most of the front line lay along a single line, to locate Private Brown.

As the owner of an Irish terrier, I can vouch for their devotion to their owners and concur with dog writer Albert Payson Terhune who suggests: 'There is a psychic side of the Irish Setter, found in almost no other dog . . .' Prince became the hero of the regiment and remained at his master's side for the remainder of the war.

*Samantha Turner, Wellington, Shropshire*

**(262) QUESTION: In *The Sound Of Music*, the Mother Superior tells Maria that the Von Trapp children's mother died seven years earlier. But the youngest, Gretl, is five years old. How can this be?**

As this 1965 film is the only video my four-year-old daughter Kalina wants to watch, after numerous viewings I feel I'm an expert on the subject. The conversation early in the film between Mother Abbess (Peggy Wood) and Maria (Julie Andrews), when she is being told to leave the convent to become governess to Captain Von Trapp's (Christopher Plummer) seven children, includes the information that the captain's wife 'died *several* years ago'.

When Maria meets the children, they offer their names and ages:

Liesl, 16 (Charmian Carr), Louisa, 13 (Heather Menzies), Friedrich, 14 (Nicholas Hammond), Kurt, 11 (Duane Chase), Brigitta, 10 (Angela Cartwright), Marta, 6 (Debbie Turner) and Gretl, 5 (Kym Karath).

One of the real mysteries in the film is why Maria arrives at the house with a large bag but is given material to make some new clothes because she has only one shabby outfit. Another is what kind of Navy captain Von Trapp is for landlocked Austria.

*Karen Hutton, Blackley, Manchester*

### (263) QUESTION: Why would anyone want to 'come up and see my etchings'?

This jocularly euphemistic sexual invitation is thought to have been first used in the US and has appeared in cartoons and jokes there from at least the twenties. It was probably current on the streets of New York as far back as the late nineteenth century.

Many of the world's greatest artists, including Picasso, Goya and Rembrandt have, at some time in their careers, used the etching technique though whether they actually invited ladies of their time to view them privately is not on record.

*Martina Adlington, Oxford University Press, Oxford*

This very old ploy to inveigle a young lady into one's boudoir leaves to the imagination what may happen after the etchings have been shown. Today's less artistic society uses the lame equivalent: 'Would you like to come in for a coffee?'

*N. G. Deed, Salisbury, Wiltshire*

### (264) QUESTION: Did George Formby ride in the TT races?

George Formby (real name George Hoy Booth), born in Wigan on 26 May 1904, was a keen motorcyclist whose enthusiasm for

238

two-wheeled travel was exemplified in his first major film, the Ealing comedy, *No Limit*. In this tale of a TT rider he refused to let anyone else do his stunts.

He joined Blackpool Home Guard as a despatch rider in the Second World War but his love of motorbikes didn't extend to real TT racing.

His father, Edwardian music hall entertainer George Formby Snr, sent his son away at the age of seven to train as a jockey, but after his father's death in 1921 and at his mother Eliza's insistence, George Jnr turned his attentions from the stables to the stage, to carry on his father's act.

*Simon Clare, Ladbrokes, London*

In the 1935 film *No Limit*, George played a TT competitor who wins against all odds. Travelling from Slagdyke, Lancashire, with a home-built Shuttleworth Snap bike, he beats all the pre-War TT aces on a fictional Rainbow machine. His co-star Florence Desmond urges him on over the famous Snaefell mountain course.

My father Jack was one of several local riders who did stunts for the film and enjoyed temporary stardom as one of those riding against George. It meant pay beyond comprehension for those days.

My mother and mother-in-law appeared as extras in crowd scenes. *No Limit* used to be shown on the island during every TT week and still turns up occasionally on TV.

A statue of George in racing leathers, playing his renowned ukulele, has been erected in Strand Street, Douglas.

*Geoff Cannell, Douglas, Isle of Man*

Though George Formby never rode in the TT races, he did compete in grass track and sand racing in his early years. The Rainbow bike he rode in the film *No Limit* was in fact a disguised Ariel.

George owned several bikes, from a little James two-stroke to a Vincent Twin. In July 1947, Norton motorcycle company presented him with a 490 cc International Norton (reg HVU 111) as a publicity stunt.

George was pictured astride the bike with his wife Beryl sitting sidesaddle on the back. Beryl was actually scared stiff of motorbikes and never approved of George riding them.

George had the Norton only ten months before selling it for £250. It now appears at classic bike shows and is probably worth at least £5,000.

*C. Blacklin, Hesketh Bank, Lancashire*

George made suggestions about performing the stunts in the film *No Limit* but the insurance company and director Monty Banks wouldn't allow him to do very much. George, in 1935, was virtually unknown outside the North and not in a position to insist. In the very first scene, he was replaced by a stunt rider who drove through a garden fence, and other stunts were performed by experienced TT riders.

After his great success in the North in the budget films *Boots Boots* and *Off the Dole*, the plan was to match him with Florence Desmond, a big star in the South, to launch him nationally. But there was tension between the two when Florence didn't get equal billing.

Riders and extras went on strike when Monty Banks was sarcastic to them and mean with their pay. The taxi driver, who got three guineas a day, stopped work when he heard that a donkey had been hired at £5 a day and free beer.

*Stan Evans, editor,* George Formby North West Newsletter, *Penketh, Cheshire*

My father Bert Gerrish was taken to the Isle of Man by film director Monty Banks to double for George Formby in his stunts for *No Limit*. These included riding up the front steps and out of the back door of The Ballacrane Hotel.

My father's cinema career spanned more than twenty years, performing stunts on horseback, swimming and diving, in cars and motorcycles and doubling for many thirties and forties stars including James Mason (whom he resembled) in *Odd Man Out*, but the ten days he spent on the Isle of Man were the best paid.

*Roger Gerrish, Beckenham, Kent*

**(265) QUESTION: What's the difference between an Admiral of the Blue, as Admiral Byng is described on his grave, and an Admiral of the Red?**

The word admiral, meaning chief or commander, came to English from the Arabic word for 'commander'. The British Fleet in the seventeenth century was divided into Red, White and Blue Squadrons, each with an admiral flying his distinctively coloured flag – hence the term 'flag officer'.

Typically, the Admiral of the White took the vanguard, the Red the centre and the Blue the rear. This ranking was replaced in the nineteenth century for the present four ranks, Admiral of the Fleet, Admiral, Vice-Admiral and Rear-Admiral.

Typically, the British tar adapted the seventeenth-century terms so that 'admiral of the blue' now refers to a publican (from the blue apron worn by tapsters), an 'admiral of the red' is a red-nosed drinker, an 'admiral of the white' is a coward (from the flag of surrender) and an 'admiral of the red, white and blue' is an overdressed doorman.

An 'Admiral of the Yellow' is a Royal Navy Captain who has never flown his flag at sea but was promoted on retirement to Rear-Admiral for the Yellow squadron, which has never existed.

*Tim Healey, Barnsley*

**(266) QUESTION: Does Newcastle United centre-forward Albert Stubbins hold the record for scoring the most hat-tricks in top flight football?**

The legendary Dixie Dean holds the record for the highest number

241

of hat-tricks in a career in league football. He clocked up thirty-seven playing for Tranmere Rovers and Everton between 1924 and 1938.

The highest number of hat-tricks in a season was recorded by George Camsell, who struck nine for Middlesbrough in Division II in 1926–27. The most top division hat-tricks in a season since the Second World War is six by Jimmy Greaves for Chelsea in 1960–61. Alan Shearer, who scored five for Blackburn in 1995–96 holds the record for the Premier League since it was formed.

Albert Stubbins scored twenty-eight hat-tricks in his career but these were all in games during the Second World War and are therefore regarded as unofficial.

*Ray Spiller, Association of Football Statisticians, Basildon, Essex*

**(267) QUESTION: Why was there a rotting hulk of a Lightning fighter in take-off position in a field adjacent to the southbound carriageway of the A1 just north of Newark?**

The English Electric Lightning parked next to the A1 at Newark-on-Trent, Notts, was XN 728, an F2A version. This aircraft finished its flying days in 1976, when it was retired from 92 Squadron at RAF Gutersloh in West Germany, 80 miles from the East German border.

Ferried to RAF Coningsby in Lincolnshire, it was used as a decoy until purchased by A1 Commercials at Newark for publicity purposes. In recent years, it was subjected to much vandalism and slipped off its trestle, so it was resting on its tail in dramatic nose-up angle.

The Lightning, designed by Teddy Petter and built by Preston-based English Electric – which also made the Canberra before merging into British Aerospace – was Britain's first supersonic fighter. It first flew in 1954 and entered RAF service as an interceptor in 1960. Up to 1968, 339 planes were built for the UK, Saudi Arabia and Kuwait before it was superseded by the American-built Phantom.

More than 100 Lightnings are still in existence, eight of which are in working condition but unable to fly without a CAA airworthiness certificate.

*Chris Norris, Lightning Preservation Group, Coddington,*
*Nottinghamshire*

As the person in charge of front-line servicing and operation of the Lightnings of 91 Squadron in Germany in 1969 to 1973, I certified the fitness for flight certificate of this aircraft, XN 728, on numerous occasions.

I wonder how many people who drove past it and saw it in such a sorry state beside the A1 are aware of the vitally important role this and the other Lightnings at RAF Gutersloh played in defending the West during the tense days of the Cold War. It was a sad end to a magnificent aircraft.

*John W. Swann, BEM, Keighley, Yorkshire*

**(268) QUESTION: For recycling, plastics are sorted into PETs, PVCs, HDPs and LDPs. What's the difference and how can they be re-used?**

The word 'plastic' covers many different materials with different characteristics. Most commonly used are: PET (polyethylene terephthalate), for fizzy drink bottles; HDPE (high-density polyethylene), bottles, crates, trays; PVC (polyvinyl chloride), cling film, toiletry, mineral water bottles; LDPE (low density polyethylene), squeezy bottles, supermarket bags, pallet wrap film; PP (polypropylene), carpets, car bumpers, battery cases, margarine tubs; PS (polystyrene), yoghurt pots, CD and cassette cases; EPS (expanded polystyrene), insulation, packaging.

For recycling, plastics have to be separated into their different types, identified by a code number in an arrowed triangle symbol with the acronym for the polymer below. Separated polymers are washed and ground into granules, to be melted and used to make new products. Recycled plastic isn't necessarily environmentally friendly. Plastic manufacture is comparatively non-polluting and low in energy consumption, so recycling plastic has less environmental benefits.

Lightweight plastic can save up to 40 per cent of fuel in transport, both when used as packaging and when used in cars and aeroplanes.

*Liz Elliot, British Plastics Federation, London*

Different plastics are sorted so that high quality products can be made from cleaned, flaked polymers. HDPE plastic bottles can be made into new bottles, furniture, compost bins and watering cans; PVC bottles into building products, window frames and knitwear, sweaters and scarves; and PET bottles into polyester fibre for filling anoraks and sleeping bags.

*Andrew Simmons, Recoup (Recycling of Used Plastic*
*Containers Ltd), Woodston, Peterborough*

## (269) QUESTION: Why are Tudor houses larger upstairs, overhanging the ground floor?

All vernacular houses built in the Tudor period had timber frames, with the upper storeys made to overhang so that the weight of the upper walls had a cantilever effect on the internal beams and floor joists to prevent them sagging.

This technique also had the beneficial effect of giving a larger floor area to the upper storeys.

*G. Dixon, Southwell, Nottinghamshire*

I was told in history lessons at school that this was because in Tudor times people had to pay tax on the area of ground on which they built their houses.

Poor people would build their house on as little land as possible so they did not have to pay so much, but make the upstairs bigger so they had more room in their house without paying for the extra space upstairs.

*S. Varian, Aylesford, Kent*

These were wooden-framed houses in which the top of each corner of the first storey was the meeting point of four pieces of timber all jointed at the same place.

Their mortise and tenon joints involved a tongue on one piece of wood going into a square hole in the other. By the time three mortises (holes) were made in the same place, there was no wood left to accommodate a further upright for the next storey. So one horizontal piece was allowed to protrude beyond the joint, allowing the connection to be spread along the beam. This also transferred some of the weight of the upper wall onto the cross members, a cantilever effect which made the top floor stronger.

*Peter Melton, Bexhill, Sussex*

**(270) QUESTION: We're often told the European Union has a map showing Britain divided into areas such as the European Region of Scotland, with England no longer so called, but divided into four 'European regions'. Does this really exist?**

For those of us who were Referendum Party members, or current UKIP candidates, acquiring a copy of this map is *de rigueur*. I have one, and farmer and broadcaster Robin Page tore one to shreds in front of an audience of 10,000 at an Alexandra Palace rally.

This cartographic abomination shows Scotland, Northern Ireland and Wales with no mention of England.

*Derek Bennett, former Referendum Party candidate, Walsall North*

This map breaks the European Union down into regions, though it also names each member state, including the United Kingdom, in bold letters.

The eleven named UK regions are Scotland, Northern Ireland, Wales, Northern, North-West, Yorkshire and Humberside, West Midlands, East Midlands, East Anglia, South-West and South-East. The name England is not specifically mentioned because, unlike Scotland, Wales or Northern Ireland, it is not a single region. The counties are defined within each region.

If there is anything ominous on this map for UK nationalists, it could be its failure to show national lines between France and the Channel Islands and between Spain and Gibraltar.

*Keith Wells, Dundee*

The regions used by the European Union for statistics, maps, etc., are chosen by member states. In the case of the UK, the EU uses the regional divisions chosen by the UK Government and used in the same way by Britain's Departments of the Environment, Transport, Trade, etc.

*William Sleath, European Commission, London*

## (271) QUESTION: What is the origin of the expression 'strapped for cash'?

Americans have used this expression since around 1850, implying the restriction of being 'tied down' through poverty.

*Partridge's Dictionary of Historical Slang* suggests it has rural roots in 'stripping' or 'strapping' a cow by milking it dry, while Robert Chapman's *Dictionary of American Slang* offers two theories, either tightening your belt (a leather strap) and going without or from 'strap', a dialect word for credit.

*David Elias, Nottingham*

246

**(272) QUESTION: My late father served on French submarines in the Second World War and always said: 'Never trust an Englishman' because of what happened at Mers el-Kebir. Why did the British attack the French there?**

There was nothing underhand about what the Royal Navy did at Mers el-Kebir, though in reporting it to Parliament, Winston Churchill called it 'a most hateful decision, the most unnatural and painful in which I have ever been associated'.

After the fall of France on 22 June 1940, most of Western Europe was under Hitler's control. The French Vichy government promised co-operation with Germany, a policy acknowledged by almost all French colonies. The lone dissenting voice of Brigadier-General Charles de Gaulle, who escaped to Britain and appealed to the French to continue the battle, rallied only a few hundred Frenchmen.

Britain stood alone. Vichy's armistice included a clause declaring the French navy couldn't be used by the Germans, but the British, just after Dunkirk, were sceptical.

On 3 July, fifty-nine French warships which had escaped to British ports were seized. But the main French fleet remained at Mers el-Kebir in Algeria, under the command of collaborator Admiral Jean Francois Darlan. Its presence was a serious threat to the Royal Navy in the Mediterranean. That same day, Admiral Sir James Somerville, on HMS *Hood*, presented Darlan with an ultimatum: his ships must either sail to British ports or to the Americas, or scuttle themselves within six hours.

Darlan refused and the British Navy launched Operation Catapult, opening fire on our former Allies, killing 1,300 French sailors and effectively crippling their fleet in less than five minutes.

In the sundering of a long partnership, the French broke off diplomatic relations with Britain, but the British action was seen both here and in the US as a gesture of resolution and defiance.

*Graeme Wormald, Bewdley, Worcestershire*

**(273) QUESTION: Who is Jane and why is she so interested in fighting ships?**

Fred T. Jane, born in Richmond, Surrey, in 1865, was interested in ships from an early age. He became a journalist and illustrator who covered naval exercises for *Pictorial World* and accumulated drawings and information on warships of the world. His first edition of *Jane's All the World's Fighting Ships* was published in 1898.

Jane was fiercely patriotic and very concerned about spies. He 'kidnapped' a pacifist MP as a practical joke and 'arrested' a suspicious German. People sent him information about suspected spies which he handed over to the War Office. Investigation of his tip-offs ultimately became the foundation for the counter-espionage system which developed into MI5.

In 1909, when the eyes of the world were on the naval arms race between Britain and Germany, Jane produced a register of Airships, Aeroplanes and Dirigibles, later developed into *Jane's All the World's Aircraft*. Both titles are still published.

*Claire Brunavs, Jane's Information Group, Coulsdon, Surrey*

Besides its authoritative listings, Jane's annual publication achieved fame for its visionary articles on defence matters. In 1903, Italian naval architect Cuniberti wrote of 'an ideal battleship for the British fleet', suggesting revolutionary naval design changes.

Three years later, HMS *Dreadnought* was launched, the world's first all-big-guns battleship, setting the standard for the next half century.

*Brian Hill, Kendal, Cumbria*

**(274) QUESTION: Why 'brand new'? Has it anything to do with bran?**

In Old English, a brand or bran was a piece of burning wood, from the Germanic *brandaz*. The words brandy and burn come from the same root.

Metalworkers referred to anything they had just made as 'bran-new' or 'brand-new', to signify that they had just emerged from the furnace or forge. In the same way, the hot iron applied as a distinguishing mark to the hide of an animal is a 'brand'. Hence the use of 'brand' to identify a particular maker's product.

A second word 'bran', the husk of a cereal, came into the language from the Gaulish *brenno*, like the Welsh *braen* and Irish *brean*, which simply referred to manure.

*Wilf Wiggins, Stockport*

**(275) QUESTION: Can an eye really be removed from its socket and replaced, as reportedly happened to a man who got his contact lens stuck?**

The eyeball is held in place by six muscles and orbital fat and connective tissue which act as packing. Removing the eye would mean severing these connections and cutting away the connective tissue. There's only about 7 mm of slack in the optic nerve so it would have to be cut to remove the eye from its socket, after which the patient would be blind in that eye for ever.

The young man who was unable to remove a contact lens probably had his eyelids held apart and then used to lift the contact lens out by gently pushing in against the eye and towards each other. As the eye is closed, the lens is folded up and pushed out by the pressure of the lids against the eye. It might have been easy to imagine that the eyeball was being 'eased from its socket'.

It would not have been necessary to carry out surgery to remove the lens, and patients who are concerned that they may have a soft contact lens stuck on their eye should first check their vision to make sure it's there. If their vision is blurred, the lens is either not in their eye, is in a corner or is folded under a lid.

Contact lenses cannot move behind the eye because the conjunctive tissue forms a sac which limits movement of anything to just under the lids.

*David Harris, Corneal Laser Centre, Clatterbridge Hospital,*
*Bebington, Wirral*

In 1950, I'm sure I saw a sailor with his eye hanging on his cheek after being kicked in the face. He was taken to the sick bay in Portsmouth Barracks and his eye was put back.

He returned to duty and in my recollection served another several years in the Navy. He was certainly not blind.

*G. J. Jones, Redhill, Surrey*


When my sister was born in 1920, the midwife didn't clean her eyes properly and she was blind. At the age of six weeks, she was operated on at the Kent Ophthalmic Hospital in Maidstone.

The eyeballs were laid on the cheek and scraped, then replaced in the socket, a minor miracle at the time. My sister had no eye problems until middle age when she needed spectacles for reading.

*Mrs K. Easter, Folkestone*


**(276) QUESTION: By what logic did seventeenth-century divines, like modern-day Christian fundamentalists, date the creation of the Earth to 23 October 4004 BC?**

James Ussher (1581–1656), Archbishop of Armagh and Primate of All-Ireland, used a mixture of Biblical chronology and Hebrew, Greek and Persian histories, with calendar adjustments, to calculate that the world was created in 4004 BC, naming the date and time as high noon on 23 October.

Genesis tells us that the world was created in six days, while 2 Peter 3:8 says: 'Be not ignorant of this, that one day with the Lord is as a thousand years and a thousand years as one day.' From this it was widely believed that Earth's potential duration was 6,000 years, 4,000 before the birth of Christ and 2,000 thereafter.

Historians of Ussher's time had identified the error in the BC1/AD transition through the discovery that the Herod of the Christmas account had died in 4 BC, pushing the date of the creation back to 4004 BC. The Jewish Year, based on lunar months, begins in autumn and is difficult to correlate to a solar calendar.

Ussher did the association by fixing creation for the first Sunday after the autumn equinox, 23 September. At the time, Britain and Ireland were still using the unreformed Julian calendar, in error by eleven days since Jesus's time. Allowing for this disparity, Ussher computed a total of just over thirty additional days since 4004 BC, fixing the creation at 23 October when 'in the middle of the first day, light was created'.

According to Ussher's scheme, the world should have ended on 23 October 1996, but it doesn't seem to have.

*Michael Kenny, Dublin*


## (277) QUESTION: Was Napoleon the dictator he is depicted in Britain, or was he a liberator?

Napoleon Bonaparte was an opportunist who played in turn the roles of Corsican separatist, democrat, liberator, autocrat and imperial emperor. He claimed to be heir to the French Revolution, or its terminator, depending on circumstances.

He installed his relatives on foreign satellite thrones and employed censorship, secret police, imprisonment and execution without trial. He even banned The Marseillaise for being too radical.

His policy of 'France before all' tried to stifle the nationalist aspirations of his fellow Europeans and he was confronted by embittered nations fighting for their own freedom. As Dutch historian Peter Geyb said, he was a conqueror with whom it was impossible to live.

In his youth, Napoleon disparaged Europe as 'a molehill' and his great ambition was to be conqueror of not merely Europe but of India and the East. Imperial France and the rest of Europe were to be the breeding ground for his armies.

He was an eighteenth/nineteenth-century Hitler who once told Austrian Chancellor Metternich that he cared not a fig for the lives of a million men.

*Tony Martin, Nunhead, London SE*

Napoleon was an opportunist but he had liberal tendencies at the start of his reign and, for its time, his Code Napoleon was a liberal set of laws.

From 1800 to 1807, his armies were treated as liberators in small German states who wanted to break away from the Prussians or Austrians, though they ended up swopping one master for another.

Napoleon found that the French army spread revolutionary and patriotic ideals, leading to a rise in German nationalism, which helped cause his downfall in the 1813 campaign. His middle and later years, when all decisions were in his hands, were characterized by dictatorship. But to his men he was an inspiration: Wellington considered him worth 30,000 men.

*M. J. Bowen, Crowborough, East Sussex*


## (278) QUESTION: Who, or what, was the original Green Goddess?

There have been several green goddesses in the world-wide pantheon but the wife of Amoghasiddhi, fifth Dhyani Buddha, must be a strong candidate to be the oldest. She is Green Tara, in the Lamaist tradition, incarnate in all good women. Tara means 'She who causes one to cross over the river of time and space to the uttermost shore', the female deity of the Buddhist religion.

The Green Taras are regarded as a group of twenty-one manifestations; Arya Tara, for example, is the protector against the eight evils of fire, theft, lightning, flood, earthquake, enemy, famine and untimely death. She is slender and graceful, usually shown seated, in the Ardhapayanka attitude, dressed and crowned like a Boddhitsatwas – one whose essence is enlightenment.

Her right hand is in a boon-conferring posture while her left holds a half-closed lotus or water lily with long, blue petals. Her right leg is often shown hanging down, supported by a lotus. Alternatively, she is sometimes shown standing and dancing.

*Tim Healey, Barnsley*

**(279) QUESTION: How do animals such as dogs seem to know when there's going to be an earthquake up to half an hour before anything untoward is apparent to humans in the area?**

Animals' ears are believed to function as pressure receivers, and there's much evidence to show that higher mammals use this mechanism. Under such a system, changes in sound pressure stimulate the ears only on their external surfaces.

Recent studies indicate, however, that many, if not most, other kinds of vertebrates may use a different mechanism for sound localization. In these animals, the ears seem to function as pressure gradient receivers. Binaural effects are still important but are generated by an interaction between two soundwaves, one of which travels through internal pathways within the animal and activates the ear from the inside. This mechanism is well known in insects.

*Olive Braithwaite, Stretford, Manchester*

**(280) QUESTION: How many aircraft did the RAF have at the beginning of the Second World War, and how many at the end?**

At the start of the Second World War in September 1939, the RAF had 3,555 aircraft available, 2,600 of which were front-line planes, organized into 196 squadrons. Types involved included 760 Ansons, 1,089 Blenheims, 1,014 Battles, 400 Hurricanes, 270 Spitfires and 172 Wellingtons.

As the Second World War came to an end in May 1945, the number of aircraft available to the RAF was 55,469 – of which 9,200 were front-line planes – in 504 squadrons.

Included were 3,403 Ansons, 1,784 Hurricanes, 5,864 Spitfires, 3,601 Wellingtons, 3,408 Mosquitos, 2,379 Lancasters, 1,514 Halifaxes, 1,621 Liberators, 1,420 Beaufighters, 1,255 Mustangs and 1,166 Typhoons.

*I. Anderson, Capel St Mary, Suffolk*

**(281) QUESTION: When I wear a wristwatch, it loses time. Why do certain people affect watches this way?**

Unusually high levels of static electricity in some people's bodies can create strange effects. In extreme cases it can generate its own magnetic field and interfere with electrical equipment.

Many offices have an office jinx who only has to go near a computer screen or fax machine to ensure a malfunction, particularly on high charge days – usually when the weather is overcast and close.

I knew of a woman called Jacqueline, from Cheshire, who experienced numerous problems, including malfunctioning watches. TVs changed channel as she passed by, vacuum cleaners and irons blew circuits and she was afraid of touching anything electrical for fear she would break it. Oxford scientist Dr Michael Shallis found she had ten times the normal level of body electricity.

In the end her problem cured itself by accident. She took up a new diet, including more greens and this dissipated her electrical problems.

*Jenny Randles, Fleetwood, Lancashire*

The idea that watches can gain or lose time due to static electricity in the body is a myth. Static electricity is electric current which is unable to run away. Any electricity will leak away in the presence of moisture, and the human body consists largely of moisture, so it's impossible for static electricity to be generated in the body.

A body might acquire a static charge from, for instance, nylon clothing, but unless the wearer was separated from the ground by insulating soles, it would soon leak away. And the watch, in close contact with the body, would acquire the same charge as the body, so there would be no electrostatic influence on the watch mechanism.

The human body is devoid of magnetism which might affect a watch. Application of a simple magnetic compass to any part of the body will show no deflection, nor is there any clinical evidence that it responds to nearby magnets.

*R. E. Bazin, Falmouth, Cornwall*

**(282) QUESTION: Among the credits in the film *Jude*, I noticed a 'footsteps editor'. What does he or she do?**

Many scenes in films are shot without sound and have the soundtrack added later (dubbed) in a recording studio while the film is projected on a screen.

The footsteps editor supervises the 'footsteps girls' (as they have been known since the thirties when they were always female), who add the sound of the footsteps to the film.

Footsteps artists, wearing footwear similar to that shown in the film, walk on small areas of gravel, wooden flooring, concrete, tarmac or whatever, in the studio while watching a playback of the film, to achieve the right effect.

If Dracula strides across a stone floor, runs across a wooden bridge and slips in a puddle on a muddy road, the footsteps editor must co-ordinate the addition of these sounds to the film.

A footsteps editor is often called the 'Foley editor' and his artists 'Foley artists' after the man who turned this process into a fine art. Foley editors sometimes have to dub dozens of sounds onto a film, using a combination of Foley artists and sound cassettes.

*Colin Craig, director, The Consulting Room, London*

**(283) QUESTION: Watching the film *North by Northwest*, shot partly around the sculptures of US presidents at Mount Rushmore, I wondered if a fifth sculpture was ever finished?**

Hitchcock's spy-thriller *North by Northwest* reaches a climax with Cary Grant and Eve Marie Saint escaping across the enormous carved faces on Mount Rushmore. This US National Memorial, in the Black Hills of south-western South Dakota, consists of 60-foot sculptures of the heads of four Presidents: George Washington, representing the nation's founding; Thomas Jefferson, for its philosophy; Abraham Lincoln, standing for American unity, and Theodore Roosevelt, as the symbol of expansion.

South Dakota historian Deane Robinson first suggested carving some of the local rock needles into huge representations of native American totems in 1926. Initial local hostility gave way to increasing support and, with the involvement of sculptor Gutzon Borglum, the idea evolved into carving the presidential effigies on Mount Rushmore.

More than $55,000 was raised by private donations and work started in July 1927. Borglum, with a team of four hundred workers, including his son Lincoln, spent fourteen years carving the mountainside and died in March 1941, at the age of seventy-four, with the project almost finished. His son completed it in October that year, weeks before the US joined the Second World War.

The idea of adding a fifth president has been the subject of much discussion over the years, the two most serious contenders being John Kennedy after his assassination and Ronald Reagan at the height of his powers in the late eighties, when the memorial was undergoing renovation. Neither plan was accepted and it seems there will be no fifth head in the foreseeable future.

*Bernie Holgate, Newham, Victoria, Australia*

## (284) QUESTION: How did the call 'Hear, hear!' originate?

This practice has become established over the course of three centuries, along with many other peculiarities of the Westminster Houses of Parliament.

If a speaker in Parliament was thought to be telling an untruth or was delivering an opinion thought unfavourable by others, he was subjected to a barrage of heckling, as he can be today. Others in the chamber who agreed with the speaker tried to persuade the shouters to quieten down to allow the speaker a fair hearing.

This began with shouts of 'Let him speak! Let's hear him!', developing into 'Hear him!' and eventually 'Hear, hear!' until the expression acquired its modern meaning of signifying agreement with what the speaker is saying.

*Kevin Meek, Bristol*

**(285) QUESTION: How many of the American states are bigger than the UK?**

The area of the UK (including inland water) is 244,101 sq km (94,248 sq miles). Of the fifty US states, eleven are larger: Alaska, Texas, California, Montana, New Mexico, Arizona, Nevada, Colorado, Oregon, Wyoming and Michigan. Alaska, at 1,700,130 sq km (656,424 sq miles) is more than seven times the size of the UK.

England alone is slightly smaller than Louisiana, the twenty-ninth largest state, Scotland is smaller than South Carolina, the fortieth largest, and Wales is smaller than New Jersey, the forty-seventh largest.

The smallest state, Rhode Island, has an area of 4,002 sq km (1,545 sq miles), less than half the size of North Yorkshire.

*Russell Ash, author:* The Top Ten of Everything,
*Dorling Kindersley Publishers, London*

Union with America is far more sensible than union with a Europe which has caused us so much grief over the centuries. The four home countries of Britain would make a very fine 'superstate' of an enlarged US. England would be by far the richest state in the union, outstripping America's jewel, California, whose population of twenty-nine million would come second to England's forty-nine million.

With Scotland's population lying sixteenth, Wales thirtieth and Northern Ireland thirty-seventh, the other home countries would

257

make a significant contribution to this fantasy world. Even in terms of area, tiny Northern Ireland would be bigger than Connecticut, Delaware and Rhode Island.

In terms of political influence, every state, regardless of size, sends two senators to Washington and a number of Congress members depending on their population. The four British states would control almost 10 per cent of the Senate and 20 per cent of Congress, making our one-vote-in-25 influence in the EU look pretty feeble. We could probably expect a Briton in the White House within twenty years of any 'Act of Union' (now wouldn't that please George III?).

Additionally, were the Republic of Ireland to become the fifty-fifth state of this fantasy union, any remaining Northern Ireland problem would disappear overnight.

*Vincent Fallon, Bury St Edmunds, Suffolk*


## (286) QUESTION: How did the term 'Bohemian' come to apply to an arty person with an other-than-normal lifestyle?

Application of the term 'Bohemian' to people who led the kind of romantically vagabond lifestyle favoured by artists, musicians, writers, actors, philosophers, etc., had nothing to do with the district of Bohemia (now in the Czech Republic), but came about because their manner of living was compared to that of the gipsy.

The term was first used in France where one word for gipsy is *Bohemien*, stemming from the belief that that area of central Europe was the gipsies' traditional home.

The word was introduced to Britain by William Thackeray's 1848 *Vanity Fair*, in which he writes of Becky Sharp: 'She was of a wild, roving nature, inherited from her father and mother, who were both Bohemians in taste and circumstance.'

*Patricia Llewelyn, Cardiff*

**(287) QUESTION: Has anyone still got a *Crackerjack* pencil?**

I can't remember the exact date of my debut but I still have the pencil given to me and my losing team mates from Plaistow Grammar School, East London, by the late Eamonn Andrews. Guest stars on the show, apart from the regular team, were Pearl Carr and Teddy Johnson, fresh from winning the Eurovision Song Contest with 'Sing, Little Birdy, Sing'.

I accompanied an old friend who won that bout to the next show when the Batchelors were starring. She no doubt still has her *Crackerjack* pen.

*Mrs Carole Lewis (née Hunt), Chigwell, Essex*

My daughter Wendy – now Mrs Wendy Richardson – faced up to the questions and held the fake groceries on a 1961 *Crackerjack* programme with Eamonn Andrews. A photograph of her and two school friends appeared in the *Radio Times* for September 1962, advertising the new *Crackerjack* series. And, yes, she still has her *Crackerjack* propelling pencil.

*Mrs J. P. Place, Hillingdon, Middlesex*

**(288) QUESTION: Were I to go out 'dressed in my best bib and tucker' what would I be wearing?**

Bib and tucker were originally women's protective clothing – a piece of cloth worn on the front of the body from neck to waist with a 'tucker' of laced frill or muslin, covering the neck and shoulders.

The saying 'best bib and tucker' began in the seventeenth century as a jocular expression and has evolved into its present meaning of wearing one's best clothes.

*Lewis Blades-Campbell, Bearsden, Glasgow*

**(289) QUESTION: In Strasbourg, my daughter noticed a street called 22 Novembre Strasse. As this is her birthday and the date of the assassination of J. F. Kennedy, she wondered what is its significance to that town?**

The strategically located city of Strasbourg, close to the Franco-German border on the River Ill, in the Bas-Rhin department of France, is the capital of Alsace and meeting place of the Council of Europe. Its population, now 450,000, has been under either German or French rule over the centuries.

Originally a Celtic village fortified by the Romans, it was part of the Frankish Empire and a free city of the Holy Roman Empire before being seized by Louis XIV of France in 1681.

In 1870, it was surrendered to Germany after the Franco-Prussian War. Alsace-Lorraine, including Strasbourg, was German-controlled until the end of the First World War when French troops led by General Gouraud returned the city to France on 22 November after a forty-nine-year absence.

The Germans re-occupied Strasbourg in 1940 during the Second World War, but on 23 November 1944, General Leclerc's troops liberated it once again for France.

*Fabiane Meyer, Strasbourg City Council*

**(290) QUESTION: What is the Parliamentary Assembly of the Council of Europe which elects judges to the European Court of Human Rights? How does it differ from the European Parliament and its European Court?**

Founded in 1949, the Council of Europe is entirely separate from the European Union. Based in Strasbourg, it aims for greater unity between its forty-seven members, facilitating their progress, and promoting pluralist democracy, human rights and fundamental freedoms.

Its members are: Albania, Andorra, Armenia, Austria, Azerbaijan, Belgium, Bosnia & Herzegovina, Bulgaria, Croatia, Cyprus, the Czech Republic, Denmark, Estonia, Finland, France, Georgia, Germany, Greece, Hungary, Iceland, Ireland, Italy, Latvia, Liechtenstein, Lithuania, Luxembourg, Macedonia FYR, Malta, Moldova, Monaco, Montenegro, the Netherlands, Norway, Poland, Portugal, Romania, Russia, San Marino, Serbia, Slovakia, Slovenia, Spain, Sweden, Switzerland, Turkey, the UK and Ukraine.

The Committee of Ministers, made up of the foreign ministers of member states, meets twice a year. They produce European Conventions, international agreements which go to national governments as recommendations. Their deputies, permanent representatives, meet once a month and can take decisions on their behalf.

The Parliamentary Assembly has 321 members, elected or chosen by the national parliaments. It holds four week-long sessions a year and has thirteen permanent committees.

One of the Council of Europe's main achievements is the 1950 European Convention on Human Rights, which established the European Commission and European Court of Human Rights, merged into one unit in 1993. This court should not be confused with the Court of Justice of the European Communities, also known as the European Court, which is the principal court of the EU.

This court interprets and applies EU treaties, decides on the legality of decisions of the EU Council of Ministers or Commission and determines treaty violations. Its decisions are binding on member nations.

*Hilary Marsden, editor*, Whitaker's Almanack, *London*

---

**(291) QUESTION: What were the top ten selling cars in Britain in 1957 before the upsurge in car ownership?**

It's frustrating that no figures were compiled by motor magazines of the time and records from the Society of Motor Manufacturers and Traders don't go back that far. The only information that can be sourced is for exports.

Based on this, the best-selling makes of the time, were: 1 Ford. 2 Rover. 3 Morris. 4 Austin. 5 Vauxhall. 6 Standard. 7 Hillman. 8 Humber. 9 Wolseley. 10 MG. The models aren't listed.

*Saul Billingsley, RAC Motoring Services, London*

**(292) QUESTION: We're told the Bible is not in chronological order. If not, why not, and what is the chronological order?**

The sixty-six books consist of the thirty-nine books of Hebrew scripture, divided into the historical books, Genesis to Esther, the poetic books, Job to the Song of Solomon, and the prophetic books, Isaiah to Malachi.

The twenty-seven books of Christian Greek scripture may be divided into the historical books, Matthew to Acts, the Letters, Romans to 3 John, and the Revelation.

These groupings aid the location of texts rather as supermarket signs indicate the location of groups of goods.

The correct chronological order for the Hebrew books is: Genesis (1513 BC), Exodus (1512), Leviticus (1512), Job (c. 1473), Numbers (1473), Deuteronomy (1473), Joshua (1450), Song of Solomon (c. 1020), Ecclesiastes (c. 1000), Jonah (c. 844), Joel (c. 820), Amos (c. 804), Hosea (c. 745), Isaiah (c. 732), Micah (c. 717), Proverbs (c. 717), Zephaniah (c. 648), Nahum (c. 632), Habakkuk (c. 628), Lamentations (607), Obadiah (c. 607), Ezekiel (c. 591), 1 Kings, 2 Kings and Jeremiah (all 580), Daniel (c. 536), Haggai (520), Zechariah (518), Esther (c. 475), 1 Chronicles, 2 Chronicles, Ezra and Psalms (all c. 460), Nehemiah and finally Malachi (both c. 443).

The order for the Christian Greek Scriptures is: Matthew (AD 41), 1 Thessalonians (c. 50), 2 Thessalonians (c. 51), Galatians (c. 50–52), 1 Corinthians and 2 Corinthians (both c. 55), Romans (c. 56), Luke (c. 56–58), Ephesians, Phillipians, Colossians and Philemon (all c. 60–61), Hebrews (c. 61), James (c. 62), Mark (c. 60–65), 1 Timothy and Titus (both c. 61–64), 1 Peter (c. 62–64),

2 Peter (c. 64), 2 Timothy (c. 65), Jude (c. 65), Revelation (c. 96) and finally John, 1 John, 2 John and 3 John (all c. 98).

*J. S. Elcock, Nottingham*

**(293) QUESTION: What is Meat Loaf's real name?**

The boy born to Mr and Mrs Aday, on 27 September 1948, in Dallas, Texas, was christened Marvin Lee but his famous nickname was given to him by a high school football coach who blurted it out after well-built Marvin accidentally stood on his toe.

Moving to Los Angeles in 1966, Meat Loaf set up a band called Meat Loaf Soul, who later became Popcorn Blizzard and at one point opened concerts for The Who.

When this band split up in 1969, Meat Loaf successfully auditioned for the part of Ulysses S. Grant in the stage musical *Hair*. In 1974, he was invited to star in a production of Jim Steinman's musical *More Than You Deserve* and in 1975 he starred as Eddie in Richard O'Brien's original Broadway blockbuster *The Rocky Horror Show* (a role he re-created for the film version *The Rocky Horror Picture Show*).

Meat Loaf resumed his partnership with Steinman in 1977 and together they created the *Bat Out Of Hell* album, which has hardly been out of the charts ever since.

*Richard Lake, Caldicot, Gwent*

**(294) QUESTION: The nearest metric equivalent to our 8 yds × 8 ft soccer goalmouth is 6½ × 2½ metres, but this isn't quite the same. Are goals a different size on the continent or do they use our Imperial measure?**

The original laws of association football, agreed by the Football Association after a series of meetings in 1863, had measurements identified in yards, as one would expect. Law 1 stated: 'The goals shall be defined by two upright posts eight yards apart.'

Measurements included in the laws are still in yards, feet and inches to this day but, in recognition of the fact that football has become a world game, the international FA Board, the only body empowered to establish or amend football laws, approved a table of metric equivalents. Thus 8 yards equates officially to 7.31 metres and 8ft to 2.44 metres. These dimensions have to be strictly adhered to.

*David Barber, The Football Association, London*

## (295) QUESTION: What is the least fattening, and which is the most nutritious: beer, lager, wine or cider?

Comparing energy and nutritional values by serving rather than per millilitre, we can regard a serving of beer, lager or cider as half a pint (287 ml) and a serving of wine as a 125 ml glass.

Most beers and lagers have similar compositions in terms of energy and nutrients, and a single serving of beer, lager, dry white or red wine contains a similar amount of energy, about 85 kcals. Most ciders contain marginally more energy and vintage cider tops the drinks list for energy content.

All these drinks contain small amounts of B vitamins and minerals such as iron and zinc. Cider and wine are better sources of iron, while beer and lager have more B vitamins. However, quantities are low compared to recommended daily values of the nutrients concerned. Seven pints of beer a day would be needed to provide the recommended daily intake of niacin, for example.

Due to the harmful effects of too much alcohol, the Government recommends that weekly intakes should be twenty-eight units for men and twenty-one units for women, with one unit being equivalent to half a pint of beer, lager or cider or one glass of wine. Therefore these drinks should not be viewed as sources of nutrients, but enjoyed in moderation, bearing in mind that the most likely effect on nutritional status will be an increase in the waistline.

*Jane Earland, Centre for Human Nutrition, Sheffield University*

We can't comment about cider and wine, but the alcohol content of UK beers is generally modest compared with most other alcoholic beverages. It is thus a long thirst-quenching drink.

Beer contains significantly less sugar than most soft drinks. The energy content of a pint of standard strength beer is about 300 kcal and the fat content is virtually zero. Beer is a good source of minerals, especially magnesium and potassium. 'A' beers contain the B group of vitamins in varying amounts.

*Brian Finnerty, Brewers and Licensed Retailers Association,*
*London*

## (296) QUESTION: Has a nightingale ever actually sung in Berkeley Square?

In 1703, when the Duke of Buckingham leased the site of the palace that now bears his name, he found it 'a little wilderness of blackbirds and nightingales'. Nightingales were said to be not uncommon between the Hyde Park and Kensington gravel pits in 1830 and in 1860 they could be found in Stamford Hill, Stoke Newington and Victoria Park.

The most recent record for inner London seems to be one that was seen and heard in full song in Kensington Gardens by Holte MacPherson on 25 April 1936. Considering these records, I have no doubt that nightingales have sung in what became Berkeley Square.

*Sid Watts, Market Harborough*

In 1964, I worked for Pearl and Dean Advertising in Dover Street. One Friday, someone came running in saying she'd heard a nightingale singing in the Square. Never having heard one, I rushed out to the square.

There were about twenty people around the entrance opposite the Rolls-Royce showrooms, all very quiet with their ears straining towards a holly bush. Just then I heard this lovely twittering above the roar of the traffic, which I assume was the nightingale.

I rushed back to work hoping my absence wouldn't be discovered but I was too late. My supervisor called me into his office and I was given the sack there and then.

On the following Monday I was forgiven and reinstated.

*Victor Nunes, London, SW16*

On my last venture into London, I made a point of walking through Berkeley Square, singing to my wife about those streets paved with stars and all that romantic stuff. So there you have it, a Nightingale singing in Berkeley Square.

*David Nightingale, Rochdale, Lancashire*

It's not generally appreciated that composer Eric Maschwitz took the title of his song from a short story by Michael Arlen, published by Collins in the early twenties.

Arlen was the pen name of Armenian writer Dikvan Kouyoumdjian who was educated at an English public school and wrote many stories, most famously 'The Green Hat', about between-wars Mayfair society.

His short story 'When the Nightingale Sang in Berkeley Square' concludes: 'That was the night the nightingale sang in Berkeley Square. A nightingale had never sung in Berkeley Square before and may never sing there again but if it does it will probably mean something.'

*Ralph Glenister, Ingatestone, Essex*

**(297) QUESTION: What is the origin of the intransitive use of the verb 'to enjoy', as used by waiters and shop assistants these days?**

The exclamation 'Enjoy!', originally inviting people to enjoy food and later other commodities, is a Yiddish construction which came to Britain from America. There, the Yiddish 'enjoy' is commonly

266

used as an intransitive verb, often duplicated as, 'Enjoy, enjoy!' Author Harry Cohen published a book with this title in 1960.

The phrase came to the attention of advertisers, who used it in various slogans, heightening its popularity and giving it the common use it has today. Enjoy!

*Yvonne Singh,* Writers' Monthly, *London N8*

### (298) QUESTION: How did the word 'taxi' become accepted all over the world for a hired car and driver?

A device to measure time and distance baffled many people, from the ancient Chinese to British, French and German inventors of the late nineteenth century. The credit finally went to Herr Bruhn of Magdeburg in Germany. In about 1890, he named his device a taxameter, *taxa* from the Latin meaning price and 'meter' from the Greek *metron* meaning measure – a measured price.

In 1910, the Bruhn Taxameter Company was operating from Gray's Inn Road, London. At the outbreak of the First World War in 1914, the company changed its name to the British Taximeter Co because of the German sounding name.

Later on, the word taxi became the name – now recognized worldwide – for a taxicab. This didn't happen overnight; as late as 1927 the Metropolitan Fare Registering Co, of Kennington Road, London, SE11, was advertising taxameters for hire.

*Phillip Warren, author,* The History of the London Cab Trade, *Taxi Trade Promotions, London SE11*

### (299) QUESTION: From what is Campari made?

Wrongly regarded by some as a vermouth, Campari is a wine derivative with a mixture of bitter medicinal herbs, made, like all good drinks, to a secret, closely guarded formula.

At the age of fourteen, country boy Gaspare Campari moved to Turin and took an apprenticeship with a liqueur distiller. Having mastered his craft, Gaspare set up business in Novarro before moving to Milan and refining his recipe for what he called 'bitters in the Dutch style' in 1842.

Campari Bitters took his fame around the world under the aegis of his energetic son Davide. As was usual then, the firm made a range of liqueurs, including Campari Cordial, for which the medicinal claims, essential for sales in the late nineteenth century, were comprehensive.

No surviving member of the Campari family is involved in the present-day business, which makes the drink at a Milanese production plant.

Campari is usually taken with ice, a round of orange (not lemon) and some water. I find it even better as an Americano (with sweet vermouth and club soda).

*John Doxat, Camberley, Surrey*

Campari isn't a wine derivative but is made by macerating sixty-eight natural herbs, spices, peels and barks in pure grain spirit.

Gaspare Campari didn't perfect his drink until 1862, when his negotiations with Milanese city planners, who wanted to compulsorily purchase his little bar to build the famous Galleria di Vittorio Emmanuele, concluded with him owning the most prestigious bar in Milan, right opposite the Duomo.

Campari is still made to Gaspare's carefully guarded secret recipe.

*Martin Watts, Campari International, Windsor, Berkshire*

When on holiday in Lanzarote some years ago, we were taken on a trip around the island, passing fields of cactus plants. We were told they were the breeding ground for the cochineal beetle. The beetle crop is harvested once a year and sold to Campari where the rich red colour from the beetle is added to the ingredients.

*G. Morris, Clyst St Mary, Devon*

**(300) QUESTION: When were gloves, masks and gowns first used in surgery?**

Taking information sourced from *The Surgeon's Glove* by J. Randers-Pehrson (1960) and *Medical Discoveries: Who and When* by J. E. Schmidt (1959), it's evident that the first surgeons and doctors tended to use gloves made of animal intestines.

Modern surgical gloves, made of rubber, were developed in 1878, though many surgeons didn't believe they were effective and continued using cotton or silk gloves even after the start of the twentieth century.

French surgeon Paul Berger is credited with the first use of the gauze mask in surgery, introducing it in October 1897. Gowns of one sort or another have always been used, usually made of cloth and nearly always left unwashed between operations.

*Wellcome Institute Library, London NW1*

My grandfather was credited with the first use of the rubber glove when he was at the Royal Free Hospital in the 1920s. There are industrial chemists on both sides of my family and my great, great-uncle on my father's side was associated with the development of the sanitary towel. My grandfather on my mother's side was one of the first women doctors.

*Jonathan Howarth, Blaenau Ffestiniog, Gwynedd*

**(301) QUESTION: An old German farmer I knew said it was impossible to find a black cow with completely white ears. Is this true?**

Genetically speaking, there's no known reason why a black cow with white ears couldn't be produced. No pedigree breed of cattle in the world is black with white ears though an occasional Hereford, crossed with a black breed, may be black and white with a white face and ears.

The Rare Breeds Survival Trust looks after more than fifty breeds of British farm livestock including two rare cattle breeds, the horned White Park and Vaynol which are white with black ears. This colour pattern is ancient and references to it occur in pre-Christian Irish and Celtic tales. The hornless British White breed has a similar colour pattern but numbers have been increased to a point where it is no longer considered rare.

*Richard Lutwyche, Rare Breeds Survival Trust,*
*National Agricultural Centre, Kenilworth, Warwickshire*

**(302) QUESTION: Was Thomas Hardy's heart really stolen by a cat? A gravestone in the churchyard at Stinsford, Dorset, where he used to preach, says his heart is buried there. What became of the rest of dear old Thomas?**

I was present at Thomas Hardy's funeral as a chorister and, as this was one of the first important services in which I took part, I have retained a great interest in the man and his works.

One of our most respected novelists, Thomas Hardy was born in Upper Bockhampton, Dorset, on 2 June 1840, the son of a master builder. After training as an architect he decided his real talent, and love, was writing. He wrote fifteen novels, including the highly acclaimed *Tess of the D'Urbervilles* and *The Mayor of Caster-bridge*, four collections of short stories, eight collections of poems and a three-part epic drama.

Hardy died on 11 January 1928. The funeral service was held on Monday, 16 January 1928, in Westminster Abbey, when his ashes were committed in a grave in Poets' Corner.

In 1978, the fiftieth anniversary of Hardy's death, I invited as my guest to our annual Old Choristers Dinner an old surgeon called Neville Taylor. When he came to the Abbey with me he asked me to show him where the remains of Hardy were laid. This I did and, as we looked at the tablet inscribed 'Thomas Hardy, died 1928' he revealed a bizarre but, he claimed, true story.

When Hardy died, it was decided that he should be buried in Westminster Abbey but the locals in Dorset wanted him to be buried in a chapel at the local Stinsford Church. It was ultimately resolved that his heart should be buried in the churchyard while his body should be cremated and the ashes buried in Poets' Corner.

A practising surgeon from Devon was commissioned to extract his heart and his assistant at the time was a young Dr Taylor, the brother of my informant. Apparently, the extraction of the heart was done in a parlour next to the kitchen and, when it was completed, the heart was placed in a receptacle by the sink.

The surgeon and his assistant were invited to have a sherry with the second Mrs Hardy in the lounge, but when they returned to the kitchen they found a very large cat chewing the heart. The young Dr Taylor rushed at it but the cat escaped out of the window and ran into the garden with the remains in its teeth. The senior doctor said to the young Dr Taylor: 'The only way we can get out of this is for you to go to a nearby village and get a sheep's heart.'

So it was that lamb's heart that was buried in a casket by the vicar, H. C. B. Cowley. The cat was ultimately buried with Mrs Hardy and so eventually Hardy's heart found its true resting place.

*Ben Gunby, Ilford, Essex*


## (303) QUESTION: What are the names for the phases of the Moon between Harvest and Hunter's Moon?

Harvest Moon, the nearest full moon to the Autumn Equinox (21 September), is so-called because farmers used its extra light to complete their harvesting by working through the night. The next full moon is Hunter's Moon, four weeks later, and there are no full Moons between these.

*Maria Blyzinsky, Curator of Astronomy,*
*Old Royal Observatory, Greenwich*

Native Indians of what today is the northern and eastern US kept track of the seasons by giving distinctive names to each recurring moon every four weeks.

There are some variations to the names but the list, beginning with the moon closest to the Autumnal Equinox, the Harvest Moon, is Hunter's Moon, Beaver Moon, Cold Moon, Wolf Moon, Snow Moon, Worm Moon, Pink Moon, Flower Moon, Strawberry Moon, Buck Moon, Sturgeon Moon and Corn Moon.

*David Leyton, Birmingham*

### (304) QUESTION: How long would a gallon of petrol last if an average car sat in a traffic jam?

Left idling, an average 1.4 litre engine with a gallon of standard unleaded (95RON) fuel in the tank, would run for about six hours. The exact time is subject to many variables, such as the condition of the engine and the amount of electric equipment – lights, radio, window controls, cooling fan, even power steering, which still needs a pump running – being used.

If you are stuck in a traffic jam for anything like this time, the most sensible thing to do is switch off the engine until you are able to move, saving both fuel for yourself and the environment for others.

*Kevin Jones, Rover Cars, Warwick*

### (305) QUESTION: How far up Mount Everest could an average person, with no climbing experience, be reasonably expected to reach?

Reaching Everest base camp (south side) at 5,500 m is an arduous but straightforward trek which any reasonably fit, well-acclimatized individual could manage. Beyond there, specialist equipment such as crampons and ice axes, and the knowledge of how to use them, is required.

In recent years, several companies have begun operating commercial expeditions to Everest, using highly experienced guides so individuals with limited experience can be led up terrain which would otherwise be beyond them.

At the highest altitudes, conditions can be extreme and an individual is very much on their own, regardless of whether an expedition is guided or not. The more experience taken to the mountain, the better able a person is to be self-reliant when the unexpected happens.

*Andy Macnae, British Mountaineering Council, Manchester*

## (306) QUESTION: A resident of Aberdeen is an Aberdonian and someone from Glasgow is a Glaswegian but what do Edinburgh people call themselves?

Scotland's capital is popularly believed to be named after the seventh-century Northumbrian king Edwin, overlord of all England except Kent. He is reputed to have built the original fort on the site of the present Edinburgh Castle. But the place names Eidyn and Din Eidyn were recorded from about AD 600, before Edwin's time.

The Scottish Presbyterians who founded Dunedin in New Zealand in 1848 took the name from Din Eidyn, their native Edinburgh. The 'burgh' of the name is the Old English *burg* – fort.

I've heard at least one reference to a person from Edinburgh as a 'Dunedin' but the most popular name is simply 'Edinburgher'.

*Adrian Room, author:* Dictionary of Placenames
in the British Isles, *Bloomsbury, London*

## (307) QUESTION: Who was this Captain Marvel, to whom Alan Shearer, Gary Lineker, David Platt and Bryan Robson have been likened?

Captain Marvel was the alter ego of schoolboy Billy Batson, who could change himself into a superhero of great power by saying the magic word 'Shazam!' – formed from the initials of various classical heroes and Gods: Solomon, Hercules, Atlas, Zeus, Achilles and Mercury.

Created by artist C. C. Beck and writer Bill Parker, he made his first appearance in February 1940, in Fawcett Publications *Whiz Comic 2*. Originally called Captain Thunder, his name was changed to Marvel just before publication. He has no connection with the equally famous *Marvel* comic.

C. C. Beck is said to have based Captain Marvel's face on then-popular actor Fred MacMurray.

Author Bill Parker was soon replaced by Otto Oscar Binder who developed a complex universe for the Captain, including Captain Marvel Jr, Mary Marvel, three Lieutenants Marvel and Hoppy the Marvel Bunny.

Captain Marvel then appeared in the comic *Power of Shazam!* published by DC Comics. His character was modernized to fit current thinking but remained much the same, a truly heroic, larger-than-life figure. The earliest Marvel stories were reprinted by DC Comics in hardback archive editions.

*Richard Davies, GOSH! Comics, Great Russell St, London*

**(308) QUESTION: What was the origin of the 'Roll Me Over In The Clover' marching song known throughout the British Army during the Second World War?**

The words and music to this song were written by Desmond O'Connor (no relation to Des O'Connor) in 1944. The song was first recorded by Billy Cotton.

*Betty Barron, Sutton Coldfield Music Library, West Midlands*

'Roll Me Over' as a popular song of British armed forces has been traced back at least 100 years. My father knew it in the First World War and I sang it on Officer Training Corps marches in the thirties, as well as during my Army service in the Second World War. It can still be heard at old comrades' reunions.

The internal rhymes in the one-line verses, of which there are usually twelve, vary according to the company present. The traditional lyrics are supposed to be sung by a female, so the verse is often sung in falsetto.

When the Canadians arrived in the UK in 1940 they brought their own version in which the words 'in the clover' were replaced by 'Canuck soldier'.

*Eric Thomas, Purley, Surrey*


## (309) QUESTION: How are things like coffee, tea and now herbs 'freeze dried'?

Freeze drying is a way of drying food whereby the water is evaporated straight from the frozen material without the ice melting and going through a liquid phase. It goes straight to steam or water vapour under high vacuum and is ducted away to be condensed off.

This has advantages over other methods, notably in retention of structure and flavour. It also makes subsequent reconstitution of the food with water quicker.

In the case of tea and coffee, there is another advantage in that as the liquid infusion is frozen in blocks and dried, the blocks can be broken up to produce granules of freeze-dried product which are attractive and easily dispersed when water is added to make a cup of tea or coffee. For herbs, the advantages lie mainly in flavour retention and in minimizing colour and flavour changes which may occur in conventional slow and/or hot drying.

*Keith Anderson, Institute of Food Science & Technology,*
*London*

**(310) QUESTION: As a child in the thirties, I recall Conservative candidates wearing red and white rosettes while Labour wore green and white. When did this change?**

Our political parties have used uniform colours only recently, since the advent of nationwide mass campaigning in the fifties and sixties. Before then, it was up to individual party organizations to decide which colour rosette their candidates should sport.

One constituency in Wales was notable for having a Labour candidate wearing blue while the Conservatives appeared with red rosettes and an apparent colour reversal of this kind is mentioned in Arnold Bennett's novel *Clayhanger*.

Even in recent years, the Labour Party's colour in north-east England has remained green, apparently in deference to the Duke of Newcastle's racing colour being red, which didn't go down well with the Durham miners.

*Stephen Bird, archivist, National Museum of Labour History, Manchester*

The use of colours to symbolize party allegiance has been in existence for two hundred years and was originally based on the racing colours of the local dignitaries supporting the particular candidates. National standardization of party colours became general in the late sixties with the arrival of colour TV.

The first election in which Conservative candidates wore almost uniformly blue rosettes was the 1970 poll, though even then some Tories in the north of the England still wore red, some in Cumbria favoured yellow and, in parts of East Anglia, some used pink and blue. The Labour Party still makes some use of green.

*Emma Winsor-Cundell, Conservative Central Office, London*

When I was Conservative agent for the constituencies of Norwich North and South in the early fifties, the party's colours were orange and purple. This posed a slight problem at elections, when allowance had to be made for the cost of an extra print run for a second colour.

*Roddy Braybrooke, Torquay, Devon*

**(311) QUESTION: Did actors Colin Firth and Martin Clunes once appear together in a children's TV programme?**

Firth and Clunes have never appeared in the same programme. Clunes's early roles were in *Doctor Who* and *All at Number 20*, while Firth appeared in *Crown Court*.

The idea that they were in the same programme probably stems from Firth's role in the 1985 LWT film *Dutch Girls*, which told the story of a boys' sixth-form boarding school hockey team on tour in the Netherlands, with a love affair between star player Truelove, played by Firth, and local Dutch beauty Romelia, played by Gusta Gerritsen.

Another character, Cone, was played by Robert Addie, who could easily be mistaken for a younger version of Martin Clunes.

*John Thurston, Stockholm, Sweden*

**(312) QUESTION: Has Patrick Moore ever seen a UFO?**

When Moore came to talk here at the University a few months ago, I asked him whether he believed in UFOs. He said he felt quite strongly that they didn't exist, and all such occurrences were explainable by other causes.

*Mike Veveris, School of Engineering, Derby University*

Of course I haven't. I've been star-gazing since the age of six, I'm now eighty-seven and in all that time I've not seen one UFO. Astronomers don't generally see UFOs. We leave that sort of thing to housewives and policemen.

*Patrick Moore, Selsey, Sussex*

**(313) QUESTION: Living on the South Coast, I can receive French radio. So why can't I get French TV broadcasts?**

British TV, like most of Europe, broadcasts in Phase Alternation Line (PAL I) but French TV, like the former USSR, broadcasts in *Sequentiel Couleur à Memoire* (SECAM L), which can't be picked up by normal British TV sets.

Many modern TV sets, however, are now multi-standard and capable of receiving both types of broadcast. I have a TV aerial aimed towards France and enjoy excellent reception.

*Malcolm Nobbs, Folkestone, Kent*

French radio is available on FM in southern Kent and parts of East Sussex because VHF radio waves travel further than UHF TV signals. The three main French TV channels – TF1, France 2 and France 3 – can be received without difficulty on the Kent and Sussex coast, between Broadstairs as far as Hastings from the nearby transmitter at Boulogne. The signal strengths fall off rapidly as you go inland.

But it's not just a matter of pointing your aerial towards France and tuning in: all you'd see would be a jumbled mass of zig-zag lines as French TV uses a different format.

Many people on the northern French coast enjoy watching British TV on multi-standard sets and VCRs, which are widely available in France to receive both formats.

*James Blackwood, Oxford*

While I was still living with my parents in Doncaster in 1974, my father came home with an old black and white TV set he had bought in a jumble sale for 50p. While trying to tune it, we obtained a discernible picture of a rugby match, the picture covering only two-thirds of the screen.

The programme wasn't being broadcast on British TV channels and the commentary was in French. We retraced the signal later that day but couldn't get it ever again. We assumed it had been the result of some freak combination of circumstances relaying the signal over an extraordinary distance.

*Julian Kirk, Slough, Berkshire*

**(314) QUESTION: Which is the fastest stretch of line on the London Underground and what speed do trains reach on it?**

Average speed on the Tube's 244 miles of track is 20.5 miles per hour. Stations in central London can be just 300 yards apart (as between Leicester Square and Covent Garden), leaving very little time to get up speed. The fastest underground stretch is on the Victoria Line between Finsbury Park and Seven Sisters where trains can reach 57 mph.

But the fastest stretch on the system is the four miles above ground on the Metropolitan Line southbound between Chalfont & Latimer and Chorleywood where trains can travel as fast as the 70 mph limit.

*Liz Connolly, London Underground*

The fastest stretch must be the non-stop section of the Metropolitan Line from Wembley Park to Finchley Road. Before locks were fitted on the door leading to the driver's cab, I occasionally sneaked the door open and saw the speedometer registering 70 mph.

*Jeffrey Phillips, Wembley Park, Middlesex*

My father retired from the Underground system as chief inspector of signal engineering in 1948, having worked on the network from 1908. He started with the London Electric Railway, later absorbed into the Metropolitan, with its 'Live in Metroland' slogan, beloved of John Betjeman.

When the line came under the London Passenger Transport

Board in 1933, separate electric locomotives pulled trains of ordinary coaches from Baker Street and Moorgate to Aylesbury, including a non-stop run from Finchley Road to Harrow on the Hill, with a running time of nine minutes, reaching 90 mph in places.

This speed was considered unsafe by the new management, one of whose first acts was to replace the 2,400 hp engines with 1,200 hp.

Drivers in those days, referred to as 'motormen', were given 'juice money', a bonus according to how little power they used per shift. This could be as much as £2 or £3 a month, so they went as fast as possible before shutting off power and coasting down the gradients.

*G. Bishop, Marhamchurch, Cornwall*

Further to the separate electric locomotives that pulled trains of ordinary coaches from Baker Street and Moorgate to Aylesbury, that line was electrified only as far as Rickmansworth. There, the electric locomotive (one named *Sherlock Holmes*, appropriately enough for trains going under Baker Street, and another *Sarah Siddons*) was replaced by a steam tank engine.

As this operation took about ten minutes, some of the effect of the rapid progress up to that point was lost. Although nostalgic to remember now, it could be slightly irritating then, especially after midnight, with the ten-mile gradient to Amersham-on-the-Hill still to come.

*M. Foley, Aylesbury, Buckinghamshire*

There are further delightful aspects of the Metropolitan Line's history that today's commuter would find hard to imagine. For one thing, Pullman cars served a full breakfast on this line.

The steam engines used the Underground in the earlier days. The Amersham ones had special condensing tanks that recycled steam, but the smoke could still be appalling in the tunnels.

At the other end of the once extensive Metropolitan empire, a quiet rural branch meandered out to Brill, near Oxford, through woodland on unfenced tramway track to pick up wagons of pigs for market at little more than walking pace. It was a very different world from today's Underground.

*Simon Stephens, Oxford*

**(315) QUESTION: Victoria Crosses were awarded to Lord Roberts during the Indian Mutiny of 1858 and posthumously to his son, Lieut. Frederick Roberts, after the Battle of Colenso in 1899. Can any other family claim this double?**

The only other VCs awarded to father and son were won by Capt. W. N. Congreve, of the Rifle Brigade, for his actions at the Battle of Colenso on 15 December 1899, and his son, Brevet Major W. Congreve DSO, MC, also Rifle Brigade, awarded posthumously for his actions in the period 6 to 20 July 1916.

Three VCs have been awarded to brothers, Major C. J. S. Gough, of the 5th Bengal European Cavalry, and Lt H. H. Gough, of the 1st Bengal European Light Cavalry, each winning a VC for his actions during the Indian Mutiny of 1857–8. Another family member, Brevet Major A. E. Gough, of the Rifle Brigade, was awarded a VC for his actions on 23 April 1903.

During the First World War, a VC was awarded to Lt R. V. Bradford MC, of the 9th Battalion Durham Light Infantry, for actions on 1 October 1916. His brother, Lt Cmdr G. N. Bradford, of the Royal Navy, won the VC for action on 22–23 April 1918. Both these awards were posthumous.

*D. J. Callaghan, Hancocks & Co Jewellers,*
*Burlington Gardens, London W1*

**(316) QUESTION: Why can't you make kiwi fruit jelly?**

It's very difficult to make jelly with kiwi fruit because the fruit contains an enzyme which prevents the jelly from setting. But it's not impossible and one way round the problem is to cook the fruit for a few minutes first, destroying the enzyme.

Despite nor being very good for making jelly, the kiwi fruit is packed with vitamin C and a variety of minerals, ideal for lunch boxes, on with luncheon meats in sandwiches. Kiwi fruits can be topped with plain yogurt and sprinkled with cinnamon for a tasty desert or stirred into a hot cereal as a natural sweetener.

New Zealand, one of the world's largest producers of kiwi fruit, has renamed it the Zespri while kiwi fruit grown outside New Zealand are still known as kiwi fruit.

*Debra Pieri, Fresh Fruit & Vegetable Information Bureau,*
*London SW7*

You can make kiwi fruit jelly if you microwave the kiwi fruit for about ten seconds first. This destroys the enzyme that prevents the jelly setting.

*Andrea Lambert, Leeds*

**(317) QUESTION: Can anyone remember the Boer War rhyme which started 'The baby's name is . . .', and listed the battles and generals of that war?**

Originally a music hall song, the chorus to this ditty was still being used as a skipping song as late as the 1940s. By that time, many of the original names had become garbled over several generations. It was also employed as a dipping chant with the name Blobbs for the selectee.

It went:

*The war, the war, the bloomin' war, has turned my wife insane.*
*From Kruger to Majuba, she's the Transvaal on the brain.*
*We went to christen our first child, last Sunday week we tried,*
*The parson said 'What's this child's name?' and my old gal*
  *replied:*

> *'The baby's name is Kitchener, Carrington, Methuen,*
> *Kekewich, White, Cronje, Plumer, Powell, Majuba,*
> *Gatacre, Warren, Colenzo, Kruger, Cape Town, Mafeking,*
> *French, Kimberley, Ladysmith, 'Bobs', Union Jack, Fighting*
> *Mac, Lyddite, Pretoria, Blobbs.'*

Two further verses referred to other Boer War icons – rolling veldt and armoured train, Spion Kop, Kroonstad, Blomfontein and Modder River.

*Terry Fairbank Weston, Sheffield*

This song, written by C. W. Murphy and Albert Hall, to a tune by Murphy, published by Francis, Day and Hunter in sheet music form at 4 shillings a copy, was sung in music halls by Charles Bignell.

*Ronald Timms, Boston, Lincolnshire*

The South African War (1899–1902), also known as the Boer War, was a conflict between the British Empire and the Afrikaner governments of the Transvaal and the Orange Free State. The European settlers in both areas were mainly of Dutch ancestry and the discovery of gold had brought in a great many *uitlanders* (or foreigners, mostly British) to the area.

The Boers, under the leadership of Paul Kruger, who became president of the Transvaal, were keen to remain independent and gave no rights to the newcomers, a situation that could not be tolerated by a British Empire keen to stamp its authority from the Cape to Cairo.

Prominent people in the song include British commanders Lord Herbert Kitchener; General Methuen, captured by Boer commandos in March 1902; General Sir George White, who held Ladysmith in a four-month siege; Herbert Charles Onslow Plumer, who led the Rhodesian Relief Force at Mafeking; Colonel Baden-Powell (better known as founder of the Scouts), who defended Mafeking during the siege; Sir Charles Warren; Sir John French (later commander of the British Expeditionary Force in France); General Sir Hector MacDonald, known as Fighting Mac, and British Commander-in-Chief Frederick Sleigh Roberts (known as Bobs), Earl of Kandahar, Pretoria and Waterford.

Sieges and battles listed include: Majuba, Lenze (Colenso), Ladysmith, Spion Kop, Bloemfontein, Kroonstad, Mafeking and Kimberley.

*John Linart, Crawley*

Though the baby in the song was fictional, some real people were lumbered with lengthy Boer War lists of names. When I was a teenager in Loughborough, we had a lodger known to us as Baden Russell who told us he had broadcast on the radio as Britain's youngest soldier in the Second World War. He'd been christened Baden Powell Brabant Plumer Ladysmith Mafeking Russell.

*Doreen Barker, Milton Keynes, Buckinghamshire*

**(318) QUESTION: What was the importance of Prince Obolensky's famous try at Twickenham in 1936?**

As husband of the Prince's niece Alexandra Obolensky, I'm aware that the most important factor was that Prince Obolensky's famous try, one of two he made that day, made a significant contribution to the first victory by England over New Zealand. It was also, I believe, the first time a prince, albeit one born in Russia, had played for England.

The legendary try, still talked of as Obo's Try in rugby circles, was unusual in that right-winger Obolensky received the ball inside the England half, feigned as if to run conventionally down the right touch-line but cut diagonally through the wrong-footed All Blacks' defence and scored in the left-hand corner.

Introduced to Obolensky before the match, the Prince of Wales was heard to observe: 'I thought I was the only prince here today.'

*Stuart Hulse, London*

Prince Alexander Obolensky (1916–40), born in St Petersburg, was brought to this country as an infant during the Russian Revolution. A fine athlete who played on the wing for Oxford University and represented England four times in 1936, his determination to be as fast on the rugby pitch as he was on the running track contributed to the development of the lightweight modern rugby boot.

His remarkable try at Twickenham is still rated as one of the greatest sporting feats this century.

Sadly, he was killed during the Second World War in a landing accident in his Hurricane fighter during RAF training.

*William Maxwell, Oxford*

## (319) QUESTION: Did air traffic control know where the US Air Force Northrop Grumman B2 Spirit stealth bomber was during its flight to the Farnborough air show?

For its starring appearance at the 1996 Farnborough Air Show, the USAF Northrop Grumman B2 Spirit long-range strategic heavy bomber flew non-stop from Edwards Air Force Base, Montana, and passed over the crowd for several minutes before flying back to Montana without landing. On nearing the venue, the pilot activated a radar beacon to allow air traffic controllers to pinpoint his location.

The plane is 69 ft long and 17 ft high with wingspan of 172 ft. Powered by four General Electric F118-GE-100 engines, it has a range of more than 6,000 nautical miles and ceiling of 50,000 ft.

The two-man crew can unleash a 40,000 lb payload of conventional or nuclear weapons, precision-guided munitions, gravity bombs or maritime armaments. At $2.2 billion each, after development costs of $20 billion, just twelve B2s have been built in the most expensive project ever for the USAF.

The plane obtains radar near-invisibility through its irregular shape, super-fine exhaust and intakes, onboard computer equipment and radar absorbent coating.

*Wesley Baines-Johnson, Streatham, London*

**(320) QUESTION: Why is morning dress worn in the afternoon?**

In the late eighteenth and early nineteenth century no self-respecting rider would venture out on a horse during the morning without wearing the correct attire, then known as a morning riding coat.

This had a continuous curve from the front to the back where it formed the tails. Another mode of the time, also worn during the day, was the dress coat, cut sharply square at the waist at the front, with the tails narrower and further round the back.

The morning riding coat, now known as 'morning dress', has evolved into formal wear for daytimes. The dress coat is formal evening wear.

*Avril Hart, fashions and textiles, Victoria and Albert Museum,*
*London*

**(321) QUESTION: What was the first tune ever played on BBC Radio 1?**

When Radio 1 began broadcasting on 30 September 1967, the No 1 record in the pop charts was Englebert Humperdinck's 'The Last Waltz'. Keith West's depressing 'Excerpt From A Teenage Opera' was at No 2 so it's no surprise that DJ Tony Blackburn kicked off with the No 3 at the time, 'Flowers In The Rain' by The Move.

*David Hutt, Pedmore, West Midlands*

Although most people believe The Move's 'Flowers In The Rain' was the first record played on Radio 1, it was preceded by Tony Blackburn's show theme, a snippet from 'Beef Eaters' by the Johnny Dankworth Orchestra.

*Howard Pizzey, Staplehurst, Kent*

The Move's 'Flowers In The Rain' caused controversy when the group promoted the record with a cartoon of then Prime Minister

Harold Wilson sitting naked in the bath. Following legal proceedings, the group had to withdraw the advertisement and apologize.

*Tony Whitehead, Guildford, Surrey*

'Theme One' by the George Martin Orchestra opened the first day's broadcasting on 30 September 1967. It was played just before 6 a.m. every morning for many years.

George produced the Beatles' *Sergeant Pepper* album, which topped the charts from early June that year, and 'Theme One' had a 'Penny Lane'-ish feel, with trumpets and violins and electronic phasing effects. But the record, on the United Artists label, wasn't a hit and is now a collector's items worth £10 in mint condition.

A decade later, drummer Cozy Powell's great version of the tune did make it into the charts.

*Frank Kilduff, Greenford, Middlesex*

### (322) QUESTION: What is the origin of the phrase 'the gravy train'?

When the word 'gravy' entered the English language in the fourteenth century it signified a spiced, stock-based sauce served with white meat. By the sixteenth century the word was applied to sauce made solely with the meat juice. By the late nineteenth century, 'gravy' was being used to describe any pleasant extra, and the First World War song 'She Was Poor But She Was Honest' included the lines: 'It's the same the whole world over/It's the poor what gets the blame/It's the rich what gets the gravy/Ain't it all a bleedin' shame'. Soon after that war the term 'gravy train' became a favourite expression among US railroad workers when they had a well-paid run that required little work. During the booming twenties it was adopted in financial circles for any high-wage low-effort endeavour.

*Liz Halbert, Glengarnock, Ayrshire*

**(323) QUESTION: What happened to all those wartime Luftwaffe aerial reconnaissance pictures of Britain? Can copies still be obtained?**

Luftwaffe aerial photographs were captured by American and British forces at the end of the war and were interpreted by a joint US/British unit known as Operation Dick Tracy. Most ended up in the US National Archives in Maryland, though the Imperial War Museum has a small collection. The Soviet Army also collected a huge amount of Luftwaffe material but much of this is believed to have been destroyed in the final stages of the war.

During the Cold War, Luftwaffe intelligence records remained secret, but in the seventies the US National Archives opened its collection to the public.

I have more than six hundred aerial photographs of the UK and Ireland taken by the Luftwaffe between 1939 and 1942, some of which have been published in a series of books. The latest of these is *Adolf Hitler's Home Counties Holiday Snaps* (ISBN 0 907683 50 9), which should be available at your local library.

*Nigel J Clarke, Russell House, Lyme Regis, Dorset*


In late 1945, my REME unit ended up with the Canadian 1st Army at Jagerhof Aerodrome, at Oldenburg, north Germany. The Map Room there was strewn knee deep with excellent quality maps in minute detail and I was shocked to find a large-scale map of Portsmouth and Southampton giving details of the dockyard and firing ranges and, to my horror, the small terrace of houses including my own home, plainly shown. Even Southwick House was shown – but not as the headquarters for D-Day.

*N. G. Cleverley, Sandbach, Cheshire*


The largest collection of Luftwaffe photographs in Britain can be seen at Keel University, Staffordshire. A limited number of photographs covering parts of Scotland can be seen at The Royal Commission On Ancient and Historic Monuments Of Scotland, John Sinclair House, 16 Bernard Terrace, Edinburgh EH8 9NX.

*John Hellis, Defence of Britain, Taunton, Somerset*

I have a photograph taken from a Dornier bomber on a raid over Britain on 18 August 1940. It shows my aunt running towards her house in Cyprus Road, Burgess Hill, Sussex, at lunchtime on that day to escape the German machine guns.

My uncle kept the cannon shell that narrowly missed her and embedded itself in the door jamb as she dashed into the house.

*K. Anderson, Freshwater Bay, Isle of Wight*

In Alfred Price's *Battle of Britain* book is an aerial map taken by a raiding Dornier aircraft over Kenley Aerodrome in 1940. I remember the wrecked Spitfire shown in the picture because I had been working on it as an armourer with 64 Squadron while it was grounded because of a glycol (engine coolant) leak.

Also in the picture is the surface shelter in which I was taking cover at the time of this air raid. When we tried to get out, we found one of its doors was jammed by an unexploded bomb, one of more than fifty around the airfield. That Dornier obviously made it back home.

*C. Morrell, Holland on Sea, Essex*

### (324) QUESTION: Of the money pledged to the BBC Children in Need appeal, how much does the BBC actually get?

BBC records show that at least 98 per cent of credit card phone pledges on the night of the appeal are honoured – but these donations make up only a proportion of the appeal's income. The amount announced on the night is normally far exceeded by the final total because so many more contributions come in after the event, as fundraisers around the country pay in their donations.

*Julia Kaufmann, BBC Children in Need,*
*Broadcasting House, London*

### (325) QUESTION: Why is a crown the symbol of royalty in Western European culture?

The creation of royalty and of bishops has always involved anointing, the pouring of oil onto the top of the head as a sign of being chosen or set apart, which is what the word 'anointed' means.

Originally, royalty and bishops wore a simple garland rather like a sweat band so that the oil didn't run into their eyes. Gradually these garlands became more ornate, taller and sometimes jewel encrusted, eventually evolving into the present-day crowns for royalty and mitres for bishops.

*Fr Christopher Jordan, St Patrick's Catholic Church,*
*Woolston, Hampshire*

### (326) QUESTION: When so many births are by induction or Caesarean, why do astrologers plot our stars from our date of birth rather than from conception?

Your birth chart describes you and your relationship with the environment at the moment you came into the world. Conception represents the beginning of a biological process but birth, the start of an independent life outside the mother, is the point astrologers find of greatest significance.

Your arrival in the world may be determined by many things, induction or Caesarean section being just two, but to astrologers the mode isn't as important as the planetary positions at the moment of birth.

*Babs Kirby, Faculty of Astrological Studies, London*

The date and precise time of birth are easily ascertainable and verified by witnesses. But in most instances, not even the mother can be sure of the exact date and time of conception, which can only be approximated. A newborn baby is already an individual, with its own character. It's arguable that the planets and stars influenced this rather than genes and other factors in the baby's body.

The fact that astrologers go for the easily available data of the birth rather than the usually unobtainable, though logically more pertinent, time of conception tells us something about the credibility of astrological theory.

*Brian Martin, Waterlooville, Hampshire*

The Earth's relationship to planetary constellations has changed over the centuries and while Eastern astrologers have kept up to date with these changes, most of their Western colleagues haven't. It's now impossible for Western and Eastern astrologers both to be correct in any particular interpretation.

The whole idea of specific constellations having a collective influence is questioned by our knowledge that while particular stars seem close to each other in our sky, they are hundreds of light years away from one another in space. Now these distances have been calculated, we can see how infinitesimally small are the effects produced by planets and stars.

One ancient people needed no modern science to tell them astrology was a mistake. More than 2,500 years ago, God told the nation of Israel: 'Do not learn the way of the nations nor be apprehensive of the signs in the sky when other nations are apprehensive of them, for the usages of the nations are superstition' (Jeremiah 10:2).

*Nick Welham, Verwood, Dorset*

**(327) QUESTION: Were Princesses Elizabeth and Margaret Rose always dressed alike, as Beatrice and Eugenie were?**

My collection of royal photographs and books, amassed over years as a keen royalist, reveal the young Princesses Beatrice and Eugenie wearing the same clothes in two out of every six pictures of them.

Pictures of the Queen and Princess Margaret when they were growing up together reveal them similarly dressed in seven out of eleven pictures, not too different from Beatrice and Eugenie.

*Julia Dawson, Fulham, London*

My memory of the young Princesses Elizabeth and Margaret Rose is that they were often dressed the same but, despite this, they had no trouble in developing very different personalities.

*Mrs Janet Raffaillac, Verriers-le-Buisson, France*

**(328) QUESTION: If every man, woman and child in Britain was each allocated a lamp-post, would there be enough for us all?**

When the Association of Street Lighting Electrical Contractors completed its last comprehensive survey of street lighting in the UK for industry journal *Highway Electrical News*, there were a total of 6,378,320 lamps in the UK, 4,984,070 in England, 796,700 in Scotland, 366,750 in Wales and 230,800 in Northern Ireland.

So the highest ratio of people per lamp is England's 9.77, with 7.94 people per lamp in Wales, 7.11 in Northern Ireland and 6.44 in Scotland.

*Vas Siantonas, Association of Street Lighting Contractors, Steyning, West Sussex*

**(329) QUESTION: My father's family claims a brother, Richard Foster, died in the twenties under the wheels of the Lord Mayor's coach. Is there any record of this?**

There's no record of such an incident during the Lord Mayor's Parades of the twenties or at any other time. However, on 10 November 1930, thirty people were injured in the ensuing panic when four Indian elephants bolted into the crowd.

The injured were treated at Charing Cross Hospital and an improvised dressing station at King's College and only two were seriously hurt: B. Moll, aged eighteen, of George St, Portman Square, whose left arm was broken, and Edward Milton, forty-three, of Shepperton Road, Islington, whose left foot was crushed.

The elephants were passing King's College when a group of students in the crowd waved aloft their red lion mascot, known as Reggie. Enraged by Reggie's realistic appearance, the elephants suddenly wheeled towards it, shrugging off their attendants' attempts to control them. The dense crowd, including women and children, were terrified and stampeded.

Meanwhile, one of the elephants seized Reggie and dashed him on the ground to be trampled by the other elephants.

*Philip Gale, Records Office, Corporation of London*


**(330) QUESTION: Is it true that women generally have a 2 per cent wider field of vision than men?**

The retina extends a good way around the inner surface of the eyeball, allowing us to see objects in the periphery of our vision. While I'm not aware of any gender differences in the extent of the retina, one's nose can limit the field of vision and may give rise to a larger field of view in women since their noses are generally smaller.

Try looking straight ahead with one eye closed, then wiggle your nose. Most people should be able to discern their nose moving out of the corner of their eye, and will realize that larger noses result in a more restricted field of view out of the one eye. Fortunately, the field of view of the fellow eye compensates for this limitation.

*Dr David Whitaker, Department of Optometry,*
*University of Bradford*

## (331) QUESTION: In what way does 'the exception prove the rule'?

This is a translation of the Latin *exceptio probat regulam* – the exception tests the rule, that is: puts it to the proof, not confirms it. The verb *probare* is the root of our word 'probe', which makes the meaning clearer. The word 'prove' has, in recent times, come to mean 'verify' rather than its earlier meaning of 'put to the test'.

*Dr Tim Healey, Barnsley, Yorkshire*

Although, in the strictest sense, the existence of any exception could be said to disprove, rather than prove, the rule, the general understanding of this expression is that knowledge of a sufficiently outstanding exception to a particular rule is in itself confirmation that for all other cases, the rule holds true.

This understanding operates on the 'man bites dog' principle. While it may generally be held that it would invariably be the dog which did the biting, should there be an occurrence of the reverse, it is sufficiently remarkable to be specifically noted.

In this case the very remarkability of the incident which goes against the rule confirms the idea that in all other cases the normal course of events can be expected.

*Owen Carmichael, Oxford*

## (332) QUESTION: Was there ever a racehorse called Christmas Day which fell on a Good Friday?

I can find no record of a horse called Christmas Day falling at any race on a Good Friday, and this is highly unlikely to have occurred as, traditionally, horse races aren't held on Good Friday or Christmas Day.

This question is probably a distortion of the famous incident during the Thorneycroft Chase at Wolverhampton on Boxing Day, 1899, when a horse called Good Friday fell, thus Good Friday fell on the day after Christmas Day, the source of many a wager between friends.

*Simon Clare, Ladbrokes, London*

**(333) QUESTION: What is the correct use of the words 'Scot', 'Scots', 'Scotch' and 'Scottish'? I understand misuse can cause offence?**

I'm a Scot and enjoy the company of other Scots, sometimes reading Scottish literature or listening to Scottish music while I'm relaxing with a glass of Scotch whisky. As a Scottish woman, I'm proud of my Scottish heritage and Scottish roots and often discuss the meaning of life with a fellow Scot – but always over a glass of Scotch.

In other words, Scotch is a term used to describe many things of Scottish origin, such as whisky, broth, eggs, even dogs and mist – but never the people, who are 'a Scot', 'the Scots', or 'Scottish'.

*Mary Buckley, Harrow*

Writer I. A. N. Henderson, in his *Angus and the Mearns*, opts for 'Scotch' and says 'Scottish' is 'a modern intrusion into the language'. He claims the word Scottish 'is a weak twentieth-century Anglicized quasi-amelioration that lacks the force and direction of "Scotch", the internationally accepted adjective'.

Scotch cattle, Scotch lamb, Scotch potatoes, Scotch barley, Scotch bluebells, Scotch thistles, Scotch whisky and Scotch men are all produced in *Angus and the Mearns*.

*Terry Smithers, Liphook, Hampshire*

I believe this is just a matter of the fashion of the day. Sir Walter Scott's list of characters in *Old Mortality* (1816) cites: 'Gilbertscleugh, Mr – a Scotch gentleman'.

And the Scot/Scotch Boswell reports Dr Johnson as saying: 'The noblest prospect which a Scotchman ever sees is the high-road that leads him to England' as well as 'Much may be made of a Scotchman if he be caught young'.

It's difficult to refute Scotland's greatest novelist and the great lexicographer. I have a first edition, published in Edinburgh in 1842, of William Anderson's *Popular Scotish* (sic) *Biography*.

The only offence likely to be taken by a Scot is if you offer anything less than a quarter gill.

*D. L. Goddard, Bournemouth*

**(334) QUESTION: Living in Denton, Manchester, as a child, any piece of high ground was always known as 'Hill 60'. What was this?**

Hill 60 is a small incline south-east of Ypres in Belgium that figured in fighting during the First World War, so named because of its height – 60 metres above sea level.

In April 1915 British forces mined and destroyed German positions and captured the hill. There followed a fierce counter attack by the Germans, whereupon both sides announced possession of Hill 60.

The propaganda value of holding the hill came to outweigh its strategic importance: because the British still held the hill the Germans were forced to launch another attack to give substance to their false claim. On 5 May, faced by gas and heavy shelling, the British retreated. Though by now partly demolished by sheer weight of explosives, Hill 60 continued to be fought over until the Allied breakthrough of 1917.

A second First World War Hill 60, one of the foothills of the Sari Bair range, featured in the Gallipoli Campaign.

*Nigel Wilcockson*, Brewer's Twentieth-Century Phrase and Fable, *Cassell, London*

Hill 60 was one of the names, along with Hellfire Corner, Menin Road and others, that my late great-uncle Will recalled from his soldiering in the Great War of 1914–18, names that intrigued me so much I decided to visit Belgium for myself.

Hill 60 is situated a few miles from the Belgium town of Ypres, a spoil heap from a deep railway cutting nearby. In the relatively flat landscape of Flanders it became an important military position overlooking much of the Ypres Salient.

Like other high ground it was fought over throughout the Great War, particularly in 1915 and again in 1917, when it saw some of the worst fighting of the war, with gas, mines and shelling all employed. Today, it's a preserved area, left to the sheep and visitors who come to remember.

*Sylvia Turnock, Biddulph, Staffordshire*

**(335) QUESTION: What happened to the Council for Education in World Citizenship, to which I belonged at school in the sixties?**

We have been preparing British young people for citizenship since 1939 and are still going strong in an increasingly interdependent world, serving more school and college students than ever. Through activities, events and publications we help them understand and confront global issues and challenges.

Originally part of the League of Nations Union, then the United Nations Association, we're now an independent charity with a membership including 1,500 schools.

Many prominent people say their contact with the Council for Education in World Citizenship (CEWC) while at school sparked their interest in public life. Michael Portillo, Virginia Bottomley, Glenys Kinnock, Jack Straw, David Steel, Lord Frank Judd, Melvyn Bragg and Jonathan Porritt have all been members.

Friends of the CEWC gather at Westminster in February each year. This year they were addressed by Douglas Hurd on the New World Order, next year it will be Nick Tate on Values and Rabbi Julia Neuberger on Moral Responsibility.

We welcome individuals and groups as members, as well as schools and colleges.

*Patricia Rodgers, Council for Education In World Citizenship,*
*London EC1A 9HY*

**(336) QUESTION: My town, South Shields, has pubs named The Eureka, The Commando, The Alum House and The Dolly Peel. Are they unique?**

The Eureka Hotel was built in the 1800s and named in honour of Archimedes. As far as I know, it's the only pub in Britain with this name.

*Lesley Barkas, The Eureka Hotel*

The pub Tetley's built in South Shields marketplace in 1952 was named The Commando in recognition of the area's long tradition of sending men into that elite force. I don't know of any other pub in the country with this name.

*Fred Bidolph, owner, The Commando*

The South Shields building now known as The Alum House opened in 1760 as an aluminium sulphate plant – an 'alum house'. It has changed hands several times, serving as offices for an engineering company, a taphouse for its neighbour, Wood's Brewery, and, in 1900, a Bass pub.

In the 1970s it was a carpet shop before reverting to a pub late in the decade and acquiring the name, The Alum House. To the best of my knowledge, it's the only pub in Britain with this name.

*Paul Newton, assistant manager, The Alum House*

Dolly Peel (1782–1857) was a formidable local heroine. She tried to hide her husband and sons from the press gang but they were found and frogmarched aboard ship to serve with the Royal Navy.

Dolly stowed away on the ship, but was discovered after three days and set to work in the sickbay. The captain intended to drop her off on the west coast of Africa, but Dolly proved such a good nurse that she was allowed to remain on board until the ship returned to South Shields. She was pardoned and her husband and sons exempted from further attention by the press gangs.

Dolly remained bitter that her family had been press-ganged and organized groups to prevent ships docking in the area. They lured ships onto the rocks knows as The Middens before boarding them and stealing their cargoes to distribute to the poor.

Dolly's descendants persuaded Earl Grey to rename one of his pubs The Dolly Peel. It is a unique name which attracts people from all over the world.

*Alan Taylor, Landlord, The Dolly Peel*


An Ormskirk pub is called the Snig's Foot. As 'snig' is a Cheshire word for snake, I imagine this must be unique: you don't get many of those.

*J. W. R. Grainger, Salt Heath, Stafford*


**(337) QUESTION: What is the radius within which you might expect, on a normal Sunday, to be able to hear the sound of Bow bells from St Mary le Bow church, Cheapside, in the City of London – the definition of a true cockney?**

Variations such as wind, street noise, rain and time of day, mean the distance changes from one day to the next.

Normally defined, the range includes the square mile of the City of London, including the Tower of London to the east, Holborn viaduct to the west, the South Bank to the south and Finsbury Square to the north. Dick Whittington's claim to have heard the bells calling him to 'turn again' when he was at Highgate Hill seems unlikely. They certainly cannot be heard from there today.

In fact, very few, if any, children are born within the range of the sound of Bow bells today.

The resident population in the area is very small and the bells' range is further restricted as they are generally muffled when tolled, out of consideration for local businesses.

*Graham Phillips, St Mary le Bow, London*

Perhaps the BBC should broadcast the sound of Bow bells rather than Big Ben, then we could all become cockneys.

*Brian Mason, Sapcote, Leicestershire*

### (338) QUESTION: Has anyone been prosecuted successfully for stealing a supermarket trolley?

Tesco has never prosecuted anyone for stealing one of its 200,000 supermarket trolleys at its 550 stores.

We buy about 10,000 to 15,000 new trolleys a year in eight different designs. Several procedures, including full-time assistants who patrol the car park and immediate area collecting abandoned trolleys, keep our stocks secure.

If they're found abandoned elsewhere, our staff will make arrangements for their collection.

We have introduced coin deposit schemes in areas where abandoned trolleys are a problem.

*Karen Marshall, Tesco, Cheshunt, Hertfordshire*

The big supermarket chains have 1.2 million shopping trolleys between them, costing an average £55 each. The six biggest chains lose £250,000 a year in lost or stolen trolleys.

Most stop short of prosecuting offenders because it's difficult to define which law has been broken and it also brings bad publicity.

They rely on the police to bring prosecutions under littering or illegal dumping laws. Stores try to make sure their trolleys go no further than the car park by employing 'trolley wallies' to collect them and scour the surrounding area for strays.

Asda spent a fortune testing self-immobilizing trolleys which cannot be wheeled outside the car park.

*Duke Manaman, Southport*

About twenty-five years ago I was a police sergeant in Newton, Powys, on early-hours patrol on a housing estate. I saw a man pushing an empty supermarket trolley, asked what he was doing with it and was told he was taking it home because he wanted the wheels. He was arrested and later fined by the local court.

*D. A. L. James, Newtown, Powys*

**(339) QUESTION: Why do so many manufacturers of battery-operated appliances, particularly toys, advise against using rechargeable batteries?**

Keith Lister, the British Toy and Hobby Association's electrical toy safety expert, says manufacturers advise against rechargeable batteries for purely commercial reasons.

By stating 'Do not use rechargeable batteries', manufacturers can reduce by around half the number of tests they have to do.

Rechargeable batteries provide a constant 1.2 volts throughout use while alkaline batteries, which start at a slightly higher 1.5 volts, drop in power during use.

Rechargeables are ideal for toys which use high power and need a lot of batteries. They are not recommended for low-drain products, such as digital clocks, remote controls or smoke alarms.

Any suggestion that rechargeables are unsafe, leak or damage toys is completely unfounded.

This Christmas, about 100 million throwaway batteries will be sold, causing a major disposal problem – something you don't get with rechargeables.

*Annie Smith, Uniross Batteries, Nailsea, Bristol*

**(340) QUESTION: How does the price of petrol relate to the average wage in Britain compared with those supposedly 'golden ages' of motoring, the thirties and fifties?**

When I bought my first car for £40 in 1935, a one-year-old Austin 7 Ruby saloon, 'run of pump' petrol was 11d a gallon.

I always bought the best National fuel at 11½d a gallon, which meant it cost five shillings to fill the tank.

There were no forecourts then and the garage man had to swing an arm over the pavement to fill the tank while the car was at the kerbside. I believe the average wage then was about £3 a week.

*H. Manning, London SE19*

When I started motoring in 1965 (no, it *wasn't* a chariot) the national average wage was £700 a year or around £13.50 a week. At that time, I was paying 4 shillings (20p) for a gallon of petrol – which meant that I could purchase a total of 67.5 gallons with my salary.

The national average rate of pay today is £22,000 a year or £423 a week. Today's average price of petrol is £5.81 a gallon. So I can now purchase 73.15 gallons of fuel.

As a percentage of my earnings, I'm paying less for petrol than I was fifty-six years ago.

*Norman A. Dean, Lask Edge, Staffordshire*

**(341) QUESTION: Did British servicemen pay income tax during the Second World War?**

There was no exemption from income tax for servicemen during the Second World War and, provided their income was above allowances and reliefs available at the time, they had to pay tax.

The standard rate of tax for the financial year before the war was the £.s.d. equivalent of 27.5p in the pound, with a reduced rate of 8.33p. The standard rate increased to 35p, with the reduced rate at 11.6p for 1939–40 and went up again the next year to 42.5p standard and 25p reduced rate.

For 1941–2 and the rest of the war years the standard rate was 50p with a reduced rate at 32.5p.

At the beginning of the war, most servicemen, like most of the working class at that time, were not paid enough to come within the income tax bracket. This changed as the country needed to increase its funds and, by the end of the war, allowance and relief levels had dropped so far, and workers' earnings, including that of most service personnel (aided by the introduction of PAYE), had increased sufficiently to bring the bulk of the working population into the tax arena for the first time.

*Peter J. Langley, Swindon*

As a REME sergeant armourer in the war, my pay at demob was 10s 6d a day. I didn't pay tax during service but soon after returning to civilian work I was contacted by the Inland Revenue and told I owed a huge amount of income tax.

We agreed that a sum of money should be deducted from my wages, which was a bit of a struggle at the time when my take-home pay was less than £10 a week.

*H. Robertson, Failsworth, Manchester*

My brother, an engineer in the Merchant Navy, was torpedoed by a German U-boat in 1942, and following his death a demand for £42 back tax was received by our family.

Even the danger money paid to these brave men was taxed, which caused great resentment.

*Mrs M. Lewis, Pontypridd*

I was an engine fitter during the war and my pay was slightly below the income tax line. However, after three years I got my good conduct stripes and my pay was increased by 3d a day. This brought me into the tax bracket and I had to pay 6d a day, so overall I was 3d a day worse off.

Some of the chaps then committed small crimes to be put on a charge and avoid the good conduct award – but my crimes went undetected, so I continued to pay for my good service.

*A. Jones, Whitwick, Leicestershire*

**(342) QUESTION: How and when were what we now know as Wagner's 'Here Comes The Bride' and Mendelssohn's 'Wedding March' first used at weddings?**

Wagner's 'Here Comes The Bride' came originally from his opera *Lohengrin*, first published on 10 December 1851. Mendelssohn's 'Wedding March' came from music he wrote for *A Midsummer Night's Dream*, published on 1 May 1844.

These pieces were first linked at the wedding in 1858 of Princess Victoria, daughter of Queen Victoria, and Prince Frederick William of Prussia, establishing a tradition that continues to this day.

*Betty Barron, Sutton Coldfield Music Library, W. Midlands*

When Vicky, Princess Royal of England, married Freddie, Prince Frederick William of Prussia, on 25 January 1858, at the Chapel Royal, St James's Palace, Mendelssohn's 'Wedding March' was played as they tripped down the aisle and its use became high fashion.

*Mrs Ida Mary Goodrick, Tadcaster, Yorkshire*

**(343) QUESTION: Ty Hyll (The Ugly House), in North Wales, is a *Tyn Un Nos*, built in one night, giving the builder ownership of the plot. Are there any other examples of this in Britain?**

One of the last built was Jolly Lane Cottage, constructed at Hexworthy, Dartmoor, by Tom and Sally Satterley and friends on one day in 1835, while local officials were at the Ram Roast at Ashburton. They completed the task between sunrise and sunset and were able to claim their hovel, on common land, under squatters' rights.

Sally was a good singer and gave several folk songs to the Revd. Baring Gould for his *Songs of the West*.

Once the inhabitants died, or moved on, the Overseers of the Poor often pulled these cottages down to exclude those who might claim poor relief from the district. Jolly Lane Cottage has now been rebuilt and looks like many other suburban villas.

*M. J. Penny, Shrivenham, Wiltshire*


Tom and Sally Satterley carefully chose to build Jolly Lane Cottage, Hexworthy, on Dartmoor, on the first Thursday in November when they knew the local farmers, who opposed all newcomers, would be at Ashburton Fair.

Sally (who died in 1901) was a remarkable woman, respected and loved by all who knew her. Her coffin was carried six miles from Hexworthy to Widdecombe by friends and neighbours, six at a time, a total of more than fifty being involved.

Sally and Tom had five daughters at Jolly Lane Cottage, one of whom, Ann Maria, married Tom Brooking at Stokenham, Devon, in 1874. Several of their descendants are members of the Brooking Family History Society, of which football pundit Trevor Brooking is patron.

*Bob Brooking, Brooking Society, Hassocks, West Sussex*

**(344) QUESTION: What has happened to the Captain Binney Medal, awarded to citizens who lost their lives defending others?**

The Binney Memorial Medal is awarded for the bravest action in support of law and order in any year in areas controlled by the City of London or Metropolitan Police by anyone other than a police officer.

This award commemorates Captain Ralph D. Binney, who lost his life in 1944 when he made a single-handed attempt to prevent the escape of smash-and-grab thieves who had robbed a jeweller's shop in the City of London.

Binney's Royal Navy friends subscribed to a trust fund and invited the Goldsmiths' Company to act as trustee. The first awards were made in 1947. The Binney family has always taken great interest in the awards and the people who have won them, and Captain Binney's daughter usually attends the presentation ceremony.

The medal isn't awarded in years when the selection committee finds no acts to justify a medal, but there have been years when two medals have been awarded.

*Sarah Fletcher, The Goldsmiths' Company, London*


**(345) QUESTION: Why do doctors and lawyers 'practise' and others 'work'?**

The basic meaning of practise, 'to perform, do, act, carry on some activity', goes back to medieval times. Its secondary meaning, 'to carry on habitually, to make a practice of', is of slightly later development.

By a slight narrowing of meaning, this developed into 'to work at, exercise, pursue an occupation, profession, or art'. Originally, this could be used to refer to any trade or employment and you could practise conjuring, piracy, fishing, and so on, as well as medicine or law. Later the general use faded out, leaving only the doctors and lawyers practising their professions. The specific use, without a grammatical object, as in 'a counsel practising at the bar', developed as early as the sixteenth century.

The sense of practise 'to perform repeatedly or continuously in order to acquire skill' is a separate branch of the meaning 'to carry on habitually', which became common only at the beginning of the seventeenth century.

*E. S. C. Weiner,* Oxford English Dictionary

**(346) QUESTION: The British know it as the English Channel, the French as *La Manche*. What do other countries call it?**

This body of water is known almost universally as either 'the English Channel' (in the Norse-derived languages, Finnish *Englannin kanaali*, Norwegian *Den engelske kanal*, Swedish *Engelska kanalen*) or simply 'the Channel' (in Danish *Kanale*, Dutch Het *Kanaal*) or some version of 'the sleeve' (in French *La Manche*, Czech *Kanal La Manche*, Italian *La Manica*, Lithuanian *La Manshas*, Polish *Kanal La Manche*, Portuguese *O Canal da Mancha*, German *Der Armelkanal*). *Manche* in French means 'sleeve' or other long, narrow object. *Le* (as opposed to *la*) *Manche* can mean a handle or shaft. Another claim is that the word is derived from the definition of the Channel as the 'arm' of the Atlantic which separates England from mainland Europe.

*Francis O'Grady, Berlitz UK Translation Services, Baldock,*
*Hertfordshire*

The English may know it as the English Channel but in the eighteenth century this waterway was known by the more accurate appellation The British Channel.

*Jonathan Webb, East Taphouse, Cornwall*

In Icelandic the English Channel is known as *Ermarsund*.

*I. S. Haroldsden, Peterborough*

**(347) QUESTION: As a child, I was told that when George V opened Parliament a 'hostage' was held at Buckingham Palace until his safe return. Was it true? Does it still happen?**

The policy of keeping a hostage at Buckingham Palace for the safe return of the sovereign dates from the time when Parliament and the monarch were in violent dispute, as occurred during the Civil War period.

The custom has had no practical value since 1834 when William IV was the last monarch to change the government to suit his own purposes. Queen Victoria tried to do so at least once, but the balance of power had shifted from Buckingham to Westminster Palace.

This practice is now simply one of the traditions of the ceremonial of the State Opening of Parliament. The role of 'hostage' is usually performed by the Vice Chamberlain of Her Majesty's Household, a post in the Whip's office.

*Bryan R. Shacklady, Lostock, Bolton*

**(348) QUESTION: My black cat has returned after an absence of four years, ten months. Is this a record?**

Amazingly, no. The world record is claimed by Mrs Greta Vindberg-Nielsen of Stockholm, Sweden, whose black and white cat Miszan disappeared in 1987, only to turn up at her house six years later.

The disappearance was never explained and the cat acted as though it had never been away, calmly walking straight to the fridge and waiting for some food. It found its old special sleeping place on a dining-room chair and dozed off.

The return was not all wonderful news, however, as Mrs Vinberg-Nielsen, thinking she would never see her beloved cat again, had already bought another cat and called it Miszan too. Miszan II was none too happy about the returnee.

In this country there are at least two other cases of cats disappearing for four years. The first being ginger and white tom

Whisky who disappeared while being cared for in 1983 when his owners Edwin and Alvena Miles of Cwmbran, Gwent, went on holiday. He returned, slightly bedraggled in 1987. The second case was that of ginger Goldie, who ran away from the Swindon home of his owner, Lilliana Stajic, on Friday 13 July 1990, when he was scared by the hammering of workmen, only to return in August 1994.

*Debbie Schofield, Cats Magazine, Manchester*

When our second son, Dominic, was born my wife had complications and had to stay in hospital with him for three months. With our other son, Matthew, then aged ten, to look after at home, I'm afraid I somewhat neglected our year-old cat, Smokey. When my wife and Dominic came home, Smokey was nowhere to be seen and we thought we would never see her again.

One day, more than six years later, I noticed a photo of a cat in a local shop with a message saying it had been found. We were convinced it was Smokey and compared the picture with our own photographs – they were identical. We were told Smokey had been fed by an old chap who had died a few months earlier and that she had been sleeping in an old car since then. After an absence of six years, nine months, Smokey was back with us.

*David Fells, Shepshed, Leicestershire*

When we moved house on 15 December 1989, our tortoiseshell cat Virgo walked out after one week and didn't return until 21 November last year when my wife found her on the doorstep: an absence of six years, eleven months.

*Charles Hewlett, Barton on Sea, Hampshire*

Possibly the most famous lost cat was a three-year-old tabby called Tabitha, belonging to actress Carol Ann Timmel, which escaped from a special carrier inside a jumbo jet. After a search, the airline, Tower Air, decided the cat must have left the aircraft or be dead and the aircraft continued its journeys, calling at Puerto Rico, Miami and Los Angeles, for twelve days.

Then the cat's owner, spurred by extensive media coverage, threatened the airline with an injunction to ground the aircraft for a second search. The airline complied and the cat was found hiding behind a rear passenger compartment. The stowaway, which had covered more than 30,000 miles, was rather dirty but in fine condition.

*Carol Bentley, Colchester, Essex*

**(349) QUESTION: My grandfather was a member of the Royal Ancient Order of Buffaloes. Does this still exist and what does it do?**

The Royal Antediluvian Order of Buffaloes was formed in 1822 among members of the acting profession, but today takes members from all walks of life. The Order is now divided into several sections, or banners, the largest of which is the Grand Lodge of England, with 2,500 branches throughout the world.

Membership is open to men of any race, colour or creed, over eighteen years old, who are loyal supporters of the British Crown. Members of overseas lodges must also be loyal to the Head of State of their country of residence. Membership is usually by invitation.

Each lodge undertakes welfare work in its own community according to its means and desires. In recent years the Grand Lodge has donated more than £70,000 to national charities, principally for medical research. It runs convalescent homes at Harrogate and Weston-Super-Mare for members and dependants, and makes cash grants to members in need.

Another fund looks after children of deceased members. The Grand Lodge of England funds more than £500,000 of benevolent activities a year, on top of what is spent by local lodges. All this money is raised by the membership's own resources.

*William Hartmann, Grand Lodge of England, Royal Antediluvian Order of Buffaloes, Harrogate, North Yorkshire*

## (350) QUESTION: How many times has *Jane Eyre* been filmed?

Charlotte Brontë's first published novel has been brought to the screen at least thirteen times. The story of harshly treated orphan Jane Eyre, who falls in love with broodingly romantic Mr Rochester, attracted seven screen versions in the silent movie days between 1910 and 1921. The first talkie was in 1934, with Virginia Bruce as Jane and Colin Clive as Rochester, followed in 1943 by a film with Joan Fontaine in the lead role and Orson Welles as Rochester.

In 1970, Susannah York was cast as Jane with George C. Scott as Rochester, followed in 1983 by a made-for-TV adaptation, led by Zelah Clarke and Timothy Dalton. A 1996 Franco Zeffirelli version starred William Hurt as Rochester with Charlotte Gainsbourg as Jane.

Aside from the main adaptations, *Jane Eyre* inspirations have gone into at least three related films: the 1943 *I Walked With A Zombie*, starring Frances Dee and Tom Conway; the 1944 *Three Sisters of the Moors*, about the Brontë Sisters, making reference to *Jane Eyre*; and the 1992 *Wide Sargasso Sea*, taken from Jean Rhys's novel, a prequel to *Jane Eyre* set in Jamaica and concentrating on Rochester's first marriage to his mad wife Antoinette.

*John Walker, editor*, Halliwell's Film Guide, *HarperCollins, London*

Early silent film versions included the 1914 film with Ethel Grandin and Irving Cummings, later a Fox director, in a two-reel IMP production and a 1915 biograph version, featuring Louise Vale.

In 1921, Mable Ballin and Norman Trevor appeared in a Hodkinson production of the Brontë novel, followed twenty-three years later by a low budget version from Monogram starring Virginia Bruce and Colin Clive.

*Brad Steel, Torquay, Devon*

Another version was the 1973 BBC TV production starring Sorcha Cusack and Michael Jayston.

*Anne Taylor, Wigan, Lancashire*

## (351) QUESTION: If every home in the country were equipped with a roof full of solar panels, how much less electricity would power stations need to produce?

There are two types of solar panel: solar collectors, which heat a domestic water supply, and photovoltaics, which produce electricity.

In a typical solar collector system, 4 square metres of flat plates can collect about 1.3 megawatt hours a year. Of the 23,506,000 UK homes, half are in blocks of flats, face the wrong way or are in the shade of taller buildings. Solar water heating could provide 15,278,900 megawatt hours a year in the remaining 11,753,000 homes.

The UK uses an average 300 million megawatt hours of electricity a year and a typical power station generates 1,000 megawatts, so solar water heating could replace 15,278 hours of power station running, the equivalent of closing two power stations.

Estimates of the amount of electricity photovoltaics could generate vary from 25 million megawatt hours to a theoretical maximum of 208 million megawatt hours. The lower figure assumes 20 square metres of panels per dwelling, while the higher figure means every part of buildings being covered with cells.

Solar electricity would give us the means to close between three and twenty-three power stations. Realistically our options lie with using energy more efficiently and employing a mixture of wind, wave and solar power.

*Paul Allen, Centre for Alternative Technology,*
*Machynlleth, Powys*

Years ago, when I was involved in a solar energy system designed for use in remote areas, the energy budget for solar cells was negative: more energy was required to produce a cell than it was capable of generating in its lifetime.

At that point, the main attraction of solar cells was as a power source in remote areas and I was aware of them being used to charge batteries used by radio telephones in remote South American villages where they are much more energy efficient than any other solution.

It's all too easy to fall into the trap of forgetting the energy needed to construct the system in the first place.

*Anthony B. Plant, South Yardley, Birmingham*

Solar electric cells have become considerably more competitive in recent years due to the commercialization of 'thin films' using minute amounts of silicon. Incorporated in buildings, they're competitive with some forms of conventional cladding and, though they add to overall construction costs, these buildings can be rented or sold at a premium.

Germany, France and Switzerland led the way and the UK has now adjusted electricity tariffs to give their owners short payback periods.

Our thin film silicon plant in South Wales produces cells which, excluding the energy used in production of the glass, pay for themselves within six to eight years.

With two in five of the world's population without access to electricity, even lower estimates for population growth and energy demand indicate an energy gap which can be closed only by renewable forms of energy, with solar playing a major part.

*Philip Bouverat, Intersolar, High Wycombe, Buckinghamshire*

**(352) QUESTION: If we have a severe frost, how come grass and trees don't die with all the other plants? Is some form of cryogenics taking place?**

Frost tolerance and hardiness is determined by several factors, the main one of which is the concentration of cytoplasm in the plant's cells. Cytoplasm is the cell's living contents suspended in an aqueous solution. Water expands when it freezes; if water freezes in a plant cell, it expands and ruptures the cell and kills it. If a plant has a very concentrated cytoplasm, there's little water to expand, or it expands only a little, which the elastic cell wall can cope with, so the cell doesn't rupture. So plants with a concentrated cytoplasm are more frost-hardy.

Some plants make a natural 'antifreeze' in winter which stops the expansion and rupturing. Cycles of freezing and thawing will also affect frost-hardiness. Repeated hard freezes and rapid thaws do most damage.

The duration of the frost is also a factor. Woody plants – trees and shrubs – have a strong outer bark which protects against frost. Grasses contain a lot of silicon which protects them.

*Geoff Hodge, Garden News, Peterborough*

**(353) QUESTION: If the Scottish National Party or Plaid Cymru ever achieved independence for Scotland and Wales and there were counties that wished to stay in the UK, how would they be treated?**

Parliament has already recognized that Wales should be treated as a single national unit. This was acknowledged by the Local

Government (Wales) Act 1972, which finally determined the status of the county of Gwent within Wales.

The national integrity of Wales is therefore acknowledged by all parties, and its constitutional future as a united country should be decided by the people of Wales.

*Sion Ffrancon, Plaid Cymru, Caerdydd/Cardiff*

The process of independence in Scotland would begin with the SNP winning a popular mandate at a General Election. Negotiations would be undertaken and an independence package put before the Scottish people at a referendum, to be accepted or rejected by democratic consent.

Scotland no longer has 'counties' as such and has been a unified nation for many centuries. All of present-day Scotland was independent before 1707 and all of Scotland moved into the Union then. There's no evidence of any part of Scotland wishing to have a constitutional future different from the rest of the country.

However, as a party strongly committed to decentralization, the SNP seeks to apply this to the governance of an independent Scotland, specifically in relation to guaranteeing the autonomy of the island communities.

*Kevin Pringle, Scottish National Party, Edinburgh*

## (354) QUESTION: Who were the Coventry Martyrs? Did they have any influence on the expression 'sent to Coventry'?

The twelve Coventry Martyrs were burned at the stake for refusing to accept the orthodox doctrines of the Roman Catholic Church. Nine members of the Protestant Lollard tendency were executed before Henry VIII's break with Rome in the 1530s.

They were: Joan Ward, burned in 1512; Master Archer; Thomas Bond; Master Hawkins; Robert Hockett (or Hatchet); Thomas

315

Lansdail; Master Wrigsham, and Mistress Smith, burned in 1520, and Robert Silkeby (or Silkesby), burned in 1522.

Three more, Laurence Saunders, Robert Glover and Cornelius Bongey (or Bungey), were burned in 1555 during Queen Mary's reversion to Roman Catholic orthodoxy. When Mary died in 1558, her sister Elizabeth I restored the Protestant faith.

The Coventry Martyrs have no relevance to the expression 'sent to Coventry', the most common explanation of which relates to Royalist prisoners captured during the English Civil War and 'sent to Coventry' to be housed at St John's Church.

*Jenni Bailey, Coventry City Council*

### (355) QUESTION: How does one steer a balloon on long distance journeys?

Steering a balloon in normal flight is very difficult but experienced balloonists learn how to use different wind directions at different altitudes. They must ascend or descend until they find the wind direction they need and simply run with it.

The art of finding the right wind is tested at numerous balloon meetings throughout the year and it's amazing to see two hundred balloons of all shapes and sizes guided around the countryside with great accuracy at events such as the Bristol Balloon Fiesta.

When Steve Fossett embarked on his epic journey, Libya denied him permission to overfly the country so he was obliged to go round it. I designed his Solar Spirit balloon – at 210,000 cu ft slightly larger than a normal one but essentially no different. He had the added advantage of radio and satellite links with meteorologists at his Chicago base to work out the position, speed and direction of his balloon, and any winds available, with great accuracy.

After take-off from St Louis, Missouri, his equipment helped him find the best wind to cross the Atlantic. In the North African area, he would have preferred to pass north of Libya, over the

Mediterranean, but the optimum winds took him south, over Niger, Chad, the Sudan and Egypt. The Libyans allowed him to overfly the south-eastern part of the country, which saved some time so he could continue what became the greatest balloon flight in history since the Montgolfier brothers put man in the air in 1783.

*Don Cameron, Cameron Balloons Ltd, Bristol*

**(356) QUESTION: I've frequently broken the 30 mph speed limit on my bicycle. Has anyone ever been caught for breaking the speed limit on a bike? What was the punishment?**

Our grandson was stopped in a police speed trap and told he had been clocked on his mountain bike at a speed in excess of 50 mph. But he was let off with a caution.

*Mrs E. H. Fensome, Spalding, Lincolnshire*

Former land speed record holder Sir Malcolm Campbell was once cautioned by police for exceeding the speed limit on his bicycle.

*Keith S. Heath, Sleaford, Lincolnshire*

One summer, with other students, I participated in a Duke of Edinburgh's Award gold cycling expedition in Snowdonia. Before we began, one of us brought up the question of breaking speed limits in urban areas and the assessor left us in no doubt that we could be fined and have penalty points added to our driving licences.

*Benjamin M.T. Shaw, Oxford*

My father often told the story of how he and my mother married on 6 June 1936, and he was stopped on his way home from work the

317

next day and accused of exceeding the speed limit on his pedal cycle. He was fined 10s (50p) which was a lot of money in those days.

*Mrs P. Marshall, Enfield, Middlesex*

Top time trialers can exceed an average 30 mph on a 25-mile run. On a training run, just past the 1,572 ft summit of Bwlch Cerrig Duon, near Trecastle, my companion's computer showed 51 mph – and we weren't even trying.

I read of a mountain biker stopped by a patrol car going downhill at 70 mph – and he got away with a caution.

*John Ridge, Carmarthen Wheelers Club*

A young lady I knew in Cambridge in the early seventies was fined for exceeding the speed limit on her bike on her way home in the early hours after a night out in Girton. She protested that her bike had no speedometer but was accused under an eighteenth-century law of 'riding furiously'.

*Clive R. Rice, Brecon, Powys*

My grandfather William Henry Melling was fined for 'riding furiously' down Penwortham Hill in Preston. This was in the early 1900s on his penny-farthing cycle when the speed limit was, I think, 4 mph.

*T. D. Roberts, Thornton Cleveleys, Lancashire*

## (357) QUESTION: Apart from price, what's the difference between pink salmon and red salmon?

Salmon, an older species than man, became an important commercial produce in the early nineteenth century after James Symes became the first man to successfully can it in 1867. Princes has been importing salmon to the UK since 1882.

The salmon family includes steel-head, trout and char, as well as the five salmon species: Chinook, Sockeye/Red, Cohoe, Pink and Chum. All five can be caught in almost every river they inhabit.

Pink salmon live only two years and reach little more than 4 lb. After six months' incubation, they drift downstream and spend two years in rich ocean feeding areas before returning to their birthplace to lay their eggs and die.

The Sockeye/Red salmon lives for four to five years and weighs an average 6 lb. It can migrate inland 700 miles, travelling more than thirty miles a day. Outside the estuary it roams thousands of miles before returning to its natal spawning stream to lay eggs and die. The largest salmon, the Giant Chinook, can live up to seven years and reach 120 lb.

In the first decade of the twentieth century, Sockeye/Reds accounted for 78 per cent of the canned salmon market and were regarded as superior because of their delectable flavour. This breed is still favoured in Japan, which consumes 45 per cent of the world's salmon, compared with Europe's 15 per cent and America's 13 per cent.

Pink salmon was first marketed in the 1880s as Princes Mountain Stream brand. In the past few years the market has grown enormously and now accounts for a quarter of the total value.

*R. Jonkind, Princes Foods, Liverpool*

## (358) QUESTION: Who was Puffing Billy?

*Puffing Billy* was the first steam locomotive built by William Hedley (1779–1843), the English inventor born in Newburn near Newcastle upon Tyne.

Hedley was a colliery viewer and lessee who, improving on earlier attempts at steam power by people such as Richard Trevithick, designed a locomotive with smooth-tyred wheels to run on smooth rails.

His engine, built at Wylam Colliery in 1813, was the first commercial steam locomotive, replacing horses to haul coal trucks 5 miles from the mine to the docks at Lemington on Tyne.

*Puffing Billy* has been preserved and can still be seen in London's Science Museum.

My wife is descended from Oswald Dodd Hedley, one of William Hedley's four sons.

*J. L. Hinds, Denton, Manchester*

## (359) QUESTION: Who has been the youngest person featured on *This Is Your Life*?

The youngest person to appear was David Butler, featured on the show hosted by Eamonn Andrews in 1962 when just seventeen. He stood in at the last minute when footballer Danny Blanchflower famously refused to take part.

David, born in 1944, had been very badly injured at eleven when he unwittingly picked up an unexploded bomb on a family picnic. He lost both legs and one hand but overcame his disabilities, learned to swim to competition level and took up motor racing and flying as soon as he turned seventeen.

During his struggle to learn to walk with artificial legs, he was befriended by legless Battle of Britain pilot Douglas Bader. Bader appeared on the programme and presented David with an RSPCA bravery medal he had just been awarded for rescuing a dog from a frozen lake. 'I must admit, I enjoy being in the spotlight,' said David. 'It gives me a kick that letters addressed to "David Butler, Hemel Hempstead" reach me without delay.'

Other guests on David's programme included boxer Freddie Mills, Formula One driver Tony Brooks and cricketer Ted Dexter.

*Jo Shawyer, Barking, Essex*

**(360) QUESTION: When the prime minister leaves the Commons after a packed Question Time, most MPs make a dash for the exit. Where do they go?**

This weekly political theatre show is the only time when it's standing room only in the Chamber. Afterwards, there's usually a sense of anti-climax, hence the stampede for the door.

Those who made fools of themselves go off to hide. Those who think they did well go off to milk the applause. Some head for the tea rooms for a bun and a bit of gossip. Most troop back to their offices wondering if it's all worthwhile.

*Tony Banks MP, House of Commons*

**(361) QUESTION: Is there anyone living in Britain who has never seen the sea?**

My father-in-law, Charles Shervington, of Harvington, near Evesham, Worcestershire, who died in 1977 at the age of seventy-three, never saw the sea. He was employed as a herdsman for a farmer and ran his own smallholding, which included some poultry. He was always busy milking cows or, in his later years, looking after his poultry. Every day was the same to him and he never took a full day off.

Although he worked very hard, he was quite content and never had any wish to visit the coast.

*D. J. Middleton, Norton, Evesham*

Seaside holidays have been popular and affordable for the working class only comparatively recently. My father, born in 1896, talked of old people living amid the Surrey Docks, in London, who had never left that island all their lives. They lived, went to school and church, worked and were buried there. Even their daily milk came from cows grazing on the island. Some people left the island only to go to The Blue, the market area around the nearby Blue Anchor pub.

*Jim Mannering, Boston, Lincolnshire*

**(362) QUESTION: I remember as a young boy reading about a tapestry being made by Queen Mary. Was it ever completed?**

Queen Mary spent eight years making not a tapestry but a carpet. It measured 108 ins by 78 ins and contained more than a million stitches. In 1950 she lent this carpet to a charity exhibition at the Victoria and Albert Museum where 90,000 people paid 6d (2½p) each to see it, after which it was sold to Canada.

Her lady-in-waiting said: 'It is the Queen's view that it is the duty of every individual to contribute something directly to help the country in its need for dollars.'

*Janice Hines, Stoke on Trent, Staffordshire*

My catalogue brochure (now a little tatty) of the 1951 Festival of Britain includes: 'Her Majesty Queen Mary's historic carpet was bought by the Imperial Order of the Daughters of the Empire for Canada for 100,000 dollars.

'The splendid gesture made by Her Majesty in presenting her carpet to the nation for dollar sale has endeared her still further to the people of this country.'

Queen Mary worked every stitch herself, taking eight years to complete the carpet from a design based on eighteenth-century flower patterns.

*Elaine Hannis, Northampton*

Queen Mary's tapestry was bought by the Canadian Imperial Order of the Daughters of the Empire for its Ottawa headquarters. A cousin of mine, living on Prince Edward Island, had a copy of it on the floor of her dining room when we visited her in 1954.

I have a fire-screen which I worked in tapestry from a special offer in *Woman's Journal* in the early fifties, a copy of one of the panels in Queen Mary's carpet, depicting a beautiful collection of flowers in a garden urn, in shades of blues, pinks, reds and green foliage with a bird on either side.

Though referred to as a carpet, it was really more a tapestry wall-hanging, measuring 108 in by 78 in (9 ft by 6 ft 6 in). When it was shipped to Canada, my penfriend there queued for hours to see it before being marched past it at speed, and expressed her disappointment at its insignificant appearance.

Far from being revered as a national treasure, when someone queried its whereabouts a few years ago it was discovered rolled up in a wardrobe.

*Mrs June Alderton, Orpington, Kent*

In June 1993, I was instrumental in getting this carpet/tapestry put on public show. When I realized the World Association of Flower Arrangers was to hold the Fourth World Flower show in Toronto, I wrote to the organizing committee about the carpet, with information gleaned from a 1957 *Woman's Journal*. It depicts a dozen eighteenth-century flower arrangements, beautifully worked by Queen Mary during the Second World War.

By then the carpet was stored at the National Gallery in Ottawa, which knew very little about it and didn't even know it had it.

Wouldn't it be generous of the people of Canada to allow it to be displayed in Windsor Castle, where Queen Mary originally intended it to be hung?

*Doreen M. G. Wadsworth, Baildon, West Yorkshire*

In the Carved Room at Petworth House, West Sussex, is a gros-point needlework panel in an eighteenth-century giltwood pillar fire-screen. The wide border design includes fruit and flowers with a centre rectangular panel containing two birds in a landscape. The signature 'Mary R, 1943' is worked in the lower right-hand corner.

*Nicky Ingram, The National Trust, Petworth, West Sussex*

**(363) QUESTION: Is it true that polar bears cover their black noses to assist their natural camouflage when stalking their prey?**

This common myth, based on Inuit (Eskimo) folklore, arose because polar bears, both captive and in the wild, often cover their noses with their enormous paws. But this is a matter of comfort, not camouflage.

A polar bear's nose is the only part of its body not covered in a thick layer of fur – even the soles of their feet are hairy. When resting, a bear covers its nose to keep it warm and help warm up the air it's breathing.

Looked at under an electron microscope, polar bear hair is solid and totally transparent, acting like a fibre optic, conducting light down the hair to the animal's black skin. It appears white because of the light reflected through it. This makes polar bear hair a favourite fishing lure for the Inuit in the Arctic.

Polar bears are adapted to survive the cold but are mammals and, given the choice, prefer temperatures of 50 to 60°F.

*Alison Ames MA, Monkey World, Wareham, Dorset*

**(364) QUESTION: Have East Fife ever beaten Forfar 5–4?**

As a long-time East Fife supporter, I'm not aware of such a score though there have been near things. In 1937–38, the season in which East Fife won the Scottish Cup, one match ended Forfar 3, East Fife 5 – if only the home side had snatched a last-minute goal.

In a League Cup match in 1964–65, the first-leg result was Forfar 4, East Fife 3. East Fife went through on aggregate to face Celtic in the quarter finals but I don't know the second leg score. Could East Fife have won 2–0, making the aggregate result East Fife 5, Forfar 4?

*Iain Anderson, Bristol*

It has never happened. The nearest score lines have been the league games: Forfar Athletic 5 – East Fife 4, at Station Park, Forfar, on

22 April 1964; Forfar Athletic 3 – East Fife 5, at Station Park, Forfar, on 23 October 1937; and East Fife 4 – Forfar Athletic 4, at Bayview, Methil, on 27 August 1958.

*Barry Stevens, Southampton*

## (365) QUESTION: How do watch manufacturers ensure their products are waterproof to the depths they claim?

Accurist watches are tested at the factory under a sampling plan to 0.35 psi (pressure per square inch) at room temperature for forty-eight hours and undergo further vacuum dry tests at our London headquarters. Some are sent to an independent testing centre and only after all these tests prove satisfactory is a batch of watches sent for sale.

Watches marked 'water-resistant' are splash-proof while others indicate a depth – 165 ft or 330 ft (50 m or 100 m) – to which they may be taken underwater.

These depths are based on static water pressure, where neither water nor watch is moving, in accordance with International Standard 2281. If you jump or dive into a swimming pool wearing a watch the pressure exerted is momentarily higher. If you swim to a depth of 100 m, pressure on a watch is considerably greater than a static pressure of 100 m.

*Robyn Steer, Accurist Watches Ltd, London*

While I was serving in HM Submarine *Oberon* in the 7th Squadron on the Singapore Station in 1965/67, my wife bought me as a first wedding anniversary present a £52.50 Rolex Oyster Perpetual Chronometer, guaranteed to a depth of 600 ft (180 m).

To test that claim, I asked our captain for permission to lash the watch to the outside of the *Oberon*'s pressure hull. We carried the watch on our next 500-foot dive and recovered it afterwards in full working order.

It's just had its first Rolex service and I've been told it's now worth at least £2,000 – not bad after all those years' wear and tear.

*Derek Lawbuary, London*

## (366) QUESTION: Are there any women in the SAS?

The rules of the SAS Association state that membership applications are allowed by any persons 'serving, or who have served in, or with, the Special Air Service Regiment, since its inception'. There are female members of the SAS Association.

*SAS Association, London SW3*

## (367) QUESTION: How many planes need to be downed for a pilot to become an 'ace'? Who were the top aces during the two world wars?

The term 'ace' was first used by the French during the First World War for a pilot who had brought down at least five enemy aircraft. The first reference in print to an air 'ace' was in *The Times* on 14 September 1917, describing Raoul Lufbery as 'the ace of the American Lafayette Squadron'.

The names of French aces were recorded in official communiqués and America and other countries followed the system though the British definition varied from three to ten combat victories and the term was never officially approved.

Top air ace of the First World War was Baron von Richthofen, the 'Red Baron', with eighty kills claimed. His brother, Lothar, claimed forty kills.

The top ten British, Irish and Commonwealth air aces of the First World War were: Edward Mannock (British), seventy-three kills; William Avery Bishop (Canadian), seventy-two; Raymond Collishaw (Canadian), sixty-two; James Thomas Byford McCudden (British), fifty-seven; Anthony Wetherby Beauchamp-Proctor (South African) and Donald MacLaran (Canadian), fifty-four; William George Barker (Canadian) and Philip Fletcher Fullard

(British), fifty-two; R.S. Dallas (Australian), fifty-one and George Edward Henry McElroy (Irish), forty-nine.

The top air ace of the Second World War was also German – Eric Hartmann, with an amazing 352 kills claimed, nearly all on the Eastern Front.

The top ten British, Irish and Commonwealth air aces of the Second World War were: Marmaduke Thomas St John Pattle (South African), fifty-one; James Edgar 'Johnny' Johnson (British), thirty-eight; Adolf Gysbert 'Sailor' Malan (South African), thirty-five; Brendan 'Paddy' Finucane (Irish), thirty-two; George Frederick Beurling (Canadian), thirty-one; John Robert Daniel Braham and Robert Roland Stanford Tuck (both British), twenty-nine; Neville Frederick Duke (British), twenty-eight; Clive Robert Caldwell (Australian), twenty-eight; and Frank Reginald Carey (British) twenty-eight.

*Russell Ash*, Top Ten of Everything, *1997,*
*Dorling Kindersley, London*

In the First World War, the top Allies' ace was Frenchman Rene Fonck, with seventy-five kills; the leading US airman, Captain Eddie Rickenbacker, had twenty-six.

During the Second World War, Ivan Kojedub of the USSR was the Allies' top ace with sixty-two; top American was Richard Bong with forty.

*Clive Pattison, aviation historian, Chiseldon, Wiltshire*

During aircrew training in the RAF Volunteer Reserve during the Second World War, various training manuals presented us with the cartoon exploits of the infamous Pilot Officer Prune, showing us behaviour to avoid. In one cartoon, the notoriously inept PO Prune had managed to write off five of our own aircraft and in the caption was saying: 'I suppose that makes me a German ace . . .'

*Mr C. Laban, Mexborough, South Yorkshire*

**(368) QUESTION: For how long does a cold or flu germ remain infectious on, say, a door handle?**

Most flu and common cold germs die quickly once they leave the body. Some remnants remain on objects for several hours, but their transfer to another body is a very remote possibility.

At the Common Cold Unit, children with colds played with toys and with volunteers who didn't have colds ... but soon caught them. Another batch of volunteers played with the same toys but were not infected.

A Dr Eliot Dick in the US got people with running colds playing poker with volunteers without colds and the volunteers were all infected. When the game had finished, another group of volunteers played with the cards and none of them caught colds.

*Dr David Tyrell, ex-Director, Common Cold Unit, Salisbury, Wiltshire*


**(369) QUESTION: In the classic *Dallas* TV series, JR's favourite drink was bourbon and branch water. What is branch water?**

In American English, a 'branch' is a stream or brook, so the nearest British equivalent of 'branch water' would be 'spring water'. JR obviously preferred a bottled mixer to the variable taste of tap water with his bourbon corn whiskey.

*David Elias, Quiz Compiler, Nottingham*


**(370) QUESTION: Why Kensington 'Gore'?**

The most common use in English of the word 'gore', with us since the sixteenth century, refers to coagulated blood, stemming from the Old English *gore*, which described animal or human dung, dirt, filth and slime. Similar words are found in Old Norse where *gor* meant slime, Welsh where *gor* is pus and Dutch where *goor* describes mud.

328

Thankfully, for people sharing the name with US politician Al Gore, there's a second meaning – 'a triangular piece of cloth', familiar to fashion manufacturers from the triangular panels of a gored skirt. This word stems from the Old English *gara*, a triangular piece of land, and Kensington Gore, the London street running between Kensington Gardens and the Royal Albert Hall, took its name from this, as did Gorebridge in Lothian.

The original use of 'gore' to describe something triangular stems from the Old English *gar*, a spear with a triangular head. This root has given us the third meaning of gore, familiar from bull-fighting, to stab or pierce.

*Tony Holgate, Chigwell, Essex*

**(371) QUESTION: My encyclopaedia says Amelia Earhart and her navigator may have survived their air crash in 1937 and died of thirst on Nikumaroro Island. What evidence is there for this?**

In 1932, Amelia Mary Earhart, born in Atchison, Kansas, on 24 July 1898, became the first woman to fly the Atlantic solo. In 1937, she and navigator Fred Noonan, forty-four, attempted the first round-the-world flight at Equator latitude in a twin-engined Lockheed Electra.

Setting off from Los Angeles on 21 May, they flew east and landed at Lae, New Guinea. From there they attempted to fly 2,500 miles to Howland Island, but on 2 July radioed that they were running out of fuel.

Further distorted messages were received and it was presumed they had landed and were transmitting from an island but searches failed to find them and it was assumed they had crashed in the ocean.

Many theories have been advanced about Amelia's fate, including a suggestion that she returned to the US and set up a new life as Irene Bolam in New Jersey, or that she was a government spy sent to photograph the Japanese-controlled Marshall Islands, and was caught and executed by the Japanese.

The idea that the pair crash-landed near, or on, the island of Nikumaroro (formerly Gardner Island, now part of the Pacific republic of Kiribati), only to die of thirst, came from a 1989 expedition conducted by The International Group for Historic Aircraft Recovery. A box which may have been the Electra navigator's bookcase and a size-9 lady's shoe were discovered, but the bookcase couldn't be positively identified and Earhart wore a size 6.

*Rachel Hutton, Manchester*

In autumn 1938, I was in Madame Tussaud's in London with my mother when a slim lady with short grey hair asked us if we knew whether there was a model of Amelia Earhart, and insisted we take her there.

As we showed her the model my mother suddenly noticed a likeness, but when we looked round the lady had disappeared. She was flesh and blood, whoever she was.

*Mrs E. R. Buckland, St Agnes, Cornwall*

## (372) QUESTION: Were The Three Stooges, the film comics, really brothers?

The violent slapstick of the Three Stooges comedy trio made a successful transition from stage to screen to be fêted by audiences for almost four decades from the mid-twenties.

Brooklyn-born brothers Moe Howard, born Moses Horowitz in 1897, and Samuel Howard (nicknamed 'Shemp'), born Samuel Horowitz in 1891, started acting as stooges for various vaudeville acts in 1923. They were joined in 1928 by Philadelphia-born musician/entertainer Larry Fine, born Lawrence Feinstein in 1902.

The advent of sound movies in the early thirties saw a huge decline in vaudeville and Shemp Howard was replaced in the Three Stooges act by another Howard (Horowitz) brother, Jerome (nicknamed 'Curly'), born in 1906. Columbia Pictures commissioned the trio to make a series of short films, and Curly, Moe and Larry became an instant success, leading to a run of more than two hundred short films.

In 1946, Curly had a severe stroke, leading to his death six years later. Meanwhile, his place in the trio was filled by the return of Shemp. The act continued until 1955 when Shemp died. For four years Moe and Larry were joined by Joe Besser and from 1959 by Joe De Rita until Larry died in 1974, followed by Moe a year later.

*Max Tyler, British Music Hall Society, Chichester*


## (373) QUESTION: How does stress cause ulcers?

There's no good scientific evidence that stress is a predisposing factor in stomach ulcers. It is now thought that the majority of ulcers are due to infection with a bacteria called Helicobacter pylori. This was discovered in 1983 by Australian gastro-enterologist Dr Barry Marshall.

Now stomach ulcers are treated by a short course of antibiotics to eradicate this bacteria rather than the reduction of stomach acid alone. About 50 per cent of the population are infected with this bacterium, however, of which about 83 per cent will not suffer any trouble.

*Dr Julia L. Newton, Gosforth, Newcastle*


## (374) QUESTION: What is the vintage car driven by Glenn Close in the film *101 Dalmatians*?

This isn't a vintage classic car but a seventies hand-built re-creation – a Panther De Ville designed and built by brilliant British car designer Bob Jankel, inspired by older vehicles.

The De Ville was inspired by the Bugatti Royale and bears some resemblance to it, though it's not a direct copy. The Bugatti was so expensive in its time that only a handful were made, mostly for heads of state and the super-rich, and they now sell for several million pounds, though they're rarely seen at auction.

Sadly, Bob Jankel's company, Panther Cars, no longer exists, but the assets were bought by a Korean firm. His other great creation was the Panther J72, inspired by the old Jaguar SS100.

These cars cannot be called replicas as they weren't intended as exact copies. But they're the closest one could get to the prohibitively expensive originals. De Villes and J72s change hands on the classic car market for £20,000 to £25,000.

*Peter Smith, Stokenchurch, Buckinghamshire*

When my family and I visited the Disney MGM studios in Florida, we were told the car driven by Glenn Close in *101 Dalmatians* was purpose-built for the film. The car and outfits worn by Miss Close are on display there, as well as special effects used in this marvellous production.

*A. Duffy, Christchurch, Dorset*

**(375) QUESTION: We know of the royal corgis, but are there any cats kept at the royal residences?**

According to Buckingham Palace officials, there are no cats kept there either as pets or as 'mousers', though there may be one or two kept as pets by royal staff in the Royal Mews.

There are also no pet cats at any of the other Royal residences. The only pets kept by the Queen are her corgis, though some shooting dogs are also kept at Sandringham.

*Bethany Hart, Kensington, London*

**(376) QUESTION: Why is there a lighthouse on top of the buildings at the corner of Gray's Inn and Pentonville Roads outside King's Cross station in London?**

This now dilapidated tower is known as the King's Cross Lighthouse but never functioned as one. Inspection of the interior has ruled out suggestions that it may have been a camera obscura, fire-watching post, bell tower, clock tower or viewing platform.

Some claim to remember it as a helter-skelter in the twenties but the tower existed in the 1870s and the fairground was further along Euston Road on the site of the present Camden Town Hall.

At the beginning of the twentieth century, its base housed an oyster bar but the tower doesn't appear to have been built to advertise it. Mid-nineteenth-century illustrations show an earlier tower which wasn't as slim as the present one. The tower was rebuilt by the Metropolitan Railway in the 1870s but there's no indication as to why this particular style was chosen. It was probably constructed as an unusual feature, an architectural conceit.

*Malcolm Holmes, Camden Borough Archivist, London*

---

**(377) QUESTION: I was in a class of fifty-three at Lingham Lane Junior School, Moreton, Cheshire, in 1948. Has anyone been in a bigger class in Britain?**

As present headteacher of Lingham Primary School, I sought to verify this information but my records go back only to 1956. However, when the term began on 4 September of that year, class 3D had fifty-four pupils and an HMI visited the school to discuss class numbers.

*D. Wright, Moreton, Wirral*

In 1935, at Mount Pleasant Infants School, Clayton-le-Moors, Lancashire, when there was no limit on class numbers and no restriction on admission of children over the compulsory school age, I taught a reception class of more than seventy children.

Everyone knew that Silver Jubilee beakers and sweets were to be given to all school children and the number in my class rose from thirty-five to nearly eighty. Children without chairs sat on every inch of floor space with others on the window ledges.

Teaching consisted solely of telling stories, singing nursery rhymes and chanting numbers one to ten. Attendance fell immediately after the beakers and sweets had been distributed.

*Mrs G. Hardy, Cheadle Hulme, Cheshire*

In July 1938, I was in a class of fifty-six at the Pinkwell Junior School, Hayes, Middlesex. Our teachers never had any difficulty controlling their classes. We all faced the front, gave regular attendance and were keen to learn.

When the war started we had no school for a time and then only for half-days. It wasn't unusual to spend the day in the school air-raid shelter and we were often kept awake at night by air raids.

*D. L. Creasey, Hayes, Middlesex*

In the late fifties, I and a colleague each had classes of sixty second-year junior children. The situation eased when another teacher was appointed and our classes reduced to forty-eight: it was heaven.

*Mrs M. A. Butler, Cardiff*

In 1950–51 a huge housing estate was built around our village and virtually overnight the population of our school almost doubled.

I was a first-year junior-school pupil and our room contained both first and second years. We sat two to a double desk with two more sitting sideways at each end. Some classrooms had forms for seating so three children were squeezed into desks designed for two.

The teacher started the first-year children on sums or reading and then taught the second years something on the same subject. After a while the school obtained some more furniture and two extra classes were put in the hall.

*M. Reynolds, Light Oaks, Staffordshire*

When I attended Beckton Road School in Canning Town, London, between 1918 and 1927, my class had seventy pupils and I recall finishing sixty-sixth in my class in 1923 because I missed some exams due to illness.

*Fred Lowe, Heverhill, Suffolk*

In 1944, aged nine, I was at North Prospect School, Plymouth, in a class of sixty. All the men were off fighting the war so our teachers were all women. We sat in five rows of six two-seater desks and the top row of twelve pupils were supposed to be the brightest but when it came to taking the scholarship (later known as the 11-plus), only three of the top-row pupils passed while in my row at the bottom, ten out of twelve of us passed.

*Len Fenn, Plymstock, Devon*

During the war, class sizes at Lady Banks Junior School, Ruislip Manor, Middlesex, increased dramatically until the summer term of 1943 when I was ten and was in a class of eighty-five. For that term, we used the school hall as our classroom.

*Raymond Richardson, Berkhamsted, Hertfordshire*

## (378) QUESTION: My father told me the Germans drink beer while in Britain we drink ale. What's the difference?

There are more than 1,000 types of beer brewed in Britain, more than in any other country, and we are also different in that most of our beer is consumed on draught in pubs.

Ale, as it was originally known, was brewed without hops. It started to be known as beer in the fifteenth century, when hops began to be used for flavouring and preservation, a practice copied from the Low Countries.

These days, beer comes in four main categories: ale, porter, stout and lager. Ales range from dark mild to bitter, offering a huge variety of flavour, aroma and appearance.

In Germany, *bier* is what we call lager, brewed, fermented and matured at a lower temperature than ale. The name lager comes from the German *lagern*, meaning to store. In the days before refrigeration, Bavarian brewers overcame the problem of spoiled beer by storing it in caves packed with ice.

Lager accounted for less than 1 per cent of the British beer market before 1960, but has now grown to more than 55 per cent.

*Brian Finnerty, Brewers and Licensed Retailers Association,*
*London*

German *bier* is normally yellow and bottom fermented (the yeast settles to the bottom of the vat) and is referred to as *pils*, rather than lager.

English ales (and porter and stout) are normally darker in colour and are top fermented (the yeast rises and is skimmed from the top of the vat). German *alt beer*, *kolsch beer* and *weizen* (wheat) beer are also top fermented, giving them their special taste.

In Germany, we have more than 6,000 different types of beer and, until recently, Germany was the second largest beer market in the world, after the US. It's now third, after the US and China. But our per capita consumption, 135 litres per head per year, is the world leader.

*Colin Bruder, Velbert, Germany*

**(379) QUESTION: Several weather stations used in the BBC's shipping forecast are automatic. How can they judge the visibility distance?**

Visibility at automatic weather stations is measured by an instrument called a transmissometer or visiometer, with a light source and sampling receiver placed a short distance apart. The receiver measures the amount of light reaching it from the light source. As visibility decreases, more light is absorbed before it reaches the receiver.

Visibility measured over this short distance can be converted to the normal visibility reported by human sight.

Comparative tests have shown these instruments to be accurate, particularly at low visibilities, when the information is most important to mariners.

*Andy Yeatman, The Met Office, Bracknell, Berkshire*


## (380) QUESTION: When did women first start shaving their legs?

Through information passed on by archaeologists and historians, it has been established that women have shaved their legs as far back as the Stone Age when, like men, they used sharpened rocks or shells in the absence of a good razor.

In Ancient Egypt, women developed a method of using hot wax and gauze, which was followed in the Middle East by a method employing cotton string laced between the fingers (a *bandandoz*) which they then ran briskly over the legs encircling and extracting the hairs.

By the eighteenth century, women had adopted a poultice of caustic lye to remove hairs.

The new age of convenient shaving was introduced in 1903 with the birth of the first safety razor with replaceable blades, invented by King Camp Gillette. Improvements and variations have continued ever since in an effort to keep the average 5,500 hairs on each leg under control.

In Britain, 31 million blades are sold for women and 470 million for men each year.

*Gwendaline Rawlings, Gillette UK, London*

(381) QUESTION: Why is the main thoroughfare of Mbabane, the capital of Swaziland, called Alastair Miller Street?

Alexander Mitchell Miller (known as Allister) was born at sea off Singapore in April 1864, the son of Scots merchant marine Captain Alexander Miller, and spent most of his early life in Tennessee, where his father had set up business.

In 1879, at the age of fifteen, he returned to Liverpool with his family, and in 1884 began working for the *Liverpool Echo*, leaving Britain in 1887 to become a sub-editor on the *Cape Argus* in South Africa. He soon moved to the *Gold Fields Times* in the Transvaal and heard that gold had been discovered in Swaziland, where Ngwenyama (King) Mbandzeni was issuing mineral rights concessions.

Mbandzeni set up a committee under Theophilus Shepstone Jnr to administer white affairs and Miller was recruited as secretary.

He struck up a good relationship with concession owner John Thorburne and became his manager when the King died in October 1889. He married Thorburne's daughter Beatrice in London that year.

Miller became the leading white settler in the country, general manager of the Swaziland Corporation, set up the Chamber of Commerce, established the *Swaziland Times* and wrote a short history of the country. His son, Allister (known as Sheikh), was a Royal Flying Corps pilot in the First World War and later founded Union Airways, which became South African Airways.

*Huw Jones, author*, Biographical Register of Swaziland to 1902,
*Bisley, Gloucestershire*


(382) QUESTION: How did the word 'suffer' come to have two such different meanings in English?

The full *Oxford English Dictionary* lists eighteen distinguishable meanings of 'suffer', all conveying the same idea of 'endure', 'permit' or 'tolerate'. Shakespeare occasionally used the word 'suffer' as a transitive verb meaning to inflict pain or to make someone suffer, but this use is now obsolete.

All modern forms of the word can be traced back to the Latin *sufferre*, through the early French *soeffrir* (spelt in several different ways), meaning to bear.

*David Elias, Nottingham*


## (383) QUESTION: Is there an absolute difference between a tornado, a cyclone and a whirlwind, or is it just a matter of degree?

A cyclone is a southern hemisphere hurricane, rotating anticlockwise. Cyclones and hurricanes are large masses of rotating air, originating over warm seas, holding millions of tons of water. Their winds are rated at Force 12 on the Beaufort Scale and can exceed 150 mph in the core rim. They can last many days.

A tornado is a local phenomenon, initiated by warm and cold weather fronts meeting and causing an updraught of rotating air which bridges the Earth's surface and the clouds. They are ephemeral, lasting from a few seconds to a few hours, though most are sustained for only thirty to forty minutes.

Wind in the air funnel can reach very high speeds, destroying houses and lifting vehicles. Film of a tornado in the American Midwest showed a residential street where houses on one side had been destroyed, while the other side suffered relatively slight damage.

Tornadoes over water are known as waterspouts and I have seen several of these in the Indian Ocean.

A whirlwind is very much less definable. It can be a minor swirl of air or wind (known as a willy-willy in Australia) up to severe localized weather conditions such as the one which brought down many trees in southern England in 1987 and was known (incorrectly) as a hurricane. Whirlwinds are usually associated with a cold front meeting warm air over land.

*Bernard Coupe, Stone, Staffordshire*

(384) QUESTION: If a rifle like a Lee Enfield .303 were fired directly upwards, how high would the bullet travel and how much time would elapse before it landed at one's feet?

Experiments on this specific question and many others regarding bullet speed and velocity were conducted before the First World War by ballistics expert R. L. Tippins on tidal mud on the Suffolk side of the River Stour. Similar experiments took place in Germany and the US.

Tippins discovered that the Lee Enfield .303 mark VII, later used in both world wars, had a muzzle velocity of 2,350 ft per second and that a bullet fired exactly vertically would rise for 19 seconds to a height of 9,000 ft. Its maximum returning velocity would be 300 ft per second, taking another 36 seconds to hit the ground. On landing, the bullet would have 30 ft lbs energy. Estimates at the time suggested it would need around 60 ft lbs to injure anyone.

On a soft pine roof board at the launch point, the bullet would cause only a one-sixteenth inch dent, like a light tap with a hammer. The bullets were very unstable in flight, depending on air conditions, and hardly ever fell at the spot from which they were fired.

*Bill Curtis, National Rifle Association Museum, Bisley, Surrey*


(385) QUESTION: What was the first cocktail? Where did the word 'cocktail' originate?

Mixed drinks of various styles have been drunk since time immemorial, but the term cocktail generally applies to a mixture of two alcoholic liquors with the possible addition of sugar or honey, fruit or fruit juice, ice and bitters.

One reference to an early cocktail, praised by the Emperor Commodus in the second century AD, refers to 'a mixture of lemon juice and powdered adders – an excellent aperitif'.

Early cocktails were often concocted with medicinal intentions in mind, unlike modern mixers that have the opposite effect.

While spirits may be sold on licensed premises only in strictly defined measures, the Licensing Act relaxes the rule if spirits are mixed together, hence the practice in cocktail bars of 'free pouring' into a glass shaker.

The first modern cocktail was the dry martini, which combines gin, dry vermouth and ice, and is served with a twist of lemon peel or an olive. The greater the proportion of gin, the drier the cocktail.

As to the origin of the name, a definitive source is unknown. Various American sources record the decoration of drinks with the tail feathers of fighting cocks, while in eighteenth-century England, a spirituous 'cock ale' was given to fighting cocks to increase their aggressiveness. The victor was toasted with a mixture of as many ingredients as the survivor had tail feathers.

*John Emmerson, member of the Bartenders' Guild, Batley,*
*West Yorkshire*

The most likely answer is the mixture of spirits known as 'cock tale', which was fed to fighting cocks to put them in fighting mood. The same drink would then be served to the punters with a tail feather put in it for every ingredient added.

*Carl Munson, Tadley, Hampshire*

I believe modern cocktails were born in New Orleans when Antoine Peychaud, a refugee from San Domingo, brought to that city a secret family recipe for a tonic called bitters.

He dispensed his tonic, mixed with brandy, from his shop at 437 Royal Street, and the popularity of mixed drinks spread rapidly through the city. The name derives from the French *coquetier*, the egg-cup he used to measure the contents of the mixture.

*John Paddon, Bolton, Lincolnshire*

**(386) QUESTION: How did the flower Sweet William get its name?**

Sweet William is the common name of the popular annual, biennial or perennial flowering herb *Dianthus barbatus*, of the pink family *Caryophyllaceae*, which comes in various colours and grows to a height of about 2 ft.

A native of eastern Russia and China, it's commonly thought to have been given its name in honour of William, Duke of Cumberland, nicknamed 'Butcher' Cumberland after he put down the Jacobite rebellion, defeating Bonnie Prince Charlie at Culloden in 1746, and savagely suppressing further resistance to the Hanoverian monarchy.

It's further claimed that just as the flower was nicknamed Sweet William by pro-Hanoverians, it was also named Stinking Billy by those still loyal to the Stuarts.

But the flower is first noted as Sweet William almost two centuries earlier in agricultural writer Thomas Tusser's 1573 publication *Five Hundreth Pointes of Good Husbandrie*.

It's actually named after St William of Vercelli because its flowers are in bloom on 25 June, his festival day.

*Lynne Hall, Hunsdon Pound, Hertfordshire*

**(387) QUESTION: Painted near our house is the slogan 'Long Live Dubcek'. Is this Britain's longest-surviving political graffiti?**

Though indistinct, the message 'Throw Attle out' can still be read on the side of a shed in Dedham, near Colchester, Essex. Another misspelled reference to Clem Attlee's premiership appeared on a barn which, until recently, stood near the shed. It said: 'Throw Atlee and his thugs out now.'

*A. W. Howard, Holton St Mary, Suffolk*

Daubed on a wall near my former home in Cheshunt, Hertfordshire, is the immortal line 'Harold Wilson is a nitwit', dating from the mid sixties. Somewhat faded, it's still discernible, despite several attempts to erase it.

*J. Westley, Kessingland, Suffolk*

When I started work for a building firm in Pokesdown, Bourne-mouth, in 1959, there was painted in yellow across the brick wall that carries the main road over the railway: 'Empire Loyalists say be British – not American puppets.' I was told this appeared during the Suez crisis. Slightly faded, it remains visible to this day.

*John F. Barrett, Christchurch, Dorset*

There's a faded message urging support for the British Party, complete with lightning logo, on a bridge in a quiet lane on the outskirts of Winsford, Cheshire. I think this may date from Sir Oswald Mosley's political party of the thirties.

As an example of the futility of this form of expression, there's a reference near the new Hulme Arch in Manchester to Viraj Mendis, the Sri Lankan taken from a Manchester church and deported: 'Viraj Mendis must stay.' It did, he didn't.

*David F. Hinman, Manchester*

Beneath a railway bridge in Bristol is a reminder from the 1936/37 elections 'Moseley (sic) will win', clearly altered to 'Moseley will swing'.

*L. F. Taylor, Bristol*

On a bridge near Huntingdon where we used to cruise our river boat a year or so ago was the slogan: 'Open the 2nd Front Now', which was often seen in the forties before D-Day when the Russians felt they were fighting the war alone.

*C. R. Brown, Higham Ferrers, Northamptonshire*

**(388) QUESTION: I was born in Hebron, Northumberland. Has it any connection with the Hebron in Palestine?**

The small village of Hebron, just north of Morpeth, Northumberland, is first mentioned as Heburn in 1251. Later mentions refer to Heborin (1264), Heburne (1346) and Hebbourn (1663).

Godfrey Watson's book *Goodwife Hot and Others: Northumberland's Past as Shown in its Place Names* suggests Hebron was originally High Borrans, the Old English name for the burial mounds made by the Celtic Ottadini tribe.

J. Hodgson's 1832 *History of Northumberland* suggests Hebron comes simply from 'He-burn', the highest stream of the Bothalburn. The population of Hebron today is just 878, a far cry from the 75,000 of the Hebron in the southern Judean Hills on the West Bank of the Jordan River.

There is, as far as we are aware, no direct connection between the two. Another UK Hebron is in Dyfed, 20 miles north of Tenby.

*Heather Mills, Morpeth Library, Northumberland*


**(389) QUESTION: Tarzan never said: 'Me Tarzan, you Jane.' What other supposed famous sayings were never actually uttered?**

Summing up his role in the 1932 film *Tarzan the Ape Man*, the first sound version of the story by Edgar Rice Burroughs, the star of the film, Johnny Weissmuller, states that the line 'Me Tarzan, you Jane' had never been said in either the film or the novel. All he did was thump his chest and say: 'Tarzan', before pointing to her and grunting: 'Jane.'

Other popular misquotations include: Captain Kirk's: 'Beam me up, Scotty' in the *Star Trek* series – the nearest he got to this was: 'Beam us up, Mr Scott'; James Callaghan's: 'Crisis? What crisis?' in January 1979, when his actual quote was: 'I don't think other people in the world would share the view there is mounting chaos'; Humphrey Bogart's: 'Play it again, Sam' in the 1942 film *Casablanca* – his real line was: 'If she can stand it, I can. Play it.'

Louis Armstrong's: 'Man, if you gotta ask you'll never know' – his actual words when asked what jazz was were: 'If you have to ask . . . shame on you.'

Abraham Lincoln's: 'The ballot is stronger than the bullet' – his 1858 speech actually used the words: 'To give victory to the right, not bloody bullets, but peaceful ballots only, are necessary.' And finally, George Bernard Shaw's: 'England and America are two countries divided by a common language'. It has been attributed to Shaw in various forms but hasn't been found in any of his writings.

*Martina Adlington*, Oxford Dictionary of Quotations,
*Oxford University Press*

A contender for the most frequent misquotation must surely be 'Till death us do part' from the wedding service. This almost always comes out as: 'Till death do us part.'

*Charles Price, Rugeley, Staffordshire*

The famous conversation between Lord Carnarvon, sponsor and Howard Carter, Egyptologist, at the opening of Tutankhamun's tomb on 26 November 1922, after 3,274 years, was called into question when I met Sergeant Richard Adamson on 6 November 1980.

A security guard from 1922 to 1932, he was one of the very few people to witness the event. I asked him: 'Did Carnarvon say: "Well, can you see anything?" And get the reply from Carter: "Yes . . . wonderful things!" With a wry smile, Adamson replied: 'No, nothing like that at all.'

*Michael Longley, Nutley, Sussex*

Addressing the Commons on 13 May 1940, Winston Churchill did not say: 'I have nothing to offer but blood, sweat and tears.' He actually offered: '. . . blood, toil, tears and sweat'.

And Hamlet, in Act 5 Scene 1, says not 'Alas! Poor Yorick. I knew him well' but 'Alas! Poor Yorick. I knew him, Horatio'.

*Tim Mickleburgh, Grimsby*


The phrase 'money is the root of all evil' is often quoted. What the Bible (in 1 Timothy 6 v10) actually says is that 'the love of money is the root of all evils'. It's not the inanimate object but our attitude towards it that causes evil.

*A. E. Harvey, Great Sutton, South Wirral*


One famous quote which was never in the text is 'Elementary, my dear Watson' supposedly from Sir Arthur Conan Doyle's stories about Sherlock Holmes. Holmes did, however, utter his other famous line 'The game is afoot' twice in the short stories and novels.

*Ben Notley, Stevenage, Hertfordshire*


Shakespeare's 'Lay on, Macduff' is generally misquoted as 'Lead on, Macduff' and 'A little knowledge is a dangerous thing' is in fact 'A little learning . . .'

'Bell, book and candle' is often called for in exorcism when they're actually used in excommunication. And as for the much characterized Mad Hatter's Tea Party, Alice in fact says 'I almost wish I'd gone to see the Hatter instead' (of the March hare).

*Louise Gibbs, Broadstairs, Kent*


**(390) QUESTION: How much money in notes would have to pass through an airport metal detector before the metal in the notes set the machine off?**

My company can program the CEIA Walk-through Metal Detector machines it supplies to airports, governments, secure establishments, etc., to detect a range of metal objects and metals in solid, sheet, foil, evaporated or sputtered (painted) form.

Metal detectors work on the cumulative mass of metal and can be programed to discover various metal objects, such as small guns, weapons and knives, or metals such as gold, silver, stainless steel, copper, lead, aluminium or combinations of these.

For security reasons, we would not want to disclose the exact amount of metal-foiled bank notes which would set off the alarm, but it's worth noting that machines exist which can detect the foil on scratchcards and even the smallest computer chips.

*Adam Hogg, Pulsar Developments Ltd, Marlow,*
*Buckinghamshire*

## (391) QUESTION: Who is or was MacPherson and what are his struts?

In 1947, Ford lured away General Motors' engineer Earle S. MacPherson to become its chief engineer. He was soon promoted to vice-president of engineering and was credited with the design of the highly efficient vehicle front suspension system, the MacPherson Strut.

The system was first used in Britain on the 1950 Consul 4 and Zephyr 6 range of large family cars. It comprises a vertical coil spring around a hydraulic shock absorber, mounted at the top in a steel and rubber block thrust bearing, bolted to a reinforced inner wing of the car.

Despite great changes in vehicle design and development, MacPherson's forty-year-old invention is lighter than most other suspension systems and is still in almost every car on the road.

*Derek Sansom, Ford Education Service, Brentwood, Essex*

## (392) QUESTION: Why 'silhouette' for a shadowy outline?

The silhouette, a solid two-dimensional form defined only by its outline, found great currency in twentieth-century posters and other decorative arts. In earlier times, silhouette profiles were cut freehand from paper, normally black, and mounted on a lighter-coloured background as shadow portraits.

This was a form of portraiture popular in the late eighteenth and early nineteenth centuries, before photography was available, as an inexpensive way of capturing a person's likeness.

Some silhouette artists were highly skilled and professional but silhouette cutting was also a popular parlour pastime.

The word silhouette came to us from French minister of finance Etienne de Silhouette (1709–67) who, in 1759, attempted to tax the rich people of his country so heavily that he was in danger of reducing some of them to poverty. As a result his name was applied, in derision, to any minimal-outline portrait.

*Antony Crolla, silhouette artist, Tenerife*

Eighteenth-century Controller General of France, Etienne de Silhouette, had his name attached to outline portraits not because he fleeced the rich but because he simplified the highly complex French tax system. But his idea attracted nothing but ridicule and he had to retire after a year.

His name became synonymous with anything reduced to its simplest form.

*K. M. Sissons, Exeter, Devon*

The *Larousse Etymologique* says silhouette comes from the ironical French *à la silhouette*, first used in France in 1759 to describe a rapid passage. It was taken from the name of Finance Minister E. de Silhouette, who had become unpopular in his business dealings and lost his job. It was later used to describe an unfinished, badly done object, as in *portrait à la silhouette* in 1782.

*Mrs C. Peaker, Milton Keynes, Buckinghamshire*

**(393) QUESTION: I have a picture of US Navy staff in 1931 commemorating the forty-second anniversary of the Samoan Disaster. What was this?**

In March 1889, seven warships were lying in Apia harbour, in what is now Western Samoa, as a political crisis blew up over possession of the South Pacific islands.

US ships *Trenton*, *Nipsic* and *Vandalia* confronted Germany's *Olga*, *Alder* and *Eber*. The British steam cruiser HMS *Calliope* stood by to represent British interests.

On Friday 15 March, the barometer fell alarmingly, and the ships prepared for a hurricane. Apia harbour was, in fact, a most unsuitable place to ride out a storm, but mutual distrust meant none dared leave. At 5 a.m. the next morning the *Eber* was thrown broadside on a reef and sank with the loss of seventy-six of her crew of eighty. Seeing his ship being forced towards the reef, the captain of the USS *Nipsic* ran her on to the beach, losing seven men. At 8 a.m. a huge wave lifted the *Alder* onto the reef with the loss of twenty of her crew.

The *Olga*, USS *Vandalia* and HMS *Calliope* were dangerously close, and the latter two collided. On the *Calliope*, Captain Kane managed, by a magnificent feat of seamanship, to steam out of the harbour and gain the open sea, where she rode out the storm.

The *Vandalia* foundered with the loss of forty-three men. The *Trenton* also sank, though all but one of her crew of 450 survived. Last to go was the *Olga*, which ran ashore without loss of life. This disaster cost the Americans fifty-one lives and the Germans ninety-six.

The *Calliope*, built in 1884, became a training ship in 1907 and was not broken up until 1951, at the ripe old age of sixty-seven.

*A. J. Smythe, Rayleigh, Essex*

Samoa, halfway between Hawaii and Australia, was discovered in 1722 by the Dutch explorer Jacob Roggeveen but remained free from imperial occupation. In June 1889, following the disaster, Germany, Britain and the US decided in Berlin that all three would share in protecting the islands, leaving King Malieota as their nominal sovereign.

*John Reilly, Naval Historical Center, Washington, DC*

**(394) QUESTION: I'm told 'Baby On Board' car stickers were intended to alert emergency services to search for a baby should there be an accident. Is this true?**

'Baby on Board' stickers became established in the early eighties after gaining earlier popularity in Germany and the Netherlands. Emergency services regard them as unnecessary. Ambulance, police and fire service personnel are trained to be on the look-out for a baby or small child after a car crash.

For optimum vision, the only sticker on a car's window should be a valid tax disc, but a Baby on Board sticker may calm down an otherwise aggressive driver.

*Rebecca Rees, AA, Basingstoke, Hampshire*

**(395) QUESTION: When reporting sick in the Army, what was the No 9 pill we were given – and why No 9?**

Among field medical equipment issued to a Medical Officer was a black enamelled tablet tin with an inventory of contents inside the lid. 'No 9' was the ninth in the list of thirteen tablets, the 'tabs cathartic' for treating constipation and the source of Army humour ever since. Most bingo callers still refer to 'Doctors Orders – No 9'.

*Lieut. Col (retd) Eyeions OBE, RAMC Museum, Aldershot*

The way it worked was this: if, at the 9 a.m. medical parade, a soldier reported sick with what was considered after a brief examination by the Medical Officer to be a frivolous complaint, he was assigned 'Medicine and Duty'.

He did, in fact, dodge duty for that day because the medicine in question was the dreaded No 9 pill which 'purged' him of his sin, physically and mentally, as he became a permanent attendant at the latrine. I never experienced it myself but I'm reliably informed it left the intestines whiter than white and the mind cleared of any doubt as to what constituted a 'frivolous complaint'.

*Ex-Sgt Harry S. Stewart (6088930), Ryde, Isle of Wight*

I recall one of my two soldier brothers in the First World War reciting: 'Oh lummy, oh lummy/What's up with my tummy/It's something I've eaten, by gum/But I won't report ill/There's that No 9 pill/And I've seen its effect on a chum.'

*Mrs E. Young, Washington, Tyne and Wear*

Just after the end of the First World War, our postman in Romsey, Hampshire, was ex-Grenadier Bill Moody, always immaculately turned out from his old-fashioned helmet to his gleaming boots.

At number 9 Mount Pleasant, we had no letter-box so Bill heralded his arrival with a sharp rat-tat! and a shout of 'No 9 – Guard's turn-out!' At the age of five, I regarded 'turn out' as something to do with appearance. Years later I learned the awesome power of No 9s and the other meaning of 'turn-out'.

*Denis Padwick, Basingstoke, Hampshire*

## (396) QUESTION: What colour was Homer's 'wine dark sea'? What wine was it?

Traditionally, Homer was thought to have written down *The Iliad* and *The Odyssey* in the twelfth century BC, around the time of the Trojan War, but modern archaeology suggests his writings were from Ionian Greece in the eighth or ninth centuries BC.

His description of the sea as 'wine dark' is as much part of his poetic language as the allusion to 'rosy-fingered dawn' also found in *The Odyssey*.

Ancient Greek wines are thought to have been similar to some of today's wines – simply fermented red grape juice like an unadulterated chianti, claret or burgundy. To these early wines, the Greeks sometimes added honey (the only sweetener available), herbs and spices, and various kinds of resin for preservation (the forerunner of today's retsina). Wines were watered down to reduce their potency.

*John Doxat, author*, The Complete Drinker's Companion, *Camberley, Surrey*

Would dilution with alkaline water have changed the colour of red wine to a kind of blue? My wine grapes produce strawberry-red juice but, with increasing dilution, it passes through pale pink to lavender. Our domestic water isn't alkaline but our garden is limestone.

*F. G. Grisley, Barry, Glamorgan*

*The Odyssey* has been translated into several languages and its original meaning may have been lost. It may be that Homer intended no colour description at all: other English translations include 'wine faced sea' and 'gloomy flood'.

The ancient Greeks used to water their wine, as many as eight-fold. The geology of the Peloponnese includes large formations of marble and limestone which would cause alkaline ground water and may have been enough to change the colour of the wine from red to a kind of blue.

If someone will give me a grant, I'll go to Greece to conduct experiments along these lines.

*Alan Crooks, Salisbury, Wiltshire*

Julian Jaynes's book *The Origin of Consciousness in the Breakdown of the Bicameral Mind* argues that the consciousness of the ancients was such that their colour spectrum was narrower than that of modern man.

He suggests this was due to a harsher daily existence that left the brain in a more constantly engaged position, trying to deal with everyday trials, and that as man has evolved and his civilization has removed many of the stresses inherent in ancient consciousness, man's colour spectrum, among other things, has expanded.

Jaynes says the ancients would have seen 'red' wine, the sea and the sky as much the same colour. The intimation of his book is that as mankind evolves, his brain expands in 'jumps' rather than as a smooth progression, and future mankind will therefore experience the world quite differently again from twenty-first century man.

*J. Drury, Hailsham, Sussex*

I have several times seen a 'wine dark sea' when holidaying in France: the sky was blue and the sea a dark red. I am a bit ancient but my life at the time was relaxed and peaceful.

*Mrs P. Smouha, London W14*

**(397) QUESTION: The first British gentlemen's convenience opened in Fleet Street on 2 February 1852. How long did ladies have to wait for similar comforts?**

The Society of Arts opened the first public water-closet 'Gents' at 95 Fleet Street, London, on 2 February, 1852. A Ladies was opened at 51 Bedford Street, Strand, nine days later.

Their main instigators were Samuel Morton Peto, the contractor who built Nelson's Column, and Henry Cole (known as the 'father of the Christmas card') who was inspired by the success of the lavatories provided at Crystal Palace for the Great Exhibition of 1851, which had reaped a profit of £1,790 in just twenty-three weeks.

The Society of Arts' 'public waiting rooms', with water-closets set in box-frames of polished wood, looked after by a superintendent and two attendants, charged 2d for basic amenities and another 2d or 3d for a hand wash, clothes brush, etc.

During the first month, the Fleet Street Gents attracted only fifty-eight customers and the Ladies just twenty-four, and the Society of Arts abandoned its experiment.

The idea was revived by City of London Corporation engineer William Haywood, who instituted the first municipal public lavatory, underground outside the Royal Exchange in 1855.

*Patrick Robertson*, New Shell Book of Firsts, *London*

**(398) QUESTION: Is Stuart Pearce the only football club manager ever to have been picked to play for England?**

Stuart Pearce was manager and captain of Nottingham Forest when he played for England. No club manager before or since him has ever been picked for England.

The closest was Terry Butcher, who played for England and managed a club side in the same year. In 1990, after his England playing career ended after the Italia '90 World Cup, he was appointed manager of Coventry City.

*David Barber, Football Association historian, London*

Stuart Pearce isn't the only manager and captain to play for England. In 1978, when Roy of the Rovers was captain and player-manager of Melchester Rovers, he not only played for England, he actually took over as manager for one match. Playing alongside Malcolm Macdonald and Trevor Francis, Roy masterminded a 4–1 victory over Holland.

At the time I was group editor of *Roy of the Rovers* comic and Roy's best friend. I can tell you that after the victory, Roy was over the moon. In fact, he was probably one of the first ever footballers to be over the moon.

*Barrie Tomlinson, St Albans, Hertfordshire*

### (399) QUESTION: How long a continuous line might the average (Bic-type) ballpoint be expected to complete?

The ball-point pen has been with us since the invention in 1938 by the Hungarian Laslo Biro of the pen named after him. His invention was relatively expensive at the time compared with other types of pen, but was very popular for its ability not to blot, the fact that it wasn't affected by air pressure or atmosphere, and its uniqueness.

In 1953, Frenchman Marcel Bich improved on the idea of the Biro, setting up his Bic company. The pen it produced, known as the Bic Crystal, was the world's first 'throwaway' ballpoint pen.

Today, the worldwide number of these pens sold is fifteen million every twenty-four hours. In the UK alone the number of ballpoint pens bought is around 300 million a year, of which at least 52 per cent are made by Bic.

The standard Bic ballpoint pen, the Bic Crystal medium, has been tested as covering a minimum straight line continuous distance of 2.2 km. The Crystal fine goes further with a minimum distance of 3.5 km. Using the Crystal medium, this means that if all the Bic pens sold in this country each year were used to draw one continuous line, this would reach between Edinburgh and London half a million times.

*Annie Magee, Biro Bic Ltd, Park Royal, London*

The Bic ballpoint wasn't the first throw-away pen of this type. The original ballpoints were very expensive, bought mainly by left-handed people who found it awkward using ordinary nibs.

Several throw-away versions were introduced in 1950 at about 5s (25p) each, including the Rolls and Rolltip. They generally shared the unpleasant characteristic of working for a few days before jettisoning their contents into your pocket.

*Bill Hewitson, Colraine, N Ireland*

Back in 1948, when I was a junior clerk in a North London branch of Lloyds Bank, our manager proudly showed us his Biro which cost him £2 12s 6d (£2.62½) at a time when my weekly wage was £3 1s 6d.

An instruction from head office told all staff to use pen and ink which was 'non fugitive' rather than Biros whose ink could be wetted and 'lifted' to copy onto another piece of paper – very handy for forging signatures.

*Patrick Courtenay, Stevenage, Hertfordshire*

**(400) QUESTION: When was the big white £5 note withdrawn from circulation? Why did you have to write your name on the back?**

All Treasury Bills (£10, £20, £50, £100 and £1,000) with the exception of the white fiver were withdrawn by the Bank of England during the war under government rules aimed at suppressing black market activities.

The £5 bills were rare and all the banks required a name and address on the back to create an air of surveillance.

In 1942, I was a very junior clerk at Lloyd's, Cox's and King's in Pall Mall, London, where my job, at close of business every day, was to complete the register of £5 Treasury Bills with details of every customer's name and address the day before they were sent for destruction.

*P. J. Richardson, Loughton, Essex*

When I worked in a bank in Brighton in 1945, part of my job was to record the full details of all incoming white fivers. There were very few of them, except on Saturdays, when the great comedian Max Miller parked his bicycle outside and deposited his week's wages, all in white fivers.

All the bank staff looked forward to his visits because he arrived dressed as he appeared on stage, in loud check plus-fours and a little white trilby set at a rakish angle. Many of our customers came to the bank on Saturdays just to be able to joke with Max.

It was a privilege to enter the great man's fivers in my log, but you won't find any signed 'Max Miller'. He always endorsed them in his real name: Henry Sargent.

*Ron Button, Haywards Heath, West Sussex*

I worked in the Bank of Scotland when these notes were in circulation and there were many forgeries. Some were of a very high standard and difficult to detect, even by those used to handling money.

We were trained to look for two features on the genuine note: the lower half of the 'f' in the 'Bank of England' heading split by a fine white line and a fine protuberance at the top right-hand side of the 'i' in the word 'five' on the black background on the bottom left-hand corner.

*D. Gardiner, Warton, Lancashire*

### (401) QUESTION: Is it true that classical goddess Diana the Huntress had a faithful companion called Camilla the Virgin?

In Roman mythology, Camilla was a favourite of the goddess Diana. According to Virgil, then-infant Camilla was fleeing with her father from his enemies when they came to a river. He tied her to his javelin, dedicated her to Diana, and threw her across the river.

In time, Camilla became a skilled hunter and was leader of a band of warriors which included other hand maidens.

She was not known to have met a prince, nor married, nor had a family.

*H. A. Barrie, Blantyre, South Lanarkshire*

In Virgil's *Aeneid*, Camilla was the virgin queen of the Volscians who was so swift she could run over a field of corn without bending a single blade, or make her way over water without getting wet. See also Pope's 'Essay on Criticism': '. . . when swift Camilla scours the plain/Flies o'er the unending corn and skims along the main . . .'

*Henry Wenstone, Hove, East Sussex*

Looking through *Bullfinch's Mythology*, I chanced upon this: 'Another battle ensued in which Camilla, the virgin warrior, was chiefly conspicuous.

'Her deeds of valour surpassed those of the bravest warriors and many Trojans and Etruscans fell, pierced with her darts or struck down by her battle-axe. At last, an Etruscan named Aruns, who had watched her long, seeking for some advantage, observed her pursuing a flying enemy whose splendid armour offered a tempting prize.

'Intent on the chase, she observed not her danger, and the javelin of Aruns struck her and inflicted a fatal wound. She fell and breathed her last in the arms of her attendant maidens. But Diana, who beheld her fate, suffered not.'

*Lorraine Kordecki, Reigate, Surrey*

### (402) QUESTION: My favourite Spoonerism is 'dum and mad' for 'mum and dad'. Who else has any classic howlers?

The 'spoonerism', an accidental (or deliberate) reversal of letters between words in a phrase, took its name in the 1890s from the Revd. William Archibald Spooner (1844–1930), Dean and Warden of New College, Oxford. He was an albino who suffered from associated health problems, including poor eyesight, but bravely overcame his disabilities and was held in high esteem by his students.

Spooner was a nervous speaker who was reputed to make errors of this type regularly. Many such utterances are touted as 'original Spoonerisms' from the end of the last century.

He is said to have spoken of 'a well-boiled icicle', 'a scoop of Boy Trouts' and to have told one student: 'You have hissed all my mystery lectures and tasted a whole worm.' But these transpositions were probably exaggerated inventions by his students.

Real transposed sounds often have some phonetic resemblance, as in 'slow and sneet'. They can affect vowels, as in 'cuss and kiddle'; the final sounds of words and syllables, such as 'hass or grash'; or whole words, as in 'mouth in her food' or 'to gap the bridge'.

*Martina Adlington, Oxford University Press*

Spoonerisms abound in our family. Pigeons 'kill and boo' in our trees, 'flutterbies' enjoy our garden, and we're careful to tie the laces of our 'shoots and boos'.

We often wonder if the good doctor really did rush in to a hatter's one day, crying 'Hush my brat it's roaring with pain' or address an audience of farm workers as 'tons of soil'.

*Revd. M. Logan, Grantham, Lincolnshire*

One of Spooner's classics came during a sermon where he is reported to have said: 'Christianity is a completely different lay of wife.'

*Gordon Goddard, Llangadog, Dyfed*

I can't vouch for its accuracy but I've been told that Dean Spooner once announced in church: 'Hymn number 365; "Kinkering Kongs Their Tatles Tike".' When asked: 'Do you know you keep reversing your consonants?' he replied, 'In dood I dee.'

He is also supposed to have once said in a sermon: 'The Lord is a shoving leopard.'

*A. Simmons, London NW5*

**(403) QUESTION: What is the origin of 'skiffle', as in skiffle music?**

In 1958, Revd. Brian Bird described skiffle as 'a simplification of jazz, with a simpler line-up which many more people can play because expensive instruments like trumpet, trombone and clarinet are replaced'.

The word 'skiffle' is believed to have originated among black Americans in the early 1920s, applied to rent parties, called 'skiffs'. Entertainment at these ad hoc events included music played on guitars which were simple wooden boxes with a few strings attached, a bass made from a tea-chest and a washboard and a can of rice for percussion. The first written use of the word is 'The Chicago Skiffle', a piece of jazz music published in 1926.

Merchant Navy brothers Ken and Bill Colyer heard this music in the Southern States in the late forties/early fifties and brought it to the UK.

*Derek Mason, Southern Skiffle Society,*
*Kingston-upon-Thames, Surrey*

**(404) QUESTION: Have the Oxford and Cambridge Boat race, two FA Cup semi-finals and the Grand National ever taken place on the same day?**

They all happened on 26 March 1949, which was also my wedding day. I believe Cambridge won the Boat Race and Russian Hero the Grand National.

Of the semi-finals, Leicester City beat Portsmouth 3–1 and Wolves drew 1–1 with Manchester United. Wolves won the replay 1–0 and went on to beat Leicester 3–1 in the final.

I recall my brother being most upset at having to miss the radio match commentaries. The groom wasn't best pleased either.

*Mrs E. Stead, Ossett, West Yorkshire*

Two friends and I went to London on 26 March 1949. We cheered on Oxford in the Boat Race but Cambridge won. All our horses in the Grand National let us down when Russian Hero won at 66 to 1, then we saw Pompey lose to Leicester in the semi-final at Highbury.

Despite all the disappointment, we came home singing: sports fans didn't cause trouble in those days.

*Roy Davis, Portsmouth*


These events all took place on 26 March 1955 – my wedding day. At the reception, my bride was very upset that I had a radio at the table to follow the Grand National. I had 6d each way riding on Irish Lizard.

And in the evening, on the way to London for our honeymoon, she couldn't believe it when I discussed football with the chauffeur.

*Don Brooks, Hockley, Essex*


All four events took place on Saturday 30 March 1968. I remember it well because I was in Kingshill Maternity Hospital, Swindon, having been in labour for twenty-four hours. The midwife kept my husband up to date with the sports news – I wasn't much interested.

My son Simon, my first child, was born late on 31 March, by caesarean. Quite a weekend.

*Frances Strange, Swindon, Wiltshire*


(405) QUESTION: Mike Harding's book *Footloose in the West of Ireland* states that in the Second World War Churchill offered de Valera an end to partition in exchange for safe waters in Eire. Is there any evidence of this?

Within a month of becoming prime minister on 10 May 1940, Churchill charged his predecessor Neville Chamberlain and Health

Minister Malcolm MacDonald with the task of reopening negotiations with Eire leader Eamonn de Valera. With the Germans overrunning France, de Valera was worried about a possible Nazi descent on Ireland and talked to MacDonald in a series of meetings in Dublin in June.

Chamberlain had failed to get agreement from Northern Ireland prime minister Lord Craigavon that the issues of defence and neutrality couldn't be separated from the question of partition but went ahead with the talks anyway.

MacDonald urged de Valera to abandon neutrality and co-operate fully with Britain in resistance to Germany. He was turned down but hints were dropped that de Valera's response may change if a united Ireland was offered. MacDonald suggested a joint council for the defence of the whole island and came up with the compromise that 'there should be a declaration of a united Ireland in principle, the practical details to be worked out in due course; this united Ireland to become a belligerent on the side of the Allies'.

But proceedings stalled and, on 26 June, MacDonald went to Dublin for the third time in ten days to present de Valera with Chamberlain's plan for the declaration of a united Ireland in principle, a joint body to work out constitutional details, a joint defence council and Eire to join the war on the British side and allow British vessels to have use of Southern Irish ports and British troops and aeroplanes to be stationed in such positions in Eire that may be agreed with the Eire government, etc.

De Valera rejected the plan because he still wanted a neutral united Ireland, which was out of the question for Britain.

On 29 June, Chamberlain went further, offering de Valera 'a declaration by the UK Government forthwith accepting the principle of a united Ireland. This declaration to take the form of a solemn undertaking that the Union is to become 'at an early date an accomplished fact from which there shall be no turning back'. This shows how far Britain was prepared to go towards Irish unity in her quest for safe waters around Eire and an end to Irish neutrality.

*Jessica Lawson, Winston Churchill's Britain at War Experience, Tooley Street, London Bridge*

I was told after the war that only one man in Northern Ireland, Lord Craigavon, knew about this treachery contemplated by Churchill. He thought about telling the Ulster people, which might have resulted in their refusing to help Britain. That would have left the Royal Navy with no Irish ports and the Atlantic wide open for Hitler's navy to plunder at will. He decided the greater of the two evils would be Hitler winning the war, so kept his silence.

As a Second World War serviceman, with two brothers in the forces and a father who had served on the Somme, I have asked myself: would we have pulled out, had we known what was contemplated? I believe we would – and this is why the people of Ulster will never trust a British government.

*Samuel Dickson, Newtownabbey, N. Ireland*

John Clive's 1983 novel *Broken Wings* is based on the true story of Dublin's Curragh Military Barracks, known as K Lines, where RAF and Luftwaffe airmen were interned.

In his notes to the book, Clive details a telegram from Churchill to the Irish President, which concludes: 'It is not possible for us to compel the people of Northern Ireland against their will to leave the UK and join Southern Ireland.

'But I do not doubt that if the government of Eire would show its solidarity with the democracies of the English-speaking world at this crisis, a Council of Defence of all Ireland would be set up, out of which the unity of the island would probably emerge after the war.'

*David Lodge, Richmond, Surrey*

As an aircrew member, operating in Catalina flying boats in the Second World War, I can confirm that de Valera gave Churchill his consent for us to fly over a few miles of Eire's territory to reach Donegal Bay before setting course for whatever area of the Atlantic we were briefed to search.

That apart, we were not permitted to fly within 7 miles of the Eire coastline.

*D. L. Johnson, Wadebridge, Cornwall*

**(406) QUESTION: My mother, now in her eighties, often talks about the hand-built HRD motorbikes she and her husband had. She says they were the best available. Is this true?**

In the opinion of most of the motorcycling public and of the company's competitors at the time, HRD machines were indeed the best available. In the twenty years during which the HRD monogram appeared on machines, most were products of the Vincent-HRD factory at Stevenage, Hertfordshire. The insignia originated with Howard R. Davies on the bikes he rode in Isle of Man TT races in the early 1920s.

Capitalizing on his racing success, he founded the HRD motorcycle company, but it failed within four years. The enterprising Philip Vincent acquired the HRD name and used its reputation to overcome motorcyclists' disinclination to try a new model.

In the drive to produce the best machine possible, the company developed its own engines during the 1930s, and by the outbreak of war the high-speed Series A Rapide V-Twin was selling well to wealthy enthusiasts, its advanced suspension and clever design features putting it ahead of its famous rival, the Brough Superior SS100.

Quality was still the major consideration when civilian production resumed in 1945 and HRDs were expensive to build and buy. Motorcycle sales dropped in the 1950s and by 1956 the struggling Vincent-HRD company had ceased trading.

We have several examples of these machines at the National

Motorcycle Museum alongside seven hundred other beautifully restored British motorcycles.

*Ken Wilson, National Motorbike Museum, West Midlands*

The original HRD motorcycles were made by Howard Raymond Davies in Wolverhampton in the 1920s. He was already famous for winning the 500 cc senior TT on a 350 cc AJS and decided to market his own supersports machines.

These appeared at the 1924 Olympia Motorcycle Show, using proprietary JAP engines and were very well received.

Despite the valuable publicity of coming second in the 1925 350 cc junior TT and winning the 500 cc event on his own machines, Davies's commercial venture failed to thrive and went into voluntary liquidation in 1927. The HRD name lived on through the thirties, forties and fifties after Philip Vincent bought the rights to make his own Vincent-HRD superbikes.

*John Edwards, Tunbridge Wells, Kent*

It would be very hard to sort out exactly which was the best of the many motorbikes on offer before the Second World War: we had so many to choose from.

I can list AJS, AJW, AKD, Ariel, Autowheel, Baker, Brough Superior, BSA, Burman, Calthorpe, Carfield, Chater Lea, Clyde, Connaught, Cotton, Coventry Eagle, Diamond, DOT, Douglas, Dunelt, Elfson, Excelsior, FN, Federal, Francis Barnett, Grindly Peerless, HRD, Humber, Ivy, James, Jardin, Levis, LGC, McEvoy, McKenzie, Matchless, Massey, Morgan, Moss, New Henley, New Hudson, New Imperial, New Knight, Newmount, Norton, NUT, OEC, OK Supreme, P&M Panther, P&P, Quadrant, Raleigh, Rex Acme, Royal Enfield, Royal Ruby, Rudge Whitworth, Scott, Seal, SGS, Sturmey Archer, Sun, Sunbeam, Triumph, Velocette, Victoria, Vincent, Vindec, W&G, Wolf and Zenith – that's seventy-one marques and there were probably more.

*J. J. Thomas, Newton Abbot, Devon*

**(407) QUESTION: Do the Scots eat more porridge oats than the English and the Welsh?**

Oats, one of the oldest known cereals, have been traced to around 3000 BC in Asia. The Ancient Greeks are thought to have been the first to make oatmeal and by the Middle Ages oatmeal and cheese was a staple part of the British diet.

Our word porridge comes from *poree*, old French for vegetable stew. The market research organization AGB Superpanel says that human consumption of porridge, or hot oat cereals, in Britain for a year is 40,925 tonnes, of which 4,139 tons are eaten in Scotland and 36,684 in England and Wales. This is an average of 0.81 kg per person in Scotland, compared with 0.71 kg in England and Wales.

Demand for oat-based cereals is expected to rise after the US Food and Drug Administration approved the claim that oats can be beneficial against heart disease.

*Priti Parmar, Quaker Oats Ltd, Southall, Middlesex*

**(408) QUESTION: Who was 'Hooky Walker'?**

Like many other cognomens ('Nobby' Clark, 'Chalkie' White, etc.) this is now used mainly in the armed services. Hooky is a common abbreviation for a leading seaman because of his badge, showing an anchor, known as a hook or killick.

The full name Hooky Walker, sometimes rendered 'Hookee' Walker, was used in civilian life in the mid-nineteenth century as an expression of incredulity, as in Dickens's *Christmas Carol* (1843): '"Buy it," said Scrooge. "Walker!" said the boy' – meaning beware its doubtful origin. The original of this expression is said to have been one John Walker, a lying informer with a hooked nose.

*Dr Tim Healey, Barnsley, South Yorkshire*

I was privileged to serve under Admiral of the Fleet Sir Harold Coulthard Walker when he was Captain of HMS *Hood* in the

Mediterranean in 1938. Despite having lost his hand in the First World War, he swam regularly and his 'Sunday best' silver hook proved very useful in latching on to any offending garments at ceremonial inspections.

When I rang the sixteen Bells for New Year 1938/9, I should, by tradition, have worn the Captain's uniform but he was a big man while I, the youngest boy on the ship at a mere sixteen years and nine months, was very small.

*Bill Cass, Crawley, Sussex*

As a Royal Marines NCO, I met Vice Admiral 'Hookey' Walker when I was drafted to Naval Party 1749 under his command when he was Commander in Chief of Naval Forces in Germany immediately after the war.

Under the Armistice, the German Army surrendered but German Navy ships were ordered off the high seas and told which port to make for. Big battleships were sent to Kiel where we Marines boarded them, immobilized them and gave them a good going over.

Walker had lost his left hand in the First World War and wore a brass hook in its place. His staff car was one of Hitler's huge bullet-proof Mercedes and I would ride with him as one of the two armed Royal Marine NCOs who always accompanied him while on duty.

'Hookey' was a very fair man, not adverse to the odd curse now and then, who could fire a rifle with the best of us.

*Bernard Slack, Ruddington, Nottinghamshire*

**(409) QUESTION: My late uncle, a 7th Armoured Division veteran, claimed its Desert Rat symbol was devised by a woman. Who was she?**

The 'Desert Rats' nickname of the British Army's 7th Armoured Division is one of the most celebrated of the Second World War.

367

Soon after General Creagh took over command of the division in early 1940, he grew dissatisfied with its white circle on a scarlet background emblem. He wanted something in the circle to symbolize the division's North African location and chose the desert rat (jerboa) because, like his men, it was a highly mobile and effective inhabitant of the desert terrain.

After much searching, his wife and her friend Mrs Peyton, wife of the General's aide, located a jerboa in Cairo Zoo and made a quick sketch of it on hotel notepaper.

Trooper K. Hill of the Royal Tank Regiment produced a final version shortly before his death in action and this image was transferred in flaming scarlet to the white circle of the divisional commander's flag and onto every vehicle and 'toby flash' (helmet marking).

By the end of 1941, the jerboa emblem was so much a part of the division's identity that when one brigade left North Africa for Burma, its members simply changed the animal's colour to green to symbolize their jungle surroundings.

Arriving back in the UK in 1943, troops were shocked to discover that the clothing firm chosen by the War Office to make their new uniforms had its own idea of what a jerboa should look like, and had produced an animal emblem that looked more like a kangaroo than a desert rat, changing its sandy colour to red-brown and the background to black.

General Erskine, who had taken over from Creagh, objected strongly but the War Office refused to sanction the expense of restoring the emblem to its original appearance.

The desert rat emblem returned to desert warfare in 1990, when the 7th and 4th divisions were part of the British contingent sent to the Gulf as part of Operation Desert Storm.

*George Worthington MM, 8th Army Veterans' Association,*
*Hyde, Manchester*

**(410) QUESTION: Most of the world's large countries seem to borrow money from the IMF. Who actually deposits any money with it?**

The International Monetary Fund was established to promote international monetary co-operation, expansion of world trade and exchange stability at a conference of twenty-nine signatory countries in Bretton Woods, New Hampshire, US, in July 1944 and began operation on 1 March 1947.

Based in Washington, DC, today's IMF has 184 member nations paying subscriptions based on their economy and balance of payments, reassessed every five years. A member's quota also determines its voting weight and access to IMF financing. Total funds of the IMF stand at around $310 billion.

Member countries may borrow from the fund for financial emergencies though there are very strict conditions for short-term loans, including limits on government spending and/or devaluation of a nation's currency. The IMF is primarily financed by subscriptions from member nations, but can increase its funds through an official lender.

*John Hutton, Twickenham, Middlesex*

**(411) QUESTION: Rooks are reputed to 'hold court' and 'serve sentence'. Is there any truth in this?**

Many country myths are based on misinterpreting and 'humanizing' animal behaviour – and this is a good example.

Several members of the crow family, particularly the magpie, appear to gather in large groups, or 'courts', apparently 'taking evidence' from birds which fly in and out until, eventually, one bird is 'sentenced' and driven out of the flock.

This behaviour is all about territorial disputes between male birds.

*Derek Niemann, Royal Society for the Protection of Birds,*
*Sandy, Bedfordshire*

Despite the sceptics, I recall that on 14 July 1978, I had the privilege of witnessing a rooks' court. At about 6.15 a.m., I was watching deer returning to their daytime plantation when 80 to 100 rooks descended on a nearby field.

They formed a circle with a lone rook being forced into the centre. The noise they made was unbelievable, as if discussing the 'case'. Suddenly, they fell silent, closed in on the defendant and attacked him. Within minutes there was but a few feathers left on the field. The rooks then dispersed not knowing that I had been watching from my hide 200 yards away.

*David Morris, Abergele, Clwyd*


In 1946, while walking in Melton Constable Park, my wife and I witnessed a 'crows' court'. In a field recently cleared of wheat, we saw a ring of about forty birds around one large crow with, cowering beside it, a sorry-looking crow with a damaged wing. The large crow strutted around, cawing. After a while, it flew a few feet into the air whereon the others attacked the injured bird, tearing it to pieces.

The local gamekeeper, a Mr Swan, said we had seen a rare sight. He said the condemned crow had either eaten another's eggs or tried to mate with another's mate. As the crows in the ring were all males, we feel its crime was probably the latter.

*Ralph Kimber, Ashtead, Surrey*

**(412) QUESTION: What was the longest Bailey Bridge constructed in the Second World War?**

Sir Donald Coleman Bailey (1901–85) was born and educated in Rotherham and took his Bachelor of Engineering degree in 1923 at Sheffield University. He literally sketched out his idea for a pre-fabricated, mobile, rapidly constructed bridge on the back of the legendary envelope in 1940.

Probably the longest Bailey Bridges built during the Second World War were the twin 5,000ft 'Tyne' and 'Tees' bridges crossing the Rhine at Rees, built in April/May 1945. They were reputed to have been the longest military bridges in the world.

Rotherham still has its own Bailey Bridge, a footbridge over the River Don at Eastwood.

*Barry Jackson, Rotherham Borough Council*


On 11 February 1945, I was a sapper in 71st Field Coy Royal Engineers, taking part in building what was then the longest Bailey Bridge in the world, over the River Maas at Gennep. It was 4,008 ft long.

*Fred Aylward, Tunbridge Wells, Kent*


The 4,008ft Bailey Bridge, built by 71, 72, 73 and 503 Field Coys, RE, plus 277 Field Park Coy RE and 149 Pioneer Coy during the advance through the Reichwald Forest, had to be so wide because of the destruction of the Roer Dams by the enemy.

*R. W. B. Heath, Orpington, Kent*


The longest Bailey Bridge built during the Italian campaign was the 1,126 ft Sangro Bridge, a 'double single' Bailey, completed by 8th Army engineers in 14 December 1943. A total of 2,494 Bailey Bridges were built in Italy, and I often wonder how many of them are still there.

*Eric Thomas, Purley, Surrey*


The longest single span ever attempted by the Royal Engineers was across the Thames for the Festival of Britain in 1951. On the day fixed for its launch, the commanding officer was suddenly called to a meeting in Germany and the remaining members of his team dropped the bridge in the river. It was rescued and successfully launched some days later.

*Peter Warmsley, Preston, Lancashire*

## (413) QUESTION: Where might one find 'the four corners of the Earth'?

The idea of 'the four corners of the Earth' was regarded as a literary conceit for the remotest parts of the globe but what began as metaphor became fact in June 1965 when Doctors Robert R. Newton and William H. Guier, of Johns Hopkins Applied Physics Laboratory, Maryland, US, published papers describing four high points, or 'corners' they had discovered while studying the shape and gravity field of the Earth through satellite observations.

Each of these high points covers an area of several thousand square miles. One is centred over Ireland and sprawls towards the North Pole; another extends across the Equator from New Guinea towards Japan; a third is south of Africa, centred about halfway to Antarctica; and the fourth, the smallest, lies just off the west coast of South America with its apex off Peru.

At the centre of these high points, the pull of gravity is 0.002 per cent greater than expected for that latitude, which means these 'corners' are an average 60 yards above the mean level surface of the planet.

*Helen Worth, Johns Hopkins University, Applied Physics*
*Laboratory, Laurel, Maryland*

## (414) QUESTION: What is the origin of the Jokers in a pack of cards and which games, other than Canasta, require their use?

When playing cards first appeared in Europe in the fourteenth century, they were tarot cards, based on eastern designs whose original purpose is unknown.

The tarot deck consisted of seventy-eight cards divided into two groups: the minor arcana of twenty-two cards each with a picture and title (Moon, Hanged Man, Judgment, etc., standing for the various forces of life and death that affected people) and the major arcana, fifty-six cards in four suits of fourteen cards each: cups (representing the Church), swords (the military), batons (the farmers) and pentacles (the merchants).

The modern deck developed from the major arcana, with numbered cards from ace to ten and four unnumbered face cards: king, queen, knight and knave. The use of playing cards became widespread after the invention of the printing press and the symbols for each suit became standardized. The tarot cups became hearts, pentacles became diamonds, batons became clubs and swords became spades. In France, the roles of knight and page were combining into what we call the jack, and the pack reduced from fifty-six cards to fifty-two.

The 'joker' was the last addition to the pack, being introduced by Mississippi river-boat gamblers for use in the game of euchre. This fifty-third card was supposedly based on the twenty-second card of the minor arcana: the fool.

*Major Donald Welsh, English Playing Card Society, Bath*

## (415) QUESTION: Does Fairlight, East Sussex, have England's most westerly view of France?

While playing cricket for Clive Vale CC on East Hill, Hastings, 3 miles west of Fairlight, Cap Gris Nez is visible on a clear day.

*R. Huggins, Rye, Essex*

Moving 4 miles west from Fairlight one comes to West Hill in the old part of Hastings from where it's possible, in exceptionally good weather conditions, to see the coast of France about 43 miles away.

*Nicky Swain, Hastings Tourist Information, East Sussex*

Standing on top of the underground reservoir at Harrow Bridge, next to the A21 on the northern outskirts of Hastings, the entire French coastline can be seen – from Cap Gris Nez to Le Touquet, including Boulogne. There aren't many days in the year when such sightings are possible because of industrial pollution over northern France.

*Henry Dallimore, St Leonards on Sea, East Sussex*

**(416) QUESTION: The Highway Code includes signs for minimum speed limits but do such things actually exist in Britain?**

Minimum speed limits apply on public roads only where they are signposted. This could be, for example, in major road tunnels where they can help regulate traffic flow. However, drivers obstructing the flow of traffic by travelling particularly slowly anywhere can, and have been, charged with the offence of 'driving without consideration for other road users'.

*Alison Langley, Department of Transport, London*

At the Clyde Tunnel in Glasgow an observant driver will see a number of minimum speed limit signs about 10 inches in diameter. Towards the tunnel exits there is the equivalent cancellation signal, permitting motorists to drive at less than 8 mph.

*Paul Parsons, Glasgow*

There is a 10 mph minimum speed limit (and maximum of 40 mph) through the Mersey Road Tunnels linking Birkenhead and Wallasey to Liverpool.

*Mrs A. T. Meacock, Oxton, Wirral*

**(417) QUESTION: Is there supposed to be a General Election every five years?**

A parliament has a five-year period which runs not from the date of the election but from the day on which the new parliament is summoned to meet under the provisions of the Royal Proclamation.

A parliament's five years expires at midnight on the last day of the fifth year since it met. After that, the law allows a maximum seventeen working days to elapse before polling day must take place.

*Chris Pond, Head of Information, House of Commons, London*


**(418) QUESTION: Was there really an aircraft called the Gnu?**

The curiously named Sopwith Gnu, introduced in May 1919, was a three-seat tourer or taxi aircraft, one of the first cabin aircraft designed for civil use, with the pilot in an open cockpit under the centre of the top wing.

Two passengers sat side-by-side in the rear cockpit under a glazed roof while the 110 hp Le Rhone engine powered the Gnu to a top speed of about 87 mph.

Only twelve Gnus were built and just four had cabins. Two enjoyed lengthy careers in the UK in the twenties: G-EADB (cabin model) and G-EAGP (open model). One was exported to Australia as G-EAIL and lasted until it was destroyed by a storm in 1946.

*Alastair Goodrum, aviation historian, Spalding, Lincolnshire*


**(419) QUESTION: Why are the wooden bits on which railway lines are laid called sleepers?**

The 'sleeper' component of a railway track spreads the load from the rails to the ballast below and maintains the gauge width between the rails.

Early railways had cast-iron rails supported on stone blocks but as rail strength improved with the introduction of wrought iron and then steel, stone blocks gave way to transverse wooden beams, first called 'sleepers' in 1789 because they lay in place below the rails.

The fifty million standard sleepers on Britain's railway lines are about 2 ft 3 ins (700 mm) apart, holding the rails at the 4 ft 8 ½ ins (1435 mm) gauge. They aren't all wood: pre-stressed concrete sleepers, weighing 300 kg each, are used under lines carrying the heaviest traffic and softwood sleepers under secondary and branch lines will be renewed in concrete or hardwood as they become due for replacement.

*Jane Terry, London*

Virtually every railway term is different on different sides of the Atlantic. Where we say platform nine, it's track nine in the US; our driver is the engineer in America; what we call points are a switch to Americans and our shunter is their switcher. A signalbox is known as a tower, a guard's van a caboose, an engine is a loco, the guard is a conductor, a carriage is a car and a van is a boxcar. They call the sleepers 'ties'.

Our terms come chiefly from the horse-and-carriage era.

*Charlie Duncan, Glasgow*

### (420) QUESTION: Which stately house was used in the film *The Go Between*?

The stately home used was Melton Constable House, off the A148 near Holt, in North Norfolk. The house was only partially restored for filming purposes and I believe after filming it again fell into disrepair.

*Rita Southgate, Bristol*

Melton Constable Hall, a seventeenth-century house in Norfolk, was owned by a local farmer. Having been unoccupied for some time it was showing signs of decay and so had to be redecorated before filming.

Despite being described as one of Britain's finest country houses, it again stood empty for some considerable time after filming, before being used as an arts centre. It was later divided into separate properties and is not open to the public. It is currently on the official English Heritage 'at risk' register.

Visitors can, however, see the green on which the cricket match in the film was played, which is at Thornage, a small village between Melton Constable and Holt. Other locations used in the film included the Tombland area of Norwich and part of the Norfolk Broads.

*The Go Between* won the Palme d'Or at the Cannes Film Festival in 1971, and Margaret Leighton was nominated for an Oscar as Best Supporting Actress.

*Tony Hillman, Darlington, Co Durham*


Seventeenth-century Melton Constable Hall, in Norfolk, was the home of Baron Hastings, whose family name was Melton and one of whose ancestors was Constable of Norfolk.

Melton Constable used to be known as 'the Crewe of East Anglia', the centre of the old Mid and Great Northern Railway in which Lord Hastings was a major shareholder, and extras used in the 1971 film were mainly former railwaymen, made redundant by the Dr Beeching axe.

Lord Hastings's eldest son married Lord Wavell's daughter but was killed in India in the war. Death duties proved the downfall of this large estate, which had been well known for its red deer herd.

*Ralph W. Kimber, Ashtead, Surrey*

**(421) QUESTION: Are you allowed to ride a bicycle on a public footpath or bridleway?**

You can cycle on bridleways but not footpaths. The 1968 Countryside Bill, backed by a powerful landowner lobby, proposed a complete ban on off-road cycling but was strongly opposed by the Cyclists' Touring Club (CTC).

After a hard campaign, cyclists won the right to ride on bridleways. Our organization stresses the need to use bridleways in a responsible, courteous and considerate fashion. Speeding through a group of ramblers or alarming a horse rider is neither grown-up nor clever and damages the reputation of all cyclists.

Some cyclists use footpaths when they are the only safe alternative to horrific main roads which, in other countries, would have been designed to allow safe cycling.

With the law as it stands, cyclists should stay off footpaths unless there is no other safe alternative.

*Peter McGrath, Cyclists' Touring Club, Godalming, Surrey*

**(422) QUESTION: When were boxed breakfast cereals first made and sold in this country?**

The first boxed breakfast cereals were sold in the UK in 1924 when W. K. Kellogg imported them from his cereal plant in London, Ontario, Canada. The first cereals made in this country were produced at the Kellogg plant built in 1938 in Trafford Park, Manchester, now the largest cereal plant in the world.

*John Mandy, Kellogg's, Manchester*

**(423) QUESTION: Was Colin Cowdrey such a good slip fielder that he could catch the ball and hide it in his pocket before turning towards the boundary to deceive the batsman?**

I saw this happen at the St Lawrence Ground, in Canterbury, when Kent played Sussex in a Benson & Hedges Cup match in May 1974.

Tony Greig was batting and the bowler was Asif Iqbal. Sir Colin was fielding at second slip when the ball flew off the edge. We all saw him put both hands in his pockets and swing round to look at the boundary. Moments later, he turned towards the batsman and took the ball out of his pocket. Greig was given out, caught Cowdrey, bowled Iqbal.

*Chris Taylor, curator, Kent Country Cricket Club, Canterbury*

Sir Colin wasn't the first to do this. I saw Walter Hammond do it in the 1930s and I've heard of other instances. I believe the trick was intended to hoodwink the crowd rather than the batsman.

It was more likely to happen in days gone by when we had proper fast bowlers.

*Charles Price, Rugeley, Staffordshire*

## (424) QUESTION: Why 'cos' lettuce?

The four main types of lettuce (*Lactuca sativa*, of the family *Compositae*), the UK's most popular salad constituent, are: crisp-heading; butterhead; loose-leaf and cos or romaine.

Like other types of lettuce, cos came originally from Asia but was eaten by the ancient Greeks, who were among the first in the Mediterranean to grow this type of lettuce. It grows particularly well in warm climates such as that of the Greek island of Cos (Kos), which gave the lettuce its name. Its cultivation spread north and west from the Mediterranean, and the cos lettuce we buy today comes mostly from Israel, Cyprus and Italy as well as being home-grown.

*Debra Pieri, Fresh Fruit & Vegetable Information Bureau,*
*London*

**(425) QUESTION: If I put two stamps marked '2nd' on a letter, will it go by first-class mail?**

Sorting machines 'read' the amount of postage on a letter automatically by the phosphor bars on the stamps, so two stamps marked '2nd' will be read as twice the 2nd price and the letter will go first class, provided it's within the weight limit.

Non-Value Indicator (NVI) stamps with '1st' or '2nd' on them are valid indefinitely. NVI stamps, available in books from post offices and 60,000 retail outlets, can be used as part payment of postage to any destination.

Underpayment of postage can be a problem. Many letters are sent to the Irish Republic bearing only a second-class stamp when they require first-class postage.

*Adam Novak, Royal Mail International, London*


**(426) QUESTION: Was the woman I took to Gibraltar on the SS *Avoceta* in 1941 to join another ship as 2nd engineer the only female engineer in the Merchant Navy?**

She was probably Victoria Drummond MBE, the first woman to qualify as a chief engineer officer in the Merchant Navy. Born in 1894, she was a remarkable woman and demonstrated immense fortitude in her chosen career, which lasted forty years. Unfortunately, she experienced considerable problems finding work on British ships and spent much of her career on foreign-registered vessels. She was awarded the MBE for her heroism in 1940 after single-handedly keeping her ship's engines going after an attack by German aircraft. Her lasting legacy is honoured by NUMAST, which presents an award in her name to women officers who make notable career achievements.

*Andrew Linnington, NUMAST, Leytonstone, London E11*


Queen Victoria's god-daughter Victoria Drummond mentions in her diary her trip on the SS *Avoceta* (one of the few voyages she undertook as a passenger) leaving Liverpool in mid-February and arriving in Lisbon on 8 March 1941. She first went to sea in the 1920s, pursuing a career considered unsuitable for her gender after completing an apprenticeship at Caledon shipyard. She joined the SS *Anchises* as 10th engineer in 1922 and sailed on forty-nine voyages.

*The Remarkable Life Of Victoria Drummond – Marine Engineer*, published by the Institute of Marine Engineers in 1994, reconstructs her life from her uncompleted memoirs, compiled by her niece Cherry Drummond (Baroness Strange).

Victoria's uniform is on display at the Institute of Marine Engineers HQ, one of whose conference rooms is called The Victoria Drummond Room in her honour.

*Joli R. Harris, Institute of Marine Engineers, London*


As a girl in the 1920s, I travelled from India with my parents aboard a British India liner on which Victoria Drummond was engineer. At each port, the embassy sent its pinnace for her to spend the day ashore. She often talked with me and she drew an albatross head in my autograph book, signing it 'VD'. I'm afraid the male engineers were not too complimentary about her work.

*E. L. Butler, Romford, Essex*


In the Second World War, my brother sailed with Victoria Drummond in the Blue Funnel liner SS *Perseus* where she was 2nd engineer in charge of fifty or more stokers. He said she ruled those hard-working men, some of them hardened drinkers who would have tussled with heavyweight champion Joe Louis if need be, with an iron fist.

He said she often boasted of her royal connections but no one believed her.

*John Kennedy, Birkenhead, Merseyside*

In the late fifties and early sixties, I worked in the crewing section of a City of London ship management company. The vessels under our management were registered with the Shipping Federation, through which we engaged officers and ratings.

On several occasions, I requested a 2nd engineer for the MV *Rampart* and was supplied with Miss Victoria Drummond, who held a chief engineer's certificate from the Panamanian authorities, but did not have a Board of Trade 2nd engineer's ticket.

She was the only female engineering officer sailing in the merchant marine at the time.

*Alan Wise, Hainault, Essex*

**(427) QUESTION: In 1915, my father scaled the clock face of the badly damaged Cloth Hall in Ypres and 'liberated' the Roman figure III, subsequently making it into a fancy fire screen when he returned home. Are there any other known souvenirs of this famous clock?**

The clock's figure I was incorporated after the First World War in the memorial to the two Price brothers, at Westwell, 3 miles from Burford, Oxfordshire. Its story was told in 1972 in the privately printed book *The History of Westwell* by the Revd. Stanley Fisher.

Lady Holland, wife of Sir Sothern, owner of the manor house near the village, lost two brothers, Royal Fusilier Harold and submariner Edward Price, in the war. Before his death, Harold had brought home the bronze figure I as a souvenir. It was suitably engraved and fixed to the south face of a monolith of Cotswold stone, brought by a team of eighteen horses from Heythrop Quarry, and erected by the village pond on a base block from Brasenose Quarry.

*Miss C. Audrey Tramaine, Burford, Oxfordshire*

The restored Cloth Hall houses the Ypres Salient Museum, including many items illustrating the costly fighting which took place in the area in the First World War.

These include the Roman V from the clock face, which was given back to Ypres by the daughter of cavalry officer Sydney Kemp MC, also a holder of the French *Croix de Guerre*, who had climbed the shell-damaged tower to take the figure. He gave the bronze item to his mother, who donated it to the Imperial War Museum. Captain Kemp's daughter returned it to the Cloth Hall at a ceremony organized by the Belgian museum's director.

*Frederick Farrow, London SW2*

At The Keep, military museum of The Devon and Dorset Regiment, where I'm a voluntary helper, we have one of the figure Vs from this clock, 'picked up' by Major R. Ewart Cree RAMC in 1917. The Roman numerals of a clock face include at least five such Vs.

*N. S. F. Lamb, Dorchester, Dorset*

### (428) QUESTION: When did snooker become more popular in Britain than billiards?

In 1927 my father, Bill Camkin, promoted the first world snooker championships at Camkin's Hall, Birmingham, but it attracted little interest until 1931 when he brought then world billiards champion Walter Lindrum from Australia and Clark McConarchy from New Zealand to play an international billiards tournament with leading British players Joe Davis and Tom Newman. As the only appearance in this country of the legendary Lindrum, the matches drew large crowds. Despite the players' reluctance, my father insisted they play one frame of snooker after each billiards session and the spectators obviously enjoyed the new game.

So, too, did Joe Davis who came to share my father's view that snooker would soon supersede the traditional billiards. Joe promoted a series of week-long challenges of best of 131 frames in Birmingham and other major cities. Horace Lindrum, Walter's nephew, and Fred Davis, Joe's brother, became leading players but none could match Joe.

These matches drew astonishing attendances with more than 15,000 watching one. By 1939, billiards was little played outside private houses.

*John Camkin, Leamington Spa*

**(429) QUESTION: Why is General Pershing's Congressional Medal of Honour in St Paul's Cathedral?**

The Congressional Medal – the highest honour the United States of America can confer – hanging on a pillar at the west end of the nave of Westminster Abbey was awarded to the Unknown Warrior. It was delivered into the keeping of the Dean of Westminster by General Pershing, then Commander-in-Chief of the US Army, on 17 October 1921.

*Dr Tony Trowles, Muniment Room and Library,*
*Westminster Abbey, London*

**(430) QUESTION: The two British women survivors of the hijacked Boeing which crashed into the Indian Ocean undid their safety belts before impact. Is this the correct procedure or were they just lucky?**

Civil Aviation Authority regulations, based on investigations of hundreds of such landings around the world over decades of international passenger flights, say seatbelts should be worn during any emergency landing. The women concerned, Elizabeth Anders and Katherine Hayes, were wearing their seatbelts when Captain Leul Abate brought the hijacked plane down after it ran out of fuel. The mistaken view that they were not is a result of misreading headlines which shortened Miss Hayes's message to her parents to a simple 'We undid belts and swam for our lives'.

In fact they undid their belts after the impact and managed to swim to the surface.

*Gordon Machin, Luton*

An Ethiopian Airlines Boeing 767 ran out of fuel after being hijacked and crashed off the Comoros Islands on 23 November 1996, causing the deaths of 127 passengers. A video shot by South African honeymooners Dolf and Marinda Gouws confirms the force of the impact, so great that the aeroplane broke into three pieces.

Had the two women concerned not been wearing their seatbelts there's little doubt that the death toll would have been higher and injuries they sustained would have been far more serious.

One of the two British women survivors was my daughter Elizabeth who, with her friend Kate Hayes, tells me that they didn't undo their seatbelts until after the impact.

They were exceptionally lucky to escape, and wearing their belts was a major factor in preserving their lives. The cameraman who died in the crash, Mohamed Amin, was reported not to have been wearing a belt – neither were the hijackers who were also killed in the crash.

*Mr Anders, Surrey*


## (431) QUESTION: Whatever happened to Tupperware parties?

Tupperware parties are still being held every day. In the UK and Ireland there are, on average, more than three thousand parties held every month. There is at least one Tupperware party held somewhere in the world every 2.5 seconds. Tupperware was invented in 1945 by Earl Tupper, in the US. It was not until 1946 that it was introduced to the public. He patented the now famous seal which keeps the containers air and liquid-tight.

Earl Tupper initially tried selling Tupperware via traditional shop outlets, but quickly found that very few people understood how to use the product. It was not until 1951 that the Tupperware company, under its far-sighted vice-president, Brownie Wise, introduced the party plan method of demonstrating Tupperware direct to the public.

The business grew rapidly and in October 1960 the first

Tupperware party was held in Britain. In the sixties the business expanded rapidly, with many households having at least one item of Tupperware.

Tupperware is the UK's original party plan selling company and is, I believe, the only member of the Direct Selling Association which can boast that it has sold by three generations. Many of the original Tupperware ladies have been joined by their children and grandchildren.

*Lynne and Mike Hughes, Authorized Tupperware Distributors,*
*Brighton*

**(432) QUESTION: I recently heard a performance of saw-playing. Is the saw just like one from a DIY shop or specially made for musical purposes?**

Any working saw bought from a hardware store is suitable. My friend, seventy-eight-year-old George Winfrey, who lives in Alexandria, Virginia, US, has been playing the saw for sixty years.

He uses a violin bow and keeps the saw in a specially made wooden box. He amuses many people with his wonderful recitals and last played in Britain in a pub in Peterborough, much to the delight of the locals. There's an annual saw players' convention in San Francisco, California, each July.

*Caron Hughes, Lincoln*

**(433) QUESTION: Why do a chimney sweep and his lad traditionally appear at weddings?**

Chimney sweeps acquired a general reputation as harbingers of good luck after one of them was supposed to have saved George III when his carriage horses bolted. The King proclaimed the sight of a sweep a sure sign of good luck.

The more prosaic explanation lies in the fact that throughout the seventeenth and eighteenth centuries the sweep's role in making the all-important household chimney safe ensured that a housewife –

'Mistress of Hearth and Home' – could keep the home warm, boil water and cook food.

Deeper, and darker, traditions link the chimney sweep's blacked appearance with early pagan traditions identifying black as a sign of fertility.

These days, the demand for sweeps to attend weddings can contribute as much as 5 per cent of a sweep's business. Charges vary from £40 to £100. I've attended more than 1,000 weddings, always making sure I'm first to see the bride as she leaves the church, as tradition demands.

I give her some advice I've picked up from other couples over the years and give her a small silver charm. I've kept in contact with many of the couples and I am pleased to report very few divorces.

The sweep's lad isn't strictly part of the tradition and I always used to take my black cat. But lately I've been pressured by my 4½-year-old son Ben to take him, too.

*Kevin Giddings, Crawley Down, Sussex*

### (434) QUESTION: Why are 'tank tops' so designated?

Most people assume this popular fashion (or non-fashion) of the late sixties and early seventies got its name because it originated as part of the uniform of the Tank Corps.

In fact, the tank top – a sleeveless pullover with scoop neckline, worn by either sex – was named after the top section of the one-piece swimming costumes seen on beaches and at local 'swimming tanks', as swimming pools were known in Edwardian days.

*Ginger Wells, Amsterdam*

### (435) QUESTION: 'Jesus wept' (John 11:35) is the shortest verse in the Bible, but which is the longest?

The book of Esther contains the longest verse in the Bible. Esther 8:9 reads: 'Then were the King's scribes called at that time in the third month, that is, the month Sivan, on the three and twentieth day thereof; and it was written according to all that Mordecai commanded unto the Jews, and to the lieutenants, and the deputies and rulers of the provinces which are from India unto Ethiopia, a hundred twenty and seven provinces, unto every province according to the writing thereof, and unto every people after their language, and to the Jews according to their writing, and according to their language.'

This verse is longer than the shortest chapter (Psalm 117), while the longest chapter (Psalm 119) is longer than the shortest book, the 2nd Epistle of John.

*David Pike, Henleaze, Bristol*

## (436) QUESTION: When Labour won the 1997 General Election, Tony Blair became prime minister without ever having held ministerial office. Was this a first in modern British politics?

From the Second World War until 1997, the UK electorate never opted for a prime minister who came to the job without having held ministerial office. John Major won the previous election having already held the position of prime minister after beating Margaret Thatcher for leadership of the Conservative Party. He had already been Foreign Secretary and Chancellor of the Exchequer.

Margaret Thatcher's Cabinet experience extended only to having been Education Secretary. Jim Callaghan had been Chancellor, Home Secretary and Foreign Secretary; Edward Heath had been Minister of Labour and President of the Board of Trade; Harold Wilson had also been President of the Board of Trade.

Sir Alec Douglas Home had been Foreign Secretary; Harold Macmillan had been Minister of Housing, Minister of Defence and Foreign Minister; Sir Anthony Eden had been Foreign Secretary, Secretary of State for War and Foreign Secretary; Clement Attlee had been Dominions Secretary and Deputy Prime Minister; and Sir Winston Churchill had held a number of ministerial offices, including President of the Board of Trade, Home Secretary, First Lord of the Admiralty, Secretary of State for War and Chancellor of the Exchequer.

Before the war Neville Chamberlain had been Chancellor and Minister for Health, and Stanley Baldwin had been President of the Board of Trade.

The last prime minister elected without having held ministerial office was Labour's first prime minister, Ramsay MacDonald, who took office on 22 January 1924 as leader of a minority government, held at the mercy of the Liberals. His office lasted a mere nine months but he did go on to become prime minister twice more after that.

Tony Blair's victory in 1997 could be held to have started a trend: when David Cameron took over from Gordon Brown in May 2010, he had never held ministerial office.

*James Campbell-Blades, Perth, Scotland*

### (437) QUESTION: What happened to 'hard labour' and 'penal servitude'? What was the difference between them?

Hard labour and penal servitude officially disappeared in 1948 with The Criminal Justice Act, which did away with the 'convict prisoner' category. From the late eighteenth century, there had been various categories of prisoner, subjected to differing regimes. Convict prisoners were the more serious offenders and were housed in special prisons such as Dartmoor. The regime in these prisons was much harsher and included 'hard labour', demeaning and arduous manual labour such as the breaking of rocks or ploughing fields without the use of horses. Convict prisoners were eventually transported, generally to Australia. In the mid-nineteenth century, however, this practice effectively ceased when Australia decided it would refuse further prisoners.

From this period the same sentence was handed out but the prisoner was subjected to penal servitude instead – put at the service of the public works depot and made available for projects such as the clearing of fields, quarrying and making breakwaters.

Although the distinction of hard labour and penal servitude survived until 1948, this was really in name only. In the period between the wars the regime became far more liberal; for example, convict prisoners no longer had to have their heads shaved or wear the exclusive arrow-marked uniforms.

*Dr Peter Davies, curator, HM Prison Service Museum, Rugby*

### (438) QUESTION: Was a grand piano once stolen from the concert hall in the BBC's Broadcasting House, London?

The story of two men in overalls walking into the Broadcasting House concert hall and casually helping themselves to a grand piano has been told for forty years – but the BBC can't confirm it ever actually happened and it's worth noting that it would probably take at least four people to manhandle a concert grand.

However, a grand piano was taken from the Royal Festival Hall on London's South Bank in 1989. A £25,000 Steinway was wheeled to a hall door by Daryl Hart, a twenty-four-year-old student, and he was assisted by passers-by who assumed he worked at the hall, in taking it more than 200 yards to Jubilee Gardens where he began using it in his busking act before security guards arrived.

He was accused of theft and taken to court but the charge was eventually dropped.

*Gillian Levy, Bristol*

The idea of a grand piano being stolen may seem outlandish but is small fry in relation to some of the more obscure items that have been stolen in past years. These include a train taken in Florida, a bungalow stolen brick by brick in Bloxwich, West Midlands, and a fire engine stolen while the firemen were in an old leather works in Hackney, putting out a blaze.

One of the most bizarre thefts was of a £200 garage, taken away piece by piece during the night, leaving behind, unmarked, the Rolls-Royce it housed.

Other items that have disappeared in recent years include a full mile of railway line and sleepers in Rotherham, the hands of the town hall clock in Wellington, Somerset, sixty cannonballs from HMS *Victory*, 50 yards of York stone pavement in Chelsea, and a 40-foot bonfire from Stanmore, Middlesex, described by police at the time as identifiable by the fact that it had a grand piano on top.

*Jason Sykes, Chadderton, Lancashire*

When I was working in the Radio Newsreel studios at Egton House, near Broadcasting House, in 1948/49, a grand piano had been taken not from Broadcasting House but from the Langham Hotel across the road, then a BBC overflow establishment.

A pantechnicon arrived and three men in overalls walked in with a trolley and took the piano. It wasn't unusual for pianos to be moved so no one questioned this impudent piece of larceny.

*Jack Nickle Smith, Taplow, Buckinghamshire*

## (439) QUESTION: What is the 'mistake' in J. M. Turner's famous picture *Rain, Steam and Speed*?

Turner probably didn't make a 'mistake', though he often produced lines of verse to accompany his work and was certainly given to poetic licence. His *Rain, Steam and Speed* clearly shows a Firefly class locomotive crossing Maidenhead Bridge.

He wished to position the locomotive in the centre of the bridge and therefore omitted the second track. He painted three distinct puffs of smoke coming from the stack when a locomotive travelling at speed would emit smoke in a continuous stream, possibly barely noticeable.

Other examples of Turner taking liberties with his subject are in

*Fisherman at Sea*, where his clouds appear to be passing behind the moon, and in *The Fighting Temeraire*, an old ship of Nelson's time which was towed up the Thames from Sheerness, in Kent, to be broken up at Deptford in London. Turner almost certainly viewed the ship – travelling westward on its last journey – from the north Kent coast so his setting sun behind it is shown in the east.

*Mike Cove, Uxbridge, Middlesex*

**(440) QUESTION: I was eighteen years and two months old when I landed on the Normandy beaches at 9 a.m. on D-Day. Who was the youngest to land on the beaches that day?**

On D-Day, the Allied invasion fleet of 1,213 warships, 864 converted merchant ships and 4,126 landing craft placed 75,215 British and Canadian and 57,500 American soldiers on the five main invasion beaches: Gold, Juno, Sword, Utah and Omaha.

In the weeks that followed, more than 2,000,000 more men were landed in France while another 7,900 British and Canadian and 15,500 US troops landed by air around the beachheads.

My father, Ken Oliver, was just under eighteen years two months when he landed on a Normandy beach with the Royal Marines in the late evening of that fateful day.

*Miss J. Oliver, Borstal, Kent*

I was eighteen years old and three weeks when I landed with the 3rd Light Infantry Division before dawn on 6 June 1944, on Sword Beach.

*Ex-Cpl E. J. Cousins, London*

I was seventeen years and seven months old when I landed with the 1st Buckinghamshire Battalion as part of No 6 Beach Group.

Bored with tapering Sten gun firing pins in a Midlands factory, I doctored my ration book and enlisted a few days after my sixteenth birthday. Looking me up and down, my sergeant said: 'If you're eighteen, I'm the Aga bleedin' Khan', but the manpower situation was so grave that the Army didn't go too deeply into recruits' backgrounds.

Soon after D-Day I joined the Black Watch and my experiences from Normandy to the Rhine were recently published by Robert Hale in the book *Fear is the Foe*.

*Stan Whitehouse, Solihull, West Midlands*

## (441) QUESTION: If the cheetah is the world's fastest animal, and the greyhound is the thirteenth-fastest, what are the other eleven and what speeds can they achieve?

The American Museum of Natural History says the fastest animals on land are the cheetah, which can reach 70 mph; the pronghorn antelope, 61 mph; wildebeest, lion and Thomson's gazelle, 50 mph; quarterhorse, 47 mph; elk and Cape hunting dog, 45 mph; coyote, 43 mph; grey fox, 42 mph; hyena, zebra and Mongolian wild ass, 40 mph; greyhound, 39 mph; whippet, rabbit, mule deer and jackal, 35 mph; reindeer and giraffe, 32 mph; white-tailed deer, warthog, grizzly bear and cat, 30 mph.

The human comes twenty-sixth at 28 mph, followed by the elephant at 25 mph.

*Jayne Rogers, Cheltenham*

## (442) QUESTION: Who was the original Svengali?

Set in Paris, George du Maurier's 1894 novel *Trilby* tells of artist's model Trilby O'Ferrall falling under the spell of musician Svengali. He uses his hypnotic skill to turn her into a famous opera singer, but when he dies her voice fails and without his guidance and control she is unable to perform. The story gave the world the name 'trilby' for the soft felt hat worn by the heroine in the 1895 stage version, in which Beerbohm Tree played an especially villainous Svengali. Trilby's beautiful feet are much admired in the novel and various styles of boot and shoe were also briefly known as 'Trilbys'.

The story, under the title *Svengali*, has been filmed many times with such stars as John Barrymore (1931), Donald Wolfit (1954) and in 1983 a television film with Peter O'Toole turning Jodie Foster into a rock star.

*David Elias, Nottingham*

**(443) QUESTION: As children, we always gave my parents the same Christmas presents: a shirt collar stud for Dad and Evening in Paris perfume for Mother. Did other children give regular presents?**

For Christmas, birthday and Mothering Sunday, my mum always had California Poppy perfume, bought in Woolworth's. Dad had a bar of Palm toffee and his favourite, a bar of Cadbury's milk chocolate-covered marzipan. The marzipan was green, in eight squares, and cost 6d (2½p).

*Christine Lewis, Rhiwbina, Cardiff*

Up to his eightieth birthday I gave my father a pair of socks, 2 oz of Three Nuns Empire tobacco, 1 lb of Merry Maid caramels and a copy of *Playboy* magazine.

*John Wood, Epsom, Surrey*

After my son was born in 1949, his Christmas present to me was a 1d box of matches, wrapped in festive paper, to light my pipe. This was my regular gift until my daughter was born in 1954, when it was upgraded to a packet of Swan Vestas from my son and Fry's Turkish Delight from my daughter.

Our grandchildren, all girls, carried on the tradition though latterly they have omitted the matches.

Then, our twenty-one-year-old granddaughter took a holiday in Turkey and brought back a large box of real Turkish Delight. Long may this tradition continue. Who cares about the waistline when you're in your seventies?

*C. Palliser, Chorley, Lancashire*


As a child, I lived by Croydon Airport, close to the Bourjois factory which manufactured the famous Bourjois rouge and Evening in Paris perfume. The scent, marketed in distinctive dark blue bottles at 1s 6d each, was available at Christmas in novelty packs like miniature Eiffel Towers. At the change of shift each day, people avoided buses used by Bourjois workers because they were pervaded by perfume smells.

In 1940, in one of the first air raids of the war, German bombers mistook the factory for part of the RAF base and scored a direct hit, causing considerable damage and some fatalities.

Bourjois, with a head office in Cavendish Square, still produces a range of make-up and Evening in Paris is still available, though it's now called Soir de Paris. I can't say whether it smells the same but, at close to £20, it's rather too expensive for most children to give their mothers.

*John Hamer, Leigh-on-Sea, Essex*


**(444) QUESTION: Was the Evening in Paris perfume factory bombed by mistake?**

In 1940, I was stationed at RAF Croydon where the Bourjois perfume factory was just outside the airfield perimeter. Each morning we would wake up to the smell of Evening in Paris.

When the bombs fell and the direct hit took place, every man and woman raced across the airfield to the factory. There were boxes of blue bottles blown all over the place and gallons of perfume poured from the huge storage tanks. The air was saturated with Evening in

Paris as we began the terrible task of extricating the dead and injured, mostly women, from the shattered factory.

I was eighteen and it was my first taste of death.

*Patrick Phelps, Hornchurch, Essex*

I was a typist at the Bourjois factory in Croydon at the time of the air raid. We girls used to chat to RAF personnel over the airfield fence and that day there was a feeling of unrest as they told us they were expecting trouble.

We were due to work overtime that evening but our bosses cancelled it. During that August night, German bombers followed our fighters inland and dropped several bombs before the air-raid warning sounded.

The next day, when I and others made our way to work, we were met by devastation. The two brothers who owned the Bourjois company had already taken two large houses in Grove Road, Sutton, as emergency offices and most of the office staff had jobs there: the few who didn't were gradually recalled.

We were told only one man from our factory was killed – the commissionaire who was shepherding the cleaners to the air-raid shelter and was machine-gunned while doing so. He died later in hospital. There was an aircraft factory nearby and we were told it suffered heavy casualties as they were working during the raid.

*Lillian Shelley, New Malden, Surrey*

I worked at the Bourjois factory, filling little blue bottles and sticking silver labels on them. I had to have my own tea cup at home because the family complained of the scent and my father wouldn't have his clothes washed with mine in case he smelled of Evening in Paris perfume.

At the time when the factory was bombed, I had just arrived home in Carshalton, so I was very lucky. I saw the planes fighting overhead but didn't realize our factory was being bombed until I went to work the next day.

The Ministry of Labour gave me the option of war work or the services and drafted me to Mitcham Works, making radios for planes and tanks.

*Lily Gould, Carshalton, Surrey*

**(445) QUESTION: Why are there two ps in sapphire?**

Our word sapphire originates from the Greek word for lapis lazuli, a semi-precious blue stone. The two syllables of this word were *sap* and *phei*, which have come down to us as 'sap-phire' and we have stopped pronouncing the first p.

It's my belief that, having stopped sounding two ps, we should stop spelling it that way, in fact, why don't we write safire, as it is in Old French? Other words in English with repeated consonants resulting from similar two-syllable construction are Matthew and saccharin.

*Leo Chapman, Simplified Spelling Society, Finsbury, London*

**(446) QUESTION: On 29 March 1965 Whitby coastguard recorded a temperature of 25°C and it remained the warmest day there for the rest of the year. Is this the earliest 'warmest day' recorded in Britain?**

That temperature at Whitby in 1965 is the earliest example of the hottest day of the year in one location but was not the hottest place in the country that year.

In the past hundred years, the earliest warmest day was 14 May 1965, when the temperature reached 28.9°C (84°F) at Kensington Palace, London. The latest warmest day was 9 September 1926, when a temperature of 32.2°C (90°F) was recorded in Camden Square, London.

The dates which have been the warmest the most times in the past century are 1 July, 11 July and 12 July, each of which has been the warmest four times.

*Andy Yeatman, The Met Office, Bracknell, Berkshire*

**(447) QUESTION: Why is the word fiasco, the Italian for flask, used to mean a humiliating failure?**

The Italian word *fiasco*, meaning literally a bottle, comes from *flasco*, the same mediaeval Latin word which gave English the words flask and flagon and itself comes from the earlier Latin *vasculum*, a small vessel, from which we get our words vase and vessel.

The English fiasco, meaning a humiliating failure, came into our language from nineteenth-century theatrical circles. In Italy, from as early as the sixteenth century, a shout of '*Far fiasco!*' (literally 'Do a bottle!') went up at the sound of any bad stage or street performance.

The explanation for this phrase is that a similar cry was used to greet bad workmanship in the glassblowing industry. There has been some suggestion that the British expression 'lose your bottle' is in some way connected with this Italian saying but I believe 'lose your bottle' comes from Cockney rhyming slang.

*Keith Waterfield, Liverpool*

The glassblowing industry was, and still is, most important in Italy and nowhere more so than in Venice, a city whose enigmatic vernacular has given us several expressions still in use.

When Venetian glassblowers were engaged in making a beautiful object, if the slightest flaw was detected, a cry of '*Far fiasco!*' went up and the article was designated a common flask. The Venetian opera house was a noisy place and a singer who failed to please was greeted with the cry, '*Ola! Ola! Fiasco!*'

*Clive Morrell, Holland on Sea, Essex*

**(448) QUESTION: Three Football League teams include County in their names. Derby County and Notts County are self-explanatory, but why Stockport County?**

Founded in 1883 as Heaton Norris Rovers, the club changed its name to Stockport County in 1889 when the town became a county borough. Stockport joined the Football League in 1900, moving to Edgeley Park in 1902 and currently play in the Football League Two division.

*Richard Thompstone, Breach, Kent*

**(449) QUESTION: Who holds the record for being an MP for the shortest time between a by and general election?**

Air Vice-Marshall Donald Bennett represented West Middlesbrough from 14 May until 5 July 1945. Because of the Armed Forces vote, the result of the 1945 election wasn't declared until 26 July, so Marshall Bennett represented his constituency for a total of seventy-two days.

*D. J. Anderson, London SW20*

**(450) QUESTION: Our local blackbird regularly sings the first line of the *EastEnders* theme tune. Is he the only *EastEnders*-loving blackbird or are there other soap-loving birds in Britain?**

Many birds are accomplished mimics, copying both the songs and calls of other birds, and all kinds of mechanical sounds such as whistles, hooters, telephone bells. They often incorporate bits of what they hear into their songs, though blackbirds are not as well known for this as starlings and song thrushes.

*Mike Everett, Royal Society for the Protection of Birds,*
*Sandy, Bedfordshire*

Our local birds must have had a better musical education as we hear them singing the first six notes of Prokofiev's *Peter and the Wolf*.

*Dennis Carrington, Hornchurch, Essex*


Some years ago, I heard a local blackbird whistle the opening notes of the song 'Little Boxes'. I would whistle it back to him and he would return the call.

*E. Booth, Chorley, Lancashire*


The blackbird in my garden has obviously been listening to Hans Christian Andersen. He sings the first line of 'The Emperor's New Clothes', the line that goes 'The King is in the altogether, the . . .' He stops after the 'the' and repeats it three or four times before starting on something else.

*Joan Insall, Sleaford, Lincolnshire*


When living in Oxford some years ago, we had a jazz-loving blackbird which regularly sang the first five notes of the 'St Louis Blues'.

*J. P. H. Lord, Witney, Oxfordshire*


Our local blackbird includes in his repertoire 'Rudolph The Red Nosed Reindeer'. I know this seems unbelievable, so I actually taped him and can play it down the phone to anyone who doesn't believe it.

*H. M. Dodd, Dronfield, Yorkshire*


Our local blackbird used to sing the first line of 'On Ilkley Moor Baht'at'. So imagine my astonishment when, in a hotel garden in Austria one day, a local blackbird sang the same song.

We have since moved and, hard as I try, I have never succeeded in teaching it to our resident bird.

*Mrs E. Rich, Dovercourt, Essex*

## (451) QUESTION: Why did French soldiers nickname Napoleon 'Father Violet'?

After Napoleon's ill-fated venture into Russia, a coalition of armies (including those of Prussia, Russia, Britain, Sweden and Austria) marched on France, outnumbered the French and took Paris on 31 March 1814. The allies refused to accept Napoleon's abdication in favour of his son and restored the exiled Bourbon dynasty.

Napoleon was exiled and given sovereign power on the Mediterranean island of Elba. He told his followers he would return to France, bringing with him some of Elba's famed violets.

Louis XVIII's restored monarchy soon made itself unpopular and when 'To the return of Corporal Violet' became a popular toast throughout France, Napoleon resolved to attempt a comeback.

Landing in Cannes on 1 March 1815, he marched north, sending his soldiers ahead to ask townspeople: 'Do you like violets?' If they answered 'Yes' it implied sympathy to his cause. If they answered 'No', the area was skirted.

The Bourbons fled and within three weeks Napoleon reached Paris and was welcomed as a hero. But the reign of 'Père Violet' lasted just 100 days, ending on 18 June when he was defeated at Waterloo by Wellington and Blucher.

Napoleon was exiled again, this time to the South Atlantic isle of St Helena, noted for its violets. He remained there until his death six years later.

*G. Cobb, Saltcoats, Ayrshire*

It was the violets not of Elba, his island of exile, but of Paris which Napoleon promised to see blooming on his return to France. After his defeat at Leipzig in October 1813, the allies of Russia, Prussia, Austria, Sweden and Britain wrote off 'Boney' as a serious threat as they advanced into France.

Yet he defeated the superior allied forces time and again, until he was forced to abdicate on 6 April 1814, because of the treachery of Talleyrand and his marshals.

Before he left for Elba, Napoleon bade a tearful farewell to his Old Guard at Fontainebleau, where the palace courtyard is still known at the Court of Farewells. He was heard to mutter that he would be back in Paris to see the violets bloom in 1815.

Invading France at the head of just 1,000 men, his Imperial troops were met by violets, the adopted symbol of the Bonapartists, in every town and village.

At Waterloo, however, only nine of Napoleon's surviving twenty-six marshals were still able to take command, and three of these he distrusted. After defeat and treacherous deals by Fouche and Marshal Davout, Napoleon was exiled to St Helena and murdered there six years later by a French royalist agent. The violet has remained the symbol of the Bonapartists.

*Michael Newbold, Cleethorpes, Humberside*

### (452) QUESTION: How small is the smallest type?

The smallest man-made objects are the probe tips of scanning tunnelling microscopes (STMs), shaped to end in a single atom. In 1990, it was announced that Eigler and Schweizer of the IBM Almaden Research Center, California, USA, had used an STM to reposition single atoms of xenon on a nickel surface, spelling out 'IBM'.

*Carole Jones, Guinness Book of Records, London*

I have a credit card-sized card, produced by Timecards of California, printed with the complete Bible. Print size is usually measured in 'points', one point being one 72nd of an inch. On this scale the typeface of the credit card Bible is about 0.05 point.

*K. J. Appleby, Cowbridge, Vale of Glamorgan*

The Monotype Corporation of Redhill, Surrey, back in the fifties, used to give away a copy of the Lord's Prayer engraved on a printer's measure of one-sixth of an inch square em. The wording was perfectly legible under a magnifying glass and was a wonderful example of the company's skill.

*D. V. Exall, Malaga, Spain*

**(453) QUESTION: Why does sub rosa (under the rose) mean in strict confidence?**

The ancient Greek god of silence was Harpocrates, Greek version of the Egyptian Harpa-Khruti (Horus), divine child of Isis, usually depicted as a naked boy on her knee, sometimes suckling at her breast but often with a finger to his lips, denoting discretion. The Greeks made him the god of secrecy.

The rose, the sacred flower of Isis, descended to the Roman Venus and ultimately became the Rosa Mystica of the Virgin Mary who is variously called a rose, a rose garden and a rosary.

She often featured in medieval paintings seated in a rose garden with the infant Jesus on her lap, his finger to his lips in the age-old gesture of secrecy, the taboo against discussing the holy mysteries.

Later still, the Jacobites adopted the white rose as their emblem when secrecy was vital to their cause. Many grew roses by the door as a secret sign of welcome within and the flower was etched on wine glasses so the faithful could drink, undetected, to 'the King over the water'. Meetings of the group were announced by the simple term '*sub rosa*'.

The Jacobites were merely adapting the Roman custom of suspending a white rose over the banquet table to indicate 'parliamentary privilege' and the custom persisted well into Victorian and Edwardian times, when ornate plaster roses graced their ceilings.

*Maisie Aller, Blackpool, Lancashire*

A rose medallion on the ceiling of Lullingstone Castle in Kent is surrounded by the inscription: 'Kentish True Blue/Take this as a token/That what is said here/Under the rose is spoken.'

*Joe Shortland, Knaresborough, North Yorkshire*

There's a Freemasons' Lodge in Weimar, which was in the former German Democratic Republic, called *Anna Amalia zu den drei Rosen*.

Freemasonry was banned under the communist regime and members would meet clandestinely in a local hotel, with a vase on the table holding three roses. The presence of the roses meant they could speak freely.

*Roy Milburn, Isle of Wight*

(454) QUESTION: We are told that when Lucifer led the revolt in Heaven, a third of the angels joined God's side, a third the Devil's and a third sat on the fence. What is the source of this information?

This comes from the Bible: Revelation 12 describes a woman giving birth and a war in heaven between Michael and Satan after which the latter is cast down to Earth. The woman represents God's heavenly organization, giving birth to a male son representing God's kingdom in Heaven. Michael represents Jesus in his heavenly position, cleansing the heavens and casting Satan to Earth, bringing woe to Earth for a short time.

Verses 3 and 4 say: 'And another sign was seen in heaven . . . a great fiery-coloured dragon, with seven heads and ten horns and upon its heads seven diadems and its tail drags a third of the stars of heaven and hurls them down to the Earth.'

The dragon is the serpent, Satan, who 'drags a third of the stars of heaven', representing angels. The proportion of 'a third' isn't literal; 'a third' is often used symbolically in the Bible; it means that a lot of angels were led astray by Satan. They could not return to God's holy organization and became demons, dragged along under Satan's control.

Satan cast them down to Earth and this refers to Noah's day, before the Flood, when Satan induced disobedient 'sons of God' to cohabit with the daughters of men. As a punishment, these angels who sinned have been thrown by God into the prison-like place called Tartarus.

The name Lucifer is used in Bibles such as the King James version which are derived from the Latin Vulgate. The original Hebrew word is *hehlel*, meaning 'shining one'. This term describes the attributes claimed by Babylon's kingly dynasty in the line of Nebuchadnezzar. The warning issued is against the king of Babylon, who was acting like Satan.

The first part of Genesis indicates that the Earth could have existed for billions of years before the first Genesis 'day', though it was not in a condition to support human life. God used his active force to prepare the Earth for habitation and made human beings on the sixth creative 'day'.

Satan means 'opposer' or 'slanderer'. It was only when the angel who became Satan saw how Adam and Eve worshipped God that he became jealous and wanted to be deified himself. That's when he rebelled and induced Adam and Eve to do the same.

*Nick Welham, Verwood, Dorset*

Isaiah 14 mentions an angel called Lucifer who wanted to 'become like the Most High' and whose subsequent rebellion 'made the world a wilderness'. The Hebrew phrases in the first chapter of the Bible shows that what God did in the six days of 'creation' was to re-create and restore the Earth and then create Adam and Eve.

In verse 1, God creates the heavens and Earth out of nothing, but

405

the Hebrew of verse 2 says 'the Earth then became emptied and desolated', loosely translated as 'without form and void'.

Lucifer's rebellion caused this devastation and archaeology bears witness to this in evidence concerning destruction of the dinosaurs and of advanced levels of technology which came to an abrupt end.

Failure to translate and explain Genesis properly has led many people to think there is no rational alternative to the theory of evolution.

*Revd. J. Willans, The Vicarage, Leigh, Surrey*

Revd. J. Willans is mistaken in his interpretation of Isaiah 14 as referring to the revolt of Lucifer. Verse four says 'Take up this proverb against the King of Babylon' and this is confirmed by Jeremiah 25 v 9.

The question is unanswerable as the Bible contains no references to a 'revolt' in heaven, only on Earth, in the Garden of Eden.

*Chris Brown, Bournemouth, Dorset*

Dante enlarged on information in the Bible to write about the battle between God and the Devil but didn't stay as close to the Biblical text as John Milton (1608–1674), Britain's great epic poet.

Fleeing from the 1665 London plague, Milton settled in Chalfont St Giles to complete *Paradise Lost* and start on its sequel, *Paradise Regained*, his justification of the ways of God to mankind.

Milton saw much evidence in Scripture of God's special government by angels, ethereal spirits, almost infinite in number. When the evil angels revolted, before the Fall of Man, there was no neat three-way split, it was a simple fight between good and evil, the heavenly battle-lines affording no luxury of indecision for fence-sitters. Their choice was either Heaven or pandemonium.

Visitors to Milton's cottage may view sixteen original editions of *Paradise Lost* and confirm the contents for themselves.

*Edward A. Dawson, curator, John Milton's Cottage and Museum, Chalfont St Giles, Buckinghamshire*

**(455) QUESTION: Geological strata from many parts of the world show signs of a great flood. Are these of similar date and duration? Has science ever proved there was a worldwide flood such as Noah experienced?**

In the 4,600 million years of Earth's existence, sea levels have changed many times and the continents have often been flooded. The Cretaceous period, for example, saw several periods when there was very little of the polar ice caps left and great sections of the continents were submerged. But there's no evidence that the whole globe was under water at any one time.

These changes were very slow by human standards, often taking hundreds of thousands of years or more, not the Biblical time of forty days and forty nights.

The last Ice Age left behind the youngest sediments coating the land surface, and these were initially thought by early geologists to be the result of Noah's Flood, which is why they were called 'diluvial' deposits (from a great deluge or flood).

*Dr Ted Nield, Geological Society, London*


**(456) QUESTION: Early film of British soldiers in the Boer War shows them singing what we were told was 'Goodbye, Dolly Gray'. Was Dolly Gray a real person? Who wrote the song?**

'Goodbye, Dolly Gray' was written by songwriters Paul Barnes and William Cobb during the Spanish-American war in 1898. It has no connection with any real Dolly Gray and the assumption of most music historians is simply that the name was convenient. It was introduced to this country as a soldiers' song in 1900 and was sung during the Boer War, achieving huge popularity, making it better known here than in the US.

It was popular again during the First World War when it was sung by Florrie Forde.

*Betty Barron, Sutton Coldfield Music Library, West Midlands*

**(457) QUESTION: Why are an army's best units known as 'crack troops'?**

This comes from the sense of crack meaning 'loud talk' or 'boast', used in some dialects from about 1450 onwards. From around 1640, the sense of 'something which is the subject of boasting', something that is 'cracked up', appears, gradually developing into 'something of superior excellence'.

This sense was used as an adjective from the 1790s onward and is still in use today in phrases such as 'crack troops' and 'crack shot'.

*Lorna Gilmour, Collins Dictionaries, Glasgow*

'Crack' and 'cracker' are words with many meanings and uses. Since the early sixteenth century 'a cracker' has been a boaster or braggart, as well as a firework that made a loud noise.

The first recorded use of 'crack regiment' comes from 1807, but a 'crack racehorse', meaning 'one that is boasted about' or 'cracked up', was mentioned in 1637. We still use the expression 'not all it's cracked up to be'.

*David Elias, Nottingham*

**(458) QUESTION: Where was the original *Skylark* of 'Any more for the *Skylark*?' fame?**

The *Skylark* was a clinker-built boat, finished in white, with a figurehead of a skylark with its wings spread back along the prow, which operated between the piers on Brighton beach, taking holidaymakers on sea trips lasting twenty minutes or so. The charge was one shilling (5p).

The captain manned the tiller and inboard engine, keeping the boat's bow nudging the beach, while the other crew member assisted passenger aboard, shouting, 'Any more for the *Skylark*?' This was in the days before the motor car was common and most holidaymakers on the packed beach had arrived by train.

These boats, owned by Frederick Collins, were very successful in the 1930s and there were three *Skylark*s in service by the outbreak of the war in 1939. I believe all three took part in the Dunkirk evacuation and only one returned to pleasure-trip duty after the war.

*John Hail, Portslade-by-Sea, Sussex*

In August 1926, I was sent to Brighton for a few weeks to recuperate with a broken arm, and I have happy memories of spending most afternoons taking sea trips on my own.

There were two *Skylark* boats, licensed to carry about seventy-six people each, boarded from the beach below the fish market, west of the Palace Pier. Each boat was white, with a huge bird stretching from the bow and I always sat right up front, leaning over the bird.

The fare was one shilling but the skippers were lenient in those days and never took my money.

*George Harris, Petts Wood, Kent*

On holiday in Scotland in 1992 we took a trip on Loch Lomond aboard a boat called the *Skylark* which, according to its skipper, had taken part in the Dunkirk evacuation in the Second World War.

*L. Poulton, Lymington, Hampshire*

**(459) QUESTION: At Regent's Park Army Barracks in 1946, I drove Churchill's wartime armour-plated Humber. Does it still exist?**

Six special Humber Pullmans were built at Coventry in 1938 with strengthened bodies and doors, armoured glass, run-flat tyres and slightly more luxurious interiors. Their occupants were supposed to have a high chance of survival from a landmine blast as well as other forms of attack.

One was for the exclusive use of the prime minister, two were for the Royal Family and the others for the heads of the armed forces. All six were based at Regency Barracks, home to 20 Squadron Royal Logistics Corps.

Churchill had other armour-plated cars including a Humber $4 \times 4$ staff car and a Daimler.

After the war, all six Humber Pullmans were sold to private buyers and I'm not aware of any having escaped the scrapyard after the 1950s.

*Wally Dugan, Beverley, East Yorkshire*

When some members of the MG Owners' Club went on a short tour of Holland, one of the visits we made was to Het National Automobiel Musiem at Raamsdonksveer.

There, among a huge collection of cars and motoring history, is displayed the Humber Pullman said to have been used by Churchill during the war. It looks in superb condition and is set against a backdrop of Churchill posters and other artefacts.

*Ruth and Raymond Shrubb, Witley, Surrey*

### (460) QUESTION: Most chicken eggshells used to be white, now they are mostly brown. Why is this?

Of the 9,504 million eggs produced every year in the UK (that's 26 million eggs a day) roughly 65 per cent go to the retail market, 20 per cent to catering and 15 per cent to processing. Hens in cages produce 86 per cent of our eggs while 11 per cent come from free-range hens and 3 per cent from hens in barns.

Generally, white breeds of hen produce white eggs and brown hens make brown eggs. Shell colour has no influence on the nutritional value or internal composition of an egg, but consumer preference has almost entirely forced the white-shelled egg off UK shop shelves.

In other countries, notably the US, the preference is for white eggs.

*Peter Sellicks, British Egg Information Service, London*

As someone who has kept chickens for fifty years, I know the colour of the bird has no relevance to that of its egg shells. Black, brown or white Leghorns and black Minorcas all lay pure white-shelled eggs while black rock lay brown- or white-shelled eggs.

*George Brown, Sandhurst, Berkshire*

**(461) QUESTION: Is anything now done in the underground factory at Hawthorn, near Box, Wiltshire, where my father worked during the war for the Bristol Aircraft Company?**

The site isn't a factory but a series of man-made caverns and tunnels created when stone was mined to build the nearby city of Bath. The underground complex has 40 miles of tunnel at various depths, of differing widths and heights, from tiny potholes to enormous caverns with floor spaces equivalent to twelve full-size football pitches.

During the Second World War, the complex was put to full military use as an underground ammunition store and workshop for vital components such as aircraft parts, produced in relative safety from Luftwaffe bombing. I believe the aero engines assembled there were used in the Brabazon aircraft after the war.

To maintain secrecy, much of what went in and out of the caverns did so through a specially constructed underground branch to Box railway tunnel. One train would enter the tunnel and pull into the complex while another similar train left the complex for the exit at the other end, giving the impression that it was the same train.

Shortly after the war the site was closed, even for storage and, though tours of the complex were conducted for several years, the area has now been sealed off for safety reasons.

*Denis Moore, Belfast*

**(462) QUESTION: When was the last time a British regiment went into battle wearing kilts?**

It's thought that the last time this happened was in the thirties on India's North-West Frontier when Highland soldiers fought rebel tribesmen. After the introduction of standard battledress in 1937, it was uncommon for Highland soldiers to engage in combat wearing kilts.

Pipers often wore kilts for ceremonial occasions in the Second World War and individual officers took them on campaigns but it is unlikely that a whole Highland regiment wore kilts in action after 1937.

*Stephen Wood, Scottish United Services Museum,*
*Edinburgh Castle*

I believe I can lay claim to being the last British soldier to go into action wearing a kilt. As Piper to the 1st (Guards) Independent Parachute Company, the Parachute Regiment, I had the honour to wear a kilt and play 'Scotland The Brave' as my unit put ashore at Port Said in November 1956 for the Suez invasion.

*Bill Edwards, Saltney, Chester*

I have a photo taken at Stammlager 21D PoW camp at Fort Rauch, Posen, Poland, in 1942 of British camp staff, which includes Company Sergeant Major McLean of the Queen's Own Cameron Highlanders, wearing a kilt.

He was taken prisoner when his unit went into action wearing kilts at La Bassee Canal, France, in May 1940.

Several of his men eventually reached prison camps still wearing their kilts, which the Germans then took as souvenirs. CSM McLean protested to the Representative of the Protecting Power (America in 1940) and had his kilt returned.

He snipped off several pieces from the heavy seams to reduce lice infestation and I obtained a couple of these snippings which I still use as bookmarks.

*Capt. W. Hutchings, Newhaven, Sussex*

The kilt was taken out of battle service in 1940 because it was considered unsuitable for mechanized warfare and cost far more to produce than standard uniform trousers. It was also suspended from service dress until after the war, the exceptions being pipers and drummers.

However, Winston Churchill gave special permission for the Liverpool Scottish to re-adopt the Forbes tartan and they were the last British unit to go to battle kilted when they formed part of a raiding force on St-Nazaire, France, in March 1942.

*Frazer Keith, Cleethorpes, Lincolnshire*

I saw the Camerons wearing kilts at Sidi Barrani, Egypt, on 9 December 1940.

*M. G. D'Arcy, Colyton, Devon*

## (463) QUESTION: What happens to deposits lost in a General Election?

Any candidate in an election has to deposit £500 with the constituency's returning officer and receives it back only if he or she gets at least 5 per cent of the total votes cast. If he or she fails to get 5 per cent, their £500 goes into the Consolidated Fund at the Treasury.

*Debbie Holgate, Chigwell, Essex*

Acting returning officers for each parliamentary constituency receive an advance from the Home Office Election Claims Unit at Liverpool to cover the cost of the election.

This advance comes from the Consolidated Fund, controlled by HM Treasury. Lost deposits are retained by an acting returning officer and sent to the Election Claims Unit.

*John A. Fielding, elections officer, Bolton, Lancashire*


By the time of the 2010 General Election, nearly £1 million was forfeited in lost deposits from candidates achieving less than 5 per cent of the vote, the biggest losers being the smaller parties. UKIP lost 458 deposits, costing it £229,000 and the Green Party suffered a £164,000 loss and another 313 Independents lost their deposits.

The Conservatives, by contrast, lost just two deposits, Labour five and the Liberal Democrats none.

*Mr S. Andrews, Sheffield*


**(464) QUESTION: What is the answer to the annoyingly common pub quiz question: There are three words in common use in the English language that end '-gry'. 'Angry' and 'hungry' are two, what is the third?**

Searching the full *Oxford English Dictionary*, I discovered about twenty words ending '-gry' of which 'unangry' is probably the one most likely to be used. Other variants of angry, including 'nangry', also exist while hungry has among its variants 'ahungry', 'land-hungry' and 'yerd-hungry'.

Words seen even less frequently include 'iggry' (hurry up), 'meagry' (thin) and 'podagry' (a plant disease). There are also variant spellings such as 'begry', 'conyngry' 'higry-pigry' and 'skugry'.

*David Elias, Nottingham*


These examples have rather spiked the guns of those clever-clogs pub quizmasters who delight in asking questions which are really updated versions of the old playground catch: 'Constantinople is a long word; can you spell it?'

The trick lies in the exact wording of the question: '... three words in common use in the English language ...' The answer being 'language'. Tedious, isn't it?

*Pauline Farmer, Sevenoaks, Kent*

We asked this on the Internet and were told of the trick, plus this, from Allan Surgenor: 'aggry' is a small glass bead found buried in Africa, resembling the adder bead of the Britons and 'gry' itself is an obsolete word, found in some old dictionaries, meaning either the grunt of a pig or the smallest unit in Locke's proposed decimal system of linear measurement.

*Gillian Armstrong, Hemel Hempstead, Hertfordshire*

## (465) QUESTION: Are there any real back-to-back houses left in Britain?

There are very few, if any, genuine back-to-back houses left in areas like Leeds, which had many of them, because they were mostly built of poor-quality brick and were not regarded as worth renovating.

A genuine back-to-back has a rear wall which is a party wall with another dwelling, unlike those in, say, *Coronation Street*, often referred to as back-to-backs, which are simple terrace houses, with small yards behind.

Elsewhere in West Yorkshire, many back-to-backs built of stone survive. Third Avenue in Keighley is a good example and there are others in Bradford.

Rose Terrace and Victoria Terrace, in Addingham, back on to each other but many of the houses have been 'knocked through' to form one home with two postal addresses.

*Mrs P. M. Clark, High Wycombe*

There are several examples of back-to-backs which have been extensively modernized in Mossley and Saddleworth, Lancashire.

*T. G. Foster, Mossley, Lancashire*

One way in which to tell a back-to-back house in Birmingham was by the number. The terraced row fronting the street would be numbered in the ordinary way, say 144, while its backing house would be 1/144. Further rows of back-to-back houses behind would be 2/144, 3/144, etc.

All occupants shared the outhouses between the rows of houses, one of which was mostly used as a washhouse but whose original use was as a brew house. These outhouses were essential because a typical back-to-back in Birmingham consists of only one room up and one down.

*Brian Mason, Sapcote, Leicestershire*

As an estate agent in Leeds, I can assure you that there are hundreds, if not thousands. We've sold in excess of fifty such houses, all dating back to the turn of the nineteenth/twentieth centuries, blowing the myth that these houses were built of poor-quality bricks.

*S. Fornear, Leeds*

As a former Leeds tourist guide, I can identify many thousands of genuine back-to-back houses still in Leeds. As Ivan Broadhead's book *Leeds* says: 'Back-to-backs were undoubtedly the characteristic architecture of Leeds and when an Act of Parliament in 1909 banned them except in areas already approved, Leeds used this neat loophole to continue building them until 1937.'

They are still very popular because they are comparatively cheap to buy, larger than you would think from the outside and, being wedged in on three sides, cosier and cheaper to heat than terrace

416

houses. I speak from experience: my first house was a back-to-back and my daughter and her husband still live in one.

*Anne Harvey, Leeds*

Some developers still build them and call them 'starter homes'. Sad, isn't it?

*K. M. Worth, Weybridge, Surrey*

**(466) QUESTION: My grandfather, in the Royal Navy for many years, referred to fizzy drinks as 'suji-muji'. Why might this have been?**

Suji Muji was fizzy but there's no way you could have drunk it. It was a powder which was mixed with water to clean paintwork on ships. But it wasn't cheap and its cost, in the fifties, led to its replacement by ordinary soda flakes. Even then, though, you were still instructed to 'suji' the paintwork.

*Albe Lechley, London*

Soogee-Moogee, which has a number of variant spellings, is established nautical slang of unknown origin, first noted in 1882, referring to a caustic soda mixture for cleaning paint and woodwork on ships and boats.

*E. C. S. Weiner, Oxford English Dictionary*

**(467) QUESTION: Was swashbuckling film star Errol Flynn a spy?**

As holder of the world's largest archive on Errol Flynn, I've studied his life and career, on and off screen, and have seen the supposed evidence from Charles Higham's 1980 book suggesting Flynn was a Nazi spy.

Comparing this with my files, including copies of FBI and CIA documents, I find no evidence that he was at any time involved with the Nazis, either in Germany or elsewhere.

The thrust of Higham's evidence is based on Flynn's friendship with German doctor Friedrich Erben. Were such an association all that was needed to incriminate a person, everyone who knew a German in the thirties could be called a spy.

There was also some speculation that Flynn may have been a spy for the Allies, but this, too, is unfounded. Flynn had only three passions in life; women, writing and, above all, yachting.

*Eric Lilley, International Errol Flynn Society, Newbury, Berkshire*

While filming *The Sea Wolves*, in Goa, India, in January 1980, I was walking on the beach with David Niven and Patrick Macnee one night, shortly after Charles Higham's book hinting at Flynn's supposed sympathies for the Nazis had been published.

Niven had shared a house, famously christened Cirrhosis by the Sea, with Flynn and I tackled him on the subject. Almost helpless with laughter, this wonderful storyteller gave Patrick and me detailed confirmation that Flynn's obsession with trying to seduce the entire cast of Hollywood's actresses gave him little time for political collaboration.

As a gentleman, Niven never named any of these women but, as far as I'm concerned, his evidence settles the argument.

*Graham Stark, London N20*

I'm sorry to have to expose the myth that David Niven and Errol Flynn shared a house. It's well documented that Niven shared a house with English actor Robert Coote, not Flynn. Niven reinvented himself many years later and his autobiographies are mostly fiction. He was certainly no hellraiser and was a moderate drinker all of his life.

*J. Sinclair, London NW10*

**(468) QUESTION: Apart from Leon Trotsky, who were the 'heroes' of whom the Stranglers sang in their hit song?**

The heroes in the song as '. . . all the Shakespearos' referring to William Shakespeare; 'that watched their Rome burn' meaning Roman Emperor Nero; 'Dear Old Lenny' is the great Lenny Bruce, popular American comedian who died of a drugs overdose in the 1960s; 'Sancho Panza' was Cervantes's fictional sidekick to Don Quixote; and 'the Great Elmyra', a character invented by Stranglers leader Hugh Cornwall, who wrote the song – plus, or course, Leon Trotsky who 'got an ice-pick that made his ears burn'.

*Gerald Wilkie, Uphall, West Lothian*

The 'heroes' in the song are reflections of the ideal of the late-1970s punk era, when anti-heroes like Sid Vicious of the Sex Pistols rejected traditional hero worship. This became somewhat ironic when people like Vicious became heroes themselves.

Recorded music at the time was dominated by 'rock dinosaurs' – Led Zeppelin, the Rolling Stones, etc. – regarded by many young people as complacent money-spinners and punk was intended to re-establish the link between musicians and their audiences.

The idea was that you didn't have to be a 'rock hero' but that anyone could get up on stage and do it themselves. It wasn't so much that anything specific happened to the heroes of The Stranglers' song, just that they were no longer important.

In a broader sense, punk postulated that all political movements, ideologies and doctrines had had their day. In this, punk was associated with political philosophies like that of Frederick Jameson whose post-modern writings spoke of the end of 'meta narratives' like the Bible, or Communism, and this also applied to influential political figures.

I doubt if The Stranglers were thinking of post-modern theory when they wrote the song but it makes for an interesting analysis.

*Simon Myers, Hove, Sussex*

Formed in 1974, The Stranglers released 'No More Heroes' in September 1977 when the group consisted of Jean Jacques Burnel (bass and vocals), Hugh Cornwell (guitar and vocals), Dave Greenfield (keyboards) and Brian Duffy (aka Jet Black), drums and percussion.

The song remained in the charts for nine weeks, climbing as high as No 8.

*Byron McGuinness, Ashton-under-Lyne, Greater Manchester*

'The Great Elmyra' wasn't invented by Stranglers leader Hugh Cornwell. The reference is to Elmyra, the noted art forger, whose 'Picassos' and 'Giacomettis' duped the art establishment and who was the subject of the Orson Welles film *F for Fake*.

*Russell Taylor, London*

**(469) QUESTION: What is the system underlying the stardates given by Captain Kirk at the beginning of *Star Trek*? I would be interested to know the stardate of my date of birth, 12 January 1964?**

Current Earth calendar dates aren't mentioned in the original *Star Trek* series, though they're occasionally referred to in the later programmes and films.

At the beginning of *Star Trek: The Motion Picture*, the words 'In the twenty-third century' flash up on the screen and we know from references in the dialogue that this movie is set not many years after the original series.

The stardate given for the first episode (in fact, the second pilot episode for the series) is 1312.4 and the stardate for the last is 5298.5: a difference of 3986.1 nnibs. The show ran for three series but I wasn't clear whether this was meant to be three years or the whole five years of the mission.

If 4,000-odd stardate nnibs represent three to five years and the first episode has a stardate of 1312.4, the system hadn't been in use for long before Kirk's departure so it would be impossible to allocate a stardate to a specific day, or year, in the twentieth century.

This is odd because I would have expected stardates to have started with the foundation of the United Federation of Planets, dated in *Star Trek: The New Generation* at 2161.

I don't think Gene Roddenberry intended stardates to be taken too seriously. He's quoted in both Stephen E. Whitfield's *The Making of Star Trek* and Michael and Denise Okudd's *The Star Trek Chronology* as saying: 'Stardates adjust for shifts in relative time which occur due to the vessel's speed and space warp capability.

'The stardates specified in the log entry must be computed against the speed of the *Enterprise*, the space warp and its position within our galaxy to get a reasonable reading.'

I think Lister, of *Red Dwarf*, had the last laugh when he said: 'Captain's Log: one.'

*Ann Davies, Didcot, Oxfordshire*

Unfortunately, it's impossible to convert your birthday into a stardate. The compilers of the *Star Trek Omnipedia* cd tried to find a link between stardates and the Gregorian calendar, only to realize that stardates were never intended to be examined too closely, and that many errors have crept into the system over the years.

*Phillip Jacey, Wallington, Surrey*

Gene Roddenberry's stardate system was based on the Julian notion used by astronomers: the last five digits of the number of days elapsed since 1 January 4713 BC.

Roddenberry added a decimal point to indicate one of ten increments in a twenty-four-hour period, e.g. 8 September 1996 (*Star Trek*'s thirtieth anniversary) would be 50335. He used this system to remind viewers that the show was set in the future.

He then added a digit to distinguish the original twenty-third century series from the *Next Generation*, set in the twenty-fourth century. The first digit of Stardate 42523.7 indicates the twenty-fourth century, the 2 indicates season 2, the 523 is a random number from 001 to 999 which progresses unevenly, and the .7 indicates one tenth of a twenty-four-hour period.

For *SD:DS9* and *ST:Voyager*, the stardates were correlated with those for *ST:TNG*. Hence *DS9*'s first episode was given the stardate 46379.1 as it opened during the *ST:TNG*'s sixth season. *ST:Voyager*'s opener is dated 48315.6 as it opened during *ST:TNG*'s eighth season.

To calculate your birthday, just work out the number of days passed since 1 January 4713 BC, remembering leap years.

*Jody McKenzie, Isleworth, Middlesex*

**(470) QUESTION: How long must an MP sit in the Commons to qualify for a pension? Does the size of that pension vary with a member's length of service?**

MPs' pensions fall under a funded final salary occupational scheme, open to all members of Parliament, Ministers and office holders. Members contribute 6 per cent of their salary for a range of personal and spouses' benefits. There's no minimum time an MP has to sit before qualifying for a pension. For every year and part-year of service as a member, the pensioner receives 1/50th of their final pensionable salary, so the pension increases as service increases.

All members receive their pensions at sixty-five, or slightly earlier if they have served more than fifteen years. If a member is under sixty-five on leaving the house their pension is deferred and increased annually in line with the Retail Price Index until they are eligible to receive it.

*Lucy Watson, Pensions Section Manager, Parliamentary Contributory Pension Fund, House of Commons, London*

**(471) QUESTION: Was Admiral Byng really shot 'to encourage the others'?**

Voltaire's callous dismissal of the fate of Admiral John Byng (1704–1757) – 'In Britain it is thought well to kill an admiral from time to time to encourage the others' – is partly true.

A fleet under Byng's command sailed for the Mediterranean in 1756 to support the British garrison on Minorca. On arrival, Byng found the garrison in Port Mahon besieged by French forces already ashore and, after an indecisive action with the French fleet covering the invasion, returned to Gibraltar. A month later, Port Mahon surrendered to the French.

Back in Britain, Byng was tried by court martial under the provisions of the 12th Article of War: 'Every person in the fleet who, through cowardice, negligence or disaffection . . . shall not do his utmost to take or destroy every ship which it shall be his duty to engage, every such person so offending and being convicted thereof by the sentence of a court martial, shall suffer death.'

Hostile public opinion and the bitter political atmosphere, together with the implacable wording of Article 12 left no room for clemency and Byng went bravely to his execution by firing squad on the quarterdeck of HMS *Monarque*.

It has never been necessary to shoot a British admiral since.

*Iain MacKenzie, National Maritime Museum, Greenwich*

Admiral Byng's execution was nothing short of political murder. The British government was slow to realize that the French troop concentration at nearby Toulon was a threat to Minorca, and finally sent Byng to defend Minorca with an inadequate force.

By the time he reached Gibraltar, the French already held every strong position on Minorca. He was ordered to take on board the officers from the Minorcan garrison and their reinforcement troops, which meant he had to leave his Marines ashore, depriving him of the possibility of fighting a successful action at sea.

Having failed to retake Minorca, Byng sent a dispatch to the Admiralty which wasn't published in the *London Gazette* for ten days, and even then had paragraphs omitted, prejudicing his case.

Byng seems to have been a weak character, as was shown in his dealings with the Governor of Gibraltar when the Admiral accepted without protest his refusal to offer further troops. He should have asserted himself at several crucial times – but to be sentenced to death for the inept orders of others seems wrong.

Admiral John Byng never married so any descendants come via nephews, nieces, aunts, uncles, brothers and sisters.

*Graham Byng, Bromsgrove, Worcestershire*

In 1757, the French held Majorca and decided to annex Minorca, a British possession which included a vast natural anchorage. Having mustered some archaic sea vessels, fitted with ancient guns, William Pitt's government sent John Byng (fourth son of George Byng, Viscount Torrington, First Lord of the Admiralty under Sir Robert Walpole) to take this pitiful fleet to the Mediterranean to relieve the besieged British at St Philip, Minorca.

When Byng encountered the far superior French navy, he called a meeting of all his officers who decided unanimously that the only sensible course was to retreat to Gibraltar to get better ships and more men. Byng withdrew without firing a shot – but what else could he have done? The French guns had twice the range of his ships and his entire fleet would have been blasted to smithereens, had it engaged the enemy.

Instead of well-earned praise for saving the British fleet and the lives of thousands of men, on arrival at Gibraltar, Byng was put in chains and sent to London for court martial.

The court acquitted him but the government needed to cover up its own blunders and Byng was shot – one of the great miscarriages of justice. As to whether Byng's execution was intended 'to encourage the others', this 'encouragement' lasted another two centuries – in the Charge of the Light Brigade and on the Somme, for example, where British forces suffered huge casualties for little purpose. It wasn't until the Dunkirk evacuation of 1940 that a military retreat was hailed as a victory.

*Fritz Kranun, France*

Admiral Byng was not the last British admiral executed. A report of Winchester Assizes dated Friday 29 July 1814, says: 'The trial which excited most interest was that of Admiral Bradley for defrauding his Majesty's Postmaster at Gosforth of £3 8s 6d.' He was accused of taking the money from postmaster J. Legge in exchange for letters which he claimed to have brought from the ship *Mary and Jane*, lying at Cowes. But there was no such ship at Cowes. He signed the receipts with a false name.

There were obvious signs of mental illness – his jailors found his conduct strange, and a Lieutenant Pitchard said that when he sailed with Bradley in HMS *Plantagenet* in 1809, he had given up command of the ship to the First Lieutenant 'in consequence of the unsettlement of Mr Bradley's mind'.

Despite this evidence – and despite excellent character references from fellow naval officers and from the Judge Advocate Moses Greetham – after a trial lasting just three and a half hours the jury returned a verdict of guilty and he was sentenced to be executed on 6 August that year.

*Ian M. Green, Padstow, Cornwall*

## (472) QUESTION: Is it true that the world's largest pyramid is not actually in Egypt?

The world's largest pyramid is not only not in Egypt, it's not even in Africa, but in Mexico, North America. The Quetzalcoatl pyramid, just over 60 miles south of Mexico City, is 177 ft tall with a base measuring 45 acres, and a volume of about 120 million cubic feet.

The largest pyramid in Egypt is Cheops (Khufu) which, although taller than Quetzalcoatl at originally 480 ft, has a base of only 13 acres. Thus the volume is about 90 million cubic feet, three-quarters that of Quetzalcoatl.

Egypt does, however, have the oldest pyramid, the Djoser Step pyramid at Saqqara, which is estimated to have been built around 2630 BC. The newest true pyramid can be found in Wadsworth, Illinois. It was built by Jim Onan and his family between 1977 and 1982 and, at five storeys high, also doubles as his home.

*Graeme Cobb, Stevenston, Ayrshire*

## (473) QUESTION: Who was the last professional to play both cricket and football for England?

The last man to accomplish this rare feat was Clement Arthur Milton, who played cricket for Gloucestershire between 1948 and 1974, and football for Arsenal and Bristol City.

Born in Bedminster, Somerset, on 10 March 1928, Milton was a right-winger for Arsenal. He moved in 1955 to Bristol City, where he helped the team gain promotion to Division 2. He played soccer only once for his country – in the 1951 2–2 home draw with Austria.

A handsome, right-hand opening batsman and right-arm, medium-paced bowler, he played in 585 matches for Gloucestershire and made 32,150 first-class runs, plus taking 79 wickets.

He made his Test debut for England against New Zealand in 1958, accomplishing the very rare feat of scoring a century in his maiden innings. But he was not a great success in subsequent Tests, never getting past 36. He always loved playing cricket, and had reached the age of forty-six before he retired and took up a full-time job as a postman. He died in April 2007.

*Alex Picker, Nottingham*

Though Milton played a total of seventy-five games for Arsenal, scoring 18 goals between 1950 and 1954, his form dipped after his disappointing display for England against Austria in 1951 and he lost his place in Arsenal's side for the 1952 FA Cup Final, which they lost 1–0 to Newcastle.

*Tony Rodgers, Hounslow, Middlesex*

Gloucestershire and Arsenal's 'Archie' Milton was a real all-rounder who, had he not chosen soccer as his winter sport, would probably have played rugby for England.

As house captain at Cotham Grammar School, Bristol, in the mid-1940s, he led Frobishers to a clean sweep in cricket as opening bat and bowler, in soccer as centre forward and at rugby as stand-off.

From the same school, John Mortimer and David Allen played cricket for Gloucestershire and England and Rusty Wood played several first-team games at wicket keeper for Gloucestershire – a record of which sports master Bert Crew was justly proud.

Like Denis Compton, Archie was also a 'Brylcreem Boy'.

*B. Blackloch, Cheltenham, Gloucestershire*

The only other player to achieve this feat since the Second World War was William Watson, born in 1920. He was right-half for Sunderland and gained four England caps in 1949 and 1950 against Northern Ireland, Italy, Wales and Yugoslavia. He represented Yorkshire at cricket and was picked for England sixteen times between 1951 and 1956, playing against South Africa, India, the West Indies and Australia.

Like Milton, he scored a century (109) on his test debut against Australia. He also made 116 against the West Indies.

*Mr C. Harris, London NW7*

## (474) QUESTION: Did the RAF use colour-blind people as special observers in the Second World War?

We have a permanent exhibition dedicated to the Pathfinders – the highly trained observers and aircrew who marked the bomb sites with flares for the following bomber aircraft – and we have been asked this question many times by our visitors.

The RAF recognized three standards of colour vision: 'normal', 'colour defective safe' and 'colour defective unsafe'.

'Safe' was where a person saw pale green as white, or orange as yellow, while seeing normally for all red and green tints.

Air Ministry Order A.746 of 1942 laid down medical standards for several aircrew categories, including sub-categories of navigator (previously known as observers).

'Normal' or 'colour defective safe' was required for all categories except that of Navigator (radio).

*Ann Cockerton, RAF Museum, Hendon*

## (475) QUESTION: Are any communities in Britain still unable to receive TV broadcasts?

I live on the Black Mountain in South Wales in a community of some six dwellings which, under normal circumstances, can receive no BBC or ITV broadcasts.

Some years ago, we decided that if the TV signal wouldn't come to us, we would go to it. About a kilometre away is a high point on which we have built a ten-metre tower, complete with aerial, so we can finally receive the elusive signal. We have to run a cable more than 1,000 metres into the hamlet, where the signal has to be amplified by a booster which takes it on to the six houses.

This exercise cost about £1,500 – and we're still expected to pay for our TV licences.

*Gordon Goddard, Llangadog, Dyfed*

## (476) QUESTION: What horsepower engine would be required to drive a boat of similar configuration and weight to the Oxford and Cambridge eights at a similar speed?

The power generated by oarsmen is normally measured by their performances on the 'ergo' rowing machine. Few are able to produce much more than 0.5 hp, measured at the oar handle over a twenty-minute period. So the sustained power of eight men over the Boat Race course is about 4 hp. The actual power during the pulling stroke is much higher than this but more than half the time is spent in the recovery stage.

The efficiency of the blades is about 80 per cent, the loss being caused by slip and by the curved path of the blade. This means the applied power of the eight rowers is about 3 to 3.5 hp, a very small amount to move an all-up weight of nearly a ton at this speed (13–14 mph) through the water.

Since propellers are quite inefficient, we may expect to require an outboard motor of between 7 and 10 hp to produce the same effect.

*D. P. Tong, Nuneaton, Warwickshire*

## (477) QUESTION: Where and when was the first pie-and-eel shop opened in this country?

The first eel-and-pie shop was opened by my great-grandfather, John Antink, in London's East End in the mid-1800s, the first of thirteen shops he opened around the capital.

In 1923, I was born in one such shop, run by my grandmother in Watney Street.

*Mrs E. I. Dallard, Wolverhampton, West Midlands*

## (478) QUESTION: When did National Service begin in Britain? Under what law were those called up prior to National Service enlisted?

Conscription was first introduced in Britain during the First World War when the Military Service Act of 27 January 1916 made unmarried men aged eighteen to forty-one liable for call-up unless their occupation exempted them. This wartime measure ended in 1919.

The first peacetime conscription in Britain was the Compulsory Training Act of May 1939. When war broke out, this was replaced

429

by the National Service (Armed Forces) Act and men aged eighteen to forty, except those in reserved occupations, were liable to be called up.

The Act was amended in December 1941 to include women and to extend the male upper age limit to fifty-one. It remained in this form until the National Service Act was passed in July 1947, coming into effect on 1 January 1949.

National Service was abolished in 1960 but the last conscripts weren't discharged until 1963. Since then the British Army has remained a volunteer force.

*Lucinda Brown, National Army Museum, Chelsea, London*

In April 1939, Prime Minister Neville Chamberlain bowed to pressure from Secretary of State for War Leslie Hore-Belisha to introduce selective conscription, giving Army training to men aged twenty.

On the outbreak of war on 3 September 1939, this was amended to include all males aged eighteen to forty 'for the Duration of the Present Emergency'. This act continued in force until March 1947.

*Edmund L. Blanford, Hastings, Sussex*

Called up on 22 January 1946, my pay book reads: 'Terms of Service . . . DPE' (Duration of the Present Emergency) and I served two years and three months in the RAF.

After the war, mobilization continued like a runaway bus. Most surprising of all was the Bounty Scheme, under which men with wartime experience were paid £125 to delay their demobilization by four years.

*Eric Smith, Walton-on-Thames, Surrey*

When I joined 978 Squad of the Royal Marines as a National Serviceman in October 1947, those who had joined for 'hostilities only' were just being stood down and the Government hadn't yet decided whether National Service should be of twelve, eighteen or twenty-four months' duration.

Because of the uncertainty, my squad was ordered to do Royal Marines regular training, which lasted twelve months. During that time the Government made up its mind that service should be for two years and I was demobilized in October 1949. Before the two-year period was confirmed, some men did only eighteen or twelve months' national service.

*J. D. W. Chase, Leigh-on-Sea, Essex*

Peacetime conscription was introduced on 27 April 1939, and I registered under the Act in June 1939. On 10 July, I was called up to serve six months with the colours plus 3½ years in the reserves and reported to No 3 Militia Training Camp at Devizes, Wiltshire. I did my basic training as a militiaman with the Royal Regiment of Artillery. Under the clothing regulations, in addition to military uniform, we were issued with a 'walking out' dress consisting of blue blazer, khaki shirt, grey flannels and Army boots.

When war was declared on 3 September 1939, the Territorial Army was embodied into the main Army and militiamen were posted to TA and regular units to bring them up to strength.

*R. Bliss, Llandysul, Ceredigion*

As one of Leslie Hore-Belisha's Militiamen, I reported for duty at Shrewsbury on 15 July 1939, and had the doubtful pleasure of having my twenty-first birthday on my sixth day in the Army. I was expected to serve six months with the colours and 3½ years in the TA.

I've always maintained that the six 'months' must have been a misprint, as I was eventually demobilized in April 1946, six years and nine months after my introduction to military life. Looking back, the one consolation was the time I spent in India, a wonderful experience despite everything.

*Peter Reese, Penarth, Vale of Glamorgan*

I served with the RAF from 1941 to 1946, then became a bus conductor. In 1947 a lot of posters appeared showing a grinning RAF bod and saying, 'Ginger's back: join the Bounty Scheme.'

On signing on again for three years, I was paid £25 and served one year at RAF Uxbridge and two years at Changi, Singapore, and Butterworth, Malaya. I got out with £100 in 1950, missing by two weeks being held indefinitely for the Korea problem.

*Harry Gummer, Romford, Essex*

## (479) QUESTION: Is it true James Dean presented Elvis Presley with a Harley-Davidson motorcycle?

This story must be one of the greatest urban myths ever. In my time at Harley-Davidson, I and my colleagues must have spoken to well over two hundred people from the UK trying to confirm whether it's correct or not.

There are many variants on this tale, the most common being that a friend of a friend finds an old Harley-Davidson in a barn. The bike is in need of restoration.

When the new owner calls us here in Milwaukee, we ask for a serial number underneath the seat to make sure the parts are correct. Next to the serial number is a small plaque inscribed: 'To James Dean from Elvis Presley.' There is a silence before the owner is asked to hold the phone for a moment. A new person picks up the phone and, after stating he is the head of Harley-Davidson, immediately offers £2.2 million for the bike. The story has been taken seriously by many people but is completely untrue.

We do actually have a bike that once belonged to Elvis, his first ever, a 1956 Harley-Davidson KH, which is housed at the Harley Museum in York, Pennsylvania. It wasn't bought from a 'friend of a friend' but came to us from Fleming Horne, a friend of Elvis, who sold us the bike in 1995.

Elvis had other motorcycles, five of which (four Harleys and one Honda) are at the Graceland Museum.

*David Elshoff, Harley-Davidson Motorcycles,*
*Milwaukee, Wisconsin*

**(480) QUESTION: What is the strongest alcoholic drink currently on sale?**

Given just how long spirits can last, it is possible that some bottles sold by the Estonian Liquor Monopoly during the inter-war period still exist. Consisting of alcohol distilled from potatoes, they had a potency of 98 per cent – this compares with 40 per cent for the average whisky.

*Tim Mickleburgh, Grimsby, Lincolnshire*

The strongest alcoholic drink intended for drinking undiluted and available worldwide is Green Chartreuse at 55 per cent alcohol. There is a Chartreuse Elixir Vegetal which is stronger, but this is almost unobtainable.

There are other spirits, such as some fine Scotch malt whiskies up to 60 per cent or more but these are best appreciated with some dilution.

Of course, there are ultra-strong spirits, made more for effect than use, which can be positively dangerous. There is no virtue in terms of quality in mere alcoholic strength. Only idiots drink purely for the alcohol without regard to taste.

*John Doxat, author:* The Complete Drinker's Companion,
*Camberley Surrey*

Scotch whisky can be very strong. At the Scotch Malt Whisky Society, we buy casks from distilleries all over Scotland and bottle at cask strength – that is, at whatever strength the whisky comes out of the cask. It varies, depending on age, but averages 57.5 per cent by volume at fifteen years old.

A new bottling list is published every two months, with about twenty different whiskies for members to choose from.

The strongest on offer is a fifteen-year-old Glenlossie from Speyside at 64.4 per cent vol. (112.7 proof). But remember, the best whiskies are not necessarily the strongest – it's all to do with personal taste.

The strongest we ever bottled was an Imperial form of Speyside at 70 per cent vol (122.8 proof).

*Pam Armstrong, The Scotch Malt Whisky Society, Edinburgh*


Holidaying in Antigua, I bought a bottle of rum which is 75.5 per cent alcohol by volume (151 per cent proof).

*D. Chevalier, Waterloo, Merseyside*


In Antigua, I have enjoyed (diluted) that Appleton 151-proof rum, produced in Kingston, Jamaica. But the strongest drink I've tasted is Austria's Stroh rum. Stroh 80 is too fierce to drink neat and is usually taken in tea as a winter drink.

*L. R. Eves, Exeter, Devon*


Spirytus Rekyfikowany, produced in Poland, is the most alcoholic drink in the world, at 96 per cent.

*B. J. Paprocki, London*


**(481) QUESTION: Does anyone regularly eat seagulls?**

Coming from a family of fishermen working the mudflats of Morcambe Bay, we used to set up nets on the sands to snare oystercatchers which, roasted with stuffing and gravy, were delicious. We also caught and ate ducks, redshank, curlews, knots and dunlin.

Some of the birds were sold locally and some were sent away to game shops in towns around the North of England.

We didn't eat seagulls because there was very little meat on them, though my father once tried a cormorant and gave up after a few mouthfuls saying the taste was too strong.

I'm not sure that netting seabirds was ever legal but it was common through many generations of fishermen in this community and accepted as one of the ways of supplementing our precarious living. It was banned in 1952.

This activity certainly didn't seem to affect the number of oystercatchers: a survey in 1995 revealed that there were 250,000 in our bay.

*John K. Manning, Flookburgh, Cumbria*

All wild birds in the UK are protected by law; only a few can be caught or killed legally and only some are palatable. Gulls can't be killed solely for eating, only under licence if they are a problem at aerodromes and a threat to air safety, or if they put public health at risk.

The regular eating of gulls, or any seabird, doesn't appear to be popular, unless you live on an isolated island where such birds might provide an important source of food.

Only one UK seabird, the gannet, can be killed for food, and then only under special licence on the island of Sula Sgeir, 40 miles north of Lewis, as the taking and eating of gannets has been a tradition there for centuries.

Gulls don't appear to have been on the menu in places like Iceland or the Faroe Islands and so they may not taste very nice.

Anyone contemplating gourmet gull-tasting should think twice as they may harbour the organisms responsible for salmonella poisoning and botulism as well as possibly carrying dangerous e-coli bacteria.

*Chris Harbard, Royal Society For The Protection of Birds,*
*Sandy, Bedfordshire*

In the early fifties, several French shellfishing boats used to anchor overnight in Newquay Bay and they regarded the cormorant, skinned and cooked in wine, as a great delicacy.

A pal and I offered to shoot them some in exchange for crabs, setting out in a punt with an outboard engine, with me on the tiller and my pal with a 12-bore gun. For a few days we kept supplies coming but after that the birds must have recognized the boat and we couldn't get within a mile of them. They were delicious to eat, dark meat, tasting just a bit fishy. These days, of course, we wouldn't consider doing such a thing.

*Reg Liddieval, Newquay, Cornwall*

Fifty years ago, I was introduced to wild fowling around the Tees estuary and used to eat whatever I shot, including, on one occasion, a greater black-backed gull.

It had a huge wingspan but, when cleaned, was only the size of a small chicken. Soaked in cold water overnight with a raw onion, it was quite palatable when cooked, though somewhat fishy.

*J. R. Kelly, Eston, Middlesbrough*

The Wine and Food Society's 1944 *Concise Encyclopaedia of Gastronomy* says: 'Black-headed gull, common gull, herring gull: these handsome birds are no longer eaten. But there was a time when, in England, gulls were netted and fattened in the poultry yard during the winter months, which may have been sufficient to make them lose their fishiness.'

They must have been highly valued as they cost 5s each when bought for the Lords of the Star Chamber in 1550, at a time when beef cost only 4s a stone.

In the seventeenth century, young black-headed gulls, known as puets, were netted and regarded as a delicacy after being fed on bullock's liver, corn or curds from the diary, which may have imparted a more pleasant flavour.

*Neville Lewis, Littlehampton, West Sussex*

Working in London in the war, a friend and I used to go to Leadenhall Market in the City during our lunch hour to see if we could buy anything 'off the ration'. There were seagulls on sale but we didn't fancy them as they had a strong fishy smell and would have been very small when prepared for the table.

In any case, I could not have eaten a creature I had seen flying so joyously over London.

*Marjorie Belches, Portchester, Hampshire*

I served ten years in the Royal Navy, where seagulls were considered to be reincarnated chief stokers. I'm told they cooked up very tough and tasted awful.

*Keith 'Jimpy' Langley, Surbiton, Surrey*

Notices in Whitby, North Yorkshire, used to read: 'Keep Whitby tidy – eat a seagull a day.'

*D. A. Edwards, Tonbridge, Kent*

## (482) QUESTION: What is the earliest recorded natural swarm from an apiary in this country?

John Croft's *Curiosities of Beekeeping*, first published in 1989, records the earliest swarm issued in Essex on 23 March 1896, and the latest in Spalding, Lincs, on 27 December 1894.

Two other swarms were noted: in Hertfordshire on 13 April and in Essex on 15 April. The earliest swarm I have experienced in fifty years' beekeeping was on 24 April.

When honey was the only sweetener and beeswax was a valuable commodity, every other cottager would own a few hives. Swarms of bees, particularly around midsummer, were an accepted and welcome phenomenon.

Swarming is a natural division of a honeybee colony; with

modern hives, beekeepers can control swarming and divide colonies when they choose.

*P. W. Tomkins, Hemel Hempstead, Hertfordshire*

Unlike other bees, honeybees don't die off in winter, leaving the new queens to hibernate away from the nest before beginning new colonies during the spring. Honeybee colonies feed through the winter on stored supplies and shared body heat.

In spring, as new young queens are about to emerge in an established hive, half the colony – as many as 10,000 to 12,000 bees – leaves with the old queen. This swarm of bees then clusters in a nearby location – bush, tree, or wall of a house – while scout bees search for a permanent home. When the scouts agree on a new location, the swarm moves there.

In the old nest, the first queen to emerge disposes of the other queens and sets up home, the cycle beginning again. Splitting the hive ensures the survival of the species.

The swarming of bees as early as 30 April is by no means unique, although May is generally the month when most swarms take place. In the case of modern hives kept by beekeepers there is normally enough room in the apiary for the bee colony to thrive without swarming naturally.

*J. K. Law, Stoneleigh, Warwickshire*

### (483) QUESTION: Can birds whistle and fly at the same time?

Birds don't whistle in the way we do. Their notes are produced by a syrinx, not larynx, with vibrating membranes making different notes at the bottom of their windpipes. Most birds make noises in flight at some time, calls of alarm, contact notes in flocks or songs in display flight.

The skylark is perhaps the bird most famous for its airborne arias, delivering a staggering range of musical notes which, exceptionally, last for nearly one hour. Swifts have a high screaming call in flight when travelling at very high speeds.

One British bird, the mute swan, whistles only when it flies because the beating of its wing feathers make a loud whistling noise as it passes through the air.

*Chris Harbard, Royal Society for the Protection of Birds, Sandy,*
*Bedfordshire*

**(484) QUESTION: How did the Custard House pub in Birmingham acquire its name?**

Title deeds show the origin of Custard House public house in 1853, at the time owned by William and Sarah Woodcock. The tavern was sold to Atkinson's Brewery after their deaths in 1880.

The inn's name is derived from the five old fields in the area known as 'Custard Fields', a not uncommon name in rural England, probably relating to an area where 'costard' apples were grown. Near the site of the pub was Custard House Farm, built in the eighteenth century and demolished around 1890. My research shows the common belief that the pub was once owned by custard manufacturers Monk and Glass is unfounded.

*Bob Marsden, Small Heath Local History Society, Birmingham*

The village of Lower Dean, Bedfordshire, used to have a Cat and Custard Pot pub, with an inn sign of a cat lapping up custard from an overturned jar. Alas, the building is now a private residence.

*A. George, Rushden, Northamptonshire*

**(485) QUESTION: Apart from Sandie Shaw in the sixties and current female chart group Alisha's Attic, have any other singers made a habit of performing barefoot?**

Ronnie Van Zant of the legendary American Deep South rockers

Lynyrd Skynyrd often took to the stage barefoot while belting out such timeless classics as 'Freebird', 'Sweet Home Alabama' and 'Call Me The Breeze'.

He was quoted on the sleeve of the band's best-selling double album *One More for the Road* as saying that he 'liked to feel the stage burn'.

I'm told Joni Mitchell often used to perform barefoot, too.

*Ian Mitchell, Flackwell Health, Buckinghamshire*

Cyndi Lauper never wears shoes in her videos and Flea of the Red Hot Chilli Peppers performs barefoot – he's often naked from head to toe.

*Glendon Swarthout, London*

Krist Novoselic, bassist in early 1990s grunge band Nirvana, was known to play many concerts barefoot.

*Richard Kelham, Crewe, Cheshire*

I saw Dolores O'Riordan of The Cranberries perform barefooted at Manchester G-Mex in July 1995. She also wore no shoes when the group performed their single 'Salvation' on *Top of the Pops*.

*Rebecca Sheridan, Northwich, Cheshire*

I recall the late great contralto Kathleen Ferrier taking off her shoes when recording, and performing.

*Robin Haig, Davidson, Scarborough, Yorkshire*

Sally Oldfield (sister of Mike) appeared barefoot to sing her hit 'Mirrors' *on Top of the Pops* in 1983 and the American singer-comedienne Connie Stephens regularly sang barefoot while appearing on *The Des O'Connnor Show* in the early 1970s.

And perhaps the greatest and most well-known barefooted songstress is the American Joan Baez. Joan not only performed in bare feet: she spends a great deal of her life barefoot.

*Peter Stevens, Carnforth, Lancashire*

## (486) QUESTION: What are the supposed 'seven stages of grief'?

Ramsey and de Groot (1977) identified nine components of grief: shock, disorganization, denial, depression, guilt, anxiety, aggression, resolution and re-integration. Shock and disorganization, and resolution and re-integration are often classified together, hence 'seven stages of grief'.

It's more accurate to term these 'components' rather than 'stages' of grief as they do not necessarily follow in any given order. Only when all the components have been successfully worked through can resolution be reached.

*R. L. Radford, Peterborough*

The seven elements are:

Shock – often a feeling of numbness which may last from a few seconds to several weeks.

Disorganisation – a bereaved person unable to do the simplest thing or organizes the funeral and then collapses.

Denial – a bereaved person behaves as if the deceased were still alive.

Depression – emerges as denial breaks down, takes the form of pining and despair, powerlessness to bring back the dead.

Guilt – real and imagined, for neglect of the deceased when alive or angry thoughts or feelings.

Anxiety – losing control of one's feelings or apprehension about the future.

Aggression – irritability towards family and outbursts of anger towards God, doctors and those in positions of responsibility.

441

These are normally followed by:

Resolution – acceptance emerges.

Re-integration – acceptance put into practice as the bereaved reorganizes their life in which the dead person has no place.

Some components such as pining and despair may reappear on occasions, such as birthdays and anniversaries.

*Catherine A. Miskimmon, Worcester*

**(487) QUESTION: In John Betjeman's children's book *Archie and the Strict Baptists*, Archie the bear likes to sit in a pew under the 'aneucapnic lamp'. What might this have been? Do strict Baptists still have them?**

My mother also wondered about this and wrote to Sir John Betjeman, who explained: '*Aneu* is the Greek for "without" and *capnicos* is the Greek for "smoke". Aneucapnic chimneys of glass for lamps of oil were shaped like this ...' He included a rough sketch of an oil lamp with a bulge in the glass chimney.

I don't think these lamps held any special significance for Baptists, unless it was in avoiding any possibility of smoke from the lamps as being too similar to incense.

*Jean Harvey, Pontllanfraith, Monmouthshire*

I can't speak for the Strict Baptists, being of the open variety myself, but I would suggest it was an oil lamp with a wide-shaped chimney, from the Greek *aneu*, meaning wide or distended, as in the medical term *aneurism*.

*L. M. Barber, Leigh-on-Sea, Essex*

**(488) QUESTION: Was the horse Moifaa, the so-called 'starved elephant' which won the 1904 Grand National, really shipwrecked and rescued from a desert island?**

In early 1899, a string of racehorses – including Moifaa – left Wellington, New Zealand, in a steamship to Liverpool. They arrived safely and went into training.

At about the same time, the SS *Thermopylae* left Melbourne, Australia, for Liverpool carrying another string of racehorses, including the famous Kiora. Rounding the Cape of Good Hope on 12 January, the *Thermopylae* hit a reef and its crew and passengers abandoned both ship and horses. Kiora managed to swim to Mouille Point, reaching land after being in the water for ten hours.

Both Kiora and Moifaa ran in the 1904 Grand National, but Kiora fell at the third while Moifaa ran on to victory – and the story of the sea rescue subsequently attached itself, erroneously, to Moifaa – perhaps because he had been sired by Natator, Latin for swimmer.

The following year, Edward VII bought Moifaa to replace his 1900 Grand National winner Ambush II but he fell at Becher's Brook on the second circuit and never raced again.

*James G. Wynes, Eastbourne, Sussex*

**(489) QUESTION: In the Kenneth Branagh film *Much Ado About Nothing*, I was surprised to see Benedick trying to put up a deckchair. Is this an anachronism?**

The deckchair scene in Kenneth Branagh's 1993 version of Shakespeare's *Much Ado About Nothing* is as much an anachronism on film as the famous chiming clock in *Julius Caesar* is on paper.

William Shakespeare was born in Stratford-upon-Avon in 1564 and wrote *Much Ado* around 1596–1599. He died in 1616. The first deckchair was manufactured by Edward Atkins of Bethnal Green, London, in 1879 and first used on ocean liners in 1884.

*Hugh Gray, Aberdeen*

## (490) QUESTION: Who originally said 'I don't mind if I do'?

This saying became embedded in the public mind after it was uttered regularly during the immensely popular *ITMA* (*It's That Man Again*) radio shows of 1939 to 1949. The star of the show was Liverpool-born comedian Tommy Handley but the line in question was used by Colonel Chinstrap, played by Jack Train, whenever there was the likelihood of a drink being offered.

*Kenneth Yeoman-Clarke, Lincoln*

Nigel Rees's dictionary of popular phrases identifies the expression as the immortal reply of Colonel Chinstrap in *ITMA* but says the idea first appeared in 1940/41 in the form 'Thanks, I will'. The Colonel was based on an elderly friend of radio commentator John Snagge.

But the phrase had existed since 1880 when *Punch* carried a cartoon with the caption: Porter: 'Virginia Water!' Bibulous old gentleman: 'Gin and water? I don't mind if I do.'

*ITMA* initiated more catchphrases than any other series. Its title was an acronym for 'It's that man again', a late thirties expression often used for Adolf Hitler, who was always bursting into the news with some territorial claim or other. Winston Churchill often spoke of Hitler as 'that man'.

*Dorothy Davidson, Upminster, Essex*

Apart from playing Colonel Chinstrap, Jack Train was also the voice of Phwaff, the German spy. Other catchphrases in the show included 'Can I do you now, sir?' and 'TTFN' (ta ta for now), by Mrs Mopp, played by Dorothy Summers; 'I go, I come back,' by Alley-Bop, the vendor of dirty postcards; 'After you, Claude'/'No, after you, Cecil,' by the removal men, and 'Don't forget the diver, going down now.'

During the stressful war years, the public latched on to these and often used them. It wasn't unusual to see important businessmen pause at a door and say: 'After you, Claude,' and get the reply: 'No, after you, Cecil.'

*ITMA* probably did as much for morale as any victory we seemed to gain, then lose, during the worst years of the war.

*Eileen Luker, Coopersale, Essex*

Colonel Chinstrap was not the first *ITMA* character to use this catchphrase. Before he appeared, resident vocal trio The Cavendish Three ('I'm Dorothy', 'I'm Pat', 'And, by the way, I'm Kay') used to reply to Tommy Handley's invitation to them to sing 'Oh, oh, we don't mind if we do' to the tune of 'Doh, mi, fa, soh, soh, fa, mi, doh'. But the Colonel soon took the catchphrase over.

*John Reed, Aylesbury, Buckinghamshire*

Surely the first person to make use of this expression was Adam.

*Rob Townsend, Helston, Cornwall*

**(491) QUESTION: Which bowler holds the record for taking the most clean-bowled wickets in Test cricket?**

England's Fred Trueman with 104 dismissals clean-bowled out of 307 Test wickets, or 34 per cent. His great partner, Brian Statham, clean-bowled 102 batsmen out of 252 Test wickets, an even better percentage at 40. And even this is exceeded by Australia's Ray Lindwall, with 99 bowled out of 228, or 43 per cent. By comparison, top Test wicket-taker Kapil Dev of India, clean-bowled only 84 batsmen out of 434 (19 per cent).

Mention should be made of England's Johnny Briggs. This slow left-arm bowler dismissed eight batsmen in one innings, taking 8 for

11 against South Africa at Cape Town in March 1889. He also bowled six batsmen in the first innings, taking 7 for 17, to make fourteen batsmen clean-bowled in the match (his other wicket was lbw). Were fielders ever so superfluous?

*James Gibb, author:* Test Match Records, *Newcastle upon Tyne*


**(492) QUESTION: In 1928, the *Daily Mail* published an edition as if it was the year 2000, with articles and advertisements foreseeing the future. How many proved accurate?**

Many of the articles and adverts in the Saturday 1 January 2000 special edition, printed in February 1928, were tongue-in-cheek, relating to problems faced by Britons in the late 1920s.

Several of its predicted news items proved astonishingly accurate including a Channel tunnel, electronic share exchanges, women in highly placed jobs (including prime minister), teleconferencing, an international court of appeal, automatic voice recorders, dishwashers, a UK population of 61 million, giant TV screens, mapping Mars and weather forecasting on TV.

Uncannily, it foreshadowed a super-telescope to improve our understanding of space and proof of life on at least one planet.

It put average life expectancy at seventy-five years but was optimistic in having some people living to 150. The abolition of diseases caused by microbes was said to be causing new worries as the population lost its natural health defences and there was a threat of a new superbug arriving from overseas.

Many predictions were wide of the mark: aerocars, a minimum speed limit of 50 mph, 'L-rays' which could steal your thoughts, electricity delivered by wireless, the removal of all rats in the country and a crime rate of just 1,984 offences a year.

Among larger predictions which didn't prove true was the discovery of an alternative race of Earthlings living in the flames of volcanoes, the draining of The Wash, the destruction of Blackpool Tower by a tidal wave, energy from the heart of the Earth's core, 'emotion machines', a four-hour working day and – best of all – crash-proof underwear for use during air travel.

*Steve Torrington, Daily Mail library, London W8*

**(493) QUESTION: Did the Russians break the sound barrier in a captured German DFS 346 rocket plane before the American Bell XI?**

The Russians would no doubt dearly have loved to have been first to break the sound barrier but even Soviet encyclopaedias admit American Charles Elwood Yeager achieved it on 14 October 1947. The Russian experimental 176 jet, designed by S. A. Lovochkin, didn't manage it until December 1948.

The invention of jet propulsion in the 1930s took many aircraft towards the speed of sound during the 1940s but the planes encountered a notional barrier in that they were insufficiently strong to withstand the massive aerodynamic stresses involved. Most nosed down as they approached supersonic speed and many simply disintegrated.

'Chuck' Yeager, born on 13 February 1923, in Myra, West Virginia, joined the Army Air Corps in 1941, was commissioned as a fighter pilot in 1943 and sent to Britain. He flew sixty-four missions during the war and was credited with twelve kills despite being shot down over France. He escaped with the help of the French Underground.

After the war, he became a flight instructor and test pilot and began flying the experimental Bell X-1 research plane. On 14 October 1947, at an altitude of 40,000 ft, over Rogers Dry Lake, California, he travelled faster than the 662 mph sound barrier but, because of Cold War secrecy his achievement was not announced until June 1948.

*Oliver Harris, Winchester, Hampshire*

**(494) QUESTION: Are there really any boys named Sioux (or Sue)?**

There's a man named Susi in the Bible. He's the father of Gaddi, one of those sent by Moses into Canaan to spy out the land (Numbers 13 v 11).

*John Ward, Bristol*

**(495) QUESTION: On whom did Bernard Cornwell base his Peninsular War character Richard Sharpe?**

As secretary of the official Sharpe fan club, and having spent time in Bernard Cornwell's company touring the battlefields of Portugal and Spain, I can tell you the character isn't based on any one person in particular, though the name Richard Sharpe was taken from an English rugby union player – whom no doubt many fans will remember.

The Sharpe novels were inspired by the Hornblower naval novels Bernard read as a boy. He always wanted to read a similar series of the same era about the infantry but, as no one else was disposed to write one, he wrote them himself – with spectacular results.

*Christine Clarke, Sharpe Appreciation Society,*
*PO Box 14, Nottingham*

**(496) QUESTION: Is any church still using prayer books so old they include prayers for the King?**

As a church organist, lots of books come my way and I have available two Prayer Books which I can date only from the Table of Moveable Feasts at the beginning. One has thirty-six years from 1868; the other twenty-nine years from 1895.

The former is in beautiful condition and contains 'plain song appropriate music by W. H. Monk'. The latter has suffered from extended use and has crossings-out of 'Victoria, Queen, and Albert Edward, Prince of Wales's substituted, over the years, by Edward and George, Kings, Our Gracious Queen Alexandra, and George, Prince of Wales.

*Susan Clark, Organist, All Saints', Wrington, Bristol*

**(497) QUESTION: The Grand Canyon is one of the Seven Natural Wonders of the World. What are the other six?**

The Seven Natural Wonders of the World are modern times' view of the most amazing natural features on Earth. They are:

The spectacular, mile-deep Grand Canyon excavated by the Colorado River in north-west Arizona, America; the 1,250-mile chain of coral reefs making up the Great Barrier Reef, in the Coral Sea off the east coast of Queensland, Australia; the 29,028 ft peak of Mount Everest, highest in the world, on the Nepal/Tibet frontier; the sky-filling phenomena of rapidly shifting areas of coloured light known as the Northern Lights or Aurora Borealis; one of the world's youngest volcanoes, Paricutin, formed in 1943 in Michoacan, west of Mexico City; the beautiful view from the sea of Brazil's Rio de Janeiro harbour, surrounded by low mountain ranges whose spurs extend almost to the waterline; and the Victoria Falls, where the Zambezi River, almost a mile wide, drops 400 ft into a gorge on the Zimbabwe/Zambia border in south central Africa.

*Katrina MacConnachy, Kirkcaldy, Fife*

**(498) QUESTION: Cardinal Richelieu's police in seventeenth-century France had a rank called 'Intendant' and our police have 'Superintendent'. What happened to our 'Intendants'?**

The British police never had 'intendants'. The hierarchical rank structure introduced in 1829 by Sir Robert Peel was based on that of the Church: Commissioner (officially Justice of the Peace, of which there were two at the time), Superintendent, Inspector, Police Sergeant and Police Constable.

Only sergeants and constables wore uniform, the higher ranks retaining plain clothes.

Superintendent came from the Latin *superintendens* – 'overseeing' – which had previously been applied to Christian ministers in some Church polities.

Intendant, from the Latin *intendere* – 'to give one's attention to' – was common in France, Spain and Portugal for a provincial or colonial officer. It still exists in many South American countries.

*Ray Seal, Metropolitan Police Museum, London*

An Intendant appears in the TV series *Star Trek: Deep Space Nine*, in the alternative universe episodes, played by the wonderfully named actress Nana Visitor, who also plays the part of Major Kira in the normal universe.

*Adrian Parsons, Scarborough, North Yorkshire*

**(499) QUESTION: Were the crocodiles, lions and other animals Ron Ely regularly fought as Tarzan in the TV series real or imitation?**

The *Tarzan* TV series of 1966–8 was well received and might have run for more than its fifty-seven episodes had it not been for the problems that beset the cast and crew.

The impressive title shot was staged at the spectacular 210 ft Iguacu Falls in Brazil, but torrential rain, landslides, mosquitoes and fever were just some of the obstacles encountered on location.

The biggest headache for executive producer Sy Weintraub was Ron Ely's insistence on performing dangerous stunts himself. Ron (then twenty-eight) shunned stuntman and wrestled real (trained) lions, crocodiles and leopards, suffering many injuries as a result. He was hospitalized several times, delaying filming and pushing up production costs.

Ron needed seven stitches in his head after being bitten by a lion;

his right bicep was torn while fighting another lion; his nose was broken and his jaw dislocated in two fights; his neck was wrenched and both shoulders and three ribs were broken in vine-swinging accidents; he was clawed and bitten by leopards, pumas and other jungle animals and his wrists were sprained in action scenes; his left hamstring and right thigh muscles were pulled; both ankles were sprained by hard landings; both feet were scratched when he fell down a hill; and his left heel was cracked and the bottom of his right foot torn on a rocky hillside.

The climate was too hostile and the film unit shot the concluding part of the series in Mexico.

*Graham Smith, Poole, Dorset*

### (500) QUESTION: The first two letters of the licence plate refer to UK regions. Is there a list?

This number plate format was introduced in September 2001. The two-letter local identifier relates to the DVLA local office where the vehicle is first registered, two numbers follow to show when it was registered, then there is a space followed by three random letters that give a unique identity.

The local identifiers are: Peterborough AA to AN, Norwich AO to AU, Ipswich AV to AY (A is for Anglia); Birmingham BA to BY, Cardiff CA to CO, Swansea CP to CV, Bangor CW to CY (C is for Cymru, Welsh for Wales), Chester DA to DK, Shrewsbury DL to DY (D = Deeside to Shrewsbury), Chelmsford EA to EY (E = Essex), Nottingham FA to FP, Lincoln FR to FY (F = Forest and Fens), Maidstone GA to GO, Brighton GP to GY (G = Garden of England), Bournemouth HA to HJ, Portsmouth HK to HY (H = Hampshire & Dorset), Luton KA to KL, Northampton KM to KY (there is no specific reason for this letter), Wimbledon LA to LJ, Stanmore LK to LT, Sidcup LU to LY (L = London), Manchester MA to MY (M = Manchester & Merseyside), Newcastle NA to NO, Stockton NP to NY (N = North), Oxford OA to OY

(O = Oxford), Preston PA to PT, Carlisle PU to PY (P = Preston), Reading RA to RY (R = Reading), Glasgow SA to SJ, Edinburgh SK to SO, Dundee SP to ST, Aberdeen SU to SW, Inverness SX and SY (S = Scotland), Worcester VA to VY (V = Severn Valley), Exeter WA to WJ, Truro WK and WL, Bristol WM to WY (W = West of England), Leeds YA to YL, Sheffield YM to YV and Beverley YW to YY (Y = Yorkshire).

*Natalie Barroccu, Press Office, DVLA, Swansea*

# Index

457